Language and Nationalism in Europe

Language and
Nationalism in Europe

Edited by

STEPHEN BARBOUR

and

CATHIE CARMICHAEL

OXFORD

UNIVERSITY PRESS

OXFORD

UNIVERSITY PRESS

Great Clarendon Street, Oxford OX2 6DP

Oxford University Press is a department of the University of Oxford.
It furthers the University's objective of excellence in research, scholarship,
and education by publishing worldwide in

Oxford New York

Athens Auckland Bangkok Bogotá Buenos Aires Calcutta
Cape Town Chennai Dar es Salaam Delhi Florence Hong Kong Istanbul
Karachi Kuala Lumpur Madrid Melbourne Mexico City Mumbai
Nairobi Paris São Paulo Shanghai Singapore Taipei Tokyo Toronto Warsaw

with associated companies in Berlin Ibadan

Oxford is a registered trade mark of Oxford University Press
in the UK and in certain other countries

Published in the United States
by Oxford University Press Inc., New York

British Library Cataloguing in Publication Data

Data available

Library of Congress Cataloging in Publication Data

Data applied for

ISBN 0–19–823671–9

3 5 7 9 10 8 6 4 2

Typeset in Minion by
Cambrian Typesetters, Frimley, Surrey
Printed in Great Britain
on acid-free paper by
Biddles Ltd., Guildford & King's Lynn

Preface

The aim of this volume is to provide a comprehensive account of the part played by language in nationalism in Europe. Either one of us could have attempted a single-authored volume on this topic, or we could have jointly written such a book. The advantage of such a work would have been uniformity of approach. However, for most areas of the continent, we would have been heavily dependent on the expertise of others, and even then most of the text would have lacked the freshness imparted by the scholar reporting directly on her or his own research or personal experience. We therefore opted very early for an edited volume, presenting at first hand research on different parts of the continent.

Since the part played by language and nationalism is so varied, the chapters of the book are quite diverse. Variety also results from the different personal and academic backgrounds of the authors; perhaps the most striking difference is between chapters written by authors who have a personal involvement in an area, who perhaps grew up there, and chapters written by more detached outside observers. Our own British perspective as editors is, we hope, tempered by the many different perspectives introduced by other contributors; the literature cited in Chapter 1 is, for example, all in English, but this bias is corrected in many later chapters. Diversity also arises from the differing academic backgrounds of the authors and of the editors: by academic training one of the editors is a linguist, the other a historian. Of the other authors, five are linguists, two social scientists.

As far as possible we have not as editors imposed uniformity of either theory or practice on the authors. The diversity, while perhaps making the book a little harder to use than a more uniform volume, contributes, we believe, to the vitality of the work. The authors' differing treatments themselves arise partly from the differing views of the phenomena current in different parts of the continent; the differences between the chapters can actually be seen as part of the data on the fascinating interrelationships between language and nationalism in Europe.

Stephen Barbour
Cathie Carmichael

London
Summer 1999

Acknowledgements

Stephen Barbour is highly indebted to Sven Gustavsson, University of Uppsala, for useful initial discussions, and for providing introductions to two of the authors of chapters, and to the British Council and Surrey University for funding a visit to Norway and Sweden for discussions.

Cathie Carmichael wishes to thank the British Council in Ljubljana and the Leverhulme Trust for awarding her a Special Research Fellowship, and the participants in the Piran Summer School run by the Ethnology Department of Ljubljana University.

We are both grateful to Middlesex University for encouraging our work, and for providing both of us with periods of sabbatical leave that helped us to complete the manuscript.

Many friends and colleagues have given us the benefit of their knowledge, or just been good listeners as our enthusiasm for the subject made us want to talk about it more and more. Particular thanks must go to Sheila Barbour, Anne Judge, Peter Trudgill, Peter Vodopivec, Mark Thompson, Sanja Malbasa, Rajko Mursic, Nebojsa Cagorovic, Igor Biljan, Christina Carmichael, Una and David John Brown, and to Chris Szejnmann and other staff and students at Middlesex University, particularly the MA Nationalism students.

Nationalism is a burning issue, and our own ideas have been fed by numerous conversations with academics, but also with people whose own lives have been deeply affected by nationalist movements. These people are too numerous to mention, and some would not wish to be mentioned, but we hope that as many of them as possible will read this book, and know that they have our grateful thanks for sharing their experiences with us, and helping to inspire us in the arduous yet rewarding and fascinating task of editing and writing *Language and Nationalism in Europe*.

Contents

List of Maps

Notes on Contributors

STEPHEN BARBOUR's research and teaching focus chiefly on German language and the linguistics of German, but also include sociolinguistic issues in several areas, particularly in northern Europe, including Britain and Ireland. His publications include *Variation in German*, with Patrick Stevenson (1990; German edn. 1998), and a number of papers on language and nationalism. He is a lecturer in German at the University of East Anglia, Norwich.

CATHIE CARMICHAEL is a specialist in the cultural history of south-eastern Europe. She has published articles on popular culture and travel literature as well as a book, *Slovenia: A Small State in the New Europe* (2000), co-written with James Gow. She teaches contemporary European history at Middlesex University.

ROBERT B. HOWELL teaches historical linguistics, early Germanic languages, dialectology, and sociohistorical linguistics, as well as Dutch and German, at the University of Wisconsin. His research focuses on explanatory models of linguistic change. He has served in various functions in the Society for Germanic Philology and the American Association for Netherlandic Studies and he is currently associate editor of the *American Journal of Germanic Linguistics and Literatures* as well as a board member of *Monatshefte*.

ANNE JUDGE is Professor of French and Linguistics at the University of Surrey. She has published extensively on language and linguistic legislation in relation to France, French within the EU, and the Francophone World. She is the co-author of a history of French style, *Stylistic Developments in Literary and Non-Literary French Prose* (1995), and is perhaps best known as co-author of the seminal *A Reference Grammar of Modern French*, first published in 1983.

CLARE MAR-MOLINERO is Head of Spanish, Portuguese, and Latin American Studies at the University of Southampton. Her teaching and research focus on Spanish sociolinguistics, particularly the areas of language policy and language and nationalism. She has published an introductory textbook on *Spanish Sociolinguistics* (1997), co-edited a book on *Nation and Nationalism in the Iberian Peninsula* (1996), and a book on *The Politics of Language in the Spanish-Speaking World* (2000). She wrote the BBC intermediate radio course *Paso Doble* (1989).

CARLO RUZZA teaches Sociology at the University of Trento, Italy. He has been a Jean Monnet fellow at the European University Institute in Florence. His research interests lie in ethno-nationalist movements in Europe, anti-racist movements, and environmental issues. He has published or co-published ten papers on the cultural and political characteristics of the Northern League.

BARBARA TÖRNQUIST-PLEWA is Associate Professor in the Department of Slavonic Studies, and coordinator of the Centre for European Studies, University of Lund, Sweden. In her teaching and research she specializes in the history and culture of Eastern and Central Europe. Her books and articles focus on the role of history, myths, and language in the construction of national identities in central Europe, Belarus, Ukraine, the Baltic States, and Moldova.

PETER TRUDGILL is Professor of English Linguistics at the bilingual University of Fribourg in Switzerland. He is a Fellow of the British Academy and Honorary President of the Friends of Norfolk Dialect. His publications include *Sociolinguistics: An Introduction to Language and Society, Introducing Language and Society, Dialects in Contact*, and *The Dialects of England*. He has carried out linguistic fieldwork in England, Greece, and Norway.

LARS S. VIKØR is a Professor of Scandinavian linguistics at the University of Oslo. His special fields of interest are: Scandinavian, particularly Norwegian, language history, language planning theory, and lexicography; language planning theory in general; Indonesian/Malay language. Among his main publications are: *Språkplanlegging. Prinsipp og praksis (Language Planning: Principles and Practice)* (1988; 2nd edn. 1994) and *The Nordic Languages: Their Status and Interrelations* (1993).

1.

Nationalism, Language, Europe[*]

STEPHEN BARBOUR

1.1. Introduction

In a book dealing with aspects of human society it is a good idea to introduce at the outset the major phenomena that will be discussed, and to say something about our understanding of the nature of those phenomena. This book deals with languages, and with the part they play in nationalism. Since the scope of any book has to be limited, we have limited our discussion to Europe.

It is obvious that nationalism is a complex social phenomenon, and that it relates to nations, which are complex social and political structures. We thus clearly have to start by outlining what we mean by nations and by nationalism.

It will be less obvious, however, that the concept of a language is a complex one. Some readers might think that a language is a rather discrete system of communication, that one language can be fairly easily delimited from another. Matters turn out to be much more difficult than this, as we shall see time and time again in the course of the book. This complexity is in fact so great, that even here, in the introductory chapter, we do need to start the discussion of what is meant by a language.

Even the concept of Europe cannot simply be taken for granted, nor can we simply restrict our discussion to Europe without providing some justification for that restriction.

This first chapter is hence devoted to providing a basis for the rest of the book by throwing some light onto the very concepts of nationalism, of distinct languages, and of Europe.

1.2. Nationalism

There can be no question that nationalism is a highly significant factor on the contemporary world scene, but, like most important social and political phenomena, it is actually very difficult to define and to discuss, so much so that we might decide that the effort needed was too great; we might accept that it is important,

* An abridged version of this paper appeared as S. Barbour, 'Reflections on Nationalism and Language', *Current Issues in Language and Society*, (1999), 5: 194–8.

and just leave matters there. The contributors to this book are, however, not prepared to leave matters there. They are, as linguists, social scientists, and historians, dedicated to an understanding of human behaviour, both for its own sake, and in the hope that perhaps better understanding might lead to an amelioration of some of the world's problems. Since nationalism is such a significant motivation in human behaviour, we feel it commands our attention.

There are, of course, many motivating factors in human behaviour, but we would claim that nationalism is particularly worthy of study. Why is it particularly significant? Its significance lies in its power to arouse passionate loyalties and hatreds that motivate acts of extreme violence and courage; people kill and die for their nations. Of course it is not alone in this: people are driven to similar extremes to protect their families, their extended families or 'tribes',[1] their home areas with their populations, and their religious groups and the holy places and symbols of their religions. However, these other loyalties are often rather easier to understand than nationalism. Parents making supreme sacrifices for their children can be seen as obeying a universal imperative in life forms, the instinct to protect one's own genetic material.[2] This instinct can also be seen at work in the urge to protect one's extended family; but then the extended family, or on a slightly larger scale the 'tribe', can also be seen, in perhaps the majority of circumstances in which human beings have existed, as essential for the survival of the individual and of the nuclear family. The nation is not generally essential to survival in this way. Of course, if the entire nation were to be wiped out, the individuals and their families would die, but the disappearance of the nation as a social unit would not in itself pose a threat to individual or family survival; only if it were to be accompanied by ethnic violence or severe economic collapse would it be life-threatening, and such cataclysmic events are not an inevitable consequence of the loss of political independence. Conversely, there is no logical connection between the gaining of political independence by a subject nation and increased life chances for its citizens. In many, perhaps the vast majority, of modern nations there is likewise no evidence that in defending the nation one is defending one's own genetic material; the notion that the citizens of modern nations are kinsfolk, while the citizens of (potentially) hostile neighbours are aliens, makes no sense in view of the highly varied genetic make-up of most modern populations.

Devotion to one's religious group, like support for one's nation, is much less obviously to the individual's advantage than is defence of the family, but we would maintain that it can be more comprehensible than nationalism. It can be seen in ideological terms as the defence of a world view and its symbols against rival world views, which are considered to be fundamentally erroneous and which, if

---

[1] The term 'tribe' is not one we favour, and will be replaced as the discussion proceeds.
[2] I do not wish to imply that all altruism can be reduced to selfish motives, or to instincts; this would be a rash claim, and excessively cynical.

successful, would force the conquered to act in ways abhorrent to their beliefs. It frequently interacts with support for a 'tribe' or other more primary unit that may be marked off from rival units by religious differences (for example, the history of Israel and Judaea, reflected in Old Testament accounts, can be interpreted in this way). While the defence of one's nation has often been seen as the defence of one's religion, and this seems to have been a widespread perception in Europe between the sixteenth and nineteenth centuries (see Chapter 2 for the British case), and while modern hostilities between nations frequently do have a religious dimension, there are many serious national conflicts that have no clear religious element; the two world wars were fought in Europe with Catholic France, Protestant Britain, and Orthodox Russia opposing Germany with its mixed Catholic and Protestant population.[3] Thus, while modern nationalisms may be linked to religion, many cases can be found without any clear religious dimension. Not only do modern nationalisms often lack a religious element; there is often (to outsiders) no obvious ideological difference between rival nations. Hence, while defence of one's religion can be seen as defence of an entire system of beliefs, a world view, it is difficult in many cases to claim that this is true of the defence of one's nation. There is in fact a good case for seeing nations as 'imagined communities', and such would be the view of some commentators (e.g. Hobsbawm 1990, and, particularly clearly, Anderson 1991).

Such imagined communities could not, of course, exist unless they fulfilled a need. We can postulate that the need to belong to a community of some kind is a fundamental human characteristic, and that nations have arisen to fulfil this need, as earlier more primary communities—local, 'tribal', and religious—have lost their significance through economic and social change. But why should this need be fulfilled by nations, rather than some other type of unit? There is strong support in the literature for a view of nations as products of particular social and economic conditions operating from around the mid-eighteenth century, as products of 'modernization' (see particularly A. D. Smith 1983). While the arguments are persuasive, it must be remembered that the strength of national loyalties remains very great at the present, when nations no longer clearly fulfil their earlier role of fundamental units of economic organization, when the most important economic decisions are arguably taken by major companies, international organizations such as the World Bank or the European Union, and a few national governments or national institutions such as the governments of the USA or Japan. What we are seeing here is perhaps the familiar phenomenon of social and political development lagging behind economic change.

To sum up, contrary to many popular views, nations in the modern sense are a relatively recent phenomenon. They are particularly important, since they are

---

[3] In the twentieth century, of course, these states did not clearly see themselves in religious terms. Only sections of the population still saw a religious affiliation as constitutive of the nation (e.g. sections of the Catholic right in France, Ulster Protestants in the UK). During the Second World War the government of the Soviet Union was militantly atheist.

considered in the current dominant political and social order to be those units with which individuals identify most strongly beyond their families; they are, for example, generally the only units in whose defence the exercise of violence is legit-imate.[4]

We are concerned then in this book with nationalism, which can be seen as a movement to defend the interests of a nation, to defend or secure its political independence (see A. D. Smith 1991: 72).

1.3. Nations and Other Communities

1.3.1. *Nations and National Identities*

Anthony D. Smith (1991: 14) provides a useful definition of a nation as: 'a named human population sharing an historic territory, common myths and historical memories, a mass, public culture, a common economy and common legal rights and duties for all members'. From this definition, which would command wide-spread agreement among social scientists, we can see that nations, in the modern sense, can only be relatively recent phenomena. Before the advent of printing, a mass public culture is scarcely conceivable. Common legal rights and duties are unenforceable unless relatively rapid travel within the territory is possible, and, while there were political units in the ancient world, such as the Roman Empire, which enjoyed relatively good communications, in most areas and in most times before the advent of modern forms of transport, such as railways, the enforcement of common rights and duties in other than very small territories was quite impractical. A nation in the modern sense cannot exist without a shared sense of identity, and for people to share an identity a certain minimum level of commu-nication between them must be guaranteed.

1.3.2. *Nations and Nation-States*

In the contemporary world there is widespread confusion between the concepts 'nation' and 'nation-state'. Nation-states are relatively easy to define; they are the fundamental units of world political organization. They are often identical to sovereign states; they are the units that have seats in the United Nations (UN); they are popularly termed 'countries' in English. It would be convenient if we could simply label them 'states', but this term is unfortunately used in some nation-states, most notably the USA, to describe units smaller than the nation-state.

It is tempting to equate nation-states and sovereign states, but this might be misleading, given the highly fluid nature of sovereignty in the modern world. Virtually all nation-states have surrendered some degree of their sovereignty to

---

[4] It goes without saying that many individuals and groups do not share this dominant perception; for certain groups of religious fundamentalists it may, for example, be perfectly legitimate to exercise violence in the name of the faith.

international organizations, but nevertheless these organizations—the UN is an excellent example here—derive their authority from the nation-states, not *vice versa*. In dealings between states there is a complex array of power relationships and agreements. At one extreme, these give wide powers to certain large states, particularly the USA, which has acquired a *de facto* right to intervene freely and openly in the internal affairs of other states, albeit *de jure* as an agent of international organizations such as the UN or the Organization of American States. At the other extreme, many small states are clearly under the tutelage of powerful neighbours or international organizations, and have in reality virtually no scope for independent action in many fields. What is generally true of nation-states is, however, that, where they lack *de facto* independence in certain fields, it has, at least in theory, been voluntarily surrendered to another state or an international organization, although in reality some kind of coercion at some period can be discovered in case after case.[5]

Most nation-states describe themselves as 'nations', so why can we simply not take them at face value and say that nation-states and nations are identical? This is not possible, since they are abstractions of a different order; a nation-state is a legally defined entity, a nation is a population. While modern populations that consider themselves to be nations generally aspire to acquire a nation-state coterminous with the nation, a definition of the nation that requires it to dominate its own nation-state is too restrictive; most commentators would agree that the majority populations of the Union republics of the former Soviet Union, such as Georgians, Lithuanians, and Ukrainians, were nations before those republics achieved independence, and that those populations of well-defined regions of states, such as Scotland, that in a majority consider that they have nation status should be recognized as such. Expressed slightly differently, an aspiration to autonomy or independence is sufficient. Although polities bearing a superficial resemblance to modern nation-states are very old, going back millennia in some parts of the world, such as China, India, and the Mediterranean basin, these very old organizations were in origin simply territories that a given élite (for example, Roman patricians or Chinese dynasties with their mandarins) was able to control. Polities of this earlier type developed into or were replaced by modern nation-states, often only slowly, and their traces survived very strongly into modern times; the Austro-Hungarian, Russian, and Ottoman Empires that survived until 1917/1918 were clearly dynastic empires whose populations had no shared sense of common national identity, and the Soviet Union, which in a real sense continued many traditions of the Russian Empire until 1991, was constitutionally a state uniting many nations. Even today it is possible to cite many cases where nation-states and nations do not easily coincide. While the governments

---

[5] There are some small states, such as Andorra and Guernsey, with some kind of clear *de jure* dependence on larger neighbours (France and Spain jointly and the United Kingdom respectively in these two instances).

of virtually all nation-states describe their polities as nations, many states contain populations that do not accept the national identity promulgated by the state; in Britain many Scots and Welsh feel they belong to a Scots or Welsh rather than a British nation, or that they have co-occurring Scottish–British or Welsh–British nationality. In Arab countries many feel they belong to an Arab nation rather than to a nation defined by one of the many Arab states stretching from Iraq to Morocco and to South Yemen.

For many people an ethnic (non-national)[6] identity is so strong that it renders the (state-orientated) national identity so weak as to be virtually unimportant; we can cite here many members of First American or African ethnic groups ('tribes').

Although nation-states and nations are not identical, they are, of course, closely connected. Anthony Smith (see particularly Smith 1991) divides nations into those that have developed chiefly from ethnic groups that have modified and extended their ethnic identities to encompass larger populations, and those that have developed within particular states where a common sense of national identity has arisen within the state to encompass a previously diverse population.

1.3.3. *Nations, Ethnic Groups, and Ethnic Identities*

We have seen above that nations frequently develop from ethnic groups (the term *ethnie*, from French, is sometimes used), and that ethnic groups and nations often share names; we can, for example, speak of a Greek ethnic group and a Greek nation. The governments of many nation-states (for example, many central and east European states) imply a complete coincidence of ethnic group and nation in their policies. Are they not then, simply, the same thing? The answer to this has to be negative. The clearest difference is territorial; both in earlier times, and in certain areas today where a nomadic economy prevails, ethnic groups can be scattered across vast territories, interspersed with other groups, and can practise a shifting lifestyle, occupying no clearly defined area. But then also in a very different environment, that of the city, ethnic mixes seem to be typical. Cities typically attract in-migration from a wide area, and unite people of different trades with different backgrounds and skills, all of which favours ethnic mix. Those states that imply identity of ethnic group and nation in their practices can be seen as projecting an anachronistic, rural ideal of ethnic purity onto their mixed urban populations, which nowadays often form a majority.[7] In dynastic pre-national states, the Ottoman Empire being a good example here, the state was not seen as the exclusive territory of a particular nation or ethnic group, and there was often a high degree of ethnic tolerance. Also in modern nations that have developed within pre-existing states rather than as an extension of a particular ethnic group, the level of ethnic tolerance may be fairly high, and there may be more clarity in the

---

[6]   We return below to the distinction between ethnic and national identity.

[7]   The idea that rural populations are, or should be, 'ethnically pure' is also mistaken, but it is perhaps not so out of step with reality as is the view of urban ethnic purity.

public mind that ethnic groups and nations are entities of a different order. In the United States, for example, while there is certainly no absence of ethnic tensions, different ethnic groups of European origin live in considerable harmony,[8] the sort of 'ethnic cleansing' experienced in Nazi Germany or former Yugoslavia in the 1990s being inconceivable, and it is a matter of everyday experience that citizens can be fully American, with an American national identity, whilst being simultaneously Irish-American, Italian-American, and so on, with one of a large number of ethnic identities. The United States was, of course, established by modern European colonialism, and such nation-states of modern colonial origin clearly demonstrate the difference between nations and ethnic groups. To give another example, Australia is clearly a nation, with a shared identity, but does its majority population of British origin represent an English-Australian, a British-Australian, or simply an Australian ethnic group? Or is it part of an English or British ethnic group found in many English-speaking areas?[9] These questions have no easy answers, and we may in fact wish to say that most Australians have complex ethnic identities.

What is an ethnic group? Ethnic groups (or *ethnies* or ethnic communities) pre-date nations in the modern sense by millennia, a situation confused by the fact that the English word 'nation' and its cognates in other languages are often popularly used to refer to ethnic groups as well as to states and nations. Unlike a nation, an ethnic group need not occupy a territory. Also, unlike a nation, its 'common myths and historical memories' may be much more plausible; since ethnic groups may be much smaller than modern nations, the often quite implausible myths of common descent that nations espouse (and that may have been created or radically adapted by modern propagandists) can have much more credible equivalents in the case of ethnic groups. And, rather than a 'mass, public culture' uniting very disparate elements, there may be a high level of shared cultural norms; and there is usually a shared language. But ethnic groups are enormously diverse in size and character. Many are very small and highly culturally coherent, and relatively isolated from other groups, such as the nomadic or tribal peoples who doubtless existed for most of human history, before the development of urban or feudal forms of organization, and that still exist in regions that have not been fully incorporated into the 'developed world', such as much of Africa, or in enclaves within the developed world such as the home areas of some of those who still identify themselves as native Americans or native Australians. It is ethnic groups of this kind that we have labelled as 'tribes', a term that is perhaps best avoided because of its implications of backwardness, and because it conceals the similarities between such ethnic groups and those of other parts of the world. Elsewhere ethnic groups may be very large; for example, the majority populations

[8] The same can sadly not be claimed for relations between European-American, African-American, and native American groups.
[9] The question of the distinction between a British and an English ethnic group will occupy us in Chapter 2.

of many nations show a high degree of cultural coherence and may share a language. In this category we can perhaps include even such large groups as the Han Chinese, numbering hundreds of millions, or the Germans, although in both these groups, particularly the former, there is a shared language only clearly in a written form. Between these very large groups and the very small ones just mentioned there are thousands of ethnic groups of intermediate size, some constituting the majority populations of nations (and in these cases very often being regarded as nations by themselves and others), many others constituting the most varied range of majority and minority groups in modern states. Many ethnic groups live in more than one nation-state.

Given that the status of a nation confers a particular kind of legitimacy, and given that it can lead to political independence with concomitant power for the group concerned, there is strong pressure on ethnic groups to redefine themselves as nations. This can lead to severe problems—for example, in Northern Ireland or Bosnia—where two or more ethnic groups with differing national aspirations live together in a single quite small territory.

This redefinition of ethnic groups as nations shows the very close link between the two categories. Indeed it is often pointless to argue whether particular populations are ethnic groups or nations, but nevertheless the distinction is useful; ethnic groups can be much smaller than nations, can lack a territorial dimension, and are usually much more focused linguistically and culturally. Many modern nations, such as the USA, and to a lesser extent some west European nations such as the Netherlands and Britain, are able to encompass various ethnic groups in relative harmony (though it would be naïve to pretend there were no tensions), and many citizens of such states have both an overarching more diffuse national identity, and a more focused and specific ethnic identity.

The high degree of cultural coherence found in an ethnic group often includes a shared religion, sometimes a distinctive religion not found in neighbouring groups, sometimes an exclusive religion not found elsewhere at all. Distinctive religions arguably delimit the Irish ethnic group and the Slav Muslim ethnic group (in the former Yugoslavia, mainly in Bosnia), and it is possible (though not uncontroversial) to regard Jews and Sikhs as ethnic groups delimited by exclusive religions. Since other religious groups may encompass many ethnic groups, even many nations (Islam and Christianity, and the major Christian denominations such as Catholicism are good examples here), it is possible to see religious groups, on the one hand, and ethnic groups and nations, on the other, as categories of different orders. A tension between a religious and an ethnic view of the group can be seen within Judaism; some members see the group as primarily religious, others see it as ethnic. Given what I have said about ethnic groups redefining themselves as nations, it is not surprising to find religious groups (or ethno-religious groups) seeking national status. Within Judaism this represents the political programme of Zionism (thoroughly understandable in the context of persecution of Jews in Europe by a number of other ethnic groups seeking exclusive occupation of territories), which, once it had come to see the Jews as a nation, set about (re)acquiring a national territory in Israel, with all the attendant problems of relations with the other groups occupying that territory.

In modern states countless individuals have complex multiple identities, encompassing occupational, class, regional, local, gender, political, and economic factors, as well as the religious, ethnic, and national factors that have concerned us here. However, in the perception of many individuals, and often in state-sponsored ideologies, ethnic and national (and sometimes religious) factors have a particular importance. This book will concentrate on such factors, but it must not be forgotten that for many people for much of the time other factors play a far greater role in their own sense of identity.

1.3.4. *Nations, Ethnic Groups, and Language*

As we have seen, the cultural coherence of an ethnic group is often partly expressed by language. This works in two ways: a distinctive language may help to demarcate the ethnic group from other groups, and a common language may facilitate communication and hence coherence within an ethnic group. Language can hence be extremely important for ethnic identity. The same applies to national identity and to nationalism, and it is the significance of language for nationalism and national identity that forms the topic of this book. We now turn to considerations of a more linguistic nature.

1.4. Language

Language is, of course, the general term for human vocal (and also written and signed) communication, but we are here concerned with the use of the term to designate distinct forms of communication used by distinct human groups. Since languages (in this sense) can differ appreciably from each other, they can form highly effective markers of different cultures and different ethnic groups and nations. It is, therefore, not at all surprising that ethnic groups and nations often use distinct languages in a highly conscious and effective fashion as markers of their distinct identities. A superficial glance at modern Europe could lead one to make two assumptions: that different languages were universally markers of different ethnic groups and nations, and that they were the most salient of such markers. These assumptions arise from the fact that a high proportion of European ethnic groups and nations bear names that resemble strongly, or are virtually identical to, the names of their languages, and that in many cases distinct languages are by far the clearest feature distinguishing one nation or ethnic group from its neighbours.

If matters were that simple this would be a very short, or very trivial (and boring) book, but of course matters are in reality much more complex. The complexity begins when we attempt to define what is meant by 'a language' and how it differs from 'a dialect'.

1.4.1. *Language, Dialect, and Language Family*

Human beings are the most mobile of the larger land mammals, and, even if only moving on foot, a single human group can spread out within a few years into an area of hundreds of square miles. Under these circumstances languages, like other human cultural characteristics, become diverse; given the fact that languages change constantly, small and then large differences can develop between different groups of language-users, and these differences can then be used to mark regional and social distinctions. Unlike other cultural characteristics, however, languages fulfil the role of essential media of communication and hence cannot become too diverse if communication is to be maintained. However, until recent times, communication took place for most people almost entirely within a local or family group. This meant that, if an original single group became divided through migration, there was little to prevent an original fairly uniform language diverging so much that communication between the two new groups became difficult or even impossible.[10] We can thus see how different languages can arise, and how they can become markers of different ethnic groups and different nations.

At this point we will introduce two entirely plausible and related working assumptions. The first is that different ethnic groups and different nations are distinguished from each other by different languages that are mutually unintelligible. The second is that language differences that arise because of geographical and social barriers within a nation or an ethnic group produce not different languages but merely different dialects[11], which are mutually intelligible.

There are cases where these two assumptions hold. For example, the Hungarian, Romanian, and Basque languages are markers of Hungarian, Romanian, and Basque ethnic groups respectively, and they are not intelligible to any appreciable extent to speakers of neighbouring languages. Within each of these languages there are different dialects in different regional groups that are mutually intelligible, though not perfectly so. These cases provide a good starting point for unravelling the complexities of the dialect–language question, but unfortunately they represent cases that are much simpler than many. In fact while dialects of the same language do tend to resemble each other more than do different languages, the reality of dialect–language differentiation is often highly complex. First of all we do find varieties that are described as dialects of a single language, but where mutual comprehensibility is very low. There is, for example, low comprehensibility between many German dialects (see Chapter 7). The reverse case is more common; there is, for example, usually a high level of mutual comprehensibility between spoken Norwegian and spoken Swedish, and between

---

[10] It is entirely possible, though unproven, that *homo sapiens sapiens* originated in a single area, with a single language, but that in the 150 thousand years or so that have elapsed since that time the hundreds of different languages that we find today could have arisen.

[11] For the moment we are using the term 'dialect' to include standard varieties or standard languages (see below).

written Norwegian (*Bokmål*) and written Danish, despite the fact that all three are considered separate languages (the full complexities of the Scandinavian situation are discussed in Chapter 5). There can also be a high level of mutual comprehensibility between neighbouring Slavonic languages—for example, between Czech, Slovak, Polish, Ukrainian, Belorussian, and Russian, and between Slovene, Serbian, Croatian, Macedonian, and Bulgarian, although between languages at the extremes of these 'continua'—for example, between Czech and Russian or between Slovene and Bulgarian—communication is not readily possible. There are even cases where speakers of certain dialects of a language may find it easier to understand dialects of a neighbouring language than to understand remote dialects of their 'own' language; thus speakers of north-western (Low) German dialects certainly understand more of north-eastern Dutch dialects than they do of the southern German dialects of Germany, Austria, or Switzerland (see Chapter 7).

A number of interesting points emerge from this complex state of affairs. First of all, it is clear that, if varieties are labelled separate languages, the notion that they are therefore necessarily absolutely different from each other and not at all mutually comprehensible is quite mistaken. There are indeed languages that are quite incomprehensible to speakers of all other languages—Basque, Hungarian, and Japanese are examples—but many languages show clear resemblances to others. Resemblances between languages may be rather obscure and only detectable by specialists. Examples are the similarities used by historical linguists to establish the various language families of the world, the best known being Indo-European, which includes most of the languages of Europe, Iran, and the northern part of the Indian subcontinent. Such similarities tell us that English is related to Hindi, and incidentally that Hungarian is related to Finnish, and Japanese to Turkish (possibly, though this latter relationship is controversial) within two other language families labelled Uralic and Altaic respectively.[12] Often, however, the resemblances are very clear, and here we are dealing with subgroups within language families, or with small relatively undifferentiated language families. Examples of subgroups are Slavonic, Germanic (German, Dutch, English, and Scandinavian), and Romance (Spanish, Portuguese, and other Iberian languages, French, Italian, Occitan, and Romanian, and others) within Indo-European, and Finnic (Finnish, Estonian, and others) within Uralic.

Within such subgroups or small families intelligibility between different languages may be high, as we have seen, although in some cases it may be low, as

---

[12] If languages are described as related, they were probably single languages, or clearly mutually comprehensible dialects, in relatively recent times, within, say, the last few thousand years; for example a single Indo-European language may have been spoken about five thousand years ago. This is relatively recent when we consider that our species may have originated about 150 thousand years ago. Given the speed of language change, the data currently available to us do not allow us to come to any clear conclusions about languages spoken before the last few thousand years, and many languages appear from current data to be quite unrelated to each other.

between English and German, or between Scandinavian languages and other Germanic languages. Why then are certain mutually quite comprehensible varieties labelled separate languages, while others have the status of dialects of a single language? And why are certain mutually poorly comprehensible varieties also labelled as dialects of a single language? There is a copious literature on this topic (see e.g. Haugen 1976; Fishman 1989), which sees the answers to these questions very much in ethnic and national identities, to which we now therefore return.

1.4.2. *Language, Ethnic and National Identity, and Nationalism*

If speakers of related but poorly mutually comprehensible varieties consider that they share an ethnic or national identity, they may accept that their varieties constitute dialects of a single language. This seems to be true for most of those who speak the diverse range of dialects that we label 'German', though some, notably Swiss-Germans, do not accept this common ethnic identity. Where the speech of such a group nevertheless contains dialects presenting severe comprehension problems to others, there may be an ambivalent attitude to the unity of the language; in the German case Low German dialects may often be considered a distinct language, but one that is still in some sense 'German', not a 'foreign' language (see Chapter 7).

Conversely, speakers of related and mutually comprehensible dialects may consider that they speak separate languages if they belong to separate ethnic groups. This sense of ethnic difference in the face of linguistic similarity may arise from a whole host of causes: Czech and Slovak ethnic groups, speaking very similar varieties, have considerably different historical experiences (see Chapter 9), while Poles and Russians belong traditionally to different Christian denominations, as well as having different histories. Croats and Serbs are similarly separated by religion, and see themselves as ethnically different; their dialects, having been considered by some to be a single language for around a century, were redefined in the 1990s as two languages, separated on ethnic lines (see Chapter 10).

We hence find that, while clear linguistic differences can delimit ethnic groups, the boundaries of languages are, in their turn, often determined ethnically. The boundary of a language often becomes particularly clear if an ethnic group comes to see itself as a nation. A nation may make a collective, conscious effort to raise its dialect, or group of dialects, to the status of a language, and may take deliberate, conscious steps to differentiate it from related varieties, as happened very clearly in the case of Norwegian in the nineteenth century (see Chapter 5). Even more radically, an ethnic group delimited on a mainly non-linguistic basis may even revive a little-spoken language to reinforce its sense of national identity; the attempted revival of Irish, and the revival of Hebrew are examples. Particularly if the nation achieves its own nation-state, its language may become the subject of large-scale language-planning. As in the Norwegian case, it may be manipulated to give greater currency to grammatical forms that are not found in the rival languages (the reintroduction of certain gender distinctions found in some

Norwegian varieties but not in Danish or Swedish), but much more commonly words of obvious foreign origin may be purged. Such language-planning is clearly impossible without some sort of administrative apparatus, and is hence easiest at nation-state level, but it represents only part of a process of standardization. Standardization with little language-planning has occurred in some very well-established nation-states, such as the United Kingdom and the Netherlands, and indeed in these two states relatively little importance is accorded to the majority language in the national identity. Standardization involves the selection of one of the dialects, or of a high-status literary variety, as the most prestigious spoken medium, termed 'standard language'. Its selection usually succeeds the establishment of a written standard, but not necessarily; selection of written and spoken standards may proceed hand in hand. Whatever the sequence of events, the written standard is usually closer to the spoken standard than it is to other spoken varieties. There is a wide variation between language areas in the extent to which other varieties are stigmatized. In some areas, such as England and France, non-standard dialects may enjoy very much lower prestige, in others, such as southern Germany and Austria, we find non-standard dialects of relatively high status. In some areas, such as Norway and German-speaking Switzerland, standard and non-standard coexist in a kind of equilibrium, known as diglossia, and non-standard forms have relatively high status.[13] It is clear that this kind of standardization process demands fairly sophisticated administration, and is hence characteristic of modern conditions, of nation-states bound together by modern communications.

We can hence see standard languages partly as products of modern nations, and nations partly as products of modern communications that allow the effective functioning of states. While certain languages, particularly those like Basque or Hungarian that are very clearly different from their neighbours, were doubtless easy to conceptualize in earlier times, it is arguable that many languages, such as the Scandinavian or Slavonic languages, were probably very vague entities when they were simply a group of dialects within a fluid, much larger dialect continuum, with a literary language that may have been scarcely used. A codified standard language, however, clearly differentiated from others, gives the language itself a kind of focus and identity that it may have not possessed before. We can hence see that the growth of nations and the sharp demarcation of languages are actually related processes.

Given that the clear conception of a particular language arises in many areas only along with the development of nations, we can see that the bases of nations are highly varied: territorial and regional, religious, as well as linguistic and administrative. They are, of course, also often based on pre-existing states and on

---

[13] Norway actually has two rival standards. In German-speaking Switzerland non-standard forms now have such high status that they are even ousting the standard in many spheres; some no longer describe this area as diglossic (see Chapter 7). The term 'diglossia' is also used where two distinct languages coexist in some kind of equilibrium.

ethnic groups, the latter also arising for regional, religious, and also linguistic reasons. In any given nation a variety of constitutive features will interact in different ways. Nevertheless there has developed a kind of ideology of the nation; because the nation fulfils a need for a sense of community, partly fulfilling the emotional needs satisfied earlier and in other places by much more tangible kinship communities, there often arises a demand that its citizens should show some demonstrable kinship. There is absolutely no utilitarian reason why citizens of a nation should be racially similar (race is in any case a difficult and even dubious concept), but nations often do develop a racialist ideology, often stronger in areas where the basis of the nation is more clearly ethnic, as in central and eastern Europe, and weaker in areas where nations developed in pre-existing states, like France and Britain, though even here it is certainly present. While a common language is useful for the coherence of a nation, a common auxiliary language is sufficient; there is no need for all citizens of a nation to be native speakers of a single language, and absolutely no need for a nation's language to be clearly distinct from all others. While the linguistically homogeneous state is extremely rare, and while a high proportion of languages are actually not sharply distinct from others, the demand for the linguistically homogeneous nation and the clearly distinct national language has become a standard part of nationalist ideology (it goes without saying that such ideology demands that nation and state be coterminous; in fact it regularly merges these two concepts).

The concept of the nation we have been discussing is particularly European, or European and American, and develops particularly clearly from the eighteenth century onwards. The ideal of a nation closely identified with a particular language is even more restricted, being chiefly European, and little more than two centuries old. One reason for writing a book on 'Language and Nationalism in Europe' is that this powerful ideal of the mutual dependence of languages and nations, which has had a great impact on the modern world, is most strongly seen in Europe. In parts of the west of the continent modern nation-states arose within the boundaries of pre-existing political units that were relatively monolingual. A good example here is the Netherlands, but Britain and France can also be cited here. All of these states did have significant linguistic minorities, but a far greater proportion of the population spoke the majority language than, say, in the Ottoman or Austrian empires to the east.[14] These western states were seen further east as models of political and economic development, and their (perceived)

---

[14] In the French case well under 50% spoke something that was *labelled* 'French/*français*' in the mid-eighteenth century, but a considerable majority spoke Romance dialects related to French, and were therefore relatively rapidly able, in the centre and north of the area, to consider themselves as French-speakers, and to learn the language, when pressure was applied upon them to do so. In a similar way, and at a slightly earlier date, speakers of Scots in Britain were able to reinterpret themselves as English-speakers (see Chapters 2 and 3). By contrast, another western state, Spain, was not able to convince speakers of some of its minority Romance dialects related to Spanish that their speech was Spanish (Castilian), and Catalan, for example, still retains the very clear status of a separate minority language (see Chapter 4).

monolingual nature was seen as essential to this, a quite plausible assumption since a shared first language can facilitate greater economic and political cooperation between citizens. In other parts of the continent multilingual states were seen by emergent ethnic and national élites as barriers to progress, their multilingual nature being viewed as an essential part of the problem. There hence emerged nationalist movements, dedicated to securing nation-states for ethnic and national groups, that were often defined as the speakers of a particular language. Such states were often constructed from parts of multi-ethnic multilingual polities, as we have seen (Greece and Albania were, for example, parts of the Ottoman Empire), or united a number of pre-existing states (for example, Italy and Germany). Particularly in the German case, an entire philosophy was developed by thinkers such as Herder and Fichte that saw language as the essential defining characteristic of a nation (see Chapter 7). As well as having native roots, this way of thinking was heavily influenced by the French case, where the common language was promoted by the revolutionary state as a means of achieving democracy and equality (see Chapter 3). Many eastern and central European nations were united by other factors beyond language, most notably by a loyalty to a particular religion, and to a historic homeland, very clear in the Greek case, for instance, even though these almost mythical homelands were often inhabited in modern times by numerous members of other ethnic groups or nations (see Chapter 11 for the strikingly multi-ethnic nature of modern Greece). In the German case the homeland was vast in comparison to most others, and ill-defined, and the nation was also sharply divided on religious lines, so a particular importance was accorded to the language as a unifying factor. Given the size of the German-speaking area, and the high prestige of its scholarship in many fields from around 1800, particularly in (historical) linguistics, the German view of language as absolutely crucial to nationalism became extremely influential, and even helped to introduce a linguistic element into national movements, Irish nationalism being a good case, which had previously placed little stress on such questions (see Chapter 2). Other factors favoured the paramount place accorded to language in nationalism in Europe; the dominance in movements of intellectuals of relatively low social status, and the decline of religion, through general secularizing trends (see particularly Hobsbawm 1990). In much of Europe, traditional élites who, if highly educated, would have been schooled in Latin and Greek, or in French, contrasted with a new intelligentsia who were versed in the local language. A new generation of schoolmasters arose able to educate the population in the local language, and often creating a bond with that population through their common use of such a language, who nevertheless saw their desire for political emancipation blocked by an aristocracy either from another linguistic group, as in the Ottoman case, or using a foreign language in its royal courts, as exemplified by the French-using German nobility and princes.

We can see, then, how a whole variety of factors have given language a crucial place in nationalism in most parts of Europe. However, the position is enormously varied, dependent on the extremely diverse histories of the various regions of the continent. This book is dedicated to exploring this fascinating diversity, both for its intrinsic interest, but also because nationalism, and in particular linguistic nationalism, is a political force of great importance not only in Europe, but in many parts of the world.

1.5. Europe

The book is restricted in its scope to Europe partly, and simply, because every book has to be limited in some way. However, we also impose this limit because Europe is, as we have seen, the area that has seen the clearest development of a large number of nationalisms in which the linguistic element is of very high importance. This is not to say that the phenomenon is not found elsewhere; it certainly is—in Japan, for example. It would also be a mistake to maintain that all European nationalisms have a clear linguistic basis; some, like Dutch nationalism or Scottish nationalism, do not (or, in the latter case, did not until recently). It is in fact the diverse role played by language in nationalism that forms much of our subject matter.

In our discussions we make two significant omissions, one region, and one category of linguistic minority.

The region we omit is the Caucasus (the modern states of Georgia, Azerbaijan, and Armenia, and the autonomous republics of Dagestan, Chechnya, Ingushetia, North Ossetia, Kabardino-Balkaria, and Karachai-Cherkessia within the Russian Federation). The omission is justified by the conventional status of the Caucasus as Europe's border, and by the extraordinary linguistic diversity of the region (approximately forty languages, the number depending, as always in this matter, on what distinguishing criteria are used), which is quite untypical of Europe, and which is partly a reflection of the fact that European styles of state administration (nation-states or even relatively unified feudal states) have been imposed on much of the region only in the course of the last two centuries.[15]

The other significant omission is the ethnic identities and languages of minorities in modern European states who do not occupy a definable territory within those states, such as immigrant minorities. This omission in no way implies that such groups are unimportant or uninteresting; it is simply that, in not occupying or claiming territories within the European states where they live, they are unlike nations (although, of course, they often see themselves as belonging to nations elsewhere, or as having complex or multiple nationality). We take seriously the

---

[15] We also omit the small Mediterranean states of Malta and Gibraltar. Both are linguistically quite unlike the neighbouring major European states, Italy and Spain, and so could not easily be included in discussion of those states. Malta is a former British colony, and Gibraltar still is under British sovereignty, and the pattern of language use in both, with a prominent role for English, resembles that in non-European areas currently or formerly under European rule, and is arguably rather untypical of Europe.

view of the nation as an 'imagined community' (but see Chapter 13), and one of the imaginary elements in its vision is often that of ethnic purity (see above). In the urban centres where European populations are increasingly concentrated it can be pure illusion: cities were perhaps never mono-ethnic in Europe; they certainly are not today. Immigrant groups will therefore be treated, where appropriate, in their role as the 'other' in nationalism, but their own attitudes can usually not be explored in detail.

Nationalism is an ideology; the unrealistic mono-ethnic vision may be part of this ideology. The complex concept of the 'national language' is another of its components. We now turn in the following chapters to an account of the fascinatingly diverse part played by language in European nationalisms.

2.

Britain and Ireland: The Varying Significance of Language for Nationalism

STEPHEN BARBOUR

2.1. The Area

In this chapter we are concerned with two states: the Republic of Ireland (sometimes also referred to in English by its Irish name *Eire*), and the United Kingdom of Great Britain and Northern Ireland (the UK), along with the UK dependencies of the Channel Islands and the Isle of Man. These two states are commonly referred to as 'Ireland' and 'Britain', but these terms are problematic, since 'Ireland' also designates the island of Ireland, part of which, Northern Ireland, is within the United Kingdom. 'Britain' is problematic, since some regard it as synonymous with 'Great Britain', which for others means only the larger of the two major islands in the archipelago, or England, Scotland and Wales. I shall refer to the two major islands, with their respective smaller offshore islands, as 'Ireland' and 'Great Britain' respectively, and I shall refer to the states as 'the Republic of Ireland' and 'the United Kingdom' or 'the UK' respectively. The term 'United Kingdom' is appropriate when referring to the state, the political structure, but 'Britain' is more appropriate when referring to national identity, since 'United Kingdom' is a cold, formal, political designation, with which, I would argue, few identify. I would even suggest that the United Kingdom is a state, a political structure, while Britain is a nation, a human population. This view is supported by the fact that many *de jure* citizens of the UK, Irish nationalists in Northern Ireland, consider their nationality to be Irish and not British.

Britain and Ireland represent that part of Europe in which the overwhelming majority of the population has English as a first language. This deceptively simple statement hides manifold complexities: unlike most other language areas that are discussed in this book, the European area where the language is used represents only part of its range; there are roughly seven times as many speakers of English as a first language elsewhere in the world than in Europe. The situation is of course further complicated by the fact that English is today the prime international language, spoken, written, or understood by many millions as a language of wider communication. The area under discussion can therefore not be simply characterized as 'the

English-speaking area', but it does nevertheless represent the European area in which English has been dominant in most geographical areas, and among most sections of the population, for several centuries. In addition, most organs of national and local government, and the highest echelons of most business enterprises, have been firmly in the hands of English-speakers, also for several centuries. This dominance of the English language in the area goes hand in hand with the political supremacy, again for several centuries, of a British government based in England, again in the hands of English-speakers. It is also mirrored by certain cultural characteristics; it would be a grave mistake to imagine that the area was culturally monolithic—no area of this size or population could possibly be so, but nevertheless there are certain cultural phenomena characteristic of Britain and Ireland. Some, like the popularity of tea, derive from the common experience of British imperialism. Others, like the importance, at least in certain areas, of strong temperance movements, are not widely shared in Europe, but are found, for example, in parts of northern Europe, and can be related to the particularly British experience of rural and industrial poverty, and to certain types of Protestantism.

In many chapters of this volume we see how national conflicts, which are consciously linked to language and 'race', also have a cultural dimension, manifest often as religious conflict, and very often a dimension of social class conflict. Britain and Ireland are no exception here. As a rather crude initial assertion, which will require extensive subsequent modification, we can see these islands as having experienced, since the collapse of the republican Commonwealth in the seventeenth century, the dominance of male English-speaking Protestants of the peculiar Anglican Church, belonging to a social élite characterized, even more than others in Europe, by landowning, or by an ideology of the landowning 'country gentleman'. This élite was educated from the nineteenth century onwards in exclusive boarding schools, the so-called Public Schools, and in the ancient collegiate universities of Oxford and Cambridge, which promoted not only English, not only standard English, but standard English pronounced with a particular prestige accent, 'received pronunciation (RP)'. All those outside this group suffered varying degrees of relative disadvantage: non-English-speakers, speakers of non-standard English, speakers of standard English with non-prestige accents, Catholics, non-Christians (such as Jews), adherents of non-Anglican Protestant denominations (Nonconformists), those with little or no land, the poor, the uneducated, or those educated in low-prestige schools. It has to be stressed that this disadvantage was only relative; the reality of power relations was extremely fluid and complex, with considerable power and influence exercised by individuals and groups beyond this élite at various times and places. Equally fluid and complex have been the attempts to challenge this power by other groups.[1]

---

[1] The view of history presented here derives from many sources, but I have been particularly influenced by Raymond Williams's writings, such as *The Long Revolution* (1961).

As we will frequently see in this volume, in the nineteenth and twentieth centuries conflicts of interest such as those described for Britain and Ireland, which social historians might interpret in class terms, are frequently seen in other terms by those involved. A common class interest may have little emotional attraction, whereas bonds to a home locality and region, or to kin and family, may have a universal appeal to human beings. It has been the achievement of successful modern nation-states to project loyalties to locality and kin, and to primary communities, onto the state's territory and population, onto the nation, the 'imagined community' (Anderson 1991). This has been achieved not only by states, but also by the leaders of many groups relatively disadvantaged by the state's policies, which then come to see themselves as subject nations fighting for independence. Movements with an economic and social basis frequently do not become movements for national autonomy or independence; if those striving for greater power lack a territorial base, then they may be seen as a social class, or a religious or cultural group if they are united a common religion or by common cultural practices. Sections of the British working class and of British Nonconformists have seen themselves as sharing class or religious goals, for example (see Hempton 1996: 117–42). If people with particular economic interests are more highly concentrated in certain regions than others, then a sense of regional identity can develop, as seen, for example, in North-East England (the traditional counties of Northumberland and Durham), with a relatively high proportion of working-class people, and, until its recent decline, relatively high levels of employment in heavy industry. In Britain and Ireland there is a complex pattern of class identities, religious or cultural identities, and regional identities: in certain regions certain coincidences of identities of these various kinds combine to create national identities that stand in opposition to a state-sponsored British national identity, which is perhaps experienced most clearly by the English-speaking, public-school-educated élite with a tradition of Anglican religious observance (although these days this observance may be only a memory for many). In Europe in general national identities can be divided, not without certain distortions and marginal cases, into those promulgated by a state and its élite (civic nationalisms), and those arising more on a popular basis from a constellation of economic, social, cultural, and regional factors (ethnic nationalisms). If such ethnic nationalisms successfully achieve statehood, then they in their turn will further their own brand of state nationalism.

For an ethnic nationalism, and indeed for state nationalisms in many circumstances, a distinct common language represents a clear advantage. Since languages are usually learnt from parents, a common, distinct language can bolster a sense of kinship. Indeed, stateless ethnic nationalisms frequently focus upon the 'national language'. Despite the generally overwhelming public dominance of English, we find in Britain and Ireland a great diversity of groups distinguished from each other on a regional, socio-economic, religious, cultural, or linguistic basis, some but not all of which see themselves as nations. As the dominance of the majority language is greater than in some other parts of Europe, we might imagine such groups would have a weaker sense of identity than in some other parts of the continent, but that seems to be not at all the case.

2.2. The Languages

I shall divide the languages spoken into 'territorial' and 'non-territorial'. I shall use the term 'territorial' to denote those languages that are, or were at some time in recorded history, quite clearly majority languages in some well-defined area of the islands. By 'non-territorial' I mean those that, despite in some cases having large numbers of speakers, never had such a clear territorial dominance in any region. The reason for the distinction is that it is only speakers of territorial languages who can, or could conceivably, lay claim to nationhood. The terms 'indigenous' and 'non-indigenous' are used sparingly, since they are very imprecise and open to dispute; basically the question 'How long must a language be spoken in an area to be indigenous?' has no answer. The indigenous/non-indigenous dimension is also of little interest to us, since some languages that could lay claim to indigenous status on the grounds of a long history in the islands, such as Romani, are non-territorial, and their speakers have no tradition of claiming to be a distinct nation in Britain or Ireland. Precisely because of their lack of role in nationalism, the non-territorial languages will not concern us further. Our neglect of them in this chapter emphatically does not mean that they are of little interest. Many of the languages concerned are highly significant to their speakers' sense of identity, and many of them are of great interest to sociolinguists and other language specialists. Our neglect of them relates solely to their lack of a role in any actual or potential nationalism within Britain and Ireland, the absence of a claim, on the part of their speakers, to part of British or Irish territory as a homeland for a nation and a language. Apart from Romani, the languages concerned have been brought into Britain at some time since the early 1800s by population movements, and, again unlike Romani, they are generally to be found in major urban centres. Most arrived from the British Commonwealth, such as a number of Indian languages; Cypriot varieties of Greek and of Turkish; Chinese languages, principally Cantonese; and Caribbean Creoles, whose status as independent languages or as varieties of English (or in some cases as varieties of French) is a complex socio-linguistic question. Many also arrived from other parts of Europe, such as Polish, Italian, Spanish, and Yiddish (for detail on non-territorial languages, see Alladina and Edwards 1991 and Trudgill 1994).

In our discussion of the territorial languages we will adopt the conventional historically based division into Germanic languages, Celtic languages, and French. Although this division derives from historical linguistics, whose findings are not necessarily relevant to contemporary sociolinguistics, the division is highly relevant to the present chapter, since languages classified as 'Germanic' stand or stood in a much closer sociolinguistic relationship to English than those not so classified: other Germanic languages may be or may have been mutually comprehensible with English, and are at present at least candidates for the status of dialects of English. In contrast, between English and languages not classified as Germanic there is an unbridgeable gulf in comprehensibility. The ideological consequences of this are considerable: Britain and Ireland contain a number of territorial languages that defy classification as varieties of the majority language, and proponents of nationalist ideologies therefore do not need to spend time and effort proving that they have a distinct language, as is often the case elsewhere; the Celtic languages are undeniably distinct from English. Map 1 shows territories in which there is a clear tradition or memory of the use of a territorial language other than English.

2.2.1. *Celtic Languages*

Before the Anglo-Saxon invasions of the mid-fifth century, the inhabitants of Great Britain and Ireland probably almost all spoke languages belonging to the Celtic subgroup of the Indo-European language family. Latin was clearly in widespread use during the Roman occupation, shown, for example, by the considerable number of Latin loanwords in Welsh, but we have no clear evidence of any sizeable number of monoglot Latin-speakers after the withdrawal of the Roman legions, although the language clearly did not disappear from use altogether (see Price 1984: 158–69). There were two clearly distinct Celtic languages, or groups of related dialects: Goidelic or Gaelic mainly in Ireland, but certainly having groups of speakers in parts of western Great Britain, at least at certain periods; and Brythonic or British mainly in Great Britain. Gaelic was well established in western Scotland by the mid-ninth century. The speakers of Gaelic, the Scots, conquered and absorbed the ethnic group known as the Picts in north-east Scotland. Some of the Picts certainly spoke Brythonic varieties, but it seems that some may have spoken a non-Indo-European language; thus the Picts may have been a linguistically diverse group who were regarded as a unit, at least by others, on the basis of shared cultural characteristics. It does not seem as if Gaelic and Brythonic have in historical times ever been readily mutually comprehensible, and on a political and cultural level there is no strong popular sense of any shared Celtic identity.

The modern Brythonic languages are Welsh, Breton, taken to Brittany by refugees from Great Britain displaced by the Anglo-Saxon invasions (see Section 3.3.3), and Cornish, which ceased to be an everyday spoken language in the eighteenth century, but which has been the subject of a revival movement since the mid-twentieth century. Welsh and Cornish have been separated by English for many centuries, and, though there are striking similarities between them, they are clearly distinct; the level of similarity between Cornish and Breton is actually higher (see Price 1984: 134–45).

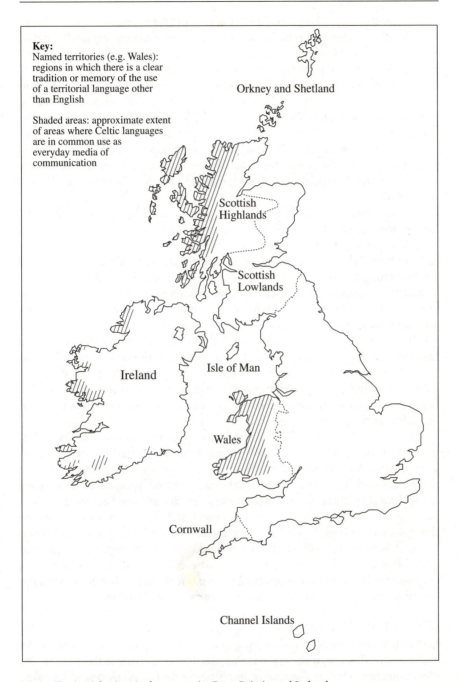

Key:
Named territories (e.g. Wales):
regions in which there is a clear
tradition or memory of the use
of a territorial language other
than English

Shaded areas: approximate extent
of areas where Celtic languages
are in common use as
everyday media of
communication

Orkney and Shetland

Scottish
Highlands

Scottish
Lowlands

Ireland

Isle of Man

Wales

Cornwall

Channel Islands

Map 1. Territorial minority languages in Great Britain and Ireland

The modern Gaelic languages are Irish, Scottish Gaelic, and Manx in the Isle of Man. The last-mentioned is no longer an everyday spoken language, its last native speaker having died in the 1970s, but it still plays a role in a local sense of Manx identity (see Price 1984: 71–83). Irish is frequently referred to as 'Gaelic', but 'Irish' is now the preferred term in Ireland, and we shall use it for that reason, but also to attempt to avoid confusion with Scottish Gaelic. Scottish Gaelic must not be confused with Scots, the Germanic varieties of Scotland. The relationship of the Gaelic languages to each other is obvious, Ulster Irish being very close indeed in every sense to south-western Scottish Gaelic. There is even a long history of written Irish functioning as the written language for speakers of Scottish Gaelic. Their modern separation is political and geographical as much as linguistic (see Russell 1995: 27–8).

Despite many borrowings from English, particularly into Welsh, and particularly in informal registers, the basic lexicon of the Celtic languages is remote from English; for example, although common origins for Welsh *haul* (sun) and English 'sun', and for Welsh *ci* (dog) and English 'hound' can be conclusively proved, no one but a historical linguist would suspect such common origins for these words. The Celtic languages also have certain grammatical characteristics that seem most exotic to English-speakers, like verb–subject–object (VSO) word order in declarative sentences, and initial mutation. The VSO word order of Celtic is seen in a Welsh sentence like *Mae Gwen yn y dref*, a word-for-word translation being 'Is Gwen in the town'; the correct translation is 'Gwen is in town'. Initial mutation means that the initial consonants of words may change depending on their grammatical relationships to preceding words, so that *ci* can become *chi, gi*, or *nghi* depending on the grammatical context (for a fuller account of the linguistics of the Celtic languages, see Ball 1993).

Apart from Manx and Cornish (modern spoken Cornish is in any case a planned creation), the Celtic languages all show substantial internal diversity. They are considered nevertheless to be single languages in each case, since they are spoken in clearly perceived geographical units, and their speakers see themselves as constituting cultural units. The unity has also in each case been cemented by adversity, as each group of speakers has experienced diverse threats to language and culture from English-speakers. Additionally, Irish, Scottish Gaelic, and Welsh now each have single codified written standard varieties, although only in the case of Welsh is a spoken standard in widespread use; in the other cases all spoken language can be viewed as dialect. In the case of Welsh and Irish, but less so in the case of Scottish Gaelic, the languages are seen as national languages.

2.2.2. *Germanic Languages*

English belongs to the Germanic subgroup of the Indo-European language family. The name of this subgroup suggests that German is the parent language of the others, but, this is not so; German is simply one of the Germanic languages, along with English, Frisian, Dutch, Yiddish, and the Scandinavian languages. The fact that English is a member of this subgroup means that English-speakers can actually have some limited comprehension of simple sentences in the other languages, particularly in Dutch, without instruction in them, but this fact has little contemporary ideological significance; the insight that some foreign languages are less alien than others seems unimportant to most English-speakers.

English derives from the speech of the Anglo-Saxon invaders from parts of what are now the Netherlands, north Germany, and Denmark, who settled in Britain from the mid-fifth century. The dialects brought into Britain at this time were quite diverse, but nevertheless a sense of a common identity and of a common language may have been present because of the clear differences between Germanic-speakers and Celtic-speakers, both linguistic and cultural, seen, for example, in the paganism of the former, and the Christianity of many of the latter. We can hence perhaps refer to the Germanic dialects of Britain at this period as 'English', without too much distortion through hindsight.

English had spread by the eighth century throughout what is now England, with the exception of much of Cornwall and parts of Cumbria, and also into south-east Scotland. Gaelic seems then by the eleventh century to have become the dominant language in Scotland, only to experience subsequent relentless pressure from English, which has now confined Gaelic as a territorial language to the Western Isles and parts of the Highlands. By the end of the eighteenth century English had replaced Cornish in Cornwall. English was spoken in small areas in Wales in the Middle Ages, including, significantly, the major towns, but English was not widely spoken in most of the country until the nineteenth century.[2] Although there were early inroads of speakers of English, and of Norman French, into Ireland, Irish remained numerically dominant in Ireland until the first half of the nineteenth century, only then to suffer a dramatic decline in favour of English, so that now Irish is the everyday spoken language of only a small minority of the population.

The overwhelming dominance of English in contemporary Britain and Ireland is hence a relatively recent phenomenon, the memory of the use of other languages remains potent, and revival and maintenance movements play a clear part in nationalisms.

Like other languages covering relatively large areas and spoken mainly by people who, until the advent of modern communications, spoke to others only within the home locality, English shows considerable dialectal diversity. Dialects representing real comprehension problems to speakers of the standard language have perhaps declined more rapidly in England than in some other European areas for a variety of reasons: the mechanization of agriculture resulting in a decline in the indigenous rural population, and the country's high level of urbanization and industrialization can be cited. It is almost certainly the case that a clear majority of native speakers of English in England now speak the standard

---

[2] Welsh even survived in parts of Herefordshire and Shropshire in England until modern times.

language, or else forms of what J. C. Wells has labelled 'general non-standard English'—forms of English that are generally mutually comprehensible and comprehensible to standard speakers, but which incorporate a number of clearly non-standard features (see Wells 1982: 2–4). Despite this linguistic levelling, linguistic differences remain significant in regional and class loyalties, and there is a high degree of awareness of regional and class accents—that is of pronunciation differences occurring in varieties that, grammatically and lexically, are either general non-standard or even standard. There is relatively low dialectal diversity in English in areas where it has replaced other languages only in the last century or two, in Ireland, Wales, and the Highlands of Scotland. In these areas, however, there are varieties of English that are easily recognized both by their speakers and by outsiders, showing strong substratum influence from the Celtic languages in pronunciation and in certain lexical and grammatical characteristics, and that can be very significant in matters of identity (see e.g. Bliss 1984).

As with other diverse languages, before the modern levelling occurred the status of English as a single language was very much the function of political factors; had not a unified state developed in England, matters might have been very different. Given the continuing institutional differences between England and Scotland, it is perhaps not surprising that the English dialects of the Lowlands of Scotland have many of the characteristics of a distinct language, and we shall indeed reserve the label 'Scottish English' for the standard language in Scotland and varieties relatively close to it, referring to more clearly dialectal varieties as 'Scots' or *Lallans* (see below).[3]

Another Germanic language, or group of dialects, which played an important role in Britain and Ireland for several centuries, is Norse. 'Norse' is used as a convenient label for the Germanic dialects of medieval Scandinavia, the Faroes and Iceland, and their modern descendants. In modern northern Europe the differences between these languages are significant, though not always clear-cut (see Chapter 5), but from a British and Irish perspective these differences have never been very meaningful, hence the use of the single undifferentiated label of 'Norse'. From the eighth until the eleventh centuries speakers of Norse visited these islands as raiders (the 'Vikings'), as traders, and as settlers. The chief areas of settlement were the large swathe of eastern and northern England known as the Danelaw; the major medieval ports of Ireland, which seem to have been Scandinavian foundations; the Hebrides, where Norse replaced Gaelic, at least partly; and the Orkneys and the Shetlands, where it replaced earlier speech, which may have been Pictish. In the Hebrides and the Irish towns Norse had disappeared again by the end of the Middle Ages, being supplanted by Gaelic in the Hebrides

---

[3] Labelling these dialects as 'English' begs a number of questions. The labels 'Anglo-Saxon', 'Anglian', or 'Germanic' may be preferable. In an otherwise excellent book, exploring many of the themes outlined here, I think Ralph Grillo (1989) is mistaken in generally treating *Lallans* as virtually a group of English dialects, and seeing it on the winning side, as it were, in an English–Celtic struggle (see esp. Grillo 1989: 49–55).

and by English and Irish in Ireland, but in the Orkneys and Shetlands, where it is known as 'Norn', it remained until the eighteenth century, having since been succeeded by varieties of English and of Scots that show clear Norn influence. Given its close similarity to English at the time (there may even have been mutual comprehensibility) and perhaps also because of strong cultural similarities between their speakers, Norse and English did not remain distinct in England. By the eleventh century they seem to have given rise to a strongly Norse-influenced English, the influence being seen in the lexicon, even extending to the pronominal system, where *they* and *them* derive from Old Norse. Norse influence is clear in modern standard English and its precursors, and is strongest in dialects not only from parts of the Danelaw area, but also from north of the Danelaw, including Scots (see Price 1984: 199–200).

2.2.3. *French*

After the Norman Conquest of 1066 French replaced English in England as the language of the aristocracy and some members of other social groups for roughly 250 years. French-speakers also penetrated the aristocracy of Scotland, and the invasions of Ireland and Wales in the Middle Ages, now popularly perceived as English invasions, were, in reality, undertaken by speakers of both Norman-French and English. Given the role played by French speakers over a long period, and given the continuing prestige of French throughout Europe and beyond, it is not surprising that all of the territorial languages of Britain and Ireland show clear French influence in the lexicon. The influence is particularly noticeable and particularly great in English, and represents one of the most decisive factors separating English (and Scots) from the other Germanic languages. The conquest of England by William Duke of Normandy brought a personal union between England and the Duke's territories in France. His successors lost their French territories over several hundred years, with the exception of the Channel Islands, which remain today in a personal union with the United Kingdom; they are not part of the UK nor of the European Union. They remained French-speaking until the twentieth century, the everyday spoken language being Norman dialects of French, the official language being standard French. Today they are overwhelmingly English-speaking, standard French being restricted to certain ceremonial contexts, and Norman French dialects being the first language of only a relatively small number of older people (see Price 1984: 207–16). Given the social dominance of French-speakers in early medieval England, as demonstrated by the thoroughgoing linguistic influence of French on English, the virtual disappearance of French as an everyday spoken medium by the fifteenth century is striking (see Price 1984: 217–19).

2.3. National Groups

In almost all parts of Europe there is, as we shall see in subsequent chapters, a certain mismatch between nations and states; people considered by themselves and others to belong to the same nation may be an indigenous population in several states, and a single state may contain a number of groups that consider themselves to belong to a number of different nations. In others there may be a closer correspondence between states and nations. At first sight there might appear to be such a close correspondence in Britain and Ireland; virtually all of the inhabitants of the Irish Republic consider themselves, and are seen by others, to belong to the Irish nation, and apart from some members of minorities, the majority of the inhabitants of mainland Britain (England, Scotland and Wales) would probably accept the label 'British'. In Northern Ireland there is, of course, a serious conflict arising from the claim to a single territory of two groups, seeing themselves as British and Irish respectively.

Only at first sight is the British situation relatively simple; as we shall see it hides manifold complexities. In most European states today there is a majority population that has only one ethnic-cum-national label for itself, even though there may be minorities who are seen or who see themselves as having more complex loyalties. In contrast, in Britain virtually the entire population has at least two ethnic or national labels that it can apply to itself. This starts with the largest single ethnic or national group, which can use both of the labels 'British' and 'English'. The view of the British situation that I propose to adopt is that of two tiers of national identity: at the level of the state I consider there to be a British national identity, which all citizens, potentially all inhabitants, can share; this is clearly a civic national identity. At a lower level I consider there to be English, Welsh, and Scottish national identities, leaving aside for the moment the identities experienced in Ulster. These second-tier identities have more characteristics of ethnic national identities, although, since England, Wales, and Scotland are separate legal entities (this is particularly clear in the case of Scotland), there is an element of civic identity also. What is important, however, is that these second-tier identities are often not shared by non-indigenous ethnic minorities; for example, residents of England who are British citizens of Asian, African, or Caribbean origin will usually be described, and will describe themselves, as 'British' but not as 'English' (Viv Edwards, personal communication; see also Crick 1997).

The vision of two-tier national identities in Britain accords with the legal structure of the state, and is in line with the thinking of many scholars—for example, Colley (1992). I adopt it here since it lends itself well to the description of the language–nationalism relationship: in England, apart from Cornwall, English is the only language that plays any part in national identity, while in Wales and Scotland it is clearly rivalled by other languages, while Ulster has a distinct pattern of rival nationalisms. This vision is, however, not uncontroversial. There is a real sense in which, over the last few centuries, English identity, relabelled as 'British', has superseded others. This is roughly the general tenor of the contributions to Schwarz (1996), a volume entitled significantly *The Expansion of England*. The situation is further complicated by the fact that the distinction between a British and an English identity is often not clear (see below).

Why do we describe these second-tier identities as national identities and not either as ethnic identities or regional or class identities? A major reason for using the 'national' label is that it is actually very frequently used by the people concerned themselves. Moreover, the identities in question are, as are national identities generally, clearly linked to national territories, which are also clearly officially defined, and not just vaguely delimited, as regions often are. Welsh and Scottish identities are also clearly linked to language, as are so many national identities, albeit, as we shall see, in very complex ways. There is also a common aspiration towards some political autonomy, or even sovereignty. I shall proceed now to a discussion of the various groups that can be seen as demonstrating national identities in Britain and Ireland, focusing particularly on the role of language in these identities. One national group, the Scots, has a long tradition of bipartite linguistic and cultural division into Highlanders and Lowlanders, and these two groups will be discussed separately.

2.3.1. *The English*

In the context of this discussion, the English, meaning members of the indigenous, English-speaking majority in England, can be seen as a national group. England is economically, culturally, and politically dominant in the United Kingdom, and many of the English refer to the state, at least on occasions, as 'England'. Nevertheless 'England' and 'Britain' or 'the UK' are not simply synonymous for this group of people; at the very least, the latter two terms sound more formal, and political, while 'England' has emotional overtones of warmth and home.[4] There has always been some awareness on the part of the English that Britain and England are distinct entities, and, with the growing prominence of nationalist movements in Scotland and Wales, this may be increasing; it has, of course, always been clearer in border areas.

Given the dominance of England in Britain, it is not surprising that English nationalism and British nationalism are often not clearly distinct from each other. The English-speaking indigenous population of England lacks generally accepted symbols of its national identity. The English language cannot easily fulfil such a function, since it is, of course, spoken as a native language by members of so many other groups. We might imagine that a specific English variety of the language could play an identifying role, but this is also problematic since, although Anglo-English is less diverse than some other languages, it is subjectively perceived as very diverse. Anglo-English with the RP accent, often perceived beyond England as a kind of typical Anglo-English, is in fact nothing of the sort; it is a variety specific to a very small social élite, around 3 per cent of the population, and evokes strongly negative reactions from many of those who do not use it. The subjective

---

[4] In many other languages, and in non-British varieties of English, the distinction between terms for England and for Britain or the United Kingdom is not consistently made. For example, many French-speakers will refer to the state as *Angleterre* (England). The terms *Grande Bretagne* (Great Britain) and *Royaume Uni* (United Kingdom) do exist and are used, but much less frequently.

diversity of Anglo-English is such that its speakers are often unable reliably to perceive its boundaries. A distinct 'r' sound in words like 'cart' (non-prevocalic 'r') is the most salient characteristic for English people of Irish or American English, and yet it is not universal in American English, and is also used by millions of speakers of Anglo-English from the south and west of England (and central Lancashire). Welsh and Scottish English are identified by monophthongs (pure vowels) in words like 'plate' and 'coat', but similar monophthongs are very wide-spread in northern England. The diversity of Anglo-English correlates with signif-icant regional and class differences and prevents the language from constituting an effective symbol of Englishness. Those of a nationalistic inclination tend to focus on real or imagined cultural characteristics such as humour and a sense of fair play, or historical memories, particularly of victory in two world wars. Many of these symbols of the nation are shared by the other national groups, and are better described as 'British' rather than 'English'.[5]

One region, the county of Cornwall, has a regionalism with a clearer linguistic dimension, and, alone of regions in England, has a political party *Mebyon Kernow* ('Sons of Cornwall') that strives for political autonomy, and to which the adjec-tive 'nationalist' is applied. Significant in this regionalism is the Cornish language, which died out in the eighteenth century in the west of the county (up to a millen-nium earlier in the east), but which is extensively documented, and which is currently being revived by enthusiasts (see Price 1984: 134–45).

2.3.2. *The Lowland Scots*

In contrast to the other nations under discussion here, there seems to have been no period in recorded history before the twentieth century in which Scotland had a clear majority of speakers of a single language. Even today we can distinguish three regions with markedly different linguistic profiles: the Highlands and Western Isles; the Lowlands; and the Northern Isles (Orkney and Shetland).

From the thirteenth century until the Reformation, Scots seems to have been the dominant language of the Lowlands. As we have seen, it is possible to view Scots as a group of northern English dialects, but before the Reformation a process of codification, separate from that under way in England, had commenced; this gives Scots, both then and now, a claim to the status of a separate language. The most popular term for this language in Scots itself is *Lallans* ('Lowland language'), and, although *Lallans* is not a common term in English, we shall use it occasionally in this section in order to avoid confusion between 'the Scots' in the sense of 'the Scottish people' and 'Scots' in the sense of 'a Scottish language'. *Lallans* can also claim the status of a distinct language, since it is not at all readily comprehensible to English-speakers from England, except perhaps those who know northern dialects. The spread of northern English dialects into the Lowlands from the

---

[5] The lack of clear linguistic self-perception among the English has been remarked upon by linguists, but is not well researched (Peter Trudgill, personal communication).

eleventh century (such dialects had possibly been used in the far south-east of Scotland from an earlier period) is not easy to understand, given that political power seems to have been in the hands of Gaelic-speakers, but it may have been furthered by the flight of English-speaking aristocrats to the Scottish royal court after the Norman invasion, and by the fact that the foundation of towns in medieval Scotland may have been undertaken partly by immigrants from northern England (see Mitchinson 1982: 16–36).

From the perspective of the nineteenth and twentieth centuries, when modern nation-states were fully established in many parts of Europe, the history of Scotland from the sixteenth to the eighteenth centuries can seem extremely paradoxical. On the one hand, we seem to see attempts by one nation-state, Scotland, to assert its independence from another, England. On the other, we see ethnic and religious tensions within Scotland: on the linguistic dimension, Gaelic-speaking Highlanders against Scots-speaking Lowlanders; on the religious dimension, Calvinist Presbyterian Protestants, strongest in the Lowlands, against Catholics, strongest in the Highlands, and Anglican Protestants (Episcopalians), strongest in some northern lowland areas. By the end of the eighteenth century these tensions had been resolved by the Calvinist local élite of Scotland accepting a political union with Anglican England, which entrenched an established position for Presbyterianism in Scotland, with Anglicanism in a relatively privileged minority position, and Catholicism defeated and marginalized (see Mitchinson 1982: 303–56). The price for all of this in political and cultural terms was the loss of Scottish political independence, and the relegation of Highland culture and the Gaelic language to the status of regional Highland peculiarities (see below), and the relegation of *Lallans* generally to the status of a group of dialects of English. The loss of status of *Lallans*, or rather its failure further to develop the status of an independent language, had started with the Reformation, when Scottish Protestants accepted English as the language of religion, in place of Latin, with few problems and no resistance (see Hardie 1996: 61–3). Throughout the period, and indeed continuing up to the present, there is a persistent desire on the part of a majority to retain a distinct Scottish identity. This is manifest to an extent by cultural production in Scots, notably the writings of Robert Burns (1759–96), which have enjoyed enormous popularity, but a distinct Scottish identity is most visibly perpetuated in the preservation of distinct legal and educational systems.

In the eighteenth century the most serious political challenges to the new Protestant British state came not from Scottish nationalists but from the Jacobites, supporters of the Stuart dynasty deposed in 1688. Their support in Great Britain came overwhelmingly from Catholics and Highlanders, only to a limited extent from Scottish Lowlanders. The Jacobites' modern popular image (in some quarters) as Scottish nationalists is almost certainly mistaken (see Mitchinson 1982: 337–56). Over the last two centuries Scotland's major political concerns have been, as in the rest of Britain, economic and social, with struggles against the ruling élite of Britain being conceived, as in England, in class terms (see above); however, given the persistent tradition of separate nationhood, the tendency to interpret social and economic issues in national terms has always been latent. It re-emerged in the late twentieth century with the large-scale exploitation of oil off the coast of Scotland, which weakened the conventional argument that an independent Scotland would not be economically viable, and with the development of the European Union, which is seen as a favourable economic and political framework for small states to enjoy at least a measure of independence (see Mitchinson 1982: 413–26).

Scottish nationalism has not allowed *Lallans* to regain, or achieve, the clear status of an independent language. It is rivalled as a national language by Gaelic, which, although it probably has fewer speakers,[6] has the great advantage of being unambiguously distinct from English. Gaelic also benefits from the reinterpretation of Scotland as a Celtic nation, which was a facet of Scottish Romanticism, and which began, interestingly enough, about the time when the defeat of the Jacobites rendered the speakers of the Celtic language, of Gaelic, politically impotent (see Trevor-Roper 1992; Chase 1996). This enthusiasm for things Celtic has led, for example, to Highland dress, such as the kilt for men, being interpreted as Scottish, but has never led Lowlanders to learn Gaelic in large numbers; it has, however, not benefited *Lallans*.

In the latter part of the twentieth century nationalism has brought some interest in *Lallans*. A translation of the New Testament is now available for the first time ever, and the European Union has accorded to *Lallans* the status of a regional language (see Hardie 1996: 65). The nationalism of Lowland Scottish people certainly does have a linguistic dimension, but a very diffuse one; there is often affection for *Lallans*, but often with little desire to increase its range of use. There may be a favourable attitude to Gaelic, which has probably not been felt in most of the Lowlands for at least about 500 years. Often Lowlanders seem to see the linguistic dimension of Scottish identity linked to dialect or non-standard forms intermediate between *Lallans* and Scottish standard English. Very often loyalty focuses merely on Scottish standard or near-standard English, varieties that differ from the English of England only in pronunciation (the contrasts here can, however, be very marked), and in the use of some specifically Scottish lexicon often arising from the distinct legal and educational systems or from the different dominant form of Protestantism (see Abrams and Hogg 1988). Scotland represents in my view the very interesting case of a non-independent nation in which the distinct national identity is nevertheless seen to a great extent in institutional terms, with distinct culture playing a lesser role, and a distinct language being of only limited importance.

2.3.3. *The Highland Scots*

After Gaelic had been restored some time in the late Middle Ages to all of the

---

[6] No statistics exist for the number of *Lallans*-speakers.

Western Isles, some areas of which had been Norse-speaking for several centuries, the Highlands and Islands remained predominantly Gaelic-speaking until the late eighteenth century. There was hence a clear linguistic divide between the Highlands and the Lowlands, but this paralleled and reinforced cultural, economic, and social contrasts; while in the Lowlands a modern money-based economy was developing, the Highlands retained the clan system, a form of patriarchal feudalism. Many clans remained Catholic after the Reformation, and there was, and is, a higher representation for Protestant denominations other than the established Church of Scotland than in the Lowlands. A high proportion of the clans sided with the Jacobites in their long struggle with the British state (see above), and the final defeat of the Jacobites in 1746 represented a disaster for many Highlanders. It was an extremely severe reverse for the Gaelic language and culture, and was exacerbated by serious loss of population, as subsistence agriculture gave way to large-scale sheep-rearing or simply recreational use of land for hunting and fishing by clan chiefs turned into modern landlords. Surplus tenants were often evicted in so-called 'clearances', or, impoverished, fell victim to starvation and disease. Thousands of Gaelic speakers emigrated to other continents or to the new urban industrial centres of England or Wales or of the English-speaking or Scots-speaking Lowlands, which experienced rapid industrialization in the late eighteenth and early nineteenth centuries (see Mitchinson 1982: 375–7). The number of speakers of Gaelic declined dramatically to reach about 65,000 in 1991, about 1.3 per cent of the population of Scotland (see Thomson 1994). The attitude of the Scottish education system to Gaelic language and culture was at best one of toleration; often they were opposed as symbols of backwardness, of Catholicism, or of disloyalty to the state (see Price 1984: 63–4). However, as we have seen above, the Romantic movement elevated selected elements of Highland culture to the status of symbols of a general Scottish identity.

Despite these reverses, a sense of Highland identity persists, alongside Highland variants of Scottish nationalism. It is currently quite strongly linked to language, although in earlier generations many people failed to transmit the language to their children, fearing, as do many in minority communities, that the home language would impede children's economic prospects (see Price 1984: 63–4). A linguistic difference from the Lowlands is also seen in the fact that, where Gaelic has ceased to be spoken, it is generally replaced by a distinctive Highland English, clearly phonetically and phonologically different from Lowland Scottish English, and relatively close to the standard language; there is no extensive use of Scots in the Highlands (see Shuken 1984). Within the Highlands and Islands there is a contemporary linguistic division between those areas (roughly the Hebrides) where Gaelic still has a noticeable presence, and the rest of the region, where Highland English dominates.

Like many minority languages, Gaelic experienced a revival in the late twentieth century; there is now radio and television broadcasting, there are Gaelic-medium schools (some even in the Lowlands) and a college, and there is some official use in the Western Isles (see Johnstone 1994: 32–82).[7]

Highland identity is perhaps best viewed as a form of regionalism rather than nationalism, since there is no movement for political independence for the Highlands. Among indigenous minority language groups in Europe, Gaelic-speakers are one of the groups that do not manifest a nationalism of their own. Perhaps this arises from the peculiar status of Scotland as an institutionalized nation that nevertheless lacks independence; Gaelic-speakers seeking to enhance the status of their language and region are hence currently channelled into Scottish nationalism rather than a Highlands or Gaelic nationalism. Were Scotland independent, we can speculate that there might indeed be a Highlands or Gaelic nationalism.

A sense of distinct non-Scottish identity has never left Orkney and Shetland, linked to the survival there, until the eighteenth century, of Norn (see Section 2.2.2), and to the modern awareness of that survival.

2.3.4. *The Irish*

As a starting point for the discussion of the nationalisms of Ireland, it is convenient to divide the indigenous population into Protestants and Catholics.[8] As we shall see, these designations are misleading. In the first place, they do not mean that members of the two groups are necessarily regular attenders at the churches of the religious denominations (though by general west European standards church attendance is relatively high), but rather that people feel that they live within either a Catholic or a Protestant tradition. Other designations, such as 'nationalists' for Catholics, are also misleading: labelling Catholics as 'nationalists' suggests that they are all active in a nationalist political movement, which is certainly not the case. Among those within a Catholic tradition there is a popular belief that this group represents the descendants of the original population of the island, the genuine Irish.

At the earliest period of which we have clear linguistic knowledge, about AD 500, Ireland was probably largely Goidelic-, Gaelic- or Irish-speaking.[9] The position changed with the Viking settlements (see above), which saw the foundation of Norse-speaking towns, which may have subsequently become English-speaking without, possibly, in some cases, ever having had an Irish-speaking majority. Further change came with medieval colonists from Great Britain, who spoke

---

[7] I am much indebted to Konstanze Gebel for a great deal of information on Gaelic.

[8] The term 'indigenous' is used here to mean almost the entire population, excluding only those of known recent origin, such as the small Chinese minority, and those who would, by the definition neither of themselves nor of others, be included in the Protestant or Catholic groups, such as Jews. The term has to be used with care, since members of the Catholic group often expressly see themselves as indigenous, and the Protestants as 'newcomers'.

[9] The language is frequently referred to as 'Gaelic'. I refer to it as 'Irish', partly because it is the most popular designation in contemporary Ireland, and partly to avoid confusion with the Gaelic of Scotland (see above).

Norman-French and English, but who seem often to have been largely linguistically and culturally assimilated to the majority population, at least after a generation or two (see Ranelagh 1994: 41, 45). From the twelfth century kings of England claimed suzerainty over Ireland, but their claims were not convincingly implemented until the sixteenth century, when a consciously Protestant English state emerged, which saw Catholic Ireland, where the Reformation had failed to take hold, as an exposed flank in its defences against its Catholic enemies in Spain or France. There followed a campaign by the English, later British, state, lasting from the sixteenth until the twentieth centuries, to neutralize the perceived threat of Catholicism in Ireland (see Ranelagh 1994: *passim*).

The configuration of religious, ethnic, and linguistic divisions was much clearer in Ireland than in other parts of the British state. In Scotland there was an ethnolinguistic divide between Highlands and Lowlands, but the different groups occupied fairly distinct geographical regions. In Ireland, in contrast, most regions contained a Catholic Irish-speaking peasant majority contrasting with Protestant English-speaking bourgeoisie and landowners. In Scotland, Anglicanism, the Protestant denomination of the British élite, was never more than a minority faith, but then the majority Protestant denomination, Presbyterianism, also had a bourgeois following, and forced the state to accept it as the established religion in Scotland. In Ireland, Anglicanism was also numerically a minority denomination, but it embraced virtually all of the more powerful sections of society; a non-Anglican, Catholic, bourgeoisie developed only in the late nineteenth century. Catholicism in Scotland was seen as a threat by the Anglican state and by Presbyterians alike, but after the defeat of the Jacobites was never more than an irritant;[10] in Ireland it was always the majority denomination. In Scotland there was a highly complex linguistic situation: an English-speaking élite did contrast with Gaelic-speaking and Scots-speaking peasantry, but the distinction between English and Scots is not always clear, and Scots-speakers and Gaelic-speakers did not feel a cultural and linguistic bond between them that could have led them to combine against English-speakers; in Ireland there was a much clearer divide between an Irish-speaking underprivileged majority and an English-speaking élite. In Wales there was a fairly clear divide between a Welsh-speaking underprivileged majority and an English-speaking élite, but it was not so clearly reinforced by religious differences: Catholics were a tiny minority, and, while Welsh-speakers tended to be non-Anglican Protestants (Nonconformists), there were also Welsh-speaking Anglicans. In any case, Nonconformism was not seen by the state to represent such a threat as Catholicism.

The lines of conflict in Ireland are then generally clearer, but an element of complexity was introduced by the plantations. These were settlements at various

---

[10] Ethno-religious tensions between Catholics and Protestants did develop after large-scale Irish immigration into industrial Scotland (and England), but only in major Scottish cities, such as Glasgow (in England it was noticeable only on Merseyside) (see Mitchinson 1982: 381).

times and places by Protestants from Great Britain that the state encouraged in order to weaken the geographical dominance of the Irish-speaking Catholic majority. The indigenous population was dispossessed in the areas in question, but then often had to be re-employed as labourers; the potential for conflict is obvious. By far the largest plantation, and the only one that is still visible by its distinct ethnic character was in Ulster, where large numbers of Scottish Presbyterians settled (see Ranelagh 1994: 55–7).

Not surprisingly there was resistance in Ireland to English domination. Modern nationalism tends to reinterpret this as a struggle of a Catholic, Irish-speaking Irish nation against colonialism by an English-speaking Protestant English nation. The reality was usually more complex; an economic struggle, or simply a struggle for survival by an impoverished peasantry, is an important theme. Discontent on the part of English-speaking Protestants against a remote state based on another island was a factor; a significant number of early national-ists were Protestants, such as Wolfe Tone (1763–98) (see Ranelagh 1984: 55, 71, 82–4).

A struggle to preserve Irish language and culture was largely insignificant until the late nineteenth century; nationalists and the Catholic Church were often indifferent to the language, seeing it as a barrier to the social advancement of its speakers. The Catholic Church's liturgical language was, of course, Latin, and its somewhat negative attitude to Irish was also coloured by the fact that Protestants sometimes evangelized through the medium of Irish. The plantations are often seen now as a blow for Irish, as indeed they doubtless often were; but some of the Scottish Protestants in the Ulster plantation were Gaelic-speakers, whose language was often mutually comprehensible with Irish, and so temporarily reinforced the position of Irish in certain areas (see Nic Craith 1995).

As we have already seen, nineteenth- and early twentieth-century Britain and Ireland experienced social movements, also found elsewhere, that can be inter-preted in various ways; one common interpretation is to see them as attempts by those excluded from political and economic power to force concessions from the political and economic élite. What is interesting about Ireland is that such politi-cal and economic aims became channelled into a nationalist movement. The fact that this happened can be explained by the clear ethno-religious gulf separating the élite from the majority, a gulf, as we have seen, that was much more pronounced than comparable divides in other regions. The Irish conflict was also more bitter, given the more extreme absolute poverty suffered by many of the underprivileged, seen in dramatic form in the famines of 1845–9. It would, however, be a grave mistake to see a simple opposition between a Catholic Irish-speaking majority and an English-speaking Protestant elite, 'the ascendancy'. Poor Protestants, chiefly found in northern Ireland, suffered similar economic hard-ships, though their position was generally better than that of poor Catholics, and adherents of non-Anglican Protestant churches, to which most of the northern working class belonged, suffered similar political disqualifications to Catholics.

Additionally, as we have seen, many middle-class Protestants identified with Irish nationalism, and even provided some of its leaders.

The subsuming of various social and political aims into a nationalist movement, rather than simply a radical political movement, has given it a particular character. It has meant that, for some at least, the independence of the entire historic territory of Ireland has been an overriding aim. The fact that only the twenty-six counties of the Republic of Ireland were granted independence from Britain in 1922,[11] and not the six counties of Northern Ireland, is a source of continuing crisis, unresolved at the time of writing, engaged in, admittedly, by only a relatively very small number of people, and affecting largely Northern Ireland, the Republic to a much lesser extent. The nationalist nature of the movement for advancement has also led to its espousal of cultural and linguistic aims, the maintenance and revival of traditional Irish cultural forms and of the Irish language. Such aims have been espoused by many individuals and groups—the Gaelic league and its founder Douglas Hyde, a Protestant and first President of the Irish Republic, being particularly noteworthy (see Crowley 1996: 99–146). Such aims are not unusual in nationalist movements, but the Irish case is most striking in the lack of success in promoting the national language; no other European language that is the first national language of a sovereign independent state is spoken as a first language by only a small minority of the population. The reasons for the weakness of Irish are many. First, unlike some languages, it has to contend with very strong rival symbols of national identity: a clearly defined national territory (an island), popular national cultural forms (music and dance), and, perhaps most significantly, a national religion (Catholicism). Even more importantly, we have to remember that the nationalist movement was very much a movement for social and political progress, and the language was seen, for monoglot speakers, as a distinct barrier to such progress; as is often the case, bilingualism was also seen as a hindrance, a popular belief that has little linguistic foundation. Even some nationalist leaders—for example, Daniel O'Connell—showed indifference to the fate of the language (see Crowley 1996: 99–112). In contrast to many other languages of subject nations, by the time Irish became a focus of interest for a local intelligentsia it was already, numerically, in a clearly minority position; a Catholic middle class sympathetic to Irish did not develop until the late nineteenth century,[12] by which time famine, emigration, and education through English had very seriously depleted the number of native Irish-speakers.

In the contemporary Republic of Ireland there is little or no hostility between Irish Catholics and a Protestant minority, largely because the latter group, though still influential, is numerically tiny, and generally now identifies itself as Irish

---

[11] The twenty-six counties were independent *de facto* as the Irish Free State from 1922. Full political sovereignty, as the Republic of Ireland, came in 1949.

[12] As we have already seen, there was also a small number of middle-class Protestant enthusiasts.

anyway. Attitudes to the Irish language are favourable on the part of most groups in the population, but, perhaps strangely, favourable attitudes do not include the desire to use the language in everyday life, or even, in many cases, to become reasonably proficient in it. Fluency in the Irish language is the preserve of a small number of enthusiasts, chiefly middle-class intellectuals, and of native-speaking inhabitants of the small areas in the west and south (the *Gaeltacht*) where the language still is the everyday medium of communication. The language has been energetically promoted by the government since independence, with depressingly poor results. For most people who use it, Irish is a second language. It lacks an informal colloquial standard form; speakers of Irish as a first language all use regional dialects. This also inhibits its use. Most Irish people seem happy with a linguistic identity focused on Irish varieties of English (see Ó Laoire 1995).

In Northern Ireland Catholics and Protestants still do identify themselves clearly as Irish and British respectively (see Section 2.3.5), and, like so much else, attitudes to the language have polarized on sectarian–ethnic–national lines. Protestants, with some exceptions, are strongly hostile to Irish, where earlier generations were not necessarily so and may have even been speakers of Irish or the closely related Scottish Gaelic. Catholics have strongly positive attitudes; indeed learning Irish has become a symbol of nationalist activism, but still only a minority is fluent (see Nic Craith 1995).

Many European nationalist movements rallied around national language, and other cultural symbols, before gaining independence; in Ireland independence was achieved without any real halt to the apparently inexorable decline of the national language. Only the contemporary general European revival of minority languages may have slowed that decline.

2.3.5. *Ulster Protestants*

Given the circumstances of the Ulster plantation, it is not surprising that there is a long history of hostility between Catholics and Protestants in the north of Ireland. Elsewhere in Ireland, Protestants were, by the beginning of the twentieth century, overwhelmingly middle class and relatively economically secure, but numerically few. They have retained a relatively privileged position in the independent Republic, which now experiences little religious or ethnic tension (see Section 2.3.4).

In the north the large Protestant working class, often, as we have seen, also experiencing some religious discrimination as well as economic disadvantage, could have made common cause with Catholic workers, but earlier inclinations to do this were stifled by the expressly nationalist, as opposed to purely economic and social character of the Catholic movement. Partly as a reaction to Protestant hostility, elements in the nationalist movement aimed to establish an officially Catholic state, and indeed the power of the Catholic Church in the Republic has been undeniable (see Hempton 1996: 72–92). Perhaps the most important element in northern Protestant attitudes was the very common antipathy found in an underprivileged population towards a group even less privileged than itself, which nevertheless seems in danger of gaining the upper hand. The movement for Irish independence hence reinforced the feeling of separate ethnicity on the part of the Ulster Protestants who came more and more clearly to see themselves as Unionist 'British', and to see Protestantism and Britishness as two sides of the same coin. As British identity in Great Britain has become less and less linked to religion, and as Scottish and Welsh nationalisms have emerged, some Ulster Protestants have become aware of the growing differences in national or ethnic identity between themselves and the inhabitants of mainland Britain, and have increasingly used the labels Ulstermen (and Ulsterwomen) for themselves, labels that always were used to some extent (see Hempton 1996: 163). Had Ireland remained united, either independent or under some sort of British sovereignty, Ulster Protestants might have come to some kind of accommodation with the Catholic majority in Ireland, but, given their relative local strength, they were able, supported by certain influential English political groups, notably within the Conservative Party, to achieve a separate partly self-governing province of Northern Ireland within the United Kingdom. This province has always suffered ethnic conflicts of some severity, since, unlike the Republic, which has a clear majority of Catholic Irish in virtually every locality, Northern Ireland, although having an Ulster Protestant majority overall, contains considerable areas with clear Catholic majorities, including the second-largest city Londonderry/Derry. Even where Catholics are in a minority, they are rarely invisible; even largely Protestant towns and villages in Northern Ireland are rarely far from another town or village that has a large Catholic minority or even a Catholic majority. Tensions are further exacerbated by the fact that Irish nationalists generally see the legitimate national territory not as the Republic, but as the entire island of Ireland. The position of the Ulster Protestants as a majority, but not a very clear majority, in Northern Ireland, and as a minority in Ireland as a whole, led to insecurity, which prompted political and economic discrimination against Catholics on ethno-religious lines (see Hempton 1996: 93–116). Given this background, it is unsurprising that Ulster has experienced political instability, and ethnic tension, accompanied by violence.

Ethnic and national identity is hence extremely problematic for Ulster Protestants. The earlier sense of Protestant Irishness, espoused by some, is rarely found, but seems to be enjoying a limited revival in some quarters, with small numbers of Protestants even learning the Irish language (see Nic Craith 1995: 41–2). The popular sense of Protestant Britishness is under severe strain, given the widespread perception in mainland Britain that Ulster people are Irish, and this has led to considerable hostility to the mainland British, particularly to the English, in Northern Ireland.

The Ulster Protestants are, then, a group with a highly complex and controversial national identity. A popular self-image as a regional group within a British nation comes up against rejection by many other British people, and is complicated by the fact that the population of mainland Britain often equates British

with English, or sees its national identity as English, Welsh, or Scottish. The particular strength of a sense of Scottish national identity causes additional problems in
Ulster, since the Ulster Protestants' links to Scotland are especially strong. It is
perhaps helpful to see the Ulster Protestants as an ethnic group, bonded, like
many others, by traditional religious affiliation. The group does, however, demonstrate that loyalty to a territory that is the characteristic of a nation; the earlier
sense of being Irish Protestants has now largely given way to a sense of being the
Protestants of the six counties of Northern Ireland. Like many nations it has serious territorial problems; all of its territory has been claimed by a rival nation
(there are parallels in the Balkans), and a large minority of the inhabitants of the
territory identify with the rival nation, a situation often found elsewhere—for
example, in Estonia with its very large Russian minority. Unlike most European
nations, it does not, however, have a distinct national language, most people
speaking, and showing loyalty to, Ulster varieties of English. Rural dialects, given
the history of the Plantation, often show strong similarity to Scots, and some are
termed 'Ulster Scots' (see Harris 1984). However, attempts to gain recognition
from the EU for Ulster Scots as a regional language, in line with the recognition
granted to *Lallans* in Scotland, have proved difficult, but progress is being made
(see Ó Riagáin 1999).[13]

Although the Catholic Irish population of Northern Ireland has a loyalty to the
Irish language, and although it has been enthusiastically learnt by some people,
one of the most remarkable features of the ethnic and national divide in Northern
Ireland is that, almost uniquely in Europe, it is very little marked at all in people's
everyday use of language; virtually everyone, whatever their ethnic loyalty, speaks
varieties of Ulster English in their everyday lives.[14] It seems that, in Britain and
Ireland, economic and social pressures have made speaking English almost an
apolitical act; the language has triumphed, but older ethnic and national divides,
often originally linked to language differences, have survived the victory of
English.

2.3.6. *The Welsh*

As we have seen, Welsh represents the only living continuation in Great Britain of
the British Celtic speech that covered most of the island before the arrival of
English-speakers. Its confinement to Wales and certain border areas of England
was complete by the early Middle Ages, but it has been remarkably tenacious in
Wales; except for certain southern areas, most of Wales had a majority of Welsh-
speakers until the end of the nineteenth century, and even today, in almost 40 per
cent of the country, over half the population speak Welsh. It must not be forgotten,
however, that most Welsh-speaking areas are relatively thinly populated, and that

---

[13] I am grateful to Kevin McCafferty for information on the status of Ulster Scots.
[14] An earlier view that there was virtually no linguistic difference between the communities now
requires modification, but it remains true that there are very few differences indeed that are immediately obvious to the layperson.

the proportion of the total population speaking Welsh is only about 25 per cent. The survival of Welsh in Wales is astonishing in view of the relative proximity to London and other major English centres of population. It becomes more remarkable when we contemplate the much more extensive spread of English in Ireland and Scotland,[15] and when we consider the dominance of English as far away as California and New Zealand.

Various sets of historical circumstances seem to have preserved Welsh: the Norman Conquest may have weakened the position of English in that the medieval kings of England who extended their control gradually to Wales were at first speakers of French, with no programme of Anglicization. Whereas in Ireland, and to a lesser extent in the Highlands of Scotland, the Reformation brought religious conflict between groups that spoke different languages, in Wales Catholicism soon became insignificant. In order to popularize Protestantism, the English authorities agreed to the publication of the Bible in Welsh, which appeared in 1588. Since then, Welsh-speaking Protestantism has been of enormous cultural significance. Whereas in Ireland the local language was relegated to a surviving earlier oral culture, with low and declining literacy in Irish, the Welsh language became central to popular religious observance with Bible-reading, preaching, and prolific hymn writing and singing in the language (see Hempton 1996: 40–58). Since there was a considerable tradition of literacy in Welsh in a written standard, and since a spoken standardized variety was used in reading aloud and in preaching in church, the language has both written and spoken modern standard forms, unlike many minority languages.

Despite this relatively strong position, Welsh suffered serious decline in the nineteenth and twentieth centuries. This occurred because, although initially a majority language in Wales, Welsh was a minority language in the United Kingdom, where, as we have seen, economic and political power was overwhelmingly in the hands of English-speakers; increasingly such power was wielded by English-speakers in Wales as well. Nineteenth-century industrialization brought many non-Welsh speakers to the industrial areas, mainly to be found in the southeast, and this certainly weakened Welsh, but not seriously in many areas where the majority remained Welsh-speaking, and where incomers actually learnt the language in order to integrate. Nevertheless the general trend has been towards fairly steep decline; it became essential for people to be bilingual. In states like the United Kingdom with a monoglot élite there is commonly an erroneous view of bilingualism as a problem, and this view was even transmitted to bilinguals who would then bring up their children to be monoglot English-speakers, in the belief that they were thereby enhancing their prospects. A view of Welsh culture as backward is dramatically seen in the *Reports of the Commissioners of Inquiry into the State of Education in Wales* of 1847, in which an official commission depicts a

---

[15] The Scottish situation is, of course, complicated by the ambiguous status of *Lallans* (see Section 2.3.2).

population trapped in barbarism by the barrier of its language. The report caused great resentment in Wales, the whole incident being dubbed the 'Treachery of the Blue Books' (see Tyson Roberts 1996). Not only did many English-speakers associate the minority language with poverty and ignorance, but this belief was also internalized by Welsh-speakers; we hence find the speaking of Welsh prohibited in school not, as in the case of Irish, because it represented supposedly alien and subversive forces, but because of a confused and damaging view of the best interests of the pupils (for an excellent account of the complexities of Anglicization in Wales, see C. H. Williams 1990).

Despite its decline, Welsh entered the modern era of revival of minority languages in a rather stronger position than many others; it had proportionally many more speakers than Irish, since Wales had not suffered Ireland's ethnic and religious conflict nor the same degree of poverty, starvation, and emigration.

Unlike Ireland, where incorporation into the British state failed because of irreconcilable economic, ethnic, and religious differences between an English-speaking élite and an originally Irish-speaking population, and unlike Scotland, which, although united with England, retained significant spheres of autonomy, Wales was institutionally incorporated into the English state in the sixteenth century. Why, then, does the sense of distinct nationhood survive? The language, and the cultural traditions transmitted through the language, seem crucial here. These have included religious observance, where the strength of non-Anglican (Nonconformist) Protestant churches has been notable (see again Hempton 1996: 49–71); popular sentiment led to the disestablishment of the Anglican Church in Wales in 1914. Nationalist action in Wales has focused particularly on the language, and has scored noticeable successes, with, for example, all official documents being available in Welsh translation, and television broadcasting for large parts of every day in Welsh (see G. A. Williams 1985: 291–4). Many Welsh-medium schools have been established, and Welsh classes for English-speakers are thriving. There is even a vital Welsh-speaking youth culture, where, for example, an Irish-speaking counterpart barely exists (Mari Jones, personal communication). Such developments do, however, encounter resentment from non-Welsh-speakers (see G. A. Williams 1985: 294).

Of the non-English nations in these islands, Wales is the least administratively separate from England, and for both historical and geographical reasons the most economically bound to England. This means that demands for political separation are relatively weak, though there is widespread support for some form of autonomy.

The linguistic situation is paradoxical; Wales is home to the strongest minority language in Britain or Ireland, but in one respect is less linguistically distinct from England than either Ireland or Scotland: while Irish (and Ulster) English, and Scottish varieties of English, encompass more or less the entire population, distinctly Welsh varieties of English are not used by most of the upper middle class, and are seen at home and in England as having low prestige. Wales is thus in some ways more like an English region, with RP accented English used by an élite, regionally accented standard and non-standard English by a majority; but then where England has traditional English dialects, Wales has a distinct language with standard and dialect forms, a considerable literature, and a vocal and informed following among educated people whose normal medium of communication is nevertheless standard English.

2.4. Conclusions: Language and Nationalism in Britain and Ireland

Speakers of English have been remarkably successful in achieving total dominance for their language in most regions and in most spheres of life in the area of Europe where it is spoken, and language issues play a relatively small part in issues of ethnic and national identity in most of the area. Over the last hundred years this has without doubt been linked to the role of English as the predominant international language. The relative lack of nationalist passion in linguistic issues (it is only relative, not absolute) has not always been a characteristic of the area; in the past English was often aggressively promulgated and resisted (see e.g. Crowley 1996: 54–146). This part of Europe is, however, although demonstrating the overwhelming dominance of one language, far from ethnically or nationally homogeneous; it is hence a salutary example, in the present volume, of how nationalism may not be linked to language in any simple sense. The nationalisms of the archipelago are related to language, but other factors, particularly traditional religious affiliation, may be more important. There is marked loyalty to languages other than English, but sometimes the memory that ancestors spoke a distinct language may suffice, given the marginal position in many regions of the traditional languages in everyday life.

3.

France: 'One state, one nation, one language'?

ANNE JUDGE

3.1. Introduction

The premiss 'one state, one nation, one language' seems an obvious one to the vast majority of French people, with the possible exception of some in areas where regional languages were and continue to be spoken. The aim of this chapter is to discover why this view of citizenship is so generally accepted and whether this is a permanent feature of French life. It is also to investigate whether there is credible political opposition to this view from the proponents of the regional languages.

Before suggesting an answer, a number of issues have to be addressed. The first is conceptual: how the French define the terms 'state', 'nation', 'people', and 'nationalism' and how these concepts relate to language (Section 3.2). The second issue is to consider the languages other than French that were spoken in France, in what contexts they were and are spoken, and their links with nationalism (Section 3.3). It is also necessary to understand how French emerged as a distinct language (Section 3.4.), how the concept of a nationally imposed 'French' language developed, and how extensive legislation ensured that it became closely identified with nationhood (Section 3.5).

The final issue to be considered is the challenge to the national and international position of French that France is facing through the increased international importance of English, and increasing internal demands for recognition of the rights of minority languages. In this respect, France must recognize that EU law restricts its freedom to protect and promote French, whilst European initiatives in the European Parliament and the Council of Europe require recognition of the rights of ethnic minorities and regional or minority languages. Thus the continued institutional and legal dominance of French is being challenged for the first time since the Revolution. Clearly France is at a linguistic crossroads. One question is whether French has ceased to be, or will cease to be, a dominant force, replaced on an international level by English. Although not always admitted, it is probably the case that most 'national' languages in Europe and elsewhere are now in a subservient position to English (see Barbour 1996). The other question is whether its traditional protectionist linguistic policies will continue to prove effective and the degree to which they are likely to be modified by pressure from the regional languages and whether this is an expression of nationalism. It is this last question that will be the main object of this chapter. Much, in fact, has changed in this respect in the last few years (Section 3.6).

3.2. The French Perception of State, Nation, People, and Nationalism

3.2.1. *State and Nation*

A state is an institutional framework and presents few problems of definition: the United Kingdom and France are states.

The French word *nation* comes from the Latin *natus* meaning 'born'. It came to mean a group of people related by birth, and was used with this sense from the early twelfth century. From 1270 onwards it was used to mean a large community, usually with its own territory, with a common historical and cultural heritage, common economic interests, and linguistic and/or religious unity. Tradition is also an important factor. In this view, a nation-state is a state comprising one nation.

In French law a nation is defined purely as a separate sovereign legal entity, made up of individuals governed by the same constitution (*Petit Larousse*, 1972). Thus, while the 'state' and 'nation' are different concepts in political and sociological terms, they are synonymous in law. Using this definition, there are two nations within the state of the United Kingdom: the English (including the Welsh) and the Scots who have their own legal system. The legal definition will, therefore, be disregarded as unhelpful in this context, since it would result in most countries being defined as nation-states, which would ignore sociological and political reality.[1] It could be argued, however, that a succession of French governments have used such a definition in relation to France.

It is true that France is a large territory that has a shared historical consciousness. There is no common official religion, but the fact that the state is officially secular could be considered a unifying factor. There is a common legal and administrative system and a common language, which are seen as the 'cement' of the nation.[2] There are also national traditions, many originally regional, that have become national if only by constant population movement since 1789: civil servants can be sent anywhere in France, and, more recently, increased mobility through transport and the power of the media has furthered cultural homogeneity.

---

[1] Crystal (1987: 34) quotes Connors (1978) as having found that in 1971, out of 132 countries studied, only twelve were true nation-states; fifty contained a major ethnic group comprising more than three-quarters of the population; and in thirty-nine states the largest ethnic group comprised less than half the population. Crystal concluded that national and state loyalties rarely coincide, and, if different languages are associated with these concepts, the likelihood of conflict is high.

[2] The term *ciment* appears in many documents in relation to French; see in particular the quote from the Ministry of Education, Culture, and Francophone Affairs (see Section 3.5.2). It is used particularly in official statements about the nature of the Francophone World.

The fact that the language is seen as a pillar of the nation-state is shown in many documents. To quote but one issued by the Ministry for Education, Culture, and Francophone Affairs:

Since the Ordinance of Villers-Cotterets of 1539, which determined that the language of the law shall be French, and the creation of the French Academy in 1635, which gave our language a protector and guardian, the French language, the cement of our national unity and the fundamental element of our heritage, has been a matter of policy.   (*Ministère de la culture et de la francophonie*) (NOR: MCCX9400007L), in relation to the Toubon law (see Section 3.5.1.)

It is worth noting that, although the national language has been French for many centuries (see Section 3.4.), this principle was enshrined in the Constitution only in 1992 in preparation for the coming into effect of the Maastricht Treaty. The Constitution now reads: 'La langue de la République est le français' (article 2). The language figures in the same article as the national anthem and the flag. French had previously been omitted, possibly so as not to upset the advocates of the regional languages. The recent need to ensure the continued importance of French within the EU has made their interests secondary to the task of strengthening the position of French in relation to English.[3] Moreover, although it is true that other languages are spoken in France, there are virtually no adult monolingual speakers of these languages.

There are no official statistics concerning the regional languages spoken in France, since speaking a regional language is viewed as a private matter, in the same way as religion is. Indeed, no official census can ask questions on religious or linguistic matters in the name of anti-racism. Such an attitude also implies that there are no linguistic problems in France. Whether or not this is a means of undermining the position of regional languages, it certainly makes it difficult to assess their vitality. The statistics in this chapter are mainly from four sources: Henriette Walter's *L'Aventure des langues en Occident* (1994), based on the most recent sociolinguistic surveys; the *Mini-Guide to the Lesser Used Languages of the EC*, published by the European Bureau for Lesser Used Languages (EBLUL 1993); Killilea (1994), commissioned by the European Parliament; and the *Euromosaic Report* (European Commission 1996).[4] It is important, however, to remember

---

[3] The original draft stated: 'Le français est la langue de la République.' Other francophone countries complained, however, at France's appropriation of the French language, claiming it belonged to francophones everywhere, irrespective of their nationality. The idea that the French language should no longer be considered the property of the French alone raises interesting points; while it strengthens the international position of French, France is no longer its sole custodian—a mixed blessing for the French.

[4] Mark Killilea prepared for the European Parliament a report on the linguistic situation in the EU, which was presented to the European Parliament in 1994. The statistics are disputed, but the report marked a positive move towards the recognition of linguistic rights in Europe. The main aim of this report was to gather data on the linguistic communities speaking minority languages in order to assess how their needs could best be served and to study their potential for production and reproduction. To obtain the necessary data, three empirical approaches were adopted: (i) questionnaires were sent out

whenever dealing with any survey that the population sample on which it is based may not be representative and questions such as 'Do you speak *X* language?' can give rise to a variety of responses from people with similar knowledge levels. Moreover, different surveys are based on different criteria, making it difficult to make a comparison between languages. Finally, the figures do not generally distinguish between the use of regional language in daily life and its use in cultural activities, in folklore and song. Such information has, therefore, been weighed against articles in newspapers, and much up-to-date information obtained from representatives of organizations dealing with the teaching of the regional languages.

Some interesting new figures have also recently come into the public domain where education in the regional languages is concerned, since Prime Minister Lionel Jospin requested Nicole Péry to draw up a report on this matter. After her appointment to government, the task was handed over to Bernard Poignant. The Poignant Report was presented to the Prime Minister on 1 July 1998 and is likely to have important repercussions (see Section 3.6.2.).

3.2.2. *'Peoples' in France, and the Appearance of New Communities*

The term *peuple* refers to persons belonging to a specific community with some points in common, but not necessarily all those listed above. There are two words in French based on the Latin *populus* to describe such communities: *peuple* and *peuplade*. *Peuple* may be used with the meaning of 'nation' as in *le peuple français* or *les peuples de l'URSS* (different nationalities within the same state). Journalists frequently refer to *le peuple corse*.[5]

Peuplade refers to a human society lacking full political organization (*société humaine incomplètement organisée* (*Petit Larousse*, 1972)). The term *peuplade* (tribe) is useful to designate early migrant groups, such as the Celtic and Germanic peoples who invaded or settled in France. These communities often integrated with others, with one of their languages generally becoming the dominant language of the new community, but not without being influenced by the others.

Thus the Gauls spread their Celtic languages through a large area of present-day France before the Roman invaders imposed Latin. The resultant language was

---

to various authorities at different levels of government; (ii) a language group respondent was nominated for each group who was responsible for giving questionnaires to a series of experts for each language group; and (iii) eight special language-use surveys were undertaken which tried to establish comparable criteria between languages, analysable in terms of numerical 'scores'. The criteria focused on use of the language within the family, within the community, at the institutional level, in terms of cultural reproduction, and in terms of the formal educational support received. Degrees of prestige and legitimacy were also examined. Only one of the eight languages chosen is spoken in France—namely, Breton. It is possible, however, to disagree with the findings for Breton, because the various sociolinguistic assumptions of the survey may no longer be valid.

[5] See e.g. the article on the murder of the French Préfet in Corsica (*Le Monde*, 10 Feb. 98, 34).

a variant of Latin, with pronunciation, vocabulary, and structural peculiarities, which is known as Gallo-Romance: Latin with a Gaulish 'substratum'. The Frankish invaders of the fifth century did not impose their own Germanic language and adopted Gallo-Romance, introducing Frankish features into it; this is called 'superstratum' influence. Gallo-Romance with a Frankish superstratum is the earliest form of French. Fig. 3.1 shows the main substratum and superstratum influences on the development of modern French. Sociolinguistic factors such as pressures in favour of spatial and social varieties have also played a major part. For further details on these, see Lodge (1993).

The speakers of some languages have been better able to resist outside influences than others. Basque is the best example of this, at least as regards grammar and phonology. Its vocabulary now contains a very large proportion of terms borrowed from Latin, but adapted to the Basque phonological system: *ikastola* (school) clearly derives from *schola*, and *izpiritu* (spirit) from *spiritus*. Despite this common vocabulary, Basque remains totally opaque to non-Basques, which is not the case for Occitan (this explains why the statistics for Basque speakers seem more consistent than for Occitan). Although this prevented the spread of the language, it also helped to preserve it and the sense of community. This leads many Basques to claim the status of a 'nation' and some to demand recognition as a 'state'.

Sometimes nationalism focuses on a language closely related to the dominant language. National identity may be rather weak in such cases, since the regional variety is not as distinctive. Thus Occitan nationalism, which includes an awareness of a *langue d'oc* substratum in the local variety of French, is the weakest in France. Where the substratum features derive from what can be seen as a regional variety of the majority language, as is the case with the *langues d'oïl*, there is no nationalism as such.[6]

3.2.3. *Language and Nationalism*

The most effective way to achieve nationhood over the past two hundred years has been through the formation of a state. There is, however, a problem where there are groups within the territorial area of the state who do not share the majority feeling of nationhood. Large-scale population mobility also presents major problems to the whole concept of the nation-state, which survives relatively unchanged only if immigration is followed by assimilation, the traditional French policy. This policy is, however, running into major problems in France, where some of the descendants of the *Magrébins*—immigrants from Northern Africa—either do not want to assimilate or cannot assimilate, mainly for cultural and religious reasons.

---

[6] Most non-French linguists would probably simply describe the *langues d'oïl* as French 'dialects' rather than minority languages. This is, however, a subject of debate among French linguists.

---

1. The Gaulish <u>substratum</u>

(+Iberian, Ligurian, Aquitain, etc. substrata)

    +2. The LATIN OF GAUL ⟶ **Gallo-Romance dialects**

                (basis of both Occitan and French)

    +3. The Germanic <u>superstratum</u> ⟶ **Gallo-Romance with Frankish features**

        4. ⟶ **MODERN FRENCH**

Fig. 3.1. The main substratum and superstratum influences on the development of modern French

It can be argued that the problem demonstrates that the nation-state is more fragile than appears at first sight.

Language has frequently played a special role in the development of nationalism.[7] It tends to be identified with a people, a culture, an approach to life. To speak a foreign language is to change one's pattern of thought, to enter a new world, to see things differently. Where people have a language, a culture, a religion, and a territory in common, they are likely to see themselves as a nation and entitled to form a state that becomes their 'home'. If the territory forms part of a larger state, the nation within may demand independence. The state is unlikely to accede to such demands for a variety of reasons. In the face of refusal, opposition to the state is likely to develop. This may be expressed democratically, through the ballot box and pressure groups. But a nationalist group may decide that it is unlikely to obtain what it wants by democratic means, and terrorism may develop, as in Corsica and the Basque country. Independence is not, however, necessarily the only outcome; there is also the possibility of becoming an autonomous political entity within the state, as is the case of the Basque country in Spain. In other cases, particularly where the status of the group is disputed—as is the case for *l'Occitanie*—recognition as a special 'region' and part of the national heritage is a

---

[7] The term 'nationalism' arose in France in the 1790s in the wake of the Revolution.

possibility. 'Regionalism' is the favoured approach of the majority of those representing the rights of regional languages in France and is part of the current political scene. Thus, in the *projet de loi Tasca*, which preceded the Toubon law (1994), the regional languages were presented in these terms:

The present proposed legislation does not oppose the use of the other languages of France, particularly the regional languages, which are equally part of our heritage and whose use is explicitly recognized in several places. But only French is designated as the common language of national public life. *(Projet du loi Tasca, Exposé des motifs,* submitted in 1993 but replaced by the Balladur government with the Toubon law).

This recognition is supposed to lead to the teaching of, and teaching in, the regional languages; their use in the media, and financial help for cultural projects.

3.3. Nationalism and the Regional Languages

3.3.1. *The Languages Spoken within the Boundaries of France*

Traditionally it has been reckoned that seven regional languages—or groups of languages—have survived in some form or other into the present: Alsatian, Basque, Breton, Catalan, Corsican, Flemish (or Dutch),[8] and Occitan. Of these, two are Germanic: Flemish, which is spoken in a small area around Dunkirk and is also an official language of Belgium, and Alsatian, which is a rather loose term applied to the Germanic varieties spoken in the *départements* of the Haut Rhin, the Bas Rhin, and the Moselle region known as *la Lorraine thioise.*[9] There is one Celtic language, Breton, spoken in the Basse Bretagne only, which includes the *départements* of Finistère and western parts of the Côtes du Nord and the Morbihan. Another is a non-Indo-European language of unknown origin, Basque. It is an official regional language in Spain but not in France. It is spoken in the *département* of the Pyrénées-Atlantiques. Catalan, spoken near the Spanish frontier, and Corsican both belong to the Romance group. Of these, Catalan is an official language in Spain. Some of these languages, such as Breton, are truly minority languages, whereas others, such as Flemish, may be majority languages elsewhere. As may be seen from Map 2, there is a problem, since linguistic frontiers do not always correspond to state frontiers. Also languages spoken in areas far from the seat of power or in remote mountain areas are more likely to survive. This is clearly the case in France.

For various reasons, not all specialists agree with the above list. For example, some people classify Occitan as one language made up of a number of dialects, while others consider Occitan as comprising several different 'languages' (*les*

---

[8] There is a good case on linguistic grounds for labelling Flemish as Dutch. Speakers of Dutch in France prefer, however, the use of the regional label '*Flamand/*Flemish', which will be used here.

[9] It is now government policy to label these languages as local spoken variants of 'German', but traditionally speakers used to prefer the regional label or 'Germanic languages' (*langues germaniques*), for obvious historical reasons.

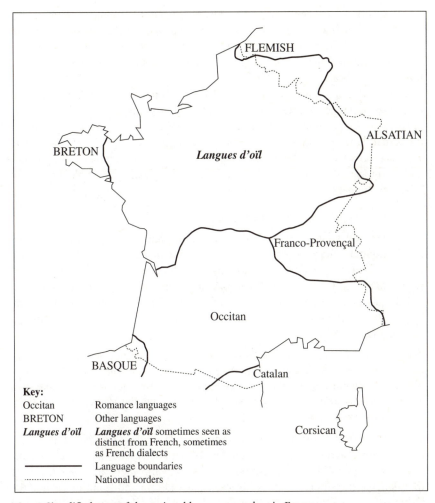

Map 2. Simplified map of the regional languages spoken in France

langues d'oc) that have a number of traits in common. Thus, some speakers of Provençal have preferred—mainly in the past—to claim separate linguistic status. There is similar disagreement as to the nature of Alsatian, seen by some as a variety of German and by others as a language in its own right, while some see Corsican as a variety of Italian. The *langues d'oïl* are even more problematic, since they belong to the same subgroup within the Romance languages as standard French. To quote Killilea (1994: 26): 'There are a certain number of dialects and *langues d'oïl* which are not yet fully recognised by the scientific community as constituting languages properly speaking ... The *langues d'oïl* enjoy even less recognition and even fewer rights than other minority languages in France.'

No mention has been made here of non-indigenous languages (*langues non autochtones*) such as Arabic. They are not seen as part of the 'national heritage' and therefore do not really enter the picture at present, although there are signs that organizations such as the European Parliament and the Council of Europe are taking up their case.

It is worth noting, however, that the Poignant Report mentions other regional languages or 'language categories', adding for the first time the Creole languages of Guyana, Guadeloupe, Martinique, and Reunion, and the Tahitian language and the Kanak language of New Caledonia as regional languages. The *langues d'oïl* such as Picard, Gallo, Poitevin, Saintongeais, Norman, Morvandiau, Champenois, and so on are listed as 'regional forms of French'. Clearly the whole concept of 'regional languages' is in the melting pot.

3.3.2. *Basque and its Ancestor, Aquitanian*

Of the very early languages such as Aquitanian, Ligurian, and Iberian, only the first is thought to have a distant surviving descendant: Basque. However, evidence of all of them can be seen in the toponymy of France; the names of important rivers are pre-Celtic: the Seine, the Rhône, the Loire, and the Garonne. But when Julius Caesar described France in his *Gallic Wars, Book 1*, he referred only to the Belgae, the Gauls, and the Aquitani as distinct nations, with the Gauls forming a loose confederation:

The whole of Gaul is divided into three parts, one of which the Belgae inhabit, the Aquitani another, and the third a people who in their own language are called 'Celts', but in ours 'Gauls'. They all differ among themselves in respect of the language, way of life, and laws. The River Garonne divides the Gauls from the Aquitani, and the Marne and Seine rivers separate them from the Belgae.

Before the arrival of the Romans, the Aquitanian language was spoken throughout Aquitaine, according to the toponymical data. It is true that from the fifth century BC some Celtic tribes penetrated the area, and there are a few traces of their language(s) in place names (for example, Calezun and Gaudun include the Celtic suffix -*dunum* meaning 'fortified place', while others such as Eauze and Lectoure bear the names of Celtic tribes, the Elusates and the Lectorates). The first contacts with Rome date from the second century BC, and in 56 BC a number of the local *peuplades* tried in vain to resist military conquest. After the conquest, most Aquitani must have adopted Latin, the language of social success, while others—gradually or suddenly—moved south to escape its impact. The term *Gascons*, which is etymologically the same word as *Basques*, refers, at least in part, to latinized Aquitani, mixed with some latinized Celts, and possibly others. Of the Aquitani, the Basques retained their language and culture more or less intact, in the isolation and remoteness of the Pyrenees.

Nothing much is known about the early forms of Basque apart from a few inscriptions, which do not go back beyond the tenth century. The first book in

Basque seems to date from 1545. There are several varieties of Basque today, but the standard form, *Euskara batua*, is a compromise variety, which is seen as a way forward by language activists, but with which the elderly often find it difficult to identify. An Academy was founded in 1919, which gave the language a single orthographic system (previously there had been two systems derived from Spanish and French respectively). It was traditionally a spoken language, used in the home, between friends and in church. In Spain it is now used in all spheres of life in its written and spoken form.

According to Walter (1994: 230–1), a survey in 1991 in the French Basque Country of 1,200 people over 15 showed that, out of a population of 237,000, 32 per cent claimed a good knowledge of the language, 23 per cent claimed some knowledge, and 45 per cent claimed no knowledge. Some degree of knowledge was thus claimed by 55 per cent. If those with a 'good knowledge' are equated with 'speakers' of the language, this is consistent with the information in the *Mini-Guide* published by the EBLUL (1993): 80,000 out of a population of 240,000. The percentage varies according to the area, with the lowest percentage in the tourist coastal area, which explains the campaigns of the Basque militant organization ETA against tourism. These figures refer only to the French Basque Country.

It is largely accepted in the European nation-states that, for a language to survive, it has to be taught and it has to be seen to have an official status within a community, which is why an association, the SEASKA, was created under the 1901 law on associations to promote education in Basque. The *ikastolak*, or Basque immersion schools, founded in 1969, were not at first recognized by the French state. Their number increased nonetheless from year to year. Such schools were imitated in other areas, which gave birth to an alternative educational system—the *écoles associatives*. Their ultimate aim is integration into the state system. They are all supposed to be apolitical and secular, and aim at being free; they were, in their early days, paid for by parents on a voluntary basis and by benefactors.

These schools had to fight to survive because of state opposition to their very existence. Thus a *préfet* in 1977 forbade the opening of a primary *ikastola* at St Palais. This led to disruptive demonstrations in Bayonne and the school was eventually allowed to open. Only strength of opinion enabled these schools to survive, and, indeed, to multiply. The problem remained financial, since the number of applicants increased to a point where the SEASKA could no longer cope—hence the intense lobbying to get recognition and financial support from the Ministry of Education. The first recognition of the *ikastolak* in the form of a government subsidy came in 1982 (1 million francs), from the Ministry of Culture (not Education), thanks to the election of a Socialist government in 1981. The first subsidy from the Ministry of Education came in 1983 (2.5 million francs). The election of a right-wing government in 1986 then slowed the process down. By the time the Socialists were back in power, the financial position of SEASKA was disastrous, but new agreements led in 1990 to sixty-one teachers in the kindergarten and primary sector being paid for by the state. In 1991 a *Convention* was signed, and then another in 1992, which included the secondary sector in the financial arrangements. Finally, in 1994, a *Protocole* signed by SEASKA and the Ministry of Education established the possibility of these schools being 'contracted' to the state. For the first time the state recognized the *ikastola* schools and the concept of teaching in Basque as valid and part of the national educational system. This general move towards the recognition of the *écoles associatives* affected all immersion schools in regional languages, and the demand for such schools is at present on the increase everywhere. The problem that remains is that the government is often unwilling to create new posts, partly because of a diminishing school population: opening a class in one context means closing one down in another. Numerous problems remain on this front.

It is interesting to note that this movement started in an area in which nationalism is much in evidence, even if only a small minority of the population accept violence as a means to an end. Although people questioned, working in Basque-speaking schools, stated that they were against violence, they admitted that most of their gains were, very regrettably, due to pressure put on the government by the extremists. Nationalism may be said to have made these schools possible, even if they state in their literature that their aim is internationalist rather than nationalist. Thus the *ikastolak* public information booklet (*Ikastola Seaska*) states: 'SEASKA, which is at the forefront of the great pedagogical movement represented by the *Ikastolak* in the seven provinces, is preparing its children for adult life in tomorrow's open-minded Europe.'

The success of the movement may be illustrated by the fact that the first *ikastola* enrolled five pupils in 1969, whereas by 1997 there were 1,630 in nursery, primary, and secondary schools. Moreover, in 1967 private bilingual schools were created. In 1997 there were 980 pupils in the nursery and primary sector and 626 in the secondary sector.

Detractors maintain they are an instrument of division within France, and that they cannot be as open and apolitical as is claimed, since the hand that fed them is essentially nationalistic in the case of Basque. Only if the state looks after such schools, will they be free of political pressures.

To address the question 'do the Basques form a nation?', it is clear they do as a whole—the Spanish and French Basques combined: there is a common history, a common culture (including a legal system, which managed to survive in France until the 1950s in a voluntary form),[10] and a language, which is for many a mother tongue. There is also an identifiable territory, although it has shrunk considerably, but, as a nation straddling two states, there are conflicting loyalties. Hence the fact that some would like to see the formation of a single state. Its symbol is 4+3=1, which refers to the four Spanish Basque provinces and the three French ones. This feeling is particularly strong on the Spanish side (see Chapter 4) for historical

---

[10] The Basques had to function within the French legal framework, but they tried to adapt it to suit their traditional system, particularly where inheritance was concerned.

reasons: between 1937 and the early 1960s the teaching of the language was forbidden, books were publicly burnt, and inscriptions on public buildings and tombs erased. While not actively promoted in France, Basque was certainly not persecuted and religious services have for centuries been held in Basque.

The Spanish Basque desire for political independence and the creation of a unified state—as against the autonomy that they currently enjoy—is strong among a section of the population, creating tensions for the French Basques. The Basque language is a potent symbol and weapon in the fight for independence led by the revolutionary terrorist movement *Euskadi ta Azkatasuua* (Basque Fatherland and Freedom) (*ETA*), formed in 1959. The French equivalent to *ETA* is the *Iparretarak*, which is, like *ETA*, committed to violence. This probably represents only a very small percentage of the Basque population (it is impossible to know with any degree of accuracy). There is also a small *Parti nationaliste basque* on the French side, which, unlike the *Iparretarak* (meaning 'those from the North'), is committed to non-violent strategies. In all three movements, language and nationalism are closely intertwined.

Most French Basques operate, however, within the normal institutional framework, maintain they are French, and are attached to French institutions (particularly the benefits of the health service and the social security system), judging by the polls. Many hold the view that the French Basque Country is too small to survive independently and recent population shifts means that the area is less homogeneous. A unification of the Spanish and French Basque Country would make for a slightly more viable entity, but this seems unlikely for a variety of reasons beyond the scope of this chapter. On the other hand, the autonomy gained by the Spanish Basque Country helps preserve the language in the French region, by strengthening its sense of identity. The French Basques also benefit from the Spanish Basque media, which help reinforce the feeling of trans-Pyrenean unity.

3.3.3. *The Gauls and the Celtic Heritage: Breton*

The recorded history of France begins with the struggle of the Gauls against the Roman invaders, and, since Victor Duruy made the study of French history compulsory in French primary schools in 1867, school textbooks have begun with a chapter on *nos ancêtres les Gaulois* (our ancestors the Gauls), even in books used in the colonies. For generations of French children 'Gaul' was symbolized by Vercingétorix, the French David against the Roman Goliath, except that in this case David lost. This is part of the national heritage and national awareness.

And yet the Gauls were once invaders themselves. They were Celts and the language(s) they spoke were Celtic languages, grouped under the label 'Gaulish'. Very little is known about the language of the Gauls (mainly toponyms and the odd inscription), since the druid priesthood refused on religious grounds to set down knowledge in writing (Julius Caesar claimed that it took up to twenty years to train a Druid, since all important knowledge had to be memorized). It appears that there were various writing systems, but these were used for unimportant matters or on coins. It is estimated that some seventy originally Gaulish words remain in French. Survivors include words common in agriculture such as *boue* (mud), *chemin* (lane), *mouton* (sheep), and an alternative to the Roman *mille* (= 1,485 metres), *la lieue* (= 2,222 metres), which survived as a unit of measurement until the arrival of the kilometre in 1795; the term survives in expressions such as *à vingt lieues à la ronde* (for miles around), *être à cent lieues de penser que* . . . (to be far from imagining that . . .). Another interesting survivor is *bouge* meaning a leather bag, which became *bougette*, a small leather bag, which gave us the English word *budget* (Walter 1994: 232–4). Gaulish words also survive in place names; it is noticeable that there are few in Provence, largely because it was the first area to be Romanized and also because the Gauls expanded into the area only at a late date and in smaller numbers. They are also less frequent in Aquitaine.

Although Gaulish is extinct, one Celtic language is spoken in France today—namely Breton. This is not a direct descendant of Gaulish, since Brittany was invaded in the fifth and sixth centuries by Celts fleeing the Germanic invasion of Britain. But it is thought that when the Bretons arrived in Armorique (*Are morica*, 'situated near the sea'), Gaulish was still spoken, despite the overpowering influence of the Roman Empire and the spread of Latin (as evoked in the comic strip, *Astérix le Gaulois*). Present-day Breton evolved from the Celtic language imported from Britain and the Gaulish language already spoken in 'Little Britain' (Brittany). Many of the inhabitants eventually became bilingual, with Latin and later French as their second language. The varying combinations of the Celtic varieties and Latin gave rise to the four major dialect groups of Breton spoken today: Cornouaillais, Léonais, Trégorrois, and Vannetais, with Vannetais regarded as the most influenced by Gaulish.

The Bretons were clearly a nation in the past, with a common territory, history, culture, and language. As in the Basque Country, the territory of the minority language has shrunk: in the ninth century it extended from the Finistère to Rennes, the present capital of Brittany, but by the twentieth century it had withdrawn behind a line from Paimpol in the north to Vannes in the south. This area is called *la Bretagne bretonnante* or *la Bretagne celtique* (Celtic Brittany).

Since the First World War, the number of *bretonnants*—Breton speakers—has been in constant decline even in *la Bretagne bretonnante*. The exact number is unknown, but was reckoned to be around 700,000 in the 1950s. According to a 1991 survey based on a sample of 1,000 carried out by Fanch Broudig for FR3 (the only TV channel with a regional language involvement), out of a total population of 1,500,000 there were 650,000 who understood Breton (450,000 for EBLUL (1993) and Killilea (1994)), of which 250,000 could speak it (300,000 for EBLUL and Killilea) and 77 per cent were in favour of it being taught. Similar figures are quoted elsewhere (see Favereau 1994).

Breton survived the Revolution mainly because it was used by the Church, which was also in practice responsible for education. According to an 1863 survey, three-quarters of the schools in the Finistère used Breton as the normal means of communication, and nearly as many in the other *bretonnants* areas. It was the educational policies of Jules Ferry that caused a steady decline,[11] but by the 1900s, because of the high birth rate, the number of Breton speakers was estimated at 1,400,000, the highest figure ever. The Church again played its part in the decline: in 1902 French became the only language apart from Latin allowed in Catholic worship, but priests continued preaching in Breton even though deprived of their livelihood as a result. It was the First World War that was the real disaster, when one-quarter of Breton male speakers were killed. This had a greater effect than the figure would suggest. Men were the force for retaining Breton; women were more likely to adopt the official language to give their children a better chance in life. The disaster of the war was compounded by a massive exodus of Bretons to Paris in search of work. An estimated 75 per cent knew Breton in 1931; this figure had dropped to 33 per cent by 1951.

Matters today are different in Brittany compared to the Basque country. After an extremely serious decline, there is in Brittany now some language revival among the very young. In the *Diwan* primary school in Tregunc, for example, the eleven older children questioned by the author all seemed to speak Breton fluently with one another and their teacher, but none had Breton-speaking parents, and few had Breton-speaking grandparents.[12] This is why the *Diwan* schools (meaning 'moment when the young shoot appears out of the earth'), which are Breton immersion schools, were created, the first one in 1977, on the Basque model. Significant progress has been made since then in terms of the number of pupils and schools (1,751 pupils in 1997), and 1997 saw the first class of students obtain their *baccalauréat*, having been educated in the *Diwan* system from kindergarten until the end of secondary school. (At the secondary level, one-third of the classes are in French, and two-thirds in Breton.) Then, in 1983, bilingual education became an accepted concept and in 1997–8, there were 4,562 pupils benefiting from such an education; there were also 907 such pupils in Catholic nursery and primary schools and thirty-three in the Catholic secondary sector. In 1993, 21,000 pupils were having some Breton taught to them in the school system.

The signing of the *Protocole* of 1994 was of particular importance, since it opened the way for *Diwan* teachers to be fully recognized and paid by the state. By 1998, sixty-five posts were being financed by the state. According to the Charter of the *Diwan* association, the ultimate aim of the *Diwan* is to be fully integrated in the state system, since it argues that its curriculum is the same. Moreover, the Charter of the *Diwan*s states that these schools are open to all, are free, are secular and apolitical, just like those in the state system.[13] The only difference is that

[11] Jules Ferry was responsible for setting up free, compulsory, and secular education for all in the 1880s.

[12] In several cases the children referred to grandparents who had forgotten their Breton, originally their mother tongue, because it had been 'brutally beaten out of them'.

[13] When questioned, neither teachers nor pupils at the Tregunc *Diwan* seemed interested—or in the case of the pupils aware—of the Breton nationalist issue. Their desire to function in Breton was 'so as to save a culture from disappearing'.

they cater for a need not fulfilled as yet by the state—namely, the right to be educated in Breton. Interestingly, the president of the *Diwan* association is an Englishman (and not a Welshman), Andrew Lincoln, and the association boasts a Romanian and a Japanese teacher of Breton, which illustrates the desire to be open rather than narrowly nationalistic. They are encouraged in their efforts by the increasing demand for places in these schools, not all from parents of Breton origin.[14]

It is difficult to say to what extent the Bretons still form a nation. At present it is clear that there is still a territory (but Breton has not been spoken throughout Brittany for centuries), a culture (albeit rather traditional), and a language trying to be reborn. The *Euromosaic* study carried out by the European Commission (1996) on a number of languages to assess their ability to reproduce themselves, concludes:

Both Breton and Sardinian are language groups which demonstrate the virtual retreat of language use within two generations . . . This is characteristic of languages with a low status and a restricted range of institutionalised use which are confronted by rapid change processes . . . In both cases the support required by the various agencies of language production and reproduction in order to confront this intensity of change has not been forthcoming.

This is why most—not to say all—new speakers have to learn it as a second language rather than as a mother tongue. On the other hand, it is hoped that the generation of children coming out of the *Diwan* schools will speak Breton to their children, thus reversing the present situation. Languages can experience dramatic revivals; Hebrew and Catalan are examples.

A problem sometimes mentioned is that Breton as a mother tongue varies from village to village, with people being more attached to the differences that confer local identity than to their common heritage. These speakers are usually elderly artisans and farmers. Young Breton speakers, on the other hand, are often intellectuals who have learnt a standardized version in the *Diwan*, or in bilingual schools, or at university. There are supposedly some 20,000 in this group. There is said to be frequent antagonism on the language issue between the two groups. This problem will disappear, however, with the elder generation, leaving room for cautious optimism.

Interestingly there have been various Breton nationalist movements but they do not appear to have helped the cause in the long term. In 1927 the *Parti auton-omiste breton* was created, which became the *Parti national breton* in 1932, which was 'separatist', and usually associated with the extreme right. It was even ready to collaborate with the Germans, who had promised to let the Bretons use their language if they did. This came to nothing, however, and, following the loss of credit by the political right during the Second World War, the regions turned to

---

[14] In the Tregunc *Diwan*, the president of the association was bilingual Flemish/French, married to a non-Breton-speaking Breton. She decided to put her children in a *Diwan* school because she is passionately in favour of bilingualism, whatever the languages.

the political left. Indeed, it was the various, mainly communist-inspired attempts that ultimately led to the Deixonne law in 1951, which allowed Breton, Basque, Catalan, and Occitan to be taught in state schools (Flemish, Alsatian, and Corsican, considered to be variants of foreign languages already taught, were excluded at first). Then the *Front de libération de la Bretagne* came into existence, a movement that was not opposed to the use of violence. Such extreme movements seem, however, to have gone into hibernation. Nowadays, 'nationalism' is reduced for most people to the development of the Breton language and culture—that is, regionalism rather than separatism. Ties with Welsh, Irish, and Scottish Gaelic speakers help them to fight a sense of isolationism and despair. These have developed thanks to EU linguistic and cultural programmes. There are plans afoot to set up a research project to investigate the features common to all the Celtic languages, in order to help speakers of one language understand the others. This is more a question of saving a worthwhile culture than of being nationalistic, since the movement itself is now enthusiastically open to all.

Breton, therefore, cannot nowadays be fully identified with Breton nationalism. Whereas nationalism is in decline, the image of the language is improving; according to the survey carried out by the Institute TMO-Ouest (in Rennes) in 1991, 92 per cent of those interviewed wished to preserve the language, and 82 per cent thought this should be done in the schools. The depoliticization of the language issue could also be its strength in the long term. It must be remembered, however, that the development of an associative school system, and the development of bilingual classes, was due originally to the gains acquired through Basque nationalism. It should also be remembered that it is not enough for the population to favour bilingual and immersion schools. Children have to be sent to these schools for the situation to be reversed.

3.3.4. *The Surviving Germanic Languages*

There are two Germanic languages in France, both spoken in border areas, neither of which is used for the expression of political nationalism. Their presence arises from the fact that political and language boundaries rarely coincide exactly. They are Dutch, or Flemish, and Alsatian.

Since Dutch/Flemish is a national language in neighbouring Belgium, not to mention the Netherlands, no great efforts have been made to keep it alive in France. As a result, the area in which it is spoken in France is steadily shrinking. It is said to be spoken by around 80,000 people in the extreme north of France. This figure given in EBLUL (1993) seems high. Henriette Walter prefers not to make a guess in *Le Français dans tous les sens* (1988), but in *L'Aventure des langues en Occident* (1994) she cites a survey carried out in 1984 in Hondschoote, a small town near the frontier, indicating considerable changes over the last three generations. According to the survey, Flemish is spoken by 38 per cent of grandparents, 25 per cent of parents are bilingual, but only 2 per cent of children are bilingual. Flemish has no official legal status, no public presence apart from a few local road signs, the result of local initiatives. It is not used as a medium of education, but, since the 1982 Circulaire Savary, it is possible to request courses in nursery and elementary schools. At secondary level it has been an optional language in a few schools (three hours per week) since 1983, and standard Dutch—of which it is a dialect or variant—is taught at a number of universities, in particular at Lille. There are no television services, and only one private local radio station broadcasts in both Flemish and French. Flemish is not mentioned in the recent preliminary report on regional languages, put forward by Nicole Péry (*Le Monde,* 4 Feb. 1998).

The Germanic dialects of Alsace and Lorraine are conveniently regarded as dialects of a single language referred to as 'Alsatian', and in Péry no separate mention is made of the Lorraine dialect. It must be remembered, however, that there are appreciable differences between the speech of these two areas, and even within these areas, no standardization having taken place.

Lorraine became French in 1766. In 1871 Alsace and Lorraine were incorporated into Germany until 1918. This period of Germanization was followed by intense Frenchification between the two world wars. The Second World War saw another Germanization followed post-war by Frenchification. Not surprisingly, the populations, traumatized by these changes, took refuge in their local speech. The creation of a European Community bringing France and Germany into a harmonious relationship, and the importance of Strasbourg, have created a happier situation. The Alsatian dialect, which had survived nearly intact until quite recently, is declining rapidly. According to Walter (1994: 327) only 17 per cent of the 3 to 10 year olds interviewed spoke Alsatian, but it is still heard in shops and restaurants. EBLUL (1993) states that in 1989 36 per cent of those entering primary school in Alsace still spoke the language and in Lorraine 20 per cent of those under 15 still spoke Lorrain, the Germanic dialect of Lorraine. Killilea (1994) claims that around 75 per cent of the population over 15 know Alsatian. This does not contradict, however, the fact that the language is declining in terms of the likelihood of its transmission from parents to children.

The figures quoted by different sources in terms of speakers, use in the media, and so on tend, in fact, to be wildly different. This is because there seems to be confusion between the concepts of Alsatian, Lorrain, and German; standard German used to function as the written form under German occupation, but there was in the past political and cultural resistance to regarding Alsatian and Lorrain as simply 'German'. And yet the claim that German is the written form of these languages appears in EBLUL (1993) and Killilea (1994). The spokesperson for *Culture et bilinguisme d'Alsace et de Moselle* makes the same claim, comparing the situation of Alsatian with that of Swiss-German. This is a debatable point from a linguist's point of view, but it seems the opinion of the new forward-looking Alsatians, who see their 'German' language as opening the door to all the other German-speaking countries. To treat Alsatian differently would, from their point of view, be backward looking. The situation today in Alsace is, therefore, a very complex one, Alsatian being used as a spoken language (including some radio and television) and German as a written language (education and newspapers).

This confusion explains why Alsatian is quoted as the most frequently taught regional language in France, with 67,000 pupils, in the *Atlas de la langue française* published by Bordas in 1995, whereas it is not mentioned in Nicole Péry's preliminary report (*Le Monde*, 4 Feb. 1998) as being taught in the state system; she only lists 467 pupils in 'associative classes' (there are no 'associative schools' as such) called *ABCM-Zweisprachigkeit*. There are now twenty of these, including two in the Moselle *département*. Alsatian is allowed in nursery schools on a voluntary basis, no more than half an hour per day, but there are no figures indicating to what extent this right is taken up. There are also some bilingual French–German classes (163 in the public sector and seven in the private sector in 1997–8). There seem to be some 4,000 pupils, in the state and private sector, enjoying some form of bilingual education.

Since knowledge of Alsatian is supposed to make learning German easier, the attitude of educationalists has changed, leading to two to three hours of German being taught in primary schools to some 80–95 per cent of the age group in Alsace and Lorraine. According to reports, the results so far have been disappointing. In the secondary system, apart from being able to study German as a foreign language, there is an option for the *baccalauréat* that comes under the heading *Langue et culture régionale* ['regional language and culture']: *Alsacien*. These two types of study, German as a foreign language, and 'regional language and culture', together account for the very high figure quoted in the *Atlas de la langue française*.

Surprisingly, the use of both Alsatian and German is in decline in the media. This is no doubt due to the expensive nature of bilingual newspapers and the lack of encouragement from the state. The decree of 10 May 1996 was promulgated to give help to regional publications. Unfortunately, in order to benefit from this help, they have to be in French. The *Culture et bilinguisme* association made a complaint to the Council of State, saying the decree was contrary to article 14 of the European Convention of Human Rights and Article 10 of the French Constitution on freedom of speech. Moreover, it was claimed that the law of 4 August 1994 (Toubon law, see Section 3.5. below) specifically states (Article 19) that this law would not affect the use of regional languages. The Council of State disregarded the complaint. Other similar complaints by other parties have met, so far, with the same response. As far as television is concerned, the need to set up a private channel is being discussed, as are links with other channels in Switzerland and Germany.

According to Andrée Tabouret-Keller, a specialist in the field, Alsatian—as against German—is on its way out; she knows of no movement pushing for it to be taught as a language separate from German in the schools. Alsatian is simply seen as a non-standard variety of German (personal communication). Alsatian (and Lorrain) is not associated with political nationalism as previously defined. In the 1970s, there existed a *Front de l'Alsace libre*, but this was a very small-scale affair (it probably developed partly in sympathy with the other nationalist movements typical of that period). There is now an *Alsace d'abord* movement, in favour of bilingualism at all levels; it is a right-wing movement, also very small. In February 1998 it issued a Charter for the Alsace Region. In other words, the extreme right is willing to play the regionalist card in Alsace (see the newspaper *Alsace*, 30 Jan. 1980).

3.3.5. *The* langues d'oc *or Occitan*

The *langues d'oc* developed from Gallo-Romance and in many ways are linguistically closer to Catalan, Italian, and even Spanish than to French. Occitan is spoken in thirty-one *départements*, but even the EBLUL (1993: 15–16) is wary of statistics: 'There are no official data on the number of speakers. Of some 12 to 13 million inhabitants in the area, it is estimated 48 per cent understand Occitan, 28 per cent can speak it, about 9 per cent of the population use it on a daily basis, 13 per cent can read and 6 per cent can write the language.'

L'Occitanie, as it is sometimes called, may have an identifiable territory comprising thirty-one *départements*, a language—or at least related languages— and an immensely rich literature going back to the eleventh century, but it is unclear as to whether it can be considered a nation. It used to be more accurate to talk of two nations, Provence and the Languedoc-Roussillon, with both regions fighting to defend their cultures, their very different history making co-operation between them difficult.

In south-western France, the thirteenth-century crusade against the Albigensian 'heretics' brought the Languedoc-Roussillon to its knees. Whilst Occitan remained in daily use up to the Second World War in the rural areas, it was no longer associated with great literature but underwent marked dialectal fragmentation, with each village having its own variant. These came to be called *patois*, a pejorative term to describe a language that is considered to be incomplete, that exists only in the spoken form, and that is used only in informal contexts. After the Second World War, the area was marked by a sense of neglect and depression. The poorest *départements* were indicated in black in schoolbooks and there were many such areas in the Languedoc. It was then that the local languages ceased to be the main means of communication for the young. In *Parler croquant*, Duneton (1982) describes how in 1941 he was, aged 6, the first monolingual French speaker at school in the area. In the same class there was one monolingual *patois* speaker, while the rest were bilingual. From then on the *langues d'oc* were relegated to the home and to rural contexts such as markets. Parents tended to speak to their children in French, even if French was an acquired language, to give them a better chance in life. The prohibition in school of languages other than French continued until the end of the Second World War, and children caught speaking regional languages at school were given 'a sign'—a marble, a necklace, a stick, etc.—which they had to carry until it was passed on to the next offender. (It must be remembered, however, that this well-documented and frequently quoted practice did not happen everywhere to the same extent.) As a result, the language was no longer transmitted from parents to children on a meaningful scale. Transmission did, however, sometimes happen between grand-parents and children, with children often acquiring a passive knowledge of the language. Politically, this area is traditionally left wing, in contrast to Provence.

Provence, on the other hand, was not colonized and crushed by the state. Moreover, in the late nineteenth century, it enjoyed a remarkable literary renais-sance. In 1854 the Provençal poet Mistral founded the *Felibrige*, a Provençal asso-ciation of writers in the language, and in 1904 he was awarded the Nobel Prize for his writings in Provençal. But Mistral and the *Felibrige* were interested only in the cultural, social, and linguistic status of Provençal and were politically conserva-tive; indeed, Provence as an area has traditionally been right wing. Thus a dictio-nary, *Lou Tresor dou Felibrige*, was published, but it was more a nostalgic attempt to revive a language then used only by peasants than an effort to extend its use to an urban context. Mistral's Nobel Prize did, however, confer on that variant of Occitan a status that later *Provençaux* were not slow to exploit.

Apart from one area being traditionally left wing while the other is right wing, there have been other sources of discord. The main one has been linguistic. Mistral's orthography was unsuitable for the other variants of Occitan, because it reflected only his variant. On the other hand, the orthography developed by Louis Alibert in his 1935 *Grammaire occitane* was suitable, since it did not reflect the dialect of one particular village but was derived from the orthography of the trou-badours in the Middle Ages, when the written language was still unified. In 1945, the Institut d'Études Occitanes in Toulouse refined the system, which is in effect a standardized form of orthography, and in 1951 Robert Laffont started using it, to the considerable disgust of some *Provençaux*.

Occitan seems, therefore, to be a language associated with two different groups inhabiting *le Midi*. The terms 'nation' and 'people' are rarely if ever used in rela-tion to this area. The term *Provençaux* has some of these connotations, and, in the south-west, terms such as *Gascon* or *Languedocien* are more likely to refer to a 'people', albeit one long ago integrated into the conceptual and cultural frame-work of France. However, the fact that the language has survived 700 years of oppression seems to indicate that there are strong regional aspirations.[15]

The differences between the south-east and the south-west culminated in the 1970s with the development of a nationalist movement in the Languedoc-Roussillon with extremists demanding independence. This was accompanied by an intense effort to revitalize the dying local language. Road signs appeared in Occitan, increasing its visibility. One of the slogans of the movement remains: *Volem viure al païs* (meaning 'we want to live in our own country'). Thus for many the use of Occitan was and is politically symbolic. Very few *Occitanistes*, propo-

---

[15] For further details on the problems of defining the Occitan language, see Hammel and Gardy (1994).

nents of the language, support political independence, however, the majority wanting no more than greater regional autonomy. Most were disappointed with the empty promises of the socialist governments in the 1980s and some are bitter. Language is clearly a political issue, and there have been a number of political movements. But these have all been very short lived.[16]

Matters seem to have greatly improved in recent times in that the old Occitan–Provençal divide is being healed. This is true on the linguistic front, since the Alibert–Laffont orthography is now generally accepted. It is especially true on the educational front, since the *Calendretas* (word meaning both 'skylark' and 'apprentice'), which are Occitan immersion schools similar to the *Ikastolak* and *Diwan* schools, are now spreading from the south-west to the Provence area. There are thirty-one in all, including one in Orange and one in Gap, as well as one each in Marseilles and Nice, opened in 1998. The solution to the original problem has been to teach written Occitan in the standardized orthography, but making a place for the *Felibrige* orthography, and allowing a diglossic situation to develop in the schoolroom—that is children are allowed (and indeed encouraged) to speak their local dialect or variant of Occitan. The number of children wishing to be taught in these schools is snowballing at present; so are the numbers wishing to follow a bilingual education in the state system. The first primary schools appeared in Bordeaux in 1982, but there has been a great increase in their number since 1989. In 1990 the Rector of the Académie de Toulouse signed an agreement with F. Bayrou, the then Minister for Education, on the promotion of Occitan in the schools and published leaflets giving details of state support. Montpellier university boasted 700 students of Occitan in 1996/7 and more *Calendretas* are to open. Altogether, 12,532 pupils were taught Occitan in 1997/8. There are clear signs of a fight to save the language, but many linguists think it is too late. On the other hand, some 20 per cent of the children have parents who are said still to speak the language.

The motivation for a return to Occitan is clearly not political, since it now unites people on both left and right of the political scene, but cultural. It stems from a desire to create schools in which the children 'will feel comfortable' and it is thought that their success has been partly a response to a generally pessimistic economic climate. Parents seek to give children some reassurance by emphasizing their roots and their identity separate from the rest of the country. The teaching methods of the 'associative' sector are also seen as more 'child oriented' and it has been noticed that the children seem to do better than those in the state system. In a country where education is considered of paramount importance, this is a strong recommendation.

Those who favour a renaissance of Occitan do not, however, want to be seen as

---

[16] The *Parti nationaliste occitan* (*PNO*) founded in 1959, the socialist *Lutte occitane* founded in 1970, and *Volem viure al païs*, founded around 1976, all demanded economic policies to ensure that people should not be forced to leave the area to find work. *Le Parti socialiste occitan/L'Union dèu poble d'oc*, founded in 1980, bridges the gap between the Provençal and Languedoc regions.

backward looking. There is an interesting research project with a new approach to regional languages called the *Latinitas*. The aim is to identify the fundamental characteristics common to all Romance languages, which would enable students to learn Occitan, Spanish, Italian, Portuguese, and Catalan extremely quickly, making the regional language a link with the outside world. There is a plan for a similar project for the Celtic languages, but the Occitan project is more advanced. This is in total contrast with the traditional approach, where dying languages were purely recorded for posterity.

3.3.6. *Franco-Provençal*

There is little published information about Franco-Provençal, which includes traits of the *langue d'oc* and the *langue d'oïl*. It is not mentioned in EBLUL (1993), but there are some statistics in Killilea (1994), since it is spoken in Italy in the Valle d'Aosta (see Section 8.2.1), in some Alpine valleys in the Piedmont region, and in two communities in the Puglia region. It is not taught in France and is, at present, too fragmented to be used as an effective political tool.

3.3.7. *Catalan*

Catalan is the official language of some 8 million people living mainly in Spain (see also Sections 4.2, 4.5.1). A 1951 survey estimated that there were 220,000 speakers in French Catalonia, mainly the *département* of the Pyrénées Orientales, in the Roussillon. EBLUL (1993) puts the number at around 180,000. It is, however, mainly spoken by elderly people, although there is a revival of interest among the young, seen in the *Association pour l'éducation et la culture catalanes 'la Bressola'*, which in 1976 established a nursery school and primary school in Perpignan and in two nearby villages. In 1981, *l'Escola Arrels*, which includes a nursery school and a primary school, was founded, which also functions entirely in Catalan. These schools have the same status and aims as the other 'associative' schools. Further primary schools were founded, bringing the total to eight by September 1997. By 1997/8, there were 196 children in eight *Bressolas*, and 1,932 pupils studying Catalan in the public sector. Perpignan is the centre of French Catalonia. As in other areas of France where there are regional languages, Catalan speakers are all bilinguals (see Marley 1995).

Like Basque, Catalan straddles a frontier. The Treaty of the Pyrenees of 1659 divided the country of Catalonia into the *Catalogne Sud* and the *Catalogne Nord*, where French became the overwhelming influence. This influence increased because the French administrative areas rarely correspond to linguistic areas (intentional at the time of the Revolution). Thus the *département* des Pyrénées Orientales includes a region that was never Catalan-speaking, and in the new Languedoc-Roussillon region all French Catalan institutions are based in non-Catalan Montpellier rather than Catalan Perpignan. In other words, the French state has denied Catalans both a geographical and an institutional identity.

Catalan has survived, however, helped by its strong presence in Spain, and has seen an intellectual revival since the 1960s. In 1960 the *Grup Rossellonés d'Estudis Catalans* was founded, which favoured a standardized version of the language. In 1967 a splinter group from this more conservative body formed the *Institut Rossellonés d'Estudis Catalans*. In 1968, the *Diades de cultura catalana* were inaugurated and in 1969 the *Universitat Catalana d'Estiu*. Poets and singers also made the language more popular. This led to a movement demanding political autonomy for the region. In 1973 two political parties, the *Acció Regionalista Catalana* and the *Esquerra Catalana dels Treballadors*, put up candidates for the legislative election. In the 1980s various Catalanist candidates stood for election, and in 1985 a new party, *Unitat Catalana*, was formed. Regionalist rather than nationalist, it does not seek independence but seeks to regain some of Catalonia's lost identity.

In France Catalan has many fewer speakers than Occitan. The terms 'nation' and 'people' are not usually used in France in connection with Catalan speakers, possibly because of the success of the anti-regionalist policies of France. But Catalan is a 'tip-of-the-iceberg language' in that it straddles a frontier and is strong in the other country, which gives it unknown and untapped potential.

3.3.8. *Corsican*

It is in Corsica that French authority has been—and still is—most resisted. Corsica was annexed in 1768 and, because of its isolation, retained its linguistic and cultural identity well into the twentieth century. According to Dorothy Carrington, the Catalan specialist in Corsican culture, it was possible in the late 1950s to meet Corsicans who spoke no French. This is no longer the case.

Originally it was excluded from the scope of the Deixonne law because it was considered to be a dialect of Italian, but the law was extended to include Corsican in 1974. According to the 1982 survey by INSEE cited in Killilea (1994), 96 per cent of the population of Corsican origin understood Corsican, and it was regularly spoken by some 86 per cent. This represented around 143,000 people.

The Corsican language is clearly associated with nationalism. The *Front de libération national corse* (*FLNC*) is an active terrorist group that regularly targets the second homes of French people. However, according to statements by their representatives in the French Parliament, a majority of the Corsican population wants to remain French. A 1996 survey revealed that 61 per cent of French people also wanted Corsica to remain part of France, but 24 per cent were in favour of independence, which implies that some French people are nowadays thinking bold thoughts on the subject.

While the French view has been canvassed, there has been no similar survey in Corsica. The French sociolinguist, P. Blanchet (1998: 30), has commented on this point: 'We are entitled to ask if the Corsicans are not the only people legitimately entitled to pronounce on the future of their community and their country, in view of the right to self-determination by democratic means provided for by the United Nations.'

The desire to protect and promote Corsican is not restricted to the separatists.

A group called the *Collectif pour la langue* has been created, bringing together cultural associations, trade unions, and the Economic, Social, and Cultural Council of Corsica. A delegation from this group recently met the official French governmental representative for the region. They drew attention to a demonstration by 5,000 Corsicans in favour of France signing and ratifying the European Charter for Regional or Minority Languages (see Section 3.5.) and indicated their intention to continue to press the government on the issue. They stressed the two resolutions of the Corsican Assembly and the broad support of the general public, pressure groups, and political parties in favour of the Charter, which would protect the regional languages, and Corsican in particular (see *Contact Bulletin* (1997: 6).

The main problem for Corsica seems to be that the most vociferous members of the community have decided on 'independence first, and the Corsican language will follow'. This has largely led to the Corsicans being ostracized by the close network of those promoting the cause of the other regional languages. There appears to be no link between Corsica and the network centred at the Institut Supérieur des Langues de la République Française in Béziers, created in September 1997, to train all future teachers of regional languages.

3.3.9. *The Regional Languages: Conclusion*

Although in decline for years, the regional languages refuse to go away. There is even some state recognition in the shape of teaching subsidies and cultural events. There are a number of reasons for this change of heart. The Algerian war and the decolonization of Africa in the late 1950s and early 1960s gave rise to the idea that the French regions had also been the victims of 'colonization'. In 1968 the political, social, and economic status quo and the domination of Paris were questioned. In the 1980s economic factors also played an important role, particularly as regards Occitan and Catalan. The European Union meant the creation of a new trading triangle linking Toulouse–Montpellier–Barcelona, with Perpignan in the middle. Paris was no longer the only centre. In addition, the new political emphasis on Brussels and Strasbourg has emphasized the regions, in contrast to the tradition of centralization. The result: French education no longer comprises two sectors, the state sector and the private sector, but now also includes a new 'associative' sector.[17]

Of the regional languages, Corsican is most closely linked with nationalism and a desire for independence, which is possibly why other regional language associations have no links with the Corsican language movements. It is true that Basque is also linked with nationalism and independence, but mainly on the Spanish side of the border. Moreover, the Basque *Ikastolak* have been a model. Breton was in the past linked with various forms of nationalism, but this movement

---

[17] Many schools in the private sector have signed contracts with the state, bringing them indirectly into the public sector.

involved only a small group of intellectuals. Occitan has been linked with nation-alism in the past but, again, only among a very small group of intellectuals. The Catalan movements have been mainly regionalist. Flemish, Alsatian, and Lorrain are not at present linked with any independence movements. The supporters of the *langues d'oïl* in northern France are still fighting for the recognition of these varieties as distinct languages, and proponents of all the languages are fighting for regional recognition within the context of the French state and nation (see Section 3.4). More people seem to think that belonging to a minority group is not incom-patible with being French. The language issue has become associated more with regionalism and a search for a new identity rather than with nationalism and independence. The concept of a regional identity is seen as enriching. Since all the regional languages—apart from the *langues d'oïl*—have links with other languages outside France, the regional languages are seen as affording an insight into other cultures. As such, they are economically desirable. This economic and political potential may reverse the trend that previously pointed to their disap-pearance. Regional languages also have a positive aura, since the associative schools—be they based on the principle of immersion, or bilingual—that promote them have the reputation of being 'more caring and child oriented' than mainstream schools.

As far as government policy is concerned, the regional languages have been gradually integrated into the state educational system. The immersion schools were allowed to function even when they were not strictly legal, because of the political explosion that would have followed any attempt to close them. The new vision of the 'associative schools' is full integration within the state system. Much more progress needs to be made to enhance the role of the regional languages in the media. A role in administrative and judicial contexts does not look a possibil-ity at present, but this will have to be addressed if significant progress is to be made to ensure their natural transmission.

3.4. The Emergence of French

The Roman conquest of Gaul was swift. In 125 BC the Romans were called in by the Greeks, who had established colonies around 600 BC in (what are now) Marseilles, Nice, and Antibes, to help end raids by the Gauls. Having achieved this in 124 BC, the Romans decided to stay and created the first Roman province, or *Provincia* (Provence), around 120 BC. In 58 BC the Gauls themselves called on the Romans for help against Germanic invaders. Having driven these back over the Rhine, the Romans again stayed on, spreading their wings further afield. They conquered the Armoricans (Gauls), who inhabited the area corresponding roughly to present-day Brittany. They also conquered the Aquitanians. Vercingetorix fought to protect the Celtic centre of Gaul, but was taken prisoner in 52 BC. The whole of Gaul was declared a Roman province in 51 BC.

After the conquest, the Gauls quickly became Romanized—and more especially

Latinized—partly because Roman policy was to make their way of life as attractive as possible. The Gaulish aristocracy became Gallo-Roman. The ease with which people could integrate into the Roman professional classes (particularly administration and the law) explains the general willingness to learn Latin. And anybody involved in trade would have needed to learn Latin. But what came to be spoken was a vernacularized form of Latin, Gallo-Romance. Gallo-Romance was, therefore, the local form of Latin—of which there were many variants—spoken with a Gaulish substratum (this label covers, therefore, a number of dialects or variants, rather than a uniform variety).[18] The concept of a written language—which Gaulish was not—was also attractive. The administration of the country was also reorganized to make it uniform in all regions. The concept of administrative and legislative unity, which characterizes France, goes back, therefore, to the Romans.

It is important to note that the administrative system created by the Romans was flexible. Thus, for example, during the second half of the third century AD, a representative of the Aquitainian *peuplades* persuaded the Roman emperor to establish an administrative entity for his people. The result was the creation of the Novempopulania region ('the nine peoples') with Eauze as its capital. France in its centralizing policies has not shown the same level of flexibility. The policy of making a Roman-style society attractive was also a success. Tacitus tells how, in AD 21, the sons of the most illustrious Gaulish families attended Roman schools whenever possible. Sidonius Apollinarius wrote in the fifth century AD that the Arvene nobility—a Celtic people in the Auvergne—had at last 'got rid of the "dross" of the Celtic language'. This means that, in the intervening period, the nobility was diglossic. Gaulish continued to be spoken in the country probably for another century and is regarded as having died out finally by the end of the sixth century, except in a few isolated areas.

Romanization had taken place throughout Gaul by the fifth century, by which time the Germanic migrations and invasions began. These were possible because of the weakness of the Roman Empire, which finally collapsed in AD 476. The non-Germanic Huns crossed the Rhine in 406 and were followed by other groups, and wars between the Germanic tribes and the Gallo-Romans continued for nearly a century. There are two important events to note. In 486, Clovis, king of the Franks, beat the Romans at Soissons and is alleged to have converted to Christianity in AD 496.[19] This is an important date in the historical consciousness of the French nation. The 1,500th anniversary of this event was celebrated in 1996. The celebrations included a visit by the Pope to Rheims, where Clovis is supposed to have been crowned in the name of God. These celebrations of rather doubtful historical facts were seen by the extreme right *Front national* as a subject for rejoicing,

---

[18] Latin was brought into Gaul by—among others—the Roman legions, themselves made up of men for whom Latin was quite often a second language, and who hence spoke varieties of Latin influenced by different substrata.

[19] Historians disagree on the exact date. They agree that it was some time between 496 and 506. The former date is the 'official' one.

echoing as they did the beginnings of the French nation. This infuriated the other political parties, for whom the anniversary was not meant to be the occasion for racist propaganda but a simple celebration of national history (in either event, however, the celebrations may be described as 'nationalist').

The conversion of Clovis ensured an alliance between the Franks and the Gallo-Roman Church, which had survived the collapse of the Roman Empire. This led to the setting-up of 'an administration based on Germanic folk-custom slightly Romanized and increasingly Christianised' (Rickard 1974: 17). In the Frankish area, the Franks often outnumbered the Gallo-Romans, but, through intermarriage and alliances of interest, the distinctions between the two peoples gradually disappeared. The Franks were, in particular, unable to impose their language except on the left bank of the Rhine and in Flanders, where Alsatian and Flemish respectively are still spoken.[20] Where they failed to impose Frankish, a Frankish superstratum was superimposed onto Gallo-Romance. In the north this gave rise to the *langues d'oïl*, of which standard French is one product, the name *français* (French) deriving from the Latin *franciscus*, originally meaning 'Frankish'.

In the south (corresponding to Provence, Languedoc, Dauphiné, and Savoie), however, Romanization and Latinization were strongest. This was an area that had been less linguistically influenced by the Gauls and it was least affected by the Germanic invasions: Aquitaine and Provence did not come under Frankish rule until 732 when Charles Martel repelled a Moorish invasion. This explains the survival of the *langue(s) d'oc* and why they are closest to Latin. Southern France, *le Midi*, still retains a sense of being special. Although obviously related to French, the traditional dialects of the *langue d'oc* are generally accepted to be a distinct language.

By the late eighth century the Gallo-Romance language spoken in the northern part of France had changed so much that it could hardly be called Latin at all. As a result, Charlemagne decided that Latin should be properly taught and established schools for young clerics in every monastery and in every bishop's house. This resulted in the great cathedral schools. These were to train not only priests but also administrators and civil servants to give the new regime a more stable basis, which implied the need for written documents. Latin became the language of law, administration, and the Church for theological matters, while the people continued to speak their Germanicized versions of Gallo-Romance. Since the two languages were mutually unintelligible, this created a problem for the Church, which decided in 813 at the Council of Tours that, in order to be understood, priests should preach in the *rustica romana lingua*.

Thus the Gauls, having abandoned Gaulish for a vernacularized form of Latin, turned to a scholastic form of Latin for administrative, judicial, academic, and

---

[20] Flemish and Alsatian are actually considerably different from each other, being Low Franconian and Alemannic (Upper German) speech forms respectively. It is possible, nevertheless, that they are both descended from Frankish speech, since the Franks may have been a confederation of Germanic-speaking peoples, speaking a variety of different West Germanic dialects.

religious purposes. It is, however, the vernacular form that emerged as French. The *Strasbourg Oaths* are generally considered to constitute the first text in French. Thus Renée Balibar (1996: 3), in her *Histoire de la littérature française*, writes:

French literature was born one winter morning at Strasbourg on 14th February 842. That day an oath of allegiance between two kings, proclaimed in two languages, representing Germanic and Romance speech, contained the seed of European vernacular literature. Once officially written down, the vernacular languages bore witness to the divisions between populations but also to their common destiny: thanks to writing, the vernacular languages were born into the world and developed through translation from one into another.

The Gallo-Romance version of Latin, influenced by the dialects of different Germanic tribes, gave rise to different languages or dialects, the *langues d'oïl*, of which there are a number of descendants, standard French being the politically successful one. The others are not referred to in EBLUL (1993) and their different status is highlighted in Killilea (1994), where they are listed in a different typeface. It is usual to refer to these *langues d'oïl* as dialects of French, since they are historically very close to the standard language. On the other hand, Picard, for example, is not easily and completely intelligible to an outsider, which logically should make it into a distinct 'language' in the same ways as Occitan is. Some speakers of *langues d'oïl* are at present fighting for their recognition as distinct languages.

Whether they are considered to be 'dialects' (i.e. politically not important) or 'languages' (i.e. worth fighting for), these languages present an educational problem in so far as they have infiltrated the standard French of the region. This is why there are intellectual groups who favour the teaching of 'languages' such as Picard, if only to help children who unknowingly produce at school a mixture of French and the local 'language', which is then termed 'bad French'. This meets with a great deal of opposition on the part of the French educational authorities, and these languages or dialects cannot, as yet, be studied as an option for the *baccalauréat*.

Killilea (1994) states that since 1981 French governments have been more sympathetic than previously, when the existence of the *langues d'oïl* was simply denied. In 1981 A. Savary, in a circular on the use of minority languages in schools, included among them the *langues d'oïl*. In 1986 a person representing these languages was appointed to the National Council for Regional Languages and Cultures. Their existence was again recognized in 1991, when they were referred to during the tabling of a Bill by Dollo in the National Assembly on the promotion of regional languages.

These languages or dialects are not generally taught, except for some short courses in universities and isolated projects in some schools.[21] Private or local radio stations broadcast a few hours in the languages, and there are numerous

---

[21] For further details, see Eloy (1998).

cultural activities, publications, plays (including a tradition of puppet theatre), and various literary activities. The issue of these languages is of importance only at a political level, in terms of a demand for recognition and respect. There is no nationalist dimension in areas that are the historical foundation of the French state. What is surprising, however, is that any clearly distinct dialects or languages (such as Picard) should have survived at all in these areas.

3.5. The Institutionalization of French as the Symbol of the Nation

There is remarkable historical continuity in the way France has evolved into an ever more centralized state. The Roman Empire was the first force for centralization, then Charlemagne encouraged the development of a powerful unified and unifying Church. Finally, the Capetian kings and their successors built a country around their Île-de-France base, gradually adding Languedoc (1229), Provence (1481), Brittany (1532), Alsace (1648), Roussillon (1659), Franche-Comté (1678), Lorraine (1766), Corsica (1768), and Nice (in 1860). Each time one of these regions became incorporated into the French state, it had to adopt French as its administrative language, although no effort was made to impose French in daily use. The Revolution occurred in an already centralized country, but one in which the provinces were linked to the Crown rather than to each other.

The task of the Revolution was to build a new kind of state. At first it seemed that language was not to be an essential part of the building process, since the States General and then the Constituent Assembly accepted and encouraged the principle of bilingualism and translation.[22] But the Convention adopted a very different policy. At first there were two opposing factions. The Girondins[23] in the Convention favoured federalism and thought that a state should satisfy all its component groups. They were against the domination of Paris and wanted to give power to the provinces and allow them to develop freely. Their opponents, the Jacobins,[24] were committed to a form of democracy based on equality of opportunity and felt this required a uniform and centralized state. The influential Condorcet, in his *Cinq mémoires sur l'instruction publique* (1791), wrote that

he who does not know how to write, and does not know arithmetic, is in a real sense dependent on a person more educated than himself to whom he constantly has to have recourse. He is not the equal of a person who has acquired knowledge through education; he cannot enjoy the same rights, to the same extent, and in the same state of independence. (1994: 62)

---

[22] In January 1790 a decree was promulgated encouraging the translation of official texts into the local languages, and, in May 1790, another decree instituted an increase in salary for bilingual teachers.

[23] The Girondins were a political group that took part in the Revolution. Their name derives from the fact that many of their most famous members in the Convention came from the Gironde region. They acceded to power in 1792, but were blamed for the military defeats in 1793, and lost power.

[24] Name given to members of an ardently republican club, which met in an old abandoned convent in the *rue Saint Jacques*.

This being the case, he concluded that state education was one of the most important duties of the state, which view was generally adopted.

Since language can be a source of inequality, it soon became obvious to the revolutionaries that everybody should speak the same language. Standard French, the language of the élite, was their obvious choice. Indeed, if one examines Condorcet's *Cinq mémoires sur l'instruction publique*, it is noticeable that the desirability of having standard French as a common language is not even questioned. A common language was also a practical necessity to enable communication in a society that was to function both horizontally and vertically, and on a national and not regional level. The regional languages were soon identified with feudalism and the lower classes and lacked political prestige. Indeed, some of the respondents to l'abbé Grégoire's 1792 questionnaire to establish the linguistic state of the nation, begged to be 'freed' from their 'patois' (any language or dialect other than standard French was defined as a dialect or a patois). To share a language that had previously been the preserve of the élite was a supreme act of democracy and the principle of 'one language, one nation, one state' became the cornerstone of the new French republic. French was the symbol of a nation that was 'une et indivisible', and all other languages were forbidden.

Achieving the goal of a common language meant setting up primary schools with the express aim of teaching *le français national*, a clear and simple form of standard French. But the revolutionaries faced many more immediate problems (military attacks from all sides) and, though they worked out an educational policy, they were unable to implement it. Napoleon I did little to further the cause. Being mainly interested in secondary and higher education, he created the *lycées* and the *grandes écoles*, which attracted the bourgeoisie who already spoke standard French. It was left to the Third Republic to implement the Jacobin policy, with the Jules Ferry educational laws in the 1880s, which made primary education in French free and compulsory.

The Jacobins' vision of a nation-state included the belief held by many contemporaries in the superiority of French over all other languages. The concept of French as a perfect language had been developing ever since French had taken over from Latin in the sixteenth century onwards, with writers and grammarians working to shape its development to make it as clear, as precise, and as elegant as possible. It was meant to assume the historic role of Latin, and, by the eighteenth century, French had become the language of international diplomacy. Those who spoke French were extremely proud of their language and the literature it had produced. Foreigners readily agreed with this, and French became the language of many of the European courts. In 1784 Rivarol won a prize offered by the Academy of Berlin for his *Discourse on the Universality of the French Language* (*Discours sur l'universalité de la langue française*):

There has never been a language in which it has been possible to write in a purer and clearer manner than ours, a language which has been more opposed to ambiguity and all kinds of obscurity, a language more sober and yet more gentle, more adapted to all kinds of style, a language more chaste in its expressions, more judicious in its figures, a language which, while loving elegance and ornamentation, is more opposed to affectation. (quoted in Wardhaugh 1987: 100–1)

This belief in the superiority of the language was to have unfortunate consequences in the long term. To adopt a language for social prestige (like the Gauls adopting Latin) is not the same as believing that the original mother tongue was an inferior jargon. This led many speakers of regional languages to feel ashamed. This shame, called *la vergonha* by today's militant Occitanists, explains why speakers of regional languages often refuse to cooperate with people wanting to learn them or linguists wishing to study them. It also explains the inferiority complex of speakers of regional French, influenced by a regional language substratum, particularly in terms of accent, in relation to standard French. It is important to realize that, even during the Revolution, not everybody wished to see their language replaced by French. The *Amis de la Constitution de Carcassonne* presented the dialects of the Languedoc as 'a single language divided into an infinite number of dialects, a little like Greek, which had four very different forms' (de Certeau *et al.* 1975: 59). In other words, the *langue d'oc* was seen as being in some way similar to Greek. There were, therefore, people for whom the concept of a nation was not automatically linked to the concept of a monolingual country and who objected from the start to the new philosophy.

Inevitably French was to take on an ambiguous role: although French was seen as the language of liberation and equality, it also became inevitably a language of repression. In the early days of the First Republic (1792–1804), when France was attacked on all sides, there were still many royalists in favour of a restoration of the monarchy, which indeed occurred in 1814. The Republicans were, quite naturally, obsessed with the idea of an uprising to re-establish the monarchy. The regional languages were linked with this idea, and they soon became a symbol of anti-patriotism, as can be seen in the following quote from Barrère, a prominent member of the Committee of Public Safety, who declared in 1794:

The voice of federalism and of superstition speaks Breton; the émigrés and those who hate the Republic speak German; the counter-revolution speaks Italian; fanaticism speaks Basque. Let us smash these instruments of damage and error . . . For our part we owe it to our citizens, we owe it to our republic, in order to strengthen it, that everyone on its territory is made to speak the language in which the Declaration of the Rights of Man was written. (Wardhaugh 1987: 102)

This became law on 20 July 1794: 'No public document may be written in any part of the territory of the Republic in any language other than French' (quoted in Wardhaugh 1987: 102).

Making a particular language compulsory, even with the best of motives, is a form of oppression, and French became the symbol of the power of the state over the regions, and—in the nineteenth century—over its colonies. Even today, in the post-colonial era, aid is closely related to language use. And, in December 1996, when people were seeking proposals for a new UN Secretary General, the English press reported that France was attempting to block the nomination of non-francophone African candidates. Sharing a language could imply sharing a certain world view. But, more cynically, it could be argued that the French government would have greater control over an African francophone.

This kind of analysis has developed since 1968, which marked the first real reaction against a traditionally Jacobin approach in France. Calvet (1974) describes how France used French to 'colonize' its regions, and then applied the same concepts outside its frontiers. Others such as Balibar (1996) have taken a similar view, but this probably still represents a minority position. The majority, and certainly all governments until the Jospin government, have backed the traditional Jacobin approach to language. Thus Toubon, when Minister for Education, Culture, and Francophone Affairs (*de la culture et la francophonie*), referring to newly established foreigners in France, wrote: 'The French language is their most important asset, the sign of their dignity, their passport to integration, the medium of a universal culture, their share in the common heritage, their part of the French dream' (*Le Monde*, 4 Aug. 1994).

This leaves no room for the regional languages, which are seen as belonging to the past. Indeed, Wardhaugh (1987: 118) quotes President Pompidou asserting in 1972 'there is no place for minority languages in a France destined to make its mark on Europe'. Nor is this an isolated comment. A linguistic survey carried out by INSEE/INED published in *Population et sociétés* (Dec. 1993) refers variously to 'the linguistic unification of France', 'the disappearance of other languages from everyday use', 'the collapse of these languages', 'the conversion to French', and 'the domination of French' to refer to the same phenomenon (Blanchet 1998: 24). And indeed one of the reasons quoted for the very short lengths of time allocated by the radio station FR3 for programmes in regional languages is that they appeal to a minority of speakers, and often 'annoy' others. As a national channel, FR3 is supposed to cater for the majority of speakers; this means that French minorities have no rights, at least in this field.

This is reflected in the Toubon law (1994), which makes no concessions to the regional languages. Article 1 asserts: 'By virtue of the Constitution French is the language of the Republic, [and] the French language is a fundamental element of the character and heritage of France'—a very Jacobin assertion indeed. This is also why the French government has refused until very recently (see *Libération*, 1 Oct. 1998) to sign the European Charter for Regional or Minority Languages, despite the fact that France already meets the demands made by the Charter in matters of education. But the fact of according legal status to the minority languages is said to be difficult to accept, for officially there are no minorities in France and all French people are therefore equal. The recognition of the concept would create a new class of citizenship, which contradicts the philosophy of the nation-state. Jean Haritschelhar (1994: 92), in an article contrasting the linguistic rights of the

Spanish Basques and their absence in France, wrote: 'For the French government to sign the European Charter for Regional or Minority Languages would demand a major change in mentality . . . Clearly, the birthplace of the Rights of Man is not to be the birthplace of any linguistic rights.'

In other words, democracy in France is geared to the majority, and leaves little room for minorities. This is what is meant by Jacobin policies. The kingdom became a state, and the state became a nation, but at a price. So far, the majority of French people—from views expressed in surveys and the media—do not question this principle. But, for a minority, the destruction of their world view as mirrored by their language is a tragic destruction of their identity, and an impoverishment of France, in which they merely seek recognition of their regional culture and language. However, this may now be changing.

3.6. Challenges to the Supremacy of French

Having established itself as the sole language of the state, French now faces a threat both externally and internally from English. Externally, English has supplanted French as the language of diplomacy and threatens the status of French in the EU. Internally, there is the incorporation of English terms and even the supplanting of French in certain contexts. The French reaction to internal encroachment was the adoption of strongly protectionist linguistic policies (Section 3.6.1). In spite of these, however, cracks in the monolingual edifice may offer hope for the regional languages (Section 3.6.2.). On the international front, close linguistic ties have developed between France and its ex-colonies, joined by other countries who wanted to avoid Russian or American influence (Section 3.6.3.).

3.6.1. *France's Protectionist Policies*

A number of governmental institutions have been created since the 1960s in an effort to defend the integrity of French. Some of these have changed name as a reflection of a changed ideological slant. Thus the *Haut comité de défense et d'expansion de la langue française* (Commission for the Defence and the Expansion of the French Language), created in 1966 under de Gaulle, became in 1973 the more politically correct *Haut comité de la langue française* (Commission for the French Language). In 1984 this committee was replaced by two new ones. The first, which studies specific linguistic problems and aims to promote a new *bon usage*, is now called the *Conseil supérieur de la langue française* (Supreme Council for the French Language). The second coordinates and disseminates the work done by the *Conseil* and is now called the *Délégation générale à la langue française* (Committee for the French Language); it was originally a *commissariat*, which implied far more control than *délégation*.

Linguistically, it has long been accepted that the main problem facing French is developing terminologies suited to the modern technological world. A first decree in 1970 allowed for the establishment of ministerial commissions on terminology; and a 1972 decree provided for ministers to publish regular lists of accepted terms in the French Official Journal, which automatically gave them force of law. In 1986 a decree provided for *all* ministries to have their own terminological commission.

Since 1990 these commissions include representatives of the Canadian Embassy, the Quebec Delegation, the Swiss Confederation, the French Community in Belgium, and the *Agence de coopération culturelle et technique* (which became the *Agence de la francophonie* in 1997), the main institution representing countries of the Francophone World (see Section 3.5.2.). The results of their deliberations are published in the French *Official Journal* and from time to time published in dictionary form (called originally 'Dictionaries of Official Neologisms' and now 'Dictionaries of Official Terms'). The fact that these terminological decrees are promulgated by the minister of the relevant department and the Minister for Education highlights the importance still attached to education in terms of language planning. A factor reinforcing these decrees is the international development of Term Banks, which are, by definition, prescriptive. France has several of these; the most important, NORMATERM, created in 1976, is dependent on the *Association française de normalisation* (*AFNOR*), which functions within the context of the International Standards Organization.

The enforcement of these decrees led to the first important linguistic law in over a century. The Bas-Lauriol law was first presented to the French National Assembly in 1973, and passed in a less rigid form in 1975. It sought to make the use of French compulsory in various domains to protect the French from misinformation arising from the use of a foreign language. It was concerned with consumer protection, contracts of employment, and the dissemination of information to the general public. Where a French term existed, this had to be used; breach of the law resulted in a fine. Enforcement was the responsibility of the *Direction de la consommation et de la répression des fraudes* (responsible for consumer affairs and the suppression of fraud) and the *Direction générale de la concurrence et de la consommation* (responsible for customer protection and competition). The *Service des douanes* (Customs Service) was also involved, since the law covered imports.

In practice, there were very few prosecutions. This ensured its replacement with a new law, the Toubon law. As before, the aim was to impose the use of French. The law covers the sale of goods and services, contracts involving the state, publicity materials, contracts of employment, and the media. A secondary aim was to impose the linguistic pronouncements of the terminological commissions and the *Académie française* (whose importance has been enhanced by recent French governments). The aim was to replace words borrowed from foreign languages by 'home-grown' French words: *sponsoriser* was to be replaced by *parrainer*. This secondary aim attracted most attention, particularly from journalists, who saw themselves possibly being imprisoned for using *franglais*.

3.6.2. *A Change in Attitude and New Hope for the Regional Languages?*

Whereas in 1975 the Bas-Lauriol law was passed without comment, this time there was not only opposition to the proposed law (passed on 1 July 1994), but parts of it were declared unconstitutional by the *Conseil constitutionnel* on 30 July 1994. The final form restricts language use in all public matters, but excludes the private domain, which is excluded under the principle of freedom of expression enshrined in the constitution. Its rejection by large sections of the country demonstrates, however, that such linguistic policies are no longer totally accept-able. A survey in March 1994 by SOFRES, and interpreted by the government as being in its favour, can also be interpreted as indicating a change in attitude. Thus, although 97 per cent were proud of their language, only 70 per cent were proud of its international status. Only 39 per cent felt that the 'defence of the French language' was a 'very important' issue for the government, while 51 per cent thought it 'important but not excessively so', and 9 per cent thought it was not particularly an important issue for government at all. As far as the role of educa-tion was concerned, 59 per cent thought the defence of the language was the responsibility of the schools, 10 per cent thought the government, and a surpris-ing 28 per cent thought the French Academy.

Furthermore, there seems to have been a fundamental change of attitude and a lack of enthusiasm for prescriptivity in relation to the borrowing of foreign words, made illegal by the Toubon law. According to the survey, 30 per cent thought the use of foreign words in French was 'useful', 19 per cent 'amusing', and 41 per cent 'modern'. Very few disapproved. The law was ridiculed by the press, who were accused of 'disinformation'.

Membership of the EU also has an impact on language policies. The EU is committed to the fundamental rights of free movement of people, goods, services, and capital, enshrined in the Treaty of Rome (1957). The detailed implementation of these rights is by Regulations and Directives. It has been suggested that articles 2 and 4 of the Toubon law relating to publicity, labelling, and marketing are contrary to EU law, in that, by insisting on the use of French on packaging and in advertising, they impose a restriction on the free movement of goods from other Member States, by increasing the cost of marketing them in France. If the European Court of Justice were to decide that French law was inconsistent with EU law in that respect, the offending Articles would have to be removed (see Judge 1994; Judge and Judge 1998).

A change in attitude may also be seen in the attitude of a number of politicians. According to Favereau (1994: 82), 'The presidency of Giscard d'Estaing marked . . . the true break, albeit a gentle one, with the Bonapartist Jacobinism inherited from the 19th century.' Mitterrand, although not living up to his election promises to help the regional languages, gradually accorded to most of them the title of 'language'. One of his ministers for Education, Alain Savary, was described as the pioneer of a new federalist approach, and, in 1993 under Chirac, another Minister of Education, François Bayrou, a fluent speaker of Occitan, declared: 'The time of shame is past. Now is the time for pride, although it comes late, and although it will be difficult. Pride does not stop at declarations . . . It implies a policy . . . Yes, [our] language will find a place in our schools' (Favereau 1994: 82). Changes in policies have been very slow, nonetheless, but they do seem to be gathering some speed at the time of writing.

Even from a governmental point of view, it is interesting to note that the approach adopted in the *circulaire*[25] of 13 March 1996 relating to the Toubon law is very different from earlier approaches. The *circulaire* states in particular, 'It [the text of the law] imposes the obligatory but not the exclusive use of French in stated domains.' It also states that the text of the law 'does not make provision for any lists of terms or expressions to be prohibited or obligatory'. These lists are available, apparently, merely for consultation.

However, the failure to sign the Charter for Regional or Minority Languages infuriated the defenders of regional languages, despite the fact it does not, in practice, offer many guarantees. Following the French Council of State's opinion that the Charter did not conform with Article 2 of the French Constitution, making French the language of the French state, strong pressure was put on the government, particularly by the Corsican language movement, *Collectif pour la langue*, for the Constitution to be amended. Minority language groups demanded the replacement of the traditional Jacobin policies and ideals with those of the Girondins. The government finally signed the Charter on 7 May 1999 but at the time of writing it has not been ratified.

It seems that France could eventually move towards a more Girondin position. The Prime Minister of France at the time of writing, Lionel Jospin, is certainly in favour of helping the regional languages. When Nicole Péry was asked to report on the situation, she pointed out that no less than fifty-two private members' bills on the issue had been drafted over the previous twenty years, without one of them ever being tabled for debate. This shows the complete lack of commitment of past governments of the left and the right to the cause of regional languages. And yet she pointed to the extraordinary *renouveau* or 'rebirth' of some of these languages, stating that 2 per cent of children in schools follow at least some courses in a regional language.

Regional aspirations are not restricted to language; some would like to see a change in the names of regions. During the 1789 Revolution, names of areas implying regional identity were replaced by neutral geographical names. The Armagnac region was renamed as the *département* of le Gers, which had no such connotations. Since the *départements* were regrouped into regions, there has been a desire to return to the old names, which reflected identities, but the Catalan-speaking area and *l'Occitanie* have no administrative existence and tend to be deprived even of their history because of not forming politically unified regions.

---

[25] Official letter sent by a minister to all those who come under the ministry concerned. It does not have the force of law.

But the specialist in Occitan, Yves Rouquette, claims that trying to define *l'Occitanie* ceases to be a problem once the traditional nineteenth-century concept of the strictly territorial nation-state is abandoned (Rouquette, n.d.: 7). Such an approach gives a whole new dimension to the concept of the regional languages at the cultural level.

With the Péry–Poignant Report demanding the signature by France of the European Charter for Regional or Minority Languages and the replacement of the Deixonne law by a new law encouraging far more bilingual education, there is a sense of revolution in the air. The appointment on 15 September 1998 of a *Chargé de missions aux langues régionales* within the *Délégation générale à la langue française*, and the appointment of the constitutional specialist Guy Carcassonne to study the constitutional implications, seem to imply the government means business.

3.6.3. *The 'Francophone' Dimension*

On the international front, the position of French as a world language weakened considerably in the course of the twentieth century. At the San Francisco meeting of the UN in 1945, France had to fight to assert its position as an official language. Matters improved only when the newly independent ex-colonial states gained access to the various international organizations and chose to use French to communicate with the outside world. For some, the choice of French was purely practical, for others it was seen, and continues to be seen, as the language of non-alignment. Some actually believe in the particularity of French as a language that has been shaped over the centuries, and others may feel that they have themselves contributed to its development. For a combination of all these reasons, a number of African leaders sought to form a new post-colonial *communauté francophone*. The leading figures were Presidents Senghor (Senegal), Bourguiba (Tunisia), and Diori (Niger). This movement led to the establishment of a number of institutions, of which the most important was the *Agence de coopération culturelle et technique (ACCT)* in 1970. Many other organizations have been created since which form a worldwide network of ties between countries that are not necessarily 'francophone', but committed to the cause of French (see Judge 1996*a,b*).

At first the French government showed little enthusiasm for becoming involved, not wishing to be accused of cultural and economic neocolonialism. In 1984 there was, however, a change of policy with the creation of the *Haut conseil de la francophonie* (Commission for the French-Speaking World). Its mission, according to article 2 of the Decree of 12 March 1984 that established the *Haut conseil de la francophonie* was 'to clarify the role of the Francophone Community and of the French language in the wider world. It assembles and compares the varieties of experience, notably in the areas of education, communications science and the new technologies.' It is presided over by the president of the French Republic and its budget comes from the Ministry of Foreign Affairs. It cooperates closely with the *Délégation générale de la langue française* and the *Conseil supérieur de la langue française* (see Section 3.5.1.).

Attitudes to *la francophonie* tend to be contradictory, as could be expected; for some it is a symbol of solidarity, a sign that France has been forgiven its colonial past and now has the aim of building on the positive aspects inherited from the past. For others it is no more than a neocolonial institution functioning with the connivance of political leaders who benefit from it.

The French themselves are not always very aware of the existence of this inter-national dimension, but all governments have been committed to it. At present the most debated issue is to determine the way forward. Past policies, particularly in relation to sub-Saharan Africa, have proved disastrous in recent years. In August 1997 Chirac announced the dismantling of the special 'African cell' exploited by presidents from de Gaulle onwards, and, in February 1998, Jospin announced the ending of special arrangements for the countries of Africa. This was presumably to improve France's tarnished image in that area rather than a rejection of the concept of *la francophonie*. The intention behind the election of Boutros Boutros-Ghali to the new post of Secretary General of *la francophonie* was certainly to enhance the organization's international profile.

3.7. Conclusions

The revolutionaries defined democracy in terms of equality and liberty, which are not totally compatible. The Jacobins opted for equality, which entailed linguistic uniformity, which in turn took roughly a century and a half to achieve. And yet, no sooner had the linguistic nation-state come into existence, with language as the symbol of both nation and state, than the monolingual edifice was threatened by the increased importance of English and by doubts as to the justification for the suppression of the regional languages in the name of equality. The right to linguis-tic freedom has now become associated with the modern concept of human rights. These rights are championed by the European Parliament and the Council of Europe, and the regional languages are staging a comeback. It could be argued that the reintroduction of the regional languages on a meaningful scale—even if it were possible—would make geographical and social mobility very difficult (as it does in Spain), at a time when the world is moving towards globalization. To this the regionalists answer that areas where there are demands for the recognition of the regional language should, by right, become areas that are optionally bilin-gual. There has thus been a slight shift away from the Jacobin to the Girondin position. Apart from the ideological problem, there is also the obvious problem of the financial cost, at least in the short term.

If the problem seems so acute in France, it is because the French state has tradi-tionally seen matters in absolute and theoretical terms.[26] A more pragmatic approach could be more successful in certain cases. For example, most Corsicans

---

[26] The term 'manichean' is extremely frequent in French, indicating this tendency to see things in black and white.

are believed to be in favour of remaining French, with the terrorists representing a small minority. But, even if there were to be a referendum that showed the majority to be against independence, it would still be necessary to satisfy linguistic demands, and bilingualism would probably achieve this. If the majority wanted independence, then it should be given in the name of human rights. The same solution could be applied to the Basque Country. Proper consultation would enable the government to measure the size of the problem, and the results would probably vary from region to region. Solutions need to be developed on the basis of consensus: the majority may have to learn to make a space for the minority.

It is important to remember, however, that most people see themselves primarily as French, and secondarily as belonging to a region. The fact that 2 per cent of the population should in 2000 be educated in a regional language is a miracle, since only thirty years previously there were none. But it is still an insignificant percentage of the whole, and the movement could peter out. The mobility of the civil service (one of the largest in the world) means that many people do not feel ties with a particular area. In this respect, Jacobin policies have been very effective. But there are areas where there has been less population mobility and where the negative policies of the state fuel rebellious thoughts that could become problematic. Democracy defined by equality is being replaced by democracy defined in terms of individual human rights. France seems to be slowly moving in this direction.

Such a move may also be in the interest of the state, given the threat posed by the National Front. The latter, although Jacobin in essence, is aiming at attracting disenchanted regionalists. Hence Catherine Trautmann, the minister for Culture and Communication, states, in a *Lettre d'information* of 1983: 'The fact that the National Front is trying to seize upon regional identities is of fundamental importance. Its aim is to exacerbate the sense of belonging to a community in order to fragment society even more and to make the community even more inward-looking.' She concludes 'we must assert that France has a pluralistic identity'. But she also states that the regional languages and cultures are no longer to be seen as the enemies of the French Republic, which makes this change of heart much easier. So, despite the new revolutionary approach, it may be that the principle of 'one state, one nation, one language' still holds, albeit in a more relaxed and civilized form. France will certainly be culturally enriched by the new departure.

4.

The Iberian Peninsula: Conflicting Linguistic Nationalisms[*]

CLARE MAR-MOLINERO

4.1. The Area

The history of language and of nationalism in the Iberian Peninsula—that is, present-day Spain and Portugal—shows many of the same features as other Western European countries, reflecting the emergence of unified states from fragmented communities and medieval kingdoms. The story of a series of conquests, the most important of which being the Roman, characterizes the development of linguistic varieties in the peninsula. What distinguishes the peninsula, however, from neighbouring European areas, is the conquest and long occupation of large parts by the Arabic-speaking Moors. The influence that the latter left on the language and culture of Spain and Portugal, and the significance of the bringing-together of potentially hostile groups during the *Reconquista* against a common enemy, cannot be overstated.

4.2. The Emergence of the Languages of the Peninsula

In this section I will trace the emergence of those linguistic varieties that are normally considered today to be separate and discrete. Unsurprisingly, it will be clear that the present linguistic map of the Iberian Peninsula owes much to the outcomes of political conflicts, of conquests and reconquests.

Prior to the Roman conquest of the Iberian Peninsula, the largest indigenous community seems to have been the Iberians, but the peninsula had also been occupied by Celtic-speaking groups, and experienced invasions by Carthaginians and Greeks. The Basque language was already spoken in the peninsula. With the exception of Basque (see Section 4.5.2, and also Section 3.3.2), however, any earlier languages were swallowed up by Latin, leaving very little trace in the peninsula's modern languages. Except, then, for Basque, all the languages we associate today with the Iberian Peninsula are derivatives of Latin and form part of the Romance

---

[*] An earlier, abridged, version of this paper appeared in Mar-Molinero and Smith (1996: 69–89).

continuum spreading across south-western Europe. While Classical Latin served as the language of writing and political power, spoken Vulgar Latin developed many diverse varieties, as the local populations created new vernaculars influenced by previous languages and their diverse geographical and environmental contexts. The fragmentation of the declining Roman Empire saw a corresponding fragmentation of Vulgar Latin. With the end of the Roman Empire, the Iberian Peninsula experienced further conquest, by a Germanic-speaking group, the Visigoths, who, however, had already been significantly influenced by the Romans, and, therefore, were bilingual and able to use Latin with their new subjects. The result is that the Visigoths left very little in the way of a linguistic mark on the development of language in the peninsula. However, one consequence of their occupation is of significance for the future linguistic and political map—that is, the establishment of Toledo (see Penny 1991), in the heart of Castile, as their capital. By the eighth century, five distinct dialect groups, all derived from Latin, had emerged on the peninsula: Galaico-Portuguese, Asturian Leonese, Castilian, Aragonese, and Catalan. What helped decide which of these groups should eventually dominate the peninsula was, as ever, a military–political event: the Moorish invasion and occupation.

During the seven centuries of Moorish presence on the peninsula, some regions experienced very little if any penetration from the Moors. Speakers of the Latin-derived Galaico-Portuguese varieties, largely because of their isolation in the far west of the peninsula, were one such community to be only minimally affected, although the Portuguese kingdom did later have some contact with Arabic-influenced varieties as it expanded southwards; the earlier Visigothic occupation had also had little effect on them. During this period Galician and Portuguese were the vehicles of a vibrant culture, and were already beginning, for political reasons, to draw apart, despite their original close similarity.

The Basques also remained largely isolated from any invading forces, although they lost territory to the encroaching Moors and others. The Basque language was also little affected, as far as we know, by Arabic or any earlier influences, although there were later some Latin and then Castilian borrowings.

Catalan, on the other hand, was the peninsular variety closest to the Latin-derived varieties spoken in other parts of Europe. Catalonia and Valencia were only temporarily invaded by the Moors. The Catalans tended to look north and seaward along the Mediterranean for their influences, trade, and status, and it was in fact during the Moorish occupation of other parts of the peninsula that they enjoyed some of their greatest international prestige in Europe.

On the arrival of the Arabs, the Asturian-Leonese variety was probably the most dominant in central Spain, also sharing a surprisingly high coincidence of characteristics with Aragonese. However, the organizing of opposition to the Moorish invaders led Castilians to a new, and never-to-be-lost, position of importance during the *Reconquista*, symbolized by the regaining of Toledo as capital of Christian Spain in 1085. Castile began to dominate the peninsula, culminating in the marriage between the Catholic Monarchs Ferdinand of Aragon and Isabella of Castile in 1469 and the final ousting of the Moors with the fall of Granada in 1492. This dominance inevitably gave status to the Castilian language, which was increasingly used, even in non-Castilian territories, as the language of culture and administration. A standard Castilian had emerged, in particular as a result of efforts by Alfonso X in the mid-thirteenth century to standardize the written language. Coinciding with the Catholic Monarchs' and Castile's political domination, the first standard Spanish (i.e. Castilian) grammar was produced, also in 1492, by Nebrija. Of equal significance to the emergence of Castilian as the dominant language on the peninsula during this period was the birth of Spain's American Empire. This was, in fact, at the outset a Castilian empire, as Galicians or Catalans, for example, were prevented from trading with, and therefore having an influence in, the New World.

The end of the fifteenth century, then, marks the birth of modern Spain. This period heralds the beginning of the imposition of Castilian hegemony, a hegemony born out of solidarity in the face of the common Moorish enemy, throughout the newly formed state and the repression of what were now perceived as minorities along the peripheries. Spanish nationalism and Castilian linguistic supremacy go hand in hand, but, nonetheless, they do not succeed in entirely eliminating non-Castilian communities. Through wars and the politics of royal marriages the various kingdoms of the peninsula were brought together, albeit still very loosely.

4.3. Portugal: A Classic Linguistically Uniform Nation-State

Attempts to include Portugal in this growing unity were not successful.[1] Portugal was established as a separate kingdom in 1134, and only briefly succumbed to Castilian dominance under Philip II in 1580–1640, thereafter remaining a separate state from Spain. In Portugal, Portuguese was the only language spoken, and this monolingual configuration has meant that language has played a very different role during the shaping of Portuguese identity. In fact, as the other developing nations of Europe experienced crises and challenges to their unity, including Spain, particularly during the seventeenth century, Portugal was able to establish a stable national identity. As Linz (1973: 46–7) has written referring to Portugal's definitive split from Spain: 'the Portuguese rebels, thanks largely to international support and the existence of a Portuguese empire, were able to create a new state sufficiently homogeneous in its European home-base to become one of its oldest pure nation-states'.

---

[1] For reasons outlined here, the role of language in Portuguese nation-building ceases to be of any great significance after 1640, and so we will not include Portugal in any further discussions in this chapter. However, for further analysis of Portuguese nationalism, see T. Gallagher (1983), Herr and Polt (1989), and Herr (1992).

The Portuguese language has a symbolic value to the Portuguese more as a marker of a supranational identity bringing Portugal and its former colonies (particularly Brazil, Angola and Mozambique) together in pan-Luso unity. The relationship of Galicia to this 'Mother' Portugal identity will be commented on later.

Portugal appears, at first sight, to constitute that rare phenomenon (to which nevertheless many states aspire in theory), the linguistically uniform nation-state. In reality, however, it harbours a number of languages, particularly those spoken by communities originating from its numerous former colonies.

4.4. The Rise of Spanish Nationalism and the 'National' Language

Initially the so-called unification of Spain, created by the Catholic Monarchs' marriage and the annexation in 1512 of Navarra, was a very loose concept, hardly akin to our present notion of 'nation'. As Siguán (1993: 20) writes:

It is ... exaggerated to say that the Catholic Monarchs aimed at achieving the unity of Spain as a nation ... Other contemporary monarchies in Europe were following the same process that leads to nation-states. Rather than stating that these states were the result of a nationalist idea, it would be fairer to say that the idea of 'nationality' emerged in the process whereby modern states were created as an ideological justification and as its representation in terms of collective consciousness.

This is reflected too in the range of languages still in use across the peninsula, although Castilian was indeed beginning to dominate. Its political superiority, as the language of the court and government and the expanding empire, was mirrored too during this period by a flourishing literary output in Castilian known as Spain's Golden Age, including authors such as Cervantes, Lope de Vega, Calderon, Góngora, and Quevedo. However, it is really not until the seventeenth century, as Spain began to abandon her imperial designs and looked inwards to the home base, that moves to consolidate Spanish national identity utilizing language policies take shape. Particularly prominent in the moves to formulate a sense of Spanish, as opposed to Castilian, identity for the monarchy and the state is the Conde Duque de Olivares, whose famous secret memorandum to Philip IV in 1624 exemplifies this awareness that strength can only be found for the king's policies by bringing political and administrative centralization to Spain. He writes,

The most important thing in Your Majesty's Monarchy is for you to become king of Spain, by this I mean, Sir, that Your Majesty should not be content with being king of Portugal, of Aragon, of Valencia, and count of Barcelona, but should secretly plan and work to reduce these kingdoms of which Spain is composed to the style and laws of Castile, with no difference whatsoever ... (quoted in Linz 1973: 43)

Clearly a major obstacle in any such centralizing policy would be the existence of different vernaculars, linked with diverse regional identities. The need for one 'national' language was hence placed on the political agenda.

The moves to impose Castilian throughout Spain via the administration and law were accelerated as a result of the repression suffered by those non-Castilian speaking communities (Aragon, Catalonia, Valencia, and Mallorca) who had backed the losing pretender (Archduke Charles) in the dispute for the Spanish throne after the death of Charles II in 1700. The successful claimant, Philip V, was the first of the Spanish Bourbon kings, who further extended a tight centralized political system, along the lines of the model being developed in France, from where he came. As a result of their and their pretender's defeat, the Catalans and others had their last residual local laws and privileges revoked. The consequence was a massive castilianization of their institutions and public life.

During the eighteenth century two spheres in particular play a significant role in furthering the position of Castilian throughout Spain: the Catholic Church, which increasingly used Castilian, and the education system. To this can also be added the effect of universal male conscription into a Castilian-speaking army. As power became centralized in Madrid, so too did the appointment of bishops, with the result that Castilian-speaking bishops were now commonplace in the non-Castilian speaking areas. While the lower clergy often resisted this loss of the use of the mother tongue, the Church had an important influence in extending the use of Castilian, in its function as both a religious and an educational institution. In a country that had conquered much of the Americas in the name of the Catholic Church and instigated the infamous Inquisition, the role of religion in ordinary people's lives cannot be underestimated.

In 1768 Charles III decreed that 'throughout the kingdom the Castilian language be used in administration and in education' (quoted in Siguán 1993: 25). This must be understood in the context of a major expansion in education during the eighteenth and nineteenth centuries, along with the accessibility of the printed word and therefore mass-produced educational materials. Increased access to education was in Spain, as in many nations, one of the principal means of providing a sense of national identity. Arguments claiming that it was necessary to learn Castilian in order to have access to the political administration or to the language of culture disguise the basic desire by the monarchy and government to give children a particular kind of Spanish character, essentially a Castilian identity.

In 1808 Spain was invaded by Napoleon. This had the effect of uniting, in a sense of solidarity against the common enemy, even those who had previously been in conflict with the central government. Arguably for the first time, a sense of Spanish (rather than Castilian, Catalan, Galician, etc.) patriotism was experienced. However, this was followed by a century of deep divisions and internal conflict, for the state was unable to build on that moment of patriotism. Linz (1973: 40) writes:

Those tensions or civil wars between liberals and partisans of the *ancien regime*, between secularizers and clericals, and later between social classes, initially had no relation to regional and linguistic differences, but, through a complex set of circumstances would be fought out largely in the lands on the periphery of the old Castilian Spain, and thereby activate their sentiments of historical distinctiveness and of grievance against the central authorities.

What is significant, however, is the lack of importance that the different sides in these conflicts paid the role of regional languages. On the one hand, the Liberals, the Federalists, and much later the left-wing supporters of working-class groups, all viewed the 'national' language as an enabling vehicle to empower people in political decision-making, and thus feared the divisive nature of promoting regional languages over Castilian. On the other hand, and surprisingly, the traditionalist Carlists, based in rural and often non-Castilian speaking regions of northern Spain, also did not appear to pay any attention to issues of local languages.

Despite this, however, the latter half of the nineteenth century sees the resurgence of cultural activities in languages other than Castilian in various parts of the peninsula, notably in Catalonia, Galicia, and the Basque Country. It needs stressing that, whilst Castilian had by now come to dominate all walks of public life in Spain, and was clearly the national language, the other languages were still spoken, to a greater or lesser extent, by their communities, and had not disappeared altogether, although in many areas they were in a classic diglossic situation *vis-à-vis* Castilian. But these cultural movements signalled new or increased literary outputs, and required focusing on the written language for the first time in many centuries. This period, then, also saw significant work in the area of codification and elaboration of the non-Castilian languages.

These cultural and linguistic 'renaissances', as they are generally called, which flourished in the second half of the nineteenth century, were stimulated by the European-wide Romantic movement. In particular, French and German writers of the time were important in influencing the development of the cultural movements in linguistic minority communities. These Romantic writers espoused a particular form of cultural nationalism, which had a profound influence on nationalist movements throughout Europe in the late nineteenth and early twentieth centuries (see e.g. Edwards 1985; Grillo 1989). The essence of their nationalism, particularly developed by German writers such as Herder and Fichte, is the notion of national spirit (*Volksgeist*), and of language as the soul of the nation. It is axiomatic in this way of thinking that the nation, defined linguistically and culturally, should also enjoy political independence. At the same time, writers influenced by the French Revolution advocated a form of political nationalism that emphasized the total coincidence between the nation and state (see Grillo 1989). Such thinking inevitably influenced the cultural revivals beginning to take shape in Catalonia, Galicia, and the Basque Country. It was also embraced by Castilian intellectuals, who were well represented by a group of writers who were producing work around the turn of the century, and who, while by no means an entirely homogeneous group, have often been called the '98 Generation. The significance of this date is that it marks the final loss of Spain's diminished world empire. The sense of national decadence and inadequacy was challenged by these writers (some of whom, while deliberately choosing to write in Castilian, were from the periphery—for example, the Basque authors Unamuno and Baroja). While these writers sharply criticized the Spain they saw around them, they supported the view that a united Spain could be great and should be regenerated and modernized, and in particular they emphasized the greatness of Castile. They were scornful of the splintering effect of the various peripheral nationalist movements. But it is this same frustration with Spain's decadence that was leading the Catalans, Basques, and others, to formulate their new nationalism and to link it to an impetus for modernization based on their local communities and detached from the problems associated with the central state.

As Spain entered the twentieth century, then, its sense of national identity was challenged both by the lingering reaction to the loss of empire and international prestige, and by the inability to modernize, and by the impatience of the linguistic minority communities on the periphery with the central state bureaucracy and administrative incompetence. Spain's political instability throughout the crises of the nineteenth century had prevented it from joining the modernizing and industrializing processes experienced by other European nations. While the imperialist past and Bourbon centralism had ensured Castilian dominance and confirmed Spanish nationalism, creating a nation-state with similarities to others in Europe, the chaotic political situation of the nineteenth century had failed to bring the linguistic minorities entirely to heel, allowing the peripheries' nationalisms to flower in the climate of cultural nationalism experienced in much of Europe. This is the legacy Spain has brought into the twentieth century, and is largely to blame for the consequent decades of repressive centralist dictatorship. Before turning to the present-day situation of Spain to discuss the current linguistic context and its relation to national identity, I would like to trace more specifically the history of the non-Castilian communities that have managed to maintain their own particular identity and separate languages despite the imposition of Castilian hegemony.

4.5. The Resurgence of Nationalist Movements on the Spanish Periphery

This discussion will centre principally on three communities: the Catalans, the Basques, and the Galicians. A brief history will be given of each language, but the focus will be on the period of the cultural renaissances in the respective regions. To a lesser extent, other regions of the peninsula can be associated with the nineteenth century's revived interest in separate, non-Castilian, identity, but this is much less marked, and often is also in some way linked with these three. There will, therefore, be passing reference to the situation of Valencia and the Balearic Islands in the Catalan context; to Navarra in the Basque context; and to Asturias and Leon in the Galician context. This is not to belittle the importance of the sense of identity that these regions may have, but it recognizes the fact that they do not have a claim to a widely spoken discrete language different from Castilian, Catalan, Basque, or Galician.[2]

4.5.1. *Catalonia*

The separate Romance language Catalan developed from Vulgar Latin and came to be recognized as a distinct language around the eleventh and twelfth centuries. At its peak, Catalan was the principal language of a large area, including not only present-day Catalonia itself, but also parts of southern France, Aragon, Valencia, the Balearic Islands, as well as enclaves in Italy, North Africa, and Greece. Its prestige during this period (eleventh to fourteenth centuries) was on a par with that of French and Italian, as well as other languages of the peninsula like Castilian and Portuguese. It increasingly replaced Latin (and later Provençal) as the language of cultural and literary production. Only in Aragon did it remain merely the spoken variety. Literary and philosophical output flourished, and, even as Catalan political power diminished in the fifteenth century to be replaced by Castilian dominance, Catalan can boast a Golden Age in letters, notably in Valencia. From the sixteenth century onwards, with the rise in Castile's power that we have noted, Catalan was on the decline, and parts of the original Països Catalans (Catalan countries) were lost (Roussillon to France, for example) or separated. Repressive laws and the increased presence of a Castilian-speaking hierarchy meant Catalan lost its prestige and became largely a spoken language only, suffering therefore dialectalizing tendencies (see Valverdú 1984). The process of Castilianization and persecution of the Catalan language continued until the nineteenth century and the *Renaixença* (see below, and see also e.g. Valverdú 1984; Ferrer 1985).

The movement known as the *Renaixença* is usually considered to take its first inspiration from a piece of lyric poetry, *Oda a la patria* written by Benaventura Aribau in 1833, and certainly the early manifestations of this movement were poetry based. However, the main thrust of the *Renaixença* took place during the second half of the nineteenth century and around the turn of the twentieth century, and became far more than a cultural expression, inspiring also a political movement. Initially literary output was seen as particularly important, reflecting the influence of the European Romantic movement, as writers exalted their past, and also particularly highlighted (even mythologized) forgotten groups and traditional cultures with their popular legends and stories. In Catalonia this encouraged writers to express themselves in their mother tongue, which had barely been used as a cultured literary language for two or three centuries. The Catalans achieved an impressive production of lyric poetry and extended this interest to the popular domain with such activities as the *Jocs Florals*, which were oral poetry competitions, modelled on the lines of similar medieval contests, and later taken

---

[2] As will be noted later, the Valencians certainly do claim that their variety is a separate language, distinct from both Castilian and Catalan. However, given its close similarity to both, particularly Catalan, I would argue that this is to a great extent a political rather than a strictly linguistic claim, which has become more relevant in the post-Franco period.

up in the Basque Country and Galicia. This cultural movement coincided with the emergence of Catalonia as an industrial society, and some of these new activities reflected new popular social concerns. As Linz (1973: 55) notes,

A complex process of social and cultural mobilization was initiated in this period with the creation of interest groups like the protectionist lobby of the Fomento del Trabajo Nacional (1867); the Liceo Opera Association (1844); cultural associations and clubs like the Ateneo (1860); the Casino Mercantil Barcelones (1864); the Juegos Florales (1859), imitating the Provençal medieval poetry competitions; new newspapers, and the like which would become even more active in the eighties and the nineties.

At first this movement was largely only a cultural and social one, not yet having a clear political dimension. Heightened cultural awareness, however, led Catalans to want to emphasize and control their separate identity in a way that the centralized governments of the Spanish state did not allow. This, of course, included the promotion of their own language, particularly through literature and other cultural activities and through the education system. In particular, in the many periods of central government crisis in the nineteenth century, Catalans felt frustrated by the Spanish state. From these experiences emerged regionalist and eventually Catalan nationalist aspirations, which, however, were preceded by a Spanish-wide Federalist movement. The nineteenth-century Federalists were inspired by such Europeans as Proudhon; they were in the main Catalans, but Catalans originally operating at national (Madrid) level, the most significant being Pi i Margall. But by the second half of the century and with increasing self-awareness on the part of the Catalan urban bourgeoisie, this federalism took on a more strictly Catalan tone. An increasing desire to protect and modernize their local industry in the midst of the traditional and largely agrarian Spanish state pushed the Catalans towards redefining their sense of identity politically as well as culturally. Valenti Almirall is usually credited with being the first of these political thinkers to promote the beginnings of modern Catalan nationalism, with the publication of his book *Lo Catalanisme* in 1866. Here Almirall looks at the nature of the Catalan character, in terms of race, national psychology, and personality. He is among the first to promote the Catalan language as a basic core value in what he describes as the Catalan nation.

Throughout the intellectual development of the ideas of the *Renaixença*, language emerges as the central issue around which the Catalans based their claims to a separate identity, and with Almirall this core value (see Conversi 1990) is also established as a central plank in their political aspirations. This is a theme taken up by the leading politician of the *Renaixença* Enric Prat de la Riba, whose book *La Nacionalitat Catalana* (1892) is the basis of much of the thinking of modern Catalan nationalism. Prat de la Riba was significantly influenced by the German Romantic writers, such as Herder, through the work of the Catalan philosopher Llorens i Barba, who introduced these ideas to Catalonia (see Conversi 1993; Siguán 1993). For Prat de la Riba, language, along with culture and territory, forms the spirit that defines the nation (Prat de la Riba 1986: 100–1). As Conversi (1993: 4–7) emphasizes, referring to Prat de la Riba's work,

Many passages emphasize language as the more visible expression of the national soul and prime bond of union between the different Catalan-speaking territories.

The Herderian link has been repeatedly revived in the Catalan academic world and society, from several perspectives, different political sides and academic milieus. Thus, linguistic theories of the deep existing links between language and thought, have reached far beyond the academic circles . . . to be reflected in many contemporary political pamphlets and programmes.

Prat de la Riba founded the Catalan bourgeois nationalist party, the *Lliga*, and in 1914 its electoral success meant he became the president of the Catalan *Mancomunitat*, which was a first step in the direction of enhanced local government for Catalonia. The latter did not have many powers, particularly compared with its later successor the *Generalitat* of the Second Republic and of today, but it continued to promote the Catalan language, setting up the *Institut d'Estudis Catalans*, under whose auspices much codification and elaboration of the Catalan language was carried out by Pompeu Fabra.

As regards the rest of the former Catalan-speaking areas of Spain—that is, Valencia and the Balearic Islands, the cultural revival of Catalan did have some impact but none in terms of political expression. Whereas in Catalonia the Catalan language had always retained its prestige even with the upper classes, in Valencia, by the nineteenth century, it was only a low-status language spoken by the rural lower classes. The context for literary output was, therefore, considerably less favourable, but some writers in Valencia did publish in Catalan, and moves to define the Valencian variety as separate from Catalan also took place at this time. Politically, though, Valencia shared the predominantly agrarian character of the rest of Spain, while not, perhaps, the country's backwardness, as Valencia's agricultural export market was expanding very successfully. But its links with Spain-wide tendencies, usually liberal, were stronger than any interest in separation or identifying with the Catalans.

In the Balearic Islands too there was revival in terms of literary output in the Catalan of the islands, but, in this very conservative agrarian area, there were no political moves away from the central state. An important event in terms of the development of the standardization of Catalan, begun at this time, was the elaboration of a dictionary of Catalan–Balearic–Valencian varieties by the Mallorcan Antoni Alcover.

4.5.2. *The Basque Country*

The origins of the Basque people and the Basque language are the cause of much speculation, much discussion, and little certainty. What is certain is that they existed well before the Romanization of southern Europe, and once covered a far wider area than the present-day region in northern Spain and south-western France (see also Section 3.3.2). It is one of the few languages in Europe (the only one in western Europe) that do not belong to the Indo-European language family; it is, in fact, a linguistic isolate, having no clear historical relationship to any other language. Place names dating back to before the Romans in such areas as Cantabria, Aragon, and even Catalonia point to this earlier extent. The Basques were forced to retreat further and further into the more inhospitable, and therefore less accessible, of their lands by the frequent wars from Roman times to the sixteenth century, which created the present political and linguistic map of the peninsula. Despite these conflicts with invading forces, the Basque language has been only a little influenced by external linguistic groups (see Diez *et al.* 1977). In return for retaining their cherished *fueros* (rights), the Basques accepted Castilian and eventually Spanish dominance more readily than the Catalans, and were able to maintain a separate but subordinate identity because of this. The Basque language continued to be spoken in much the same way as Catalan, as an oral variety in a diglossic situation, Castilian being the language of power. Unlike the Catalans, the Basques did not have a significant medieval literary written corpus in Basque to serve as a basis for maintaining the unity of the language. Far more than Catalan or Galician, Basque has suffered from divisions into dialects and subdialects, some almost mutually incomprehensible. To some extent this also reflects the geographical terrain, with many isolated mountain and valley settlements where contact was minimal. This dialectal fragmentation of the language has been an impediment right up until the present day. Politically, too, the Basques were divided, never having a strong kingdom, as the Catalans did in the Middle Ages. The communities in Viscaya and Guipuzcoa had no one leader, and were rigidly separate from the Kingdom of Navarra, the latter being only partially Basque-speaking. Whereas Barcelona has always served as a brilliant centre for all things Catalan, the Basques have not had such a clearly defined focus.

As with Catalonia, the nineteenth century saw an increased awareness of Basque culture and eventually a form of Basque nationalism; as did Catalonia too, the Basque Country, unlike the rest of Spain, experienced major industrial and economic development parallel with other parts of nineteenth-century Europe. But, besides these similarities, there are very many differences between the two regions, as their different histories already suggest. The two most obvious differences between the modern nationalisms that developed in the two regions are, first, the role that language played in constructing their identity, and, second, the very different reactions of the industrial bourgeoisie in the two regions. The contrasting levels of popular involvement in the two regional movements are also significant, with the Basque movement being backed by a very small group of committed intellectuals.

While in Catalonia it could be argued that the cultural and political nationalist movements grew out of the industrialization process taking place, in the Basque country the opposite is almost the case. The Basque urban bourgeoisie was content to work with Madrid, and in fact the major Spanish banking élites were Basque ones, intricately bound in with the Spanish state's economy and political fortunes. The Basque language was barely spoken in urban areas, or by the middle class, and, while it was indeed middle-class intellectuals who wished to revive the Basque identity, they had to rely on the 'pure' Basques of the isolated rural areas as their base.

In both Catalonia and in Galicia, cultural revivals preceded political expressions of regional identity. In the Basque Country it was largely a radical political manifesto that, along with cultural representation, inspired Basque nationalism at the turn of the century. The father of modern Basque nationalism was Sabino Arana (1865–1903). As Conversi (1993: 6) writes, 'He formulated the first political programme aimed at the rebirth of the Basque nation, founded its first political organization, wrote its national anthem, designed its flag, coined its name, and defined its geographical extension.' Arana and his followers saw Basque urban society with its modernizing industrialization and influxes of immigration as threatening the essence of Basque identity, which he set out to reconfirm and define. It was unrealistic to place too much importance on the role of language, as Basque was not a widely spoken language, even compared with Catalan or Galician. In fact, it was only used as a way of excluding those who were clearly not Basque by birth or descent. In this early nationalist thinking, the most important common value for the Basques was to be race. Evangelista de Ibero, a major writer of this Basque movement, wrote in 1906 when defining and contrasting the meanings of 'nation' and 'state':

1. What is a nation? The ensemble of men or peoples who have a same origin, a same language, a same character, the same custom, the same fundamental laws, the same glories, the same tendencies and aspirations, and the same destinies.
2. Of all these properties, which constitutes essentially a nationality? In the first place, the blood, race or origin; in the second place, the language. The other qualities are nothing but the consequence of the other two, most specifically of the first. (quoted in Linz 1973: 37)

This emphasis on race ('blood' and 'origin') contrasts significantly with Prat de la Riba writing at same time about Catalan nationalism, where the emphasis is, above all, on the bonding effect of language:

We saw the national spirit, the national character, the national thought; we saw the law, we saw the language; and from the law, the language and the organism; the national thought, the character and the spirit, bring the Nation; that is a society of people who speak a language of their own and have the same spirit that manifests itself or is characteristic for the whole variety of the whole collective life.

. . . we saw that Catalonia had a language, a law, an art of its own, that it had a national spirit, a national character, a national thought: Catalonia was therefore a nation. (quoted in Linz 1973: 37)

The choice of race and not language as the prime core value (see Conversi 1990) in Basque nationalism is a significant difference compared with Catalonia, and one that also characterized the two regions' nationalisms in the twentieth century. With the use of the Basque language being less widespread and with little in the way of a literary tradition, it is not surprising that the literary cultural movement in the Basque Country was on a far smaller and less wide-reaching scale than its Catalan counterpart. The nationalist movement, however, did focus its political aspirations with Arana, founding and leading the *Partido Nacionalista Vasco (PNV)*, which shared many similarities with Prat de la Riba's *Lliga*.

The Basque nationalists have always regarded Navarra as part of the Basque Country (in the same way as they claim the three French Basque provinces). However, Navarra has in fact been politically separate from the Basque Country for many centuries, the Kingdom of Navarra being the last such to be annexed by the Crown of Castile in 1512. Like the Basques, Navarra enjoyed its own special local laws, *fueros*, but, unlike the Basque laws, these remained in place even under Franco. Since a part of the Navarrese population has always been Basque-speaking, particularly in some of the provinces in the Pyrenees, there has existed an uneasy relationship with Basque nationalism, with a partial recognition of some shared culture and language and some support for Basque nationalist parties. As well be seen later, even today Navarra recognizes this linguistic situation in its present Statute of Autonomy.

4.5.3. *Galicia*

As has been seen already, the earlier form of the language spoken in Galicia was Galaico-Portuguese, a Romance variety that emerged from the Roman occupation, which had come later to this part of the peninsula than any other. Claims that Galician and also Portuguese were strongly influenced by the Celtic languages spoken in this area on the arrival of the Romans are hard to substantiate, although their significance in terms of popular beliefs in the construction of Galician national identity should be noted. It is generally considered that the separation of Galician from Portuguese took place around the eleventh century, although this was a very slow and gradual process, and it can be said that both shared in the success of Galician lyrical poetry, which was widely acclaimed in the Middle Ages (twelfth to fourteenth centuries). The importance of Santiago de Compostela, in Galicia, as a place of pilgrimage meant that this literary production was known further afield than the Iberian Peninsula and was in turn influenced by the Provençal troubadours. The Castilian king Alfonso X was known to have written in Galician, reflecting the high regard for Galician letters during this period.

The historical–political reasons why Galicia and Portugal separated have left their mark too in the linguistic development. As the kingdom of Portugal was established from the beginning of the twelfth century, a national language for all the purposes of state evolved. The Galaico-Portuguese variety that was spoken there underwent influence from the Mozarabic (Arabic-influenced Romance varieties) spoken in the southern areas that the Portuguese kings annexed. This move southwards also changed the focal centre of the new kingdom to Lisbon, and away from the influence of Galicia. As Portuguese blossomed and developed as a national language of an important empire, Galician shrank into an oral form only, increasingly dominated by Castilian. The political domination of Galicia by Castile was even stronger than the domination of Catalonia, as was the subordination of the Galician language to Castilian, partly because there was a less strong written tradition (the lyrical poetry was essentially an oral genre) to build on, and because Galicia did not have the same political power base as the Catalans had. The early adoption of Castilian by the Church in a region where religion was so important also furthered the near demise of Galician.

The nineteenth-century cultural revival in Galicia, her *Rexordimento*, differs significantly from that which took place in Catalonia and the Basque Country, in that it was restricted to literary and cultural production. The political awareness that followed these movements in the other two regions was much slower to emerge in Galicia, and we can only really talk of a political articulation of Galician nationalism from well into the twentieth century. The principal explanation for this is the economic condition of nineteenth-century Galicia, which was an extremely poor agricultural society, suffering high levels of emigration to other parts of Spain, Europe, or, above all, Latin America. Galicia was a backward and traditional society not experiencing the challenges of modernization or industrialization that were taking place in Catalonia and the Basque Country. It was also geographically very isolated, a feature that has always helped to shape Galician history.

Nonetheless European-wide influences such as Romanticism did lead Galician intellectuals to examine their historical and cultural roots and rediscover pride in their region and language. Some important writing was produced in Galician (although, again, mostly poetry). *Xogos Florais* were held modelled on the Catalan Jocs Florals, and the poetry read at these was published. The most famous writer of this movement is Rosalía de Castro, who, however, reverted to publishing only in Castilian towards the end of her life. By the turn of the century a Galician Royal Academy had been established with the aim of standardizing and codifying Galician. The need to decide on norms for the written language and to represent Galician identity was important not only, as in the other regions, to overcome the diversity of the dialects, but, particularly, in the case of Galician, because of its ambiguous position in relation to Portuguese. This latter relationship continues, as we will see, to present a dilemma in present-day Galicia.

Linguistic frontiers are often unclear, often blurred areas along a continuum, and therefore it is no surprise to discover important Galician-speaking communities beyond the political confines of Galicia, particularly in western Asturias. In the latter case, this has been an important factor in the explanation of why the Asturian–Leonese language did not develop as strongly as its early history might have suggested. Squeezed by the emerging Castilian, on the one hand, and by the then robust Galician–Portuguese varieties, on the other, Asturian–Leonese never emerged as a linguistic rival to either. Claims for a discrete language in this area do still exist today, as we will note later, but the stronger influence of Galician, as well, of course, as the dominance of Castilian, have helped prevent these varieties from taking any significant hold.

4.6. Language and Nationalism in Twentieth-Century Spain

4.6.1. *The Crisis of Nationalism*

As we have seen, the political situation in Spain at the beginning of the twentieth century was highly volatile, with a traditional, conservative, and highly centralized political system, conflicting with a desperate need for the economy to be modernized and for industries to be built up to compete with the rest of Western Europe. The tensions in the regions reflected this economic and social instability, heightened by the newly rediscovered cultural awareness of their different identities. The history of this period reflects these uncertainties with waves of social unrest, particularly in Catalonia, a certain prosperity and liberalizing of the social and political structures during the First World War, as neutral Spain benefited as a provider to the warring factions, a process that allowed a certain increase in Spanish industrialization. This was followed, as economic recession set in, by a period of military dictatorship (Primo de Rivera 1923–31), which inevitably reinforced the centralist nature of the regime. However, in 1932 the abdication of the King and the proclamation of a Republic (the Second Republic 1932–6) led Spain to a few years of enormous political and social change, much of which was replicated later on the death of Franco. There were radical changes during this period, which sought to reform Spain's agriculture, to secularize the state (and therefore radically alter the education system), and to give greater powers to the regions. Statutes of local autonomy were passed for the Catalans, the Basques, and the Galicians, although the outbreak of the Civil War meant that only the Catalans, who were the first to receive theirs, properly experienced this decentralizing policy. These attempted reforms reflect the cleavages that cut through Spanish society in the nineteenth century—religious splits, cultural–regional splits, social–political splits—and that, it is essential to stress, do not necessarily correspond. The fact that, for example, the cultural aspirations of the Catalan bourgeoisie were not the same as the anti-Catholic anarchist working-class movement also active in Catalonia has a lot to do with why the success of the peripheral nationalisms was not greater. The 1936–9 Civil War was, amongst other things, a bloody manifestation of Spain's multiple identity crises.

It was forces of centralism that won the Civil War, and the years that followed saw harsh repression by the Franco dictatorship of the minorities on Spain's periphery. During this regime the language question was a highly political topic. The use of minority (non-Castilian) languages was seen as anti-patriotic. These languages were, therefore, proscribed from public use and ridiculed. A situation, once again, of enforced diglossia existed in the regions, such as Catalonia, shutting down the enormous expansion in the use of minority languages that had taken place during the Republic. The regime carefully chose to refer to these languages as 'dialects' (with the exception of Basque). It was claimed that the non-Castilian languages were inferior, and they were characterized as the speech only of the uneducated and peasantry. All the patriotic rhetoric of the dictatorship centred around the concept of *lo castellano* (things Castilian); anything challenging this was considered dangerously subversive.

In the early part of the Franco period infringements of the laws prohibiting the use of languages other than Castilian were heavily punished with fines and imprisonments. But in 1966 the dictatorship relaxed its attitudes a little with the passing of the so-called Freedom of Expression Law, which removed the stricter forms of censorship in favour of prior, self-censorship. As a result, private organizations were now allowed to teach mother-tongue languages other than Castilian, and publishing was once more permitted in these. To some extent this reflects the confidence of the Franco regime, as it judged that it had little to fear from unflattering views published in non-Castilian languages, given the inevitably limited readership. The regime deliberately encouraged a certain type of media coverage in non-Castilian languages of a sort that might in fact seem to trivialize their cultures—reports on dance competitions or local fiestas or how to cook local dishes—leaving 'serious' news and politics to be reported in Castilian.

Franco died in 1975. The period that followed, known as the *Transición*, contrary to his and many other commentators' expectations, heralded the introduction of a respectable democratic system of government. A remarkable volume of legislation was passed, including the 1978 Constitution (approved by national referendum), and the speed with which the change from forty years of dictatorship to Western-style democracy took place should not be ignored in any evaluation of the outcomes of the social and legal transformations that have since occurred.

4.6.2. *The 1978 Spanish Constitution*

The Constitution that was introduced after Franco's death is a masterpiece of compromise and consensus. Not least is this true in the very definition of what Spain is, with the ambiguities between the central state and the many regions within this state that cherish first and foremost their own separate cultural identities. In this vein of compromise the second article of the Constitution reads: 'The Constitution is founded on the indissoluble unity of the Spanish Nation, the common and indivisible homeland of all Spaniards, and it recognizes and guarantees the right to autonomy of the nationalities and regions which make up the Nation and the solidarity amongst all of them' (Spanish Constitution 1978, author's translation).

By the legal nicety of using 'nation' and 'nationality' to mean different, but undefined, concepts, the Constitution tries to please both Spanish patriots and the regions. However, to refer to the identity of the different regions as 'nationalities' was certain to enrage many centralist-minded Spaniards. The juxtaposition of 'indissoluble', 'indivisible', and 'solidarity' with 'autonomy' continues this deliberate attempt to satisfy all. As a result of this Constitution, Spain is now divided politically into seventeen Autonomous Communities, all with delegated powers of a greater or lesser magnitude. The Catalans, Basques, and Galicians were the first to receive the Statutes of Autonomy, but eventually the entire state has been organized in this way. The relationship between the central government and the autonomous regions has continued to be uneasy, but it has gone a long way to meeting regionalist demands. The radical terrorist Basque nationalist group *ETA*, which enjoyed a degree of popular support during the Franco years, has certainly seen this support drastically diminished with the changed political structures of the present system. While the Catalans always want more control, particularly over their finances and taxes, they have used their demands as ways of creating pacts with the central government when this is in need of parliamentary support. The Socialist Party (*PSOE*), which has always historically favoured strong central government, was prepared to listen to major demands from the Catalans, in return for their votes.

As well as attempting to recognize Spain's plurinational nature in the Constitution, its drafters also set out to acknowledge Spain's multilingual/multicultural configuration with the Article 3 language clause, in which linguistic rights are enshrined. The first clause of Article 3 states: 'Castilian is the official Spanish language of the State'. Significantly this talks about 'state' and not 'nation' as well as 'Castilian' and not 'Spanish', an important statement acknowledging the existence of various 'Spanish' languages. This has been bitterly disputed by many, not only on the political right, for example, Salvador (1987: 92), who claims: 'With notable impropriety, the third article of the Constitution refers to "Spanish languages", in a shoddy drafting which ignores the fact that the adjective "Spanish" when applied to the language constitutes a complex lexeme with a unitary value which, through tradition and usage, means one thing: "the Castilian language" ' (author's translation). This clause, however, goes on to say: 'All Spaniards have the duty to know it [Castilian] and the right to use it.' Few if any national constitutions worldwide prescribe the duty to know a language. However, what is 'know'? Is it something purely passive requiring no active competence? How can it be demonstrated that a citizen does or does not 'know' a language? This is highly ambiguous and awaits legal interpretation and clarification.

Clause 2 declares: 'The other Spanish languages will also be official in the respective Autonomous Communities in accordance with their statutes.' This enabling definition of Spain's minority languages is, thus, qualified by the highly prescriptive constraint of limiting their official status to their own territorial space. This clear geographical limitation means realistically that the future role of the minority languages will always take second place to Castilian. It could even be argued that it contravenes the spirit of later articles of the Constitution that claim equality for all Spanish citizens. Those Spanish citizens whose mother tongue is not Castilian could argue that they do not have equal linguistic rights to those who are Castilian mother-tongue speakers. A native Catalan speaker cannot insist on the right to use Catalan in official contexts in, for example, Madrid. Native Basque-speakers cannot expect the Spanish state to provide Basque teaching to their children if they happen to live in, for example, Seville. On the other hand, throughout the Spanish state, Castilian may be used and must be provided for. I have argued elsewhere (see Mar-Molinero and Stevenson 1991; Mar-Molinero 1994) that this policy to promote linguistic pluralism in fact creates linguistic reservations and supports the subordination of the peripheries to the Castilian core.

The third clause appears to confirm a belief in linguistic pluralism when it states: 'The richness of Spain's different linguistic varieties is a cultural heritage which shall be the object of special respect and protection.' The exact meaning of words such as 'respect' or 'protection' needs legal interpretation if it is not simply to sound like hollow rhetoric. However, it is probably fair to say that this final clause has permitted a new and imaginative understanding of Spain's linguistic map. It has allowed Autonomous Communities in their Statutes to define their local linguistic variety, and, even when this is not considered a discrete separate language from Castilian, its own particular features can be recognized and protected. This has inspired work on lexical and phonological features in, for example, Andalusia and the Canary Islands in order to draw up guidelines on what constitutes these regions' respective language varieties. The implications of this for such areas as education and the media is very significant, raising such issues as those of standard-versus-local language varieties, and forms of acceptable literacy.

4.6.3. *Current Language-Planning in Spain*

Despite these ambiguities in the constitutional framework there is no denying the substantial advances that have taken place since 1978 in the promotion and status of Spain's minority languages and cultures. These efforts are supported not only by Article 3 of the Constitution but also by the relevant Autonomy Statutes in each region and, in particular, by the local Linguistic Normalization Laws. There are many similarities between the regions in their legal frameworks and the areas of linguistic activity through which local languages are promoted, but there are also important differences of a sort similar to those characteristics that we noted in their nineteenth-century cultural revival movements. The greatest activity in terms of language-planning efforts is at present taking place, as would be expected, in those areas that have historically shown the keenest sense of their own identity and nationalist aspirations—that is, Catalonia, the Basque Country, and Galicia. However, a more limited degree of minority language protection and promotion has also taken place in Asturias, Aragon, Navarra, Valencia, and the Balearic Islands. The case of Valencia is an interesting one, since one way of determining which 'languages' to identify for the purposes of the second clause of Article 3 is to see into which language the Constitution has been officially translated. Five versions of the Constitution have been published: Castilian, Basque, Galician, Catalan, and Valencian. However, the text of the last two is exactly identical. Nationalist aspirations on the part of the Valencians meant that a separate version was published. Such concessions to minority community demands are certainly unusual in Spanish history.

By far the most active and apparently successful language promotion programmes are taking place in Catalonia, which is unsurprising, given it is the largest and wealthiest of the three relevant communities. Today the Autonomous Community of Catalonia has more than six million inhabitants, of whom approximately 90 per cent claim to understand Catalan, whilst over 60 per cent admit to speaking it in some form (CIS 1994). As in the Basque Country and Galicia, the local government has set up a Directorate to coordinate language promotion programmes and is encouraging the teaching of and through the medium of Catalan, the development of modern terminologies in Catalan, the use of the local language in all government and administration and official public use, as well as through the media. The results are spectacular: the rise in the number of schools offering some or much of their curriculum through Catalan is sharp; most public notices, street names, menus, bank cheques, entrance tickets, and so on are in Catalan (sometimes exclusively, sometimes bilingually). There are two Barcelona and one Gerona daily papers in Catalan, two television channels entirely in Catalan and a third giving some programmes in Catalan, there are also numerous Catalan local radio stations. Theatre, cinema, and written publications flourish in Catalan. Much of this includes translations from languages other than Castilian.

As we have seen, Catalan has always been a language of all sections of the Catalan population, including, significantly, the upper and middle classes, and in this sense it is importantly different from Basque and Galician. This has meant that the language serves as a symbol of social mobility and acceptance, with the ensuing favourable attitudes to its use and teaching. This has undoubtedly helped overcome its single greatest obstacle, which is the large non-Catalan speaking immigrant population now found resident in Catalonia. This has obviously diluted the spread of the language, and especially in the urban industrial areas where these immigrant groups are concentrated. However, unlike Basque, but like Galician, Catalan's accessibility to Castilian speakers has helped provide a very high incidence of passive knowledge of the language by the region's population.

However, Catalan shares, albeit to a lesser degree, with Basque and Galician (and in fact with many other minority languages) the challenge of mass communications in modern technological societies. Satellite television, international travel, computer technology, multinational business creating the so-called global village inevitably weaken the role of lesser-used languages and strengthen the position of world languages, such as, above all, English. Castilian is, of course, a widely spoken world language, and therefore to compete with it or aspire to equal bilingualism (as stated in the Language Laws' objectives in the respective Autonomous Communities) is arguably an impossible goal.

With currently less than two and a half million inhabitants the Basque community is the smallest of the three where a minority language is being promoted. Fewer than 25 per cent of these claim to speak Basque (CIS 1994), reflecting partly the difficulty in learning the language for speakers of Castilian, a difficulty that they do not encounter in learning Catalan or Galician. The language has considerably less prestige and status than Catalan within its community. A development dating back to the 1960s was the introduction of Basque schools, teaching Basque and providing a curriculum through the medium of Basque. These schools are known as *Ikastolak* and were an important attempt to promote Basque identity, originally as largely clandestine groups, and then increasingly throughout the 1960s and 1970s as private organizations, often working as non-profit making parents' cooperatives. However, with no strong literary tradition the codification of the language and selection of a standard variety from various competing dialects is very recent and was a divisive feature in the move to consolidate Basque identity. All of this has made the teaching of Basque and the use of it in public life very much more difficult. The Basque Country also has an important non-Basque immigrant population, who have been slow to want to learn Basque, which has, unlike Catalan, been associated with rural areas and backward traditionalism. There have, nonetheless, been successes, as Basque is promoted through the education system (there are now state-funded *Ikastolak*), and used in local government wherever possible. But the obstacles to the learning of Basque create the sense that its promotion is above all symbolic rather than practical.

Galicia has not been affected by immigration, and therefore a very high percentage speak the language, some 90 per cent of its nearly three million population (CIS 1994). However, Galician continues to lack status and therefore is not used for social advancement or for more academic purposes, except by a tiny minority of middle-class intellectuals. The language-planning activities, similar in conception to the Catalan and Basque ones, are attempting to counter these attitudes. However, an important difference in the case of Galician is the existence of a society that has known heavy emigration, leading in general terms to a conservative 'holding' mentality, particularly with womenfolk waiting for the return of the perceived head of the family. Such a predominantly rural society has not encouraged belief in cultural independence and confidence. Moreover, what changes are now taking place as a result of the new language policies must also be seen in the context of a counter-movement by the so-called Reintegrationists, a small but vociferous group who romanticize the need to return Galicia and Galician to the fold of 'Mother Portugal'. Neither the Reintegrationists nor the isolationists (those who see Galician culture and language as separate from either of their larger neighbours) are able substantially to counter the influence and dominance of Castilian.

4.7. Conclusions

Clearly issues of national and group identity are present in all these activities to promote and protect minority language rights in Spain, as they are also in the Castilian centre's determination to allow linguistic independence only up to a certain point. By limiting the promotion of non-Castilian languages to discrete geographical areas, the continued domination of Castilian as the 'national' language is ensured. The minorities' cultural identities are only acknowledged when they are linked to territorial identities. In a world of increasingly changing populations this is a questionable principle.

Indeed the linguistic map of Spain needs to be analysed with two other elements in mind; the role of ever-increasing groups of immigrants, and the effect of a more closely integrated European Union. On the one hand, the likely change in political power structures within the EU seems to point to the emergence of a Europe of the Regions, where the traditional national state centre will be increasingly bypassed through a relationship between the European supranational centres of power and the local regional centres. This is viewed by Catalans, Basques, and Galicians as a real possibility for the strengthening of their particular cultures and languages, and is to some extent backed up with EU resources such as regional aid and initiatives like those pursued by the EBLUL and the Mercator Project (Coulmas 1991).

On the other hand, however, a major principle of the EU is the encouragement and right of the freedom of movement of persons between the member states. This policy must have language implications, above all challenging the notion that linguistic and cultural identity can be tied to one geographical space. Added to this is the situation of the significant numbers of non-European immigrants many of whom do not speak as their mother tongue the language of any member state. Spain has only recently begun to experience the social and cultural effects of such immigration, largely with groups from North Africa and Latin America. In the case of the latter, of course, language is not an issue, but it is becoming a very serious one in the case of the former. If Spain is to honour the spirit of the European Community's 1977 directive encouraging all member states to provide at least some mother-tongue education for the children of immigrants, this will put a strain on the delicate balance arrived at between the present national language and the indigenous minority languages, a balance by no means viewed by all as ideal.

The Catalans, in particular, are pushing this relationship to its limit with attempts since 1993 to increase the amount of compulsory teaching in Catalan that would be offered in their schools (see Mar-Molinero 1995). The ensuing tussle with the Supreme Court in Madrid in order to test the measures' constitutionality is putting in jeopardy the hard-won right to almost complete self-determination in the formulating of educational policies, which has allowed the various Autonomous Communities to promote their own sense of identity. It is, perhaps, though, a logical conclusion of this tension: given that equal status for the co-official languages is the stated goal of the communities where a second language is spoken, and given the unequal dominance of Castilian, only positive discrimination in favour of the minority language, it could be argued, would ever make this aim possible. The accusations of discrimination that are now being heard from non-Catalans who feel that the language normalization programme to promote Catalan has gone far enough should come as no surprise.

Language is indeed the symbol of many of these identity crises, throughout Spain's history and also today. And while the most significant arena for this discussion has been in the peripheries where languages other than Castilian are spoken, it should not be forgotten that there are many areas of Spain where a variety labelled as 'Castilian' is spoken, but the cultural identity is not Castilian, but, for example, Andalusian, Estremaduran, or Aragonese. However, it is likely that precisely the lack of a separate linguistic identity has been the main reason that these regions have been more subordinated to the Spanish–Castilian nation-state than other communities on the periphery. As Linz (1973: 99) writes, 'Spain today is a state for all Spaniards, a nation-state for a large part of the population, and only a state but not a nation for important minorities.'

5.

Northern Europe: Languages as Prime Markers of Ethnic and National Identity

LARS S. VIKØR

5.1. The Area

I discuss together as 'Northern Europe' five independent states. From east to west they are Finland, Sweden, Denmark, Norway, and Iceland. In addition I include two territories that are largely autonomous, but not fully independent: the Åland Islands (under Finnish sovereignty) and the Faroe Islands (under Danish sovereignty). One might also include Greenland, which is also under Danish sovereignty, but this island belongs more to America than to Europe geographically as well as ethnically, and it will therefore be excluded from the present discussion.

The joint treatment of these states is justified by much shared history, which manifests itself in strong linguistic and cultural links. Traditionally, the overwhelming majority of the population in each state is Lutheran Protestant by religion, and the majority languages of each state but Finland show striking similarities and share a relatively recent common origin, and even Finland experienced long domination by Swedish speakers, Swedish still being the first language of a significant minority.

All the five states are regarded as established and consolidated nation-states by their own citizens as well as by the world outside, and in all of them a distinct language is considered crucial to national identity, although only Iceland is linguistically homogeneous. Even the Faroese consider themselves a separate nation, and they have a separate language to prove it! Only in the case of Åland may it be doubted whether the (semi-)autonomous status corresponds to any sense of a separate national identity, although this status is linguistically motivated: Åland is constitutionally defined as monolingually Swedish. We shall return to this problem later; here, we only make the preliminary statement that there seems to be full correspondence between statehood and national identity in these countries. The clearest and most important exception to this are the Sámi, who definitely regard themselves as a separate 'people', often using the word 'nation' about themselves, although they have no state of their own, and no territory which is exclusively theirs: they live in the north of Norway, Sweden, and Finland (and some also on Russian territory in the Kola peninsula). But they have many other symbols of nationhood, first and foremost a separate language (or several separate languages—this we will discuss in more detail presently), and, besides, they are culturally distinct from the majority populations, there is a separate Sámi flag, there is a Sámi 'parliament' in each of the three countries, and so on.

5.2. The Languages

The languages of the area belong to two language families: Uralic and Indo-European. The Uralic languages are Finnish and Sámi, which belong to different subgroups within the Finnic branch of the family, and are not mutually intelligible. The Indo-European languages all belong to the Germanic branch of the family, where they make up the North Germanic subgroup. Swedish, Danish, and Norwegian are mutually intelligible, at least when there is a will to understand on the part of the interlocutors. They are usually grouped together under the name Scandinavian. Faroese and Icelandic are not mutually intelligible in speech, but they are codified in such a way that they resemble each other quite closely in writing. They may be grouped together as 'insular Nordic'. There are many differences between Scandinavian and insular Nordic. The former experienced a much greater influx of loanwords from Low German between the fourteenth and sixteenth centuries, when the North German Hanseatic League of trading cities dominated the Nordic economies. Low German influence virtually transformed the vocabularies and derivation patterns of Danish, Swedish, and Norwegian.

The use of the terms 'Nordic' and 'Scandinavian' is often inconsistent in English. I choose here to use 'Nordic' in a strictly geographical sense, to designate the whole area and all its languages regardless of language families. I use 'Scandinavian' as a linguistic term in a narrower sense, to include only Swedish, Danish, and Norwegian, as indicated above.

While the Nordic area consists of five independent states, these states have developed close cooperation in many fields, both officially and at the grassroots level, and they are often perceived by their own citizens as well as by the outside world as a supranational unit with an identity of its own, in spite of the linguistic diversity. In the final section of the chapter we shall briefly discuss this Nordic identity in relation to the separate national, ethnic, and linguistic identities.[1]

5.3. The Historical Background

The earliest state formations in the Nordic area took place during the Viking

---

[1] For detail on many aspects of the languages and their histories, see Wessén (1965), Haugen (1976b), Vikør (1993), Karker *et al.* (1997).

Age—from the ninth to the eleventh centuries. There emerged three kingdoms: Denmark, Norway, and Sweden. But they were rather loosely organized; people's identity was probably more tied to their local communities than to a 'national' community. For instance, the laws differed from region to region; only in the late Middle Ages were the laws unified at state level.

Shortly before 1400, the three kingdoms were united under one Crown, the so-called Union of Kalmar (1396), which in fact then embraced the whole Nordic area: Finland was already a part of Sweden, while the Faroes (since 1035), Iceland (since the 1260s), and Greenland (since 1261) belonged to the realm of Norway. But this union—brought about by dynastic coincidences and centred in Denmark—was artificial, and from around 1450 Sweden established itself again during protracted wars with Denmark, being clearly recognized as independent by the Danish king in 1523. The wars were resumed later, however, and in the seventeenth century Sweden established itself as the leading power of the area. Norway with its dependencies remained under Danish rule, and Finland under Swedish rule.

These wars, although basically dynastic, did much to foster a sense of ethnic and national identity among Swedes and Danes—particularly the sense of difference, indeed of nationalist antagonism, towards the other people. The linguistic consequences of this will be examined in the following section. Suffice it here to say that the periods of inter-Scandinavian wars subsided around 1720, and a century of peace ensued. But the Napoleonic Wars brought about new changes: In 1809 Russia forced Sweden to cede Finland, which was made into a grand duchy directly subordinate to the Tsar. In 1814 the Swedes (then on the winning side in the war against Napoleon) similarly forced the Danish king to cede Norway. An attempt by the Norwegian élite (officials and rich merchants) to establish a sovereign state failed, but they succeeded in acquiring a high degree of home rule.

The rest of the nineteenth century was peaceful. This was the era of Romantic nationalism, and in all the countries this current gained ground and conquered the hearts and minds of nearly everyone in the non-independent territories (Norway, Finland, Iceland, the Faroes). A cultural nationalism unfolded, leading to demands for political independence towards the end of the century. In the twentieth century, these hopes were fulfilled for Norway (1905), Finland (1917), and Iceland (home rule 1918, full independence 1944). The Faroes achieved home rule in 1948, while the Åland Islands were granted their special status as a semi-autonomous, monolingually Swedish part of Finland in 1921.

Only the Sámi made no headway, but remained under harsh oppression linguistically and culturally. In the 1980s, however, things began to change, not because of a renewed Romantic nationalism, but because of the rise of ethnicity as a political issue in Europe, and an international upsurge in movements for the rights of aboriginal peoples. The Sámi have received official recognition in so far as they are now represented by their own 'parliaments' (since 1973 in Finland, 1989 in Norway, and 1993 in Sweden). The quotation marks around the word 'parliaments' are motivated by the fact that these bodies (although elected by popular franchise) are only advisory in relation to the 'real' national parliaments.

5.4. Language and Nationalism in Northern Europe

5.4.1. Denmark and Sweden

A sense of language as a bearer of identity has probably always existed, but this identity was in pre-modern times probably more ethnic and local than national. The Icelandic historian Snorri Sturluson wrote in the early thirteenth century that his work would tell about people 'who have spoken the Danish tongue'. 'Danish' then must have meant 'Scandinavian' or 'North Germanic' in modern terms. Why he called it 'Danish' is not altogether clear, but the reason was probably that the Danes were the Nordic people that had the most intensive contacts with other peoples, and that the common designation 'Danish' for the Scandinavian language of the time was given by these other peoples, whether English or Germans.

Although Sweden and Denmark existed as kingdoms during the Middle Ages, there is little evidence that language was an element in the loyalty that one owed to—to whom? Not the nation, but rather to the king, the noblemen under whose sway one happened to live, and to the Church.

People spoke their respective dialects, and no standard spoken language seems to have existed. In writing, the most popular medium was the runic alphabet—a set of characters used by the Germanic-speaking peoples for epigraphic purposes in pre-Christian times, but also in Scandinavia in the Christian Middle Ages. The clergy, however, wrote with Roman characters, and mostly in the Latin language. The earliest extant longer texts in the indigenous languages were law texts, which were written down in the thirteenth century. These laws were regional, written in a language based on the dialect of the region in question.

The use of the indigenous languages in writing increased from the fourteenth century onwards, especially in religious literature intended for laypeople and propagandistic literature that was clearly nationalistic in content, arising from the struggles between the two countries from 1450. A kind of national written standard also gradually evolved, greatly helped by the invention of printing. The first printing presses were set up in Denmark and Sweden shortly after 1480, but an even more decisive event was the introduction of Lutheranism as the state religion in 1527 in Sweden and 1536 in Denmark. This reform paved the way for the translation of the Bible into the national languages (1541 in Sweden, 1550 in Denmark), and the language used there became very influential in subsequent developments.

We may safely say that from this period language played a dominant role as a marker of identity in the two countries—although the spoken language was vastly pluriform, including both sharply differing dialects of the Scandinavian language(s) and non-Germanic languages such as Finnish and Sámi. However, tolerance of language variation seems to have been quite high—there was little linguistic pressure and coercion (with one notable exception which I shall return to presently). The symbolic function of the language was particularly stressed at the political centre, in the written form used by State and Church, and the only demand placed on the rest of the people was that they accept this unifying linguistic standard as 'theirs', although most of them could not use it. The linguistic basis of the standards was, as one might expect, upper-middle-class speech in the respective capitals: Copenhagen and Stockholm.

The animosity between the two countries, and the relative closeness of their standard languages (dialectal differences within each of the two countries were greater than the difference between the two standards), made it imperative to stress the difference between them in the standardization process. This was particularly important to the Swedes, who after all had been the dominated party in earlier times. This is the reason why the Danish letters *æ* and *ø* were rendered as *ä* and *ö* in Swedish—a difference which even today it seems impossible to abolish, because it still serves as an identity marker. In sixteenth-century Sweden, the official written language as used by the royal chancery showed many Danish influences, notably the use of the central vowel, written *e*, in unstressed syllables, where Swedish speech to a large extent had preserved the Old Scandinavian so-called full vowels *a* and *o*. The Bible, on the other hand, was translated into a more archaic form of Swedish, where the old full vowels were employed, and this latter standard won out in the seventeenth century, conquering the chancery and all other areas of use. Today, the use of *a* and, to a lesser extent, *o* in unstressed final syllables is a marker of Swedish in contrast to Danish.

The most conspicuous case of language planning with a political end, however, took place in the late seventeenth century in Scania and the neighbouring regions Blekinge and Halland in the extreme south of present-day Sweden. These districts were originally Danish, both politically and linguistically. They had been conquered by Sweden in the inter-Scandinavian wars that ended in 1660. The population, especially in Scania, still considered itself Danish, however, and several insurrections were harshly suppressed. In this situation, the Swedes started a linguistic reschooling of the Scanians, prohibiting the use of Danish altogether, and sent a host of teachers and clerics from the rest of Sweden southwards in order to teach and enforce Swedish in all areas of written language use. The dialect of the area, it must be added, was of an intermediary kind, forming a part of a linguistic continuum between areas of clearly Danish and clearly Swedish speech—it could equally correctly be called 'East Danish' or 'South Swedish'.

The assimilation process in fact succeeded; after one or two generations the Scanians were Swedicized linguistically and probably also accepted a Swedish identity as their own. (Recently, a regional Scanian ethnicity movement has called this acceptance into question, however.)

The Swedish treatment of the Scanians perhaps shows some of the roots of linguistic nationalism. The most important element of this ideology is the desire to stress the difference from another linguistic entity that in some way may be perceived as threatening or challenging one's own autonomy.

During the eighteenth century, Danish and Swedish were consolidated as the national standard languages of the respective countries. In fact, Danish was now more under pressure than Swedish, since the Danish ruling class was under strong German linguistic and cultural influence, while French and Latin, too, were prestigious languages. As a reaction to this, we see a Danish language movement unfolding: Early in the century, the playwright and historian Ludvig Holberg ridiculed the use of foreign languages as a prestige symbol. From the middle of the century onwards a purist movement directed against Romance (French) and Latin words unfolded (many of the 'Danish' words advocated instead were, however, loan translations from German). Towards the end of the century, Danish established its place in the state education system, and the government promoted a model for spelling to be used in schools. A codification of spelling also took place in Swedish in 1801, commissioned by the Swedish Academy, which had been created in 1786 in order to 'develop the purity, strength and nobility of the Swedish language'.

When Romanticism, with its emphasis on language and culture as markers of national identity, was imported from Germany, it was influential in both countries, but it did not change the role of language as a marker of identity in Sweden and Denmark, since this role was already well established. Neither Danes nor Swedes had to assert their linguistic identity in the face of external oppression, and their languages were not threatened in any way. The standard varieties of the languages made even more headway than before through improvements in the education system, subjecting the traditional dialects to such strong pressure that many of them were eradicated in the course of the twentieth century. In this way, the use of standard Danish and standard Swedish became the marker *par excellence* of national identity, although linguistic variation still exists, based upon regional, social, and generational differences.

While Swedish has enjoyed a position of absolute dominance over the last few centuries, not only being unchallenged at home, but also dominant as the majority language in Scandinavia as a whole, the Danes have continuously felt the pressure from German dominance, especially highlighted by the Schleswig conflict. Schleswig had been a part of the Danish kingdom since medieval times, but linguistically German had expanded steadily through the centuries, so that the territory was linguistically divided by the middle of the nineteenth century. Then the influence of Romantic nationalism made itself felt, along with a mounting conflict between the Danish king and the German duke of Holstein about supremacy over Schleswig. Increasingly, linguistic allegiance became a token of political loyalty. A short war in 1848 secured the area for Denmark, and, while it had not mattered very much before which language had been used in churches, schools, and so on, a policy of Danicization now set in, creating sharp reactions from the German-minded part of the population. A new war with Prussia in 1864 severed the whole of Schleswig from Denmark, and in 1871 it followed Prussia into the new German Empire. An even more ruthless Germanization was the result, and in Denmark one of the major issues in national politics became the 'liberation' of Schleswig. The Folk High School movement, stressing the values of Nordic culture and the desirability of using the mother tongue in all kinds of education, became a powerful instrument of anti-German agitation in Schleswig. This continued for two generations, until Germany lost the First World War. Then, in 1920, Schleswig was divided following a referendum, the northern part uniting with Denmark, the southern part remaining within Germany. Although there remains a German minority in the north and a Danish one in the south, the language question in Schleswig has by now been reduced to a movement for the preservation of a cultural heritage, without any political overtones. A treaty between the two countries in 1955 granted full linguistic rights for both minorities in the country where they lived.

But the anxiety of the Danes about their large southern neighbour remained after the settlement of the Schleswig conflict, and it is typical that anti-German reaction has regularly taken a pan-Scandinavian direction. Pan-Scandinavianism in Denmark—and in Norway and Sweden—came to the fore in the 1850s and 1860s, openly connected with the Schleswig conflict. A private conference of prominent cultural figures from the three countries in Stockholm in 1869 tried to promote a spelling reform moving Danish and Swedish towards each other. Some of the proposals were in fact implemented later, but pan-Scandinavian enthusiasm did not reach far enough into society at large really to influence developments. In the 1930s and 1940s a new wave of anti-German pan-Scandinavianism swept Denmark, understandably enough in view of the Nazi threat that loomed large in those years. A minor spelling reform was the result, removing initial capitals from nouns (German-style *Großschreibung*) and introducing the character *å* for the earlier *aa*—both these measures bringing written Danish closer in appearance to Swedish and Norwegian (this movement and its modest results are thoroughly described in Jacobsen (1973)).

All this, however, may be seen as small ripples on a large and calm sea. The Danish and Swedish national and linguistic identities have been taken for granted for many generations now, and they seem quite secure even in the face of Anglo-American pressure and of relations with the European Union. But the development of the EU may bring these questions to the fore again. In Denmark, which has been an EC member since 1973, a debate on questions of national and linguistic identity has unfolded during recent years, notably in connection with the two referenda on the Maastricht Treaty in 1992 and 1993, but there is a more general preoccupation with these things to be discerned too. We shall return briefly to this in the final section of this chapter.

5.4.2. *Norway*

The Old Norse written language, which was in extensive use in Norway from the twelfth till the fourteenth century, experienced a decline after the passing of power into the hands of Danish monarchs from 1380 onwards. The fifteenth century was a transition period, when modified versions of Old Norse (often called Middle Norwegian, although it did not form a consolidated language variety) competed with Swedish and increasingly with Danish. The latter language eventually won out. Although some ancient law texts in Old Norse were in use until 1604, and the peasants in certain districts still tried to write letters in it, Danish had conquered the field for all practical purposes by the time Lutheranism was introduced in 1536. The Bible, therefore, was never translated into Norwegian (before modern times). It is probable that most people regarded Danish as the standard version of their own language throughout the period of Danish rule (until 1814). The fact that mutual comprehensibility between the Norwegian dialects and the Danish standard was possible (albeit not without difficulties) contributed to this. In any event, it is difficult to speak of Norwegian national identity before 1814, although a Norwegian regional loyalty can be clearly discerned. The idea that the Norwegian dialects were a language directly descended from Old Norse and thus separate from Danish was harboured only by a few individuals, as far as we now know.

From 1814 everything changed. Norway was suddenly a national entity, although the struggle for independence was defeated. But it was clearly perceived by everyone that, whatever the Norwegians were, they were not Swedes. When the Norwegian constitution had to be amended to suit the needs of the forthcoming union with Sweden, the Parliament saw to it that the 'Norwegian language' be made the only official one in Norway. But this was only a way of designating the Danish language as used in Norway. The Danes themselves were not happy with it, telling the Norwegians that they should use the correct name of their common language. Norwegian, it was stated, only existed in the dialects of Norway; the standard language was Danish and only that.

The nineteenth century was Norway's age of nation building, and the language question played an important role in this process. From the 1830s there emerged two opposing views on how Norwegianness was to be defined—in general as well as linguistically. One might express the crucial difference between the two conceptions by asking the question: 'How old is Norway?' (Jahr 1989:12).

One answer to this question was: Norway is 1,000 years old. Modern Norway is a continuation of the medieval independent state. The foundations of Norwegian national identity, therefore, have to be found in cultural and linguistic continuity between medieval and modern times. This continuity could not be found in the upper-middle-class culture of the times, which was imported from Denmark or from the European continent through the mediation of Danish upper-class culture. One had to study popular culture, which had medieval roots and had survived through the centuries of Danish rule scarcely influenced by urban upper-middle-class culture. Therefore the 1840s saw the beginnings of a large-scale collecting and recording of this popular culture, which was expressed in local dialects as far as it was verbal (ballads, fairy tales, legends).

The linguistic consequence of this view was that a standard language worthy of the name 'Norwegian' had to be founded on the popular dialects—since these dialects had developed directly from Old Norse, unlike Danish, which belonged to another branch of Scandinavian. This assumption, originally based on loose impressions by observers from the upper middle class whose linguistic insights were scarce, was given credence by the self-taught linguist (dialectologist) Ivar Aasen (1813–96), himself of farming stock and therefore, unlike a large majority of educated people at the time, a native speaker of a Norwegian dialect.

Aasen spent many years travelling around in the country doing research into the rural dialects—partly for academic reasons, but chiefly for the reason that, by comparing them, he could find their common basis and prove that they were separately descended from Old Norse. On the basis of systematic comparisons aided by the methods of comparative linguistics, which were being meticulously developed by German linguists (Bopp, Grimm) at that time, he codified a common standard for them, which he called *Landsmål* ('the language of the country' or 'of the countryside'), but which today is called *Nynorsk* (New Norwegian). A grammar (1864) and a dictionary (1873) from Aasen's hand—both maintaining a very high professional level—were the foundations for this new written language (his methods are briefly described in Haugen 1972: 191–214). Soon, from the 1860s onwards, it became a vehicle for a cultural emancipation movement among the rural population, inspiring poets and prose writers, and being taught in the Norwegian Folk High Schools (a school type imported from Denmark, stressing the local popular culture as the basis of sound education). In 1885 it was formally acknowledged by the Parliament to be on a par with Danish.

But there was another answer to the question 'How old is Norway?' It was that Norway was a new nation, not directly derived from the medieval kingdom—which, after all, had been based on a very different type of culture (more or less feudal). To function in the modern world, Norway would have to base its identity on the modern culture existing in the country, namely that represented by the urban upper middle classes (civil servants and business people)—like other countries in contemporary bourgeois Europe. Popular rural culture has the same value here as in other countries, but it could never function as a nucleus of identity in the modern world.

The linguistic consequence of this view was to accept that Danish as spoken and written by Norwegians was in fact the language of Norway, which only needed some adjustments in the lexicon to cover aspects of Norwegian nature and culture and some idiomatic Norwegianization in order to be fully acceptable. The pronunciation norms must be different from those of Danish, since the languages are phonetically considerably different, but even before 1814 Norwegians pronounced Danish in a distinctively Norwegian fashion. That was not seen as a problem; the written form was regarded as much more important, and that was to remain identical with Danish except in small details. The large differences from the dialects were no problem, since such differences were just as great in many other countries, and the dominant idea was that a standard language was a language for the cultural and socio-political élite. The dialects, in this view, should have the same humble position as dialects in other countries.

Within this view, there were nuances in the degree of willingness to accept Norwegianizing reforms in the standard. The leading advocate of a reformist course from the middle of the century onwards was the teacher Knud Knudsen (1812–95). He was of the opinion that the standard language had to be based on a spoken form of Norwegian, and he then advocated the more or less standardized upper-middle-class speech that was not regionally restricted, but that, in principle, could be used all over the country; in other words, it was nationwide. Knudsen wanted to reflect the systematic deviations from Danish pronunciation in the orthography, thus altering the written shape of the language. He attacked the Danicizing pronunciation used by Norwegian officials in formal situations, and urged that they should base the written language on their more casual everyday speech, which was most clearly Norwegian in phonetics and phonology. He met with much conservative opposition from people contemptuously called 'Danomans' by their adversaries, but the basic elements of his policy won through around the turn of the century, formally confirmed by an official reform in the 'Dano-Norwegian' standard in 1907. From then on, it was based on the speech of the urban upper middle class of Norwegians. Its autonomy was symbolically confirmed in 1919, when a Norwegian novel in this language variety was for the first time translated into Danish. Since 1929, the variety has officially been called *Bokmål* ('Book Language' or 'Literary Language').

Around 1900, then, there were two standard languages in Norway, both aspiring to the designation 'Norwegian'. We use the names *Bokmål* and *Nynorsk* consistently here for practical reasons, even though different names for them have been used in different periods and by different groups—partly ideologically loaded names. Thus, the adherents of *Nynorsk* long insisted on calling *Bokmål* 'Norwegio-Danish', while even prominent adherents of the latter standard used the name 'Dano-Norwegian' without embarrassment—among them Knud Knudsen. This indicates that the reformers within the *Bokmål* camp were conscious that their language, in all respects a fully suitable modern standard language, lacked something in Norwegianness, and thereby was weakened in its competition with *Nynorsk*.

They had good reason to feel like that. *Nynorsk* expanded rapidly in the Norwegian countryside from the 1890s until the 1920s, although it never really gained a foothold in the towns and cities. There were two main reasons for its successes. One was its Norwegianness, which was an important asset in the ideological climate of this period, the years preceding and following the dissolution of the union between Norway and Sweden in 1905. But no less important was the appeal of *Nynorsk* to the rural population as a more genuine linguistic expression of their culture as opposed to urban upper-middle-class culture. Not only was their national identity better expressed through *Nynorsk*, but also their social and regional identity. The *Nynorsk* language community has always been tolerant towards regional variation in usage integrating dialectal particularism in a striking way in a national unity directed against the 'foreign' *Bokmål*.

By the 1880s, however, a third current began to make itself felt. There were those who feared a lasting linguistic and cultural cleavage, because it could endanger the fragile unity of the new nation. Their alternative was to acknowledge both strands of Norwegian national identity, the urban, upper-class, foreign-influenced one, and the indigenous, rural, popular one, and gradually integrate them into a single unity where all these elements had their place. Linguistically, this could be done by moving the two standards towards each other. They were similar enough to make such a policy possible. While *Nynorsk* was based on more traditional dialects of the western Norwegian countryside and the mountain valleys of southern Norway, *Bokmål* has south-eastern urban upper-middle-class speech as its main foundation. However, in the south-east and the north, dialects were spoken that were linguistically intermediate between the two standards. To change the base of the two standards towards these dialect groups might be a way to find common ground for them. The south-east was, moreover, the most populous part of the country, and the new fused standard would become more representative of Norwegian speech as a whole than the two existing ones, when all dialects were considered together.

In 1917 both standards were reformed so as to absorb many forms from these dialects, while still retaining most of the usual traditional forms as optional alternatives. This met with strong resistance in the *Bokmål* camp, because the reform transgressed the sociolinguistic boundary between upper middle class and popular speech, thereby 'vulgarizing' the standard—although one of the intentions behind the introduction of the dialect forms was to 'Norwegianize' the language further and thus remove the 'Danish' stigma. From now on, the language struggle took on a sociolinguistic and socio-political character, while the question of Norwegianness receded into the background. Although most *Nynorsk* adherents still viewed *Bokmål* as half Danish and therefore unsuited to be a standard language in Norway, the *Bokmål*-using majority rejected this view. To them, the traditional 1917 *Bokmål* standard was fully Norwegian.

The 1930s saw an intensification of the rapprochement policy, resulting in further reforms of both standards in 1938. Now, many of the optional rapprochement forms from 1917 were made compulsory—thus bringing the development towards fusion a step further. Before resistance could develop, the Second World War started, and the Germans occupied Norway in 1940. The language struggle subsided for the time being. After 1945 resistance mounted again, mostly urban-based and supported by the political right. But now, a new tendency manifested itself: Since all the linguistic factions had with a few individual exceptions been loyal to the national cause during the war, the argument that *Bokmål* was less 'national' and 'Norwegian' than *Nynorsk* definitely lost its force—and so did the nationally inspired motivation for the rapprochement policy. The war simply brought about a new definition of Norwegianness—the expression 'good Norwegians' now simply meant 'anti-fascists'. At the same time, a social process of urbanization, industrialization, and internationalization took place, making the old cleavages of the language struggle less and less important. Only in the 1960s did leading *Nynorsk* protagonists understand this and start to revise their policy and ideology to suit the new situation. But by then *Nynorsk* had been ousted in many places where it had expanded before the war, particularly in the north, and the percentage of school children learning *Nynorsk* as their first written language declined from 32 per cent in 1946 to 20 per cent in 1965—and further declined to 16.4 per cent in 1977, when a stabilization set in; at the time of writing it stands at between 16 and 17 per cent. In parallel with this, the movement to reform *Bokmål* stopped and was even formally reversed by a parliamentary decision in 1981, when traditional forms that had lived on in written usage in spite of official disapproval were admitted in the official standard again. The language-planners by now admitted that they had underestimated the established socio-stylistic norms of linguistic usage. But the development is not unidirectional. The use of dialects in speech outside strictly local and private contexts has expanded markedly since the 1960s, and the trend towards more informality in linguistic usage, even in writing, has to a certain extent strengthened many of those popular forms that had been formerly introduced in the standard for reasons of language politics.

It is fair to say that *Bokmål* now, for most—if not all—of its users, functions as a national symbol in just the same way as Danish and Swedish do in their respective countries, and most *Nynorsk* users accept this, too. But *Nynorsk* also represents a crucial element of the national heritage—important parts of the Norwegian 'literary canon', for instance, are written in Nynorsk—and it is still dominant in many regions, especially in western Norway. Formally, the standards are equal; the state has the obligation to use both according to a specified set of rules. About 10–15 per cent of the population probably use *Nynorsk* at present. The varieties are so close to each other that all Norwegians can understand both of them in speech as well as in writing; the differences are mostly morphological, partly also lexical and idiomatic. This is an asset as well as a problem for *Nynorsk*: an asset because it can be used on a par with *Bokmål* everywhere, but a problem because its autonomy may be called into question by its opponents (something that regularly happens). A terminological expression of this fact is that *Bokmål* and *Nynorsk* are officially called *målformer* (standard language varieties), not *mål* or *språk* (languages).

While *Nynorsk* was originally codified as an apparently more adequate expression of Norwegian national identity, one may ask what kind of identity it represents now—since this asset had been taken from it. It is clear that the *Nynorsk* users do regard this language variety as part of their identity; it represents something that *Bokmål* lacks. If not, it would not have survived. A definite answer cannot be given, but it seems that the feeling of regional identity and solidarity it gives to those who come from or live in the *Nynorsk*-using regions is very important. Norway is a country where regionalism has always been strong, as we have already seen—but then a regionalism without any single trace of separatism. The idea of unity in diversity has always been exceptionally strong in Norway, and the strength of *Nynorsk* must have something to do with this: after the *Nynorsk* movement had to give up its dreams of replacing *Bokmål*, it has continued to fight hard for its existence alongside *Bokmål*. Through its literary tradition, containing folk literature as well as *belles lettres*, it has a register of expressions—and indeed a particular expressiveness—which is not matched by *Bokmål*; many *Bokmål* users support *Nynorsk* for this reason. The rural/urban dichotomy is also important: the rural population of Norway has been and is still very self-assertive, not accepting a position as peripheral and backward, and *Nynorsk* is one of many symbols of this rural assertiveness. Even this is to a large part a question of identity. In Norway, then, it is particularly important to realize that national identity is only one strain in a whole web of interrelated identities—and that this fact has a profound influence on the linguistic profile of the country.[2]

5.4.3. *Finland*

Finland has, unlike the other Nordic countries, no history of separate statehood in the Middle Ages. It was gradually absorbed by the Swedish realm, and the south-west coast was populated by Swedes starting before the Viking Age, while the Finns expanded in the rest of the country, pushing the original Sámi population northwards. The designations Swedes, Finns, and Sámi are exclusively ethno-linguistically based; politically they were all Swedish citizens.

Finnish was first written in the fourteenth century, and it was extensively used during the early Lutheran period in the sixteenth. The New Testament was translated into Finnish by the Lutheran cleric Michael Agricola in 1548; he also recodified the language and modernized it, thereby earning a place in Finnish linguistic history that is comparable with that of Luther for German. As the Swedish state became more centralized and consolidated under the Vasa dynasty, Finnish was pushed aside and Swedish became more and more the leading language for formal use. But Finnish was still used for ecclesiastical purposes, by the official Church as well as by the very influential Pietist movement. That was inevitable, since most people did not understand any other language; Swedish belonged exclusively to the educated élite, except in the coastal areas of early Swedish settlement. Still, it gives food for thought that the Swedes did not find it necessary to enforce the use of their language in Finland as they did in Scania. The most important reason besides the lack of mutual intelligibility and the practical difficulties emanating from this must have been that Finnish was not the language of a rival power or the vehicle of a political independence movement, and therefore was not perceived as a threat.

---

[2] On the position of *Nynorsk*, and the self-image of its users, see Oftedal (1981) and Venås (1993).

This situation continued after the inclusion of Finland in Russia. The tsars were relatively liberal as far as Finland was concerned, allowing the Finns a high degree of autonomy, and they did not interfere with the linguistic situation. Thus Swedish remained the official standard language of the country.

A Finnish language movement started to unfold from about the middle of the nineteenth century. This movement was not nationalist, directed against Russian overlordship, but purely linguistic and cultural, directed against the supremacy of Swedish. Still, the movement did foster a consciousness of Finnish nationhood, stimulated by the national romanticist idea that a separate language was a fundamental requirement for a separate nation. Like the *Nynorsk* movement in Norway, the Finnish language movement had an ethnic and national dimension, but also a social content; the social emancipation of the masses who spoke Finnish from the power of the élite minority that spoke Swedish was an important motive behind the movement. As in other countries, the movement started with folkloristic and artistic manifestations, which culminated in 1835, when the folklorist Elias Lönnrot published the great epic cycle *Kalevala*—based on popular traditions, but edited as a work of art. *Kalevala* is the Finnish national epic *par excellence*, fulfilling a role in the formation of national identity comparable to that of the saga literature in Iceland.

But great writers like Johan Ludvig Runeberg and Zacharias Topelius—although writing in Swedish!—also contributed crucially to the development of a Finnish (or Finlandic) national identity. This highlights a conflict similar to the struggle in Norway during the same period. While the 'Fennomans' firmly associated Finnish nationality with the Finnish language, which was unique to Finland and the only language for the great majority of the population, the 'Suecomans', like the 'Danomans' in Norway, maintained that an imported language that had carried the 'high culture' of the country for several generations must be regarded as a congenial expression of the national identity of that country. This was a more difficult position in Finland than in Norway, however, considering the indisputable autonomy of Finnish as a separate language, not even belonging to the Indo-European language family.

Finland is characterized by a discrepancy between linguistic and national identities, which makes it advisable to introduce a terminological distinction between Finns and Finlanders: Finns are the majority Finnish-speaking population, while the term 'Finlanders' designates citizens of the country regardless of ethnolinguistic background. The Swedish speakers of Finland are usually called Finland-Swedes, and we follow this tradition here, but 'Swedish-speaking Finlanders' would actually be a preferable term, reflecting better their own sense of their identity.

From 1810 until the 1830s, the codification of what would become the modern Finnish standard language took place, leaning more towards eastern Finnish dialects than the earlier standards, which were chiefly based on the western ones. This was not unnatural, as the capital was now Helsinki, while in earlier centuries it had been Turku; it played a role, too, that the eastern dialects were less influenced by Swedish than the western ones. The issue was very controversial at the time, though, implying different ideological and cultural attitudes: east Finnish was supported by the rich and 'authentically Finnish' folklore in the eastern areas, while the proponents of west Finnish referred to the literary traditions of the established standard. Culturally (irrespective of language), western Finland was strongly influenced by Sweden, eastern Finland more by Russia. In any event, the reformed and more eastern-inspired (but still compromising) standard was generally accepted after the publication of *Kalevala* (see Klinge 1985).

In 1863, under the regime of the liberal tsar Alexander II, Finnish was officially put on an equal footing with Swedish (with a transition period of twenty years). During the following decades it expanded steadily, as education facilities grew, the flow of printed media increased, and the language was elaborated to suit new functions lexically (on a rather puristic basis), syntactically, and stylistically. When Finland became independent in 1917, the tables had definitely been turned: Finnish was the national standard language for all purposes, while Swedish had been relegated to minority status.

The constitution of the new state, which was adopted in 1919, prescribed a strict formal equality between Finnish and Swedish as national languages and granted the users of both languages extensive linguistic rights, which were specified in a separate language law. However, the antagonism between the two groups ran high in the 1920s and 1930s—because of the strong nationalist currents at the time, which were not very conducive to tolerance towards intra-national language variation, and reinforced by the social barrier between the traditional Swedish-speaking élite and the Finnish majority, which was receding, but nonetheless still existed. Only after the Second World War did the situation calm down, and the official bilingualism of the country was generally accepted.

Today Finnish is used by 95 per cent of the population, Swedish by 5 per cent, mostly in certain southern and western coastal areas. A special case is constituted by the Åland islands, which are wholly Swedish-speaking. They opted in a referendum for a return to Sweden after Finland became independent in 1917, but international negotiations secured a compromise solution: they remained part of Finland, but were granted home rule and—uniquely in Finland—a constitutionally guaranteed position as monolingually Swedish.

While the language movement certainly contributed greatly to Finnish or Finlandic nationhood, the linguistic and national identity of the citizens of Finland now seems settled. There is still a certain animosity towards Swedish among certain groups of Finns, based on the by now unfounded prejudice that the Finland-Swedes are a kind of upper middle class. From these circles one may hear the argument that Finnish is the only linguistic expression of nationhood, and that the country should be monolingual. The emergence of similar attitudes elsewhere in Europe and the world in recent years may have stimulated this kind of thinking in Finland too, until now regarded as an international model as far as linguistic democracy and human rights are concerned. But still most Finnish-speakers accept that Finnish and Finland-Swedish are both elements in national identity.

The Finland-Swedes have, however, an autonomy problem in two directions (see Reuter 1992). Their national loyalty towards Finland has at times been called into question by sections of the Finnish majority. On the other hand, their linguistic position *vis-à-vis* the Swedish of Sweden is also to a certain extent insecure. Linguistically, the difference is clearest at the phonetic level. The written language is basically the same as the Swedish of Sweden, but with some idiomatic and lexical deviations. However, there has been a debate among Finland-Swedes on whether they should establish linguistic autonomy from Sweden-Swedish, by letting their language absorb more Finlandisms (Finland-Swedish dialectalisms) and Fennicisms (influences from Finnish), or whether they should keep the close connections with the Swedish of Sweden. The prevailing policy, supported by a great majority of the Finland-Swedes, is to prevent the language from drifting apart from Sweden-Swedish. They thus prefer to be a part of the realm of the dominant Scandinavian language, rather than establishing their variety as an autonomous minority language—which they fear would weaken their position greatly in relation to Finnish. The Finland-Swedes are, therefore, ardent Scandinavianists or Nordists.

While the Finns probably derive much of their national identity from their language, the Finland-Swedes experience a split between their national identity, which is securely Finlandic, and their linguistic identity, which is crucial to them as a group. Their only distinguishing feature is their language; they are ethnically and culturally otherwise indistinguishable from the Finns. Although they are comparatively privileged as a minority, they experience societal pressure towards Finnish, something that may be inevitable in a situation where the numerical majority is as overwhelming as it is in Finland (see Reuter 1981; Tandefelt 1992). In mixed marriages Finnish is most often dominant. Finland-Swedish youth have a much greater need to learn Finnish than Finnish youth have to learn Swedish, in order to function in society; the compulsory learning of Swedish continues in Finnish schools, but is a frequent target of criticism at all levels from the parliament downwards. Finnish (and English, but not Swedish) is the language of popular culture. The percentage of Swedish speakers in Finland is slowly diminishing: 11 per cent in 1920, 6 per cent in 1990, amounting to just under 300,000 people. But their language loyalty and desire to maintain their language is very strong, and they profit from extensive institutional support for their language, as well as from the central position of Swedish in inter-Nordic contacts.

In Åland, the Swedish language has a different position: it is used by the whole population, and it is the only reason for the autonomous status that the islands have. The Ålandic population traditionally did not feel like Finlanders at all, but today Finlandic nationality is accepted by them; political separatism is dead. But they cherish their linguistic Swedishness as well as their political semi-autonomy.

Language, therefore, is a formative element in their regional identity as Ålanders.

We must also mention that there are Finns who do not regard themselves as Finlanders at all: the Finnish-speaking minority in Tornedal in northern Sweden and the so-called Kven minority in the extreme north of Norway. Tornedal lies at the border between Finland and Sweden and remained Swedish when Finland was given to Russia in 1809. The local Finnish dialect is still alive there, among perhaps 20,000 people, but they regard themselves as a purely ethnolinguistic, not national, minority (see Wende 1992). The Norwegian Kven were almost extinguished as a linguistic group because of extreme assimilative pressure in the first half of the twentieth century, but a revival movement among them has asserted itself in recent years (see Lindgren 1990).

5.4.4. *The Sámi Ethnic Group and the Sámi Language*

The Sámi, formerly known as Lapps, a designation rejected by the group, are ethnically and linguistically quite distinct from their Scandinavian and Finnish neighbours and overlords. The problems they have with language and identity lie mainly on two levels. First, there are sharp differences between varieties of the Sámi language, making it doubtful whether these varieties should be called 'languages' or 'dialects'. Secondly, the concerted assimilative pressure to which generations of Sámi have been exposed render the relationship between the Sámi language(s) and Sámi identity very problematic.

The number of Sámi speakers is estimated to be approximately 30,000–35,000, more than half of them living in Norway, about a third in Sweden, only a few thousand in Finland, and still fewer in the Kola peninsula in Russia. On linguistic grounds, seven Sámi 'dialects' have been postulated in Norway, Sweden, and Finland, while two others are spoken in Kola. The most important 'dialect' is North Sámi, which is by far the strongest in terms of numbers of speakers—probably more than 90 per cent of those using Sámi in everyday life, according to Hætta (1993: 94). It is geographically based in the Norwegian provinces of Finnmark and Troms and the adjacent extreme northern areas of Sweden and Finland. This area, especially the communities of Karasjok and Kautokeino in inner Finnmark, are the centre of gravity of the Sámi language and Sámi ethnicity generally, since these are the only districts where a majority of the population is Sámi-speaking. Here we find the leading educational institutions teaching Sámi, the centre for the cultivation of the language, the headquarters of the Sámi organizations, and the elected Sámi parliament of Norway. As a written language, North Sámi is also totally dominant among the 'dialects'.

The other Sámi varieties are spoken by small groups of people, living dispersed among the majority populations, sometimes being occupationally distinct as reindeer-herders—the only occupation from which the majority populations are debarred. There is a kind of linguistic continuum between the varieties, which is one reason for calling them dialects. But this continuum is now more apparent than real, because the majority population has occupied the whole territory that formerly was Sámi, so that there is no continuous Sámi speech area any more. Thus, mutual intelligibility between the Sámi varieties is now low or non-existent. At any rate, between North Sámi and South Sámi, which is spoken in the central parts of Norway and Sweden, no comprehension is possible. Between these we encounter three other varieties as we move southwards: Lule Sámi, Ume Sámi, and Pite Sámi. At the other end of the North Sámi area there is a clear language boundary between North Sámi and the Eastern Sámi (Finlandic, Kola) varieties.

It is customary among Sámi, linguists and laypeople alike, to call the Sámi varieties 'dialects'. One argument for this might be that only North Sámi has been developed into a written standard language. However, four other varieties have also been codified in writing, and to a certain extent taught in schools—namely, South Sámi, Lule Sámi, and the Finlandic varieties Enare Sámi and Skolt Sámi. (The two Kola varieties have also been codified, with Cyrillic characters.) There has been some criticism on the part of speakers of those varieties of the term 'dialect' in this context. As to the linguistic rights laid down in the existing laws on Sámi, they only extend to the North Sámi areas, and a further elaboration of these rights—for instance, for South Sámi speakers—is probably impeded by the 'dialect' designation.

Historically, the Sámi, as an aboriginal population, have always been economically oppressed by the majorities, but linguistically and culturally they were left alone until Christian missions started to integrate them into the modern nation-states from the seventeenth and eighteenth centuries onwards. Both Swedish and Danish/Norwegian missionaries and clerics used Sámi for proselytizing purposes, both in speech and in writing; they made the earliest descriptions of Sámi grammar and vocabulary and codified North Sámi, Lule Sámi, and South Sámi in writing. Later, professional linguists from the majority populations modernized the spellings, while the Sámi élite has more recently taken the matter of language cultivation into its own hands.

But the evolution of modern nationalism and improvements in schooling have made things tougher, particularly from the last decades of the nineteenth century onwards; there has been strong pressure towards linguistic and cultural assimilation, most markedly in Norway. The idea that the unified Norwegian nation should have a unified Norwegian language had detrimental consequences for Sámi-speakers, who were not regarded as citizens with full rights unless they knew and used Norwegian.[3]

After the rise of social democracy, this policy continued, since Norwegian was now considered the agent of modernization in the Sámi areas. Only in the 1960s did the trend change; Sámi was again allowed and then made compulsory for Sámi children in primary schools, the Sámi organized themselves to struggle

---

[3] The effects were, however, even harsher for the Finnish-speaking Kven minority in northern Norway, which was almost totally assimilated; they were actually the primary target of the pressure, because of Norwegian fear of Finnish expansionism in the 1920s and 1930s—periods of intense nationalism in both countries.

politically for their ethnic and linguistic rights, and an ethno-cultural revival set in and intensified after 1980. In 1992 the linguistic rights of Sámi-speakers were enshrined in law in Norway and Finland, whereby Sámi was made an official language on a par with Norwegian or Finnish in the North Sámi core area.[4]

Past pressure towards assimilation has, however, led to the situation that virtually nobody is monolingual in Sámi any more—all have a working knowledge of, and more often than not a mother-tongue level of competence in, the majority language of the country where they live. Only in the nuclear Sámi area in the north of Norway do we still find people with a deficient knowledge of the majority language (Norwegian), and they are elderly people. On the other hand, the knowledge of Sámi is often deficient among many Sámi people, since it has been a deliberate policy in many districts to force the children to speak only the majority language, and this has been widely practised even within families: many parents have been ashamed of their language, or in any case they have viewed mastery of the majority language as necessary for the future of their children. Thus, there are now many thousands of people of Sámi parentage and with a professed Sámi identity who have not mastered the Sámi language. This is especially the case in the coastal areas, where the cohesive forces existing in the reindeer-herding districts have been absent.

This raises the question of whether the Sámi language is an important part of Sámi identity at all. The prevailing view is that this is indeed the case, and that the survival of a language community, where Sámi is used actively both privately and in official and cultural spheres, is necessary for the continuation of Sámi identity. The exact nature of Sámi identity is another and somewhat different question. In general, the Sámi profess their allegiance to the states they live in, provided that these states acknowledge their rights as a separate ethnic group, including certain territorial rights in their core areas. These questions are, however, still unsettled, not only between the Sámi and the ethnic majorities, but also among the Sámi themselves, many of whom see their Norwegianness, Swedishness, or Finnishness as more important than their Sámi identity, while many others are of the opinion that the Sámi should be recognized as a separate nationality within the states of Norway, Sweden, and Finland. A desire for political separation from these states, however, has seldom been voiced, because of the obvious difficulties this would lead to, both in assessing which areas such a state should encompass, and the problems of viability such a mini-state would be confronted with. The problem of assessing who really is a Sámi and who is not, in a population where much intermingling between the ethnic groups has taken place, is large enough in itself. For registration for Sámi parliamentary elections, the criterion used is not the mastery of the Sámi language, but only documented Sámi ancestry, and the subjective declaration that one regards oneself a Sámi. Sámi ethnicity in fact represents the

---

[4] On the status of Sámi and the struggle of its speakers against Norwegian, Swedish, and Finnish dominance, see Keskitalo (1981) and Jernsletten (1993).

clearest challenge in northern Europe to the whole concept of an ethnically based nation-state.

5.4.5. *Iceland, and the Faroes*

Old Icelandic was in fact a dialect of Old Scandinavian, with its nearest cognate dialects in south-western Norway. Iceland was populated chiefly from Norway, but also from Scotland and Ireland, in the decades around AD 900. The Celtic linguistic impact was slight, however, leaving only a few loanwords. Medieval Iceland was an independent political entity, a kind of republic with a national assembly of chieftains (the Alþing) as its only nationwide political institution (having a legislative and judicial mandate, but no executive power). But the Icelandic Church was subordinated to the Norwegian archdiocese of Nidaros (now Trondheim) from 1152, and in 1262 the country submitted to the Norwegian king after decades of internecine wars (the East Icelanders in 1264). The country followed Norway into the union with Denmark, and remained under Danish control until it received home rule in 1918. It acquired full independence in 1944.

From the late Middle Ages, Icelandic and Scandinavian developed along widely different lines, and, while the historian Snorri Sturluson in the thirteenth century stated that all Scandinavians including the Icelanders spoke 'the Danish tongue', Icelandic was a separate language unintelligible to Scandinavians by the sixteenth century. The language had remained morphologically and lexically almost unchanged since the heyday of Icelandic saga literature in the thirteenth century, while the phonology had changed markedly. But these changes left few traces in the spelling, since the writing and reading traditions in Iceland were very strong. The Lutheran reformation did away with Latin as the language of the Church, but Latin had in any case been much less dominant in this country than elsewhere. When the new Lutheran Bible translations came, it was undisputed that the language must be Icelandic, and that the printing must take place in Iceland, which had a printing press as early as the middle of the sixteenth century, a hundred years earlier than Norway.

The linguistic identity of the Icelanders was, therefore, something to be taken for granted. Although Danish was used for official purposes, nobody disputed the autonomy of the Icelandic language. But Iceland was as undeniably a part of the Danish realm, and a feeling of national separateness arose only under the influence of Romantic nationalism after 1800—which coincided with a period of economic growth and the rise of an indigenous urban bourgeoisie. The result was a movement unfolding from the 1830s onwards for a larger degree of Icelandic political autonomy, leading to a gradually increased influence on the part of the Icelanders in the running of their own country. In linguistic matters, this movement caused a strong purism—which had its roots back in the eighteenth century, but which gained momentum in the nineteenth. The target was the spoken and to some extent the written language of the urban bourgeoisie, which was Icelandic, but very receptive to Danish and Low German loanwords. The language reform movement entailed a campaign against these words that led to almost full victory, making Icelandic one of the world's prime examples of a consistent and successful purism. It is even more astonishing that this policy has persisted even after the full victory of Icelandic as the all-purpose language of the Icelandic people.

Iceland is practically the only example in Europe (and possibly in the world) of a linguistically homogeneous nation-state. One hundred per cent of the Icelanders speak Icelandic as their first language and use it as their dominant language in all spheres of life, while it is not spoken anywhere outside Iceland. The language is even without dialectal variation, except for a few characteristic, but minor, pronunciation differences. Thus language is one of the prime ingredients of Icelandic nationhood, besides the ancient literature and culture, and the geographical isolation of the island. Even so, there is a constant feeling that this identity is being threatened by larger linguistic entities, formerly Danish, nowadays English, since Anglo-American cultural influences are strong in Iceland. This is the prime motive behind the persistent purist drive, besides a concern that continuity with the language and literature of the medieval golden age might be disrupted if structural changes arose through the adoption of too many loanwords. This, it is felt, would threaten national identity. In scarcely any other country is the production of indigenous neologisms undertaken on such a large scale and in such a systematic and organized fashion as in Iceland, and probably nowhere else does this policy have such enthusiastic backing among the public at large, although ordinary people often have difficulty in living up to the high standards that they continue to support in theory. It is not uncommon that loanwords are used in everyday life while indigenous neologisms have a formal and literary ring. One example is the word for tractor, which in formal Icelandic is *dráttarvél* (pulling-machine) (cf. the literal Latin meaning of *tractor*), while ordinary people simply say *traktor*. (On different aspects of Icelandic language policy, see Eiríkur Rögnvaldsson 1988; Baldur Jónsson 1988; Jón H. Jónsson 1988.)

Iceland is also notable for its attempts to contain the use of English in the media, and in commercial and scientific contexts, by legislation. Most people agree with this, but the lengths to which it should be taken are controversial (see Ari P. Kristinsson 1992).

The Faroes have a background similar to Iceland, but nevertheless their situation is different. These islands were also populated from Norway, as early as the ninth century, and they were politically a part of Norway from the eleventh century onwards. The inhabitants spoke dialects close to the contemporary speech of Iceland and south-western Norway. Linguistically and ethnically, they were probably regarded as Norwegians. Like Icelandic, Faroese developed in its own direction from the late Middle Ages onwards, constituting itself as a separate language in relation to both Norwegian and Icelandic—while the political alignment shifted to Denmark through Norway's subordination under the Danish

Crown, and the islands remained Danish, like Iceland, after the separation of Norway in 1814. Like Norway, the Faroes did not have its own language codified and used in writing; Danish was the only official and written language used. We know that, in the late eighteenth century, the Faroese dialects were regarded as 'Norwegian', with no autonomy of their own. Only after 1800 were these dialects explored and used in writing in a more or less standardized form, at first with a rather phonemic spelling. At that time, it became clear that they constituted an independent language, which must be called Faroese.

This language was codified in a very etymologically inspired form by the cleric V. U. Hammershaimb around 1850. He deliberately chose to lift the standard above dialectal differences by approaching it as closely as possible to Old Norse and Icelandic. This was meant to enhance the dignity of the language. At first, it was used only for folkloristic purposes, while people still wrote Danish for all 'serious' purposes. Only at the end of the century did a language-revival movement arise, promoting Faroese as a general standard language in opposition to Danish. This was part of a national movement aiming at Faroese autonomy and eventual independence.

By this time, language was very much a part of Faroese ethnicity and nationhood, and it has remained so ever since. As in Iceland, a purist policy has been followed, but it is more difficult to promote here, because the Danicisms are more ingrained in the speech of ordinary people, and because of the continued Danish influence, Danish remaining an official language in the islands, formally on a par with Faroese. All Faroese learn Danish early in school, and they are all bilingual, unlike the Icelanders. Very many of them have migrated to Denmark, or have lived there for part of their lives. The result is that there has developed a cleavage between speech, which is strongly influenced by Danish, and writing, which is more 'purely' Faroese. Unlike the Icelanders, the Faroese are not unanimous in their support of purism; many resent the tendency to import Icelandicisms to replace Danicisms and contend that these are just as un-Faroese as the Danish words they are designed to replace (see Clausén 1978).

Even so, the linguistic separateness of the Faroese is an important component in Faroese identity. The issue of national independence has often been hotly debated, and in 1946 a slight majority voted for independence in a referendum. But this result was set aside because the percentage voting was so low (in fact one-third of the electorate voted for independence, one-third voted against, and one-third abstained). Today the idea of independence is viewed as unrealistic by most Faroese, because of the heavy economic dependence on Denmark, but it does surface from time to time when a crisis places a strain on relations between the two countries. But the ideology of a separate ethnic and national identity and its strong connection with the Faroese language is deeply ingrained, and seems set to remain so. Danish is fully accepted as the nation's second language, but the motives for this acceptance are solely instrumental, not integrationist (see Poulsen 1981, Sandøy 1992).

5.5. Conclusions: New Challenges

While language in the Middle Ages seems to have been primarily a mark of ethnicity, the growth of nation-states and national identities to a large extent used, if not to say exploited, language as a tool and a symbol. The forming of a Danish and a Swedish nation led to the codification of the Danish and the Swedish languages, while a continuation of the Nordic union of 1396 might have resulted in a common standard language for all of Scandinavia, probably mostly based on Danish. This Danish and Swedish 'nationalization' of the language varieties paved the way for analogous developments in the other ethnic groups and new national communities later on. The Finns, the Sámi, the Faroese, and the Icelanders all had languages sufficiently different from Scandinavian to be accepted as separate linguistic entities, and, along with larger and smaller cultural differences, this helped them to establish themselves as separate nations whether they acquired independence (Finland, Iceland), home rule (the Faroes), or the recognition as indigenous ethnolinguistic groups with certain linguistic and other (not yet fully clarified) rights (the Sámi). The Norwegians have had the greatest difficulties with their linguistic identity; in their case, different perceptions of the relations between language and nationality have created a linguistic cleavage that still persists, but now based more on established linguistic and cultural traditions than on an internal nationalist struggle.

Today, the national and ethnolinguistic identities of northern Europe are firmly established, but the content of these identities is constantly changing as the relations with the external world change. On three levels we may discern a challenge to the linguistic and national identities in this part of Europe.

First, there is the ideology of Nordism, an extension of the earlier pan-Scandinavianism. Pan-Scandinavianist ideas were already being voiced in the eighteenth century, and gained momentum in the middle of the nineteenth. The idea of uniting the Scandinavian languages as a part of the development of a supranational pan-Scandinavian identity was raised, and there were attempts made to put such an idea into practice. However, such attempts have always failed. Modern Nordism is still a potent ideology, encompassing all the Nordic countries and peoples, but its aims and methods are more modest. On the political and cultural level, it is practised through the creation and maintenance of numerous networks at the grassroots level, supported by political cooperation in order to strengthen contacts, such as the abolition of passport controls between the countries in 1952. Thus, Nordism is evoked as a supranational identity that is to supplement, not suppress, the national identities.

Linguistically, the same kind of pragmatic cooperation is exercised with the aim of preventing the Scandinavian languages from drifting further apart (through terminological cooperation, for example), and to strengthen the teaching and comprehension of other Nordic languages in each country. Linguistic pluralism in northern Europe is now seen as an asset in itself, and the strengthening and preservation of the linguistic minorities are regarded as positive and important tasks for the Nordic movement. However, a linguistic asymmetry is unavoidable: only the Scandinavian languages (that is, Danish, Norwegian, and Swedish) can possibly serve as languages of inter-Nordic communication (besides the major international languages, especially English). The strengthening of Swedish in Finnish schools and of Danish in Icelandic schools is, therefore, strongly desired by Nordists, but controversial in the countries concerned. Only tiny, albeit dedicated, minorities in the Scandinavian countries will take the trouble to learn Finnish or Icelandic. Therefore, there is a constant disagreement between those who wish to use English in inter-Nordic contacts, and those who insist on Scandinavian, because they see English as a threat to the Nordic identity they want to uphold.

More controversial is the second challenge—namely, the intrusion of English in the Nordic societies. It may be compared with the great influx of Low German words into the Scandinavian languages between the fourteenth and sixteenth centuries (see Section 5.2). But this process took place over several generations, the new words gradually 'trickling through' from urban to rural speech, long after the Hansa's mercantile power had disappeared; at the beginning of modern language cultivation, the new vocabulary structures were firmly established. Today there is a general feeling of massive pressure. Anglo-American cultural and linguistic influence pervades everybody's lives nowadays in some way or other. In certain domains of life, such as science, technology, commercial life, and youth culture, the national languages run the risk of being relegated to the position of 'secondary languages' in relation to English—in any case, many people believe this to be happening. The purely linguistic pressure on the vocabulary and phraseology of the Nordic languages is also marked, although the extent of this pressure may be exaggerated by those who most strongly oppose it. A reaction against this 'anglomania' has shown itself in all the countries, by far the strongest in Iceland, but it is also marked in Norway, and somewhat weaker in Finland, Sweden, and Denmark. On the other hand, English is associated with modernity and internationalism in many quarters where the national languages are regarded as 'traditional' and 'provincial'.

This conflict is highlighted by the present arguments about the relations between the Nordic countries and the EU, since an identity conflict between the national entities and the Union will probably be inevitable. On the one hand, many want to integrate with the international world where English, and secondarily French and German, for some even Spanish and Italian, are the languages of culture, the chief ingredients in a future European identity. The economic integration of Europe, the abolition of national borders, and the free movement of people throughout the area are bound to put the national identities under pressure. But such pressure always elicits two opposite reactions: support and resistance. We may expect increasingly strong confrontations between the European, the national, and the regional and local identities in the future, linguistically expressed by a pressure on the national languages both from above (primarily from English) and from below, from localized popular speech and minority languages. The national languages themselves will, according to the fears of many, increasingly run the risk of sharing the fate of the dialects, ending up as dominated languages only fit for private use and traditional culture. But this fear in itself will elicit a more active policy for strengthening and promoting them. The outcome of this struggle, as far as the present author can see, is completely open.[5]

Finally, I shall briefly mention the third perceived challenge, from the recent non-European (and south-eastern European) immigrant communities. There are people who experience these as a threat to the linguistic and national identities of the countries, although the immigrants concerned do not exceed 5 per cent of the population in any of the countries. Their presence in any case stresses the fact that the Nordic countries have ceased to be ethnically, linguistically, and culturally homogeneous—if they ever were (homogeneity is a relative concept). But in fact these new communities do not exert any pressure on the majority populations, since their languages and cultures are without prestige. On the contrary, they are themselves exposed to assimilative pressure from the majorities, although less harshly than the Sámi were in former times. They do, however, by their very presence, challenge the prevailing idea of the unity between nation, state, language, and culture—a unity which has never existed anyway (except possibly in Iceland), but which has formed our ideology and our mentality over the last two centuries. In this, the Nordic countries are in a position resembling that of the rest of Europe, although the conflicts generated tend to be less violent than in some other countries.

[5] On the position of the Nordic languages in the EU, see Simonsen (1996).

6.

The Low Countries: A Study in Sharply Contrasting Nationalisms

ROBERT B. HOWELL

6.1. The Area and its Languages

This chapter will focus particularly on the development and use of the Dutch language, since the other major language of the Low Countries, French, is treated exhaustively in Chapter 3.

Standard Dutch (*Algemeen Nederlands* (*AN*)) serves as the official language of the Netherlands and of the northern provinces of Belgium. While the speakers of Dutch in the Netherlands (now numbering roughly 14.5 million) and in Belgium (now numbering roughly 6 million) shared in many respects a common history and culture until the Dutch revolt against the Spanish Habsburg rulers in the sixteenth century, the relationship between language and nation in the two countries could hardly contrast more sharply. In the Netherlands, where Dutch was standardized in the course of the sixteenth and seventeenth centuries, the language has long enjoyed general acceptance as the official language of the Dutch Republic and, in turn, of the Kingdom of the Netherlands. In Belgium, on the other hand, speakers of Flemish[1] dialects had to accept French, at first *de facto* and later by law, as their standard language.

The negotiation of linguistic conflicts between speakers of Flemish and the approximately 4 million speakers of French in Belgium's Walloon provinces and in Brussels has been the source of heightened nationalist feelings, particularly in the last 150 years.

When Antwerp fell into Spanish hands in 1585, the southern Netherlands (modern Belgium)and the northern Netherlands were definitively torn asunder. In the north, the Dutch Republic blossomed as a thriving economic power in

---

[1] The term 'Flemish' is used here to denote those dialects of Dutch spoken in Belgium, namely the Germanic varieties spoken in the provinces of East and West Flanders, Brabant, and (Belgian) Limburg. While this usage is potentially misleading, given the fact that the dialects of East and West Flanders alone can also be called 'Flemish' in contrast to Brabants and Limburgs, there is no other satisfactory English term, and it in fact corresponds to the common use of *Vlaams* in Belgium as a cover term for all Dutch dialects in the country.

which a standard language based largely on dialects of the most powerful province, Holland, developed in the course of the seventeenth century. In the Habsburg southern Netherlands, however, French predominated as the written language both in French-speaking Wallonia and in the Germanic-speaking provinces of Flanders,[2] Brabant, and Limburg. Not until the late nineteenth century and the first half of the twentieth century did Dutch gain full status as an official language in these provinces.[3] The secure position of Dutch in the northern Netherlands contrasts sharply with the long struggle for recognition in the south, and largely accounts for the fact that language and nationalism are so closely linked in Belgium while the relationship between language and national consciousness in the Netherlands is less obvious.

Because there is so much popular confusion surrounding the relationship between Dutch and German, on the one hand, and Dutch and Flemish, on the other, it is important from the outset to define these terms as precisely as possible. The modern designations Dutch and German refer to the two major standard languages of the West Germanic dialect continuum, which stretches from the North Sea coast to the Alps and beyond in the south.[4] Prior to the onset of the standardization process for both languages in the sixteenth century and to the concurrent rise of the Dutch Republic, the clear terminological distinction between Dutch and German did not exist. Speakers of continental West Germanic dialects typically referred to their language using local developments of primitive Germanic *þeudisk- ('[language] of the people'), often modified by adjectives for 'low' and 'high' referring to the geographical altitude of a given dialect speaker's homeland. Words such as *nederduuts* (Low Dutch/German) functioned until the seventeenth century and beyond as common cover terms for northern West Germanic dialects spoken from Dunkirk to Riga.[5] This general use of variants of *duuts/diets/deutsch* to refer to all speakers of continental West Germanic languages is reflected in the semantically narrowed modern English designation 'Dutch', originally a term applied to merchants and immigrants from the Low Countries and from northern Germany alike (see van der Wal and van Bree 1992: 186).

In the Netherlands, the term *Hollands*, the name of the speech of the central and most populous province(s), is often popularly used in synecdochic fashion to

---

[2] 'Flanders' is often used to denote the entire Dutch-speaking northern part of Belgium. We use it in the more precise, and earlier, sense of the area of the province of Flanders (modern East and West Flanders) in north-eastern modern Belgium.

[3] After the Congress of Vienna (1814–15), the northern and southern Netherlands were reunited under King Willem I, and Dutch was imposed as a standard language. This unified Kingdom of the Netherlands existed from 1815 to 1830.

[4] Frisian also enjoys the status of a standard language in the province of Friesland in the Netherlands, but even in this province Dutch is also recognized, and the use of Frisian for official purposes, in schools, and so on, remains limited.

[5] Such dialects did not undergo the second or High German sound shift, and hence have forms such as Dutch *pond* and *tien* (English 'pound' and 'ten') corresponding to (High) German *Pfund* and *zehn*.

refer to both spoken and written varieties in the country much the way speakers of English often call the Netherlands 'Holland'. In like fashion, Dutch speakers in Belgium use the term *Vlaams* (Flemish), when referring to their own vernacular, even outside the provinces of West and East Flanders. This very common and traditional use of *Vlaams* today, even to designate the standard language, when *Nederlands* (Dutch) would in fact be more appropriate, has led to the frequent assumption that Flemish and Dutch are two separate languages. In fact, the inhabitants of the Netherlands and Flemish-speaking provinces of Belgium all speak variants of Dutch, since they all have standard Dutch as their standard language or *cultuurtaal*.[6] The definition of a language used here, therefore, proves to be primarily political/sociolinguistic in nature and only secondarily linguistic, and it follows very closely the concepts outlined by Goossens (1976; 1977a: 36–52; 1977b: 11–30).

In the province of Frisia in the Netherlands both Dutch and Frisian are recognized as official languages. The low degree of mutual comprehensibility between spoken Frisian and Dutch dialects has no doubt long contributed to the general feeling that Frisian and Dutch are, indeed, different languages. But the fact that a codified standard Frisian serves alongside Dutch as an officially recognized language in schools, churches, and in public administration allows us to characterize Frisian without qualification as a separate language rather than as a variant of Dutch. Nonetheless, the status of Frisian is constantly threatened by Dutch. Immigration of monolingual speakers of Dutch into the province, nearly universal Dutch/Frisian bilingualism among speakers of Frisian, and a low level of complete literacy in Frisian, all weaken the position of Frisian in the province. Among inhabitants of Frisia, 94 per cent understand spoken Frisian, 73 per cent speak Frisian, 65 per cent can read it, but only 10 per cent can write the language, a clear indication of its vulnerability as a functioning standard language (de Vries *et al.* 1994: 232).

Two sets of enclaves that currently fall outside the modern borders of Belgium and the Netherlands, but in which Dutch has historically played an important role as a standard language, are worthy of note, though they will not be considered here in detail. The first of these are the areas of northern France around Dunkirk, Calais, and Artois that originally belonged to the province of Flanders, where the Germanic/Romance linguistic border extended as far south as the river Somme prior to the seventh century. Romance has expanded at the expense of western Low Franconian dialects from the seventh century onward, a process accelerated significantly by the extension of French political influence over the area starting in the thirteenth century and made permanent in 1713 by the Treaty of Utrecht. Although this Westhoek could be characterized as Dutch-speaking in the eighteenth century, the shift to French is today nearly complete, with only about

---

[6] The term *cultuurtaal* is particularly useful in the early modern period when the concept of standard language imposed by the modern nation-state is not really fully developed.

30,000 'French-Flemings' having an active command of the dialect, and another 70,000 possessing passive knowledge (Camerlynck 1993: 312).[7]

Several enclaves now within the borders of Germany also used Dutch as a standard language, at least in certain domains, from the sixteenth until well into the nineteenth centuries (see Heida 1976; Kremer 1983; Vekeman and Ecke 1993; Bister-Broosen 1993). This acceptance of Dutch as opposed to German resulted in part from large-scale immigration during the Reformation primarily from Flanders and Brabant, and the success of Calvinism (versus Lutheranism) in these areas of heavy southern Dutch settlement, and also arose in part from strong economic ties between these areas and the thriving cities of Holland. Three major areas employed Dutch as a standard language: the area around Emden in East Frisia, the region surrounding Bentheim, Lingen, and Steinfurt to the south, and part of the Rhineland near Kleve. In all of these areas Dutch has yielded to German, though the local dialects still exhibit considerable lexical influence from standard Dutch (Bister-Broosen 1993: 320–1).

6.2. The Status of the Languages

In the Netherlands Dutch serves as the unquestioned major language, sharing official status with Frisian only in the province of Frisia. In Belgium the situation is much more complicated. Until the 1870s, French was the single official language, and large segments of the Flemish-speaking populace acquired excellent skills in French in order to be able to function in official bureaucracies, the educational system, non-local commerce and various other public domains. French-speaking Wallonians, on the other hand, rarely learned Flemish. In the course of the nineteenth century, however, the Flemish Movement gathered strength and succeeded through a series of linguistic laws passed from 1878 onwards in elevating Dutch to the status of the official language of the Flemish-speaking provinces. In Belgium's Francophone areas the legal inroads made by Flemish led to the development of a Wallonian nationalist movement. French remains the official language of Wallonia. German serves as the protected official language of some 60,000 speakers in a small area of Belgium, along the eastern border of the French-speaking province of Liège (see Barbour and Stevenson 1990: 224–30). Interestingly, most of the dialects of this area are Low German, and hence linguistically close to Dutch. Their status as German dialects arises from historical links between the area and Germany, and illustrates once again that distinctions between languages can owe more to politics and history than to linguistic considerations.

The secure position of the Dutch language in the northern Netherlands has

---

[7] For further information on the situation in French Flanders see Section 3.3.4. Excellent sources on the topic are Verbeke (1970), Camerlynck (1993) and de Vries *et al.* (1994: 213–16). The sources quoted in Section 3.3.4 give rather different figures from those quoted here.

tended to limit its role in national identity. In Belgium, on the other hand, language provides the major criterion separating Flemings and Wallonians. We therefore see Dutch playing two very distinct roles in the construction of national identities in two geographically contiguous modern nation-states.

6.2.1. *Dutch*

The history of the standardization of Dutch and of the political partition of the Low Countries yields important insights into the role of language in the modern Netherlands and Belgium, and therefore merits rather detailed discussion. The fact that the standardization process resulted in the inclusion of both northern and southern linguistic features in the standard language of the northern Netherlands made the eventual adoption of the northern Dutch standard in Belgium more feasible. The partition of the Netherlands simultaneously secured the future of Dutch in the Netherlands while gravely endangering the linguistic position of Flemish speakers in the south. Both of these developments prove crucial to understanding the modern situation, where the status of Dutch provides the dominant theme in the question of nationalism in Belgium, while in the Netherlands language is only one of many components of national identity.

I shall now devote considerable space to the history of Dutch, since it provides an interesting counter-example to the many instances described in this book where language standardization and the development of a national identity seem to go hand in hand. I shall argue here that the beginnings of the standardization process in Dutch are, to an extent, independent of the development of a national consciousness, and can be seen to be crucially dependent on economic and demographic factors.

The fact that the rapid emergence of a super-regional written form of Dutch in the sixteenth and early seventeenth centuries closely parallels the rise of the Dutch Republic can lead one to the overly simplistic conclusion that the process of standardization is a direct reflection of growing Dutch nationalism during the Eighty Years War against the Habsburgs. Close scrutiny of the history of the Dutch language reveals, however, that the roots of the standardization process can be traced to the thirteenth century and that a number of socio-historical factors contributed over the following three centuries to the growing need for a translocal written language. The Dutch Revolt and the establishment of the Dutch Republic simply magnified the need for a national written standard and provided a milieu that accelerated the process. In what follows I would like to discuss briefly and chronologically four major developments that strongly promoted the use of super-regional written varieties of Dutch prior to 1568 and then place them in the socio-historical context of the young Dutch Republic. These four developments would be (1) the rise of large, economically powerful and culturally influential cities first in Flanders, then in Brabant, and, finally, in Holland, and the resulting growth of a large and relatively literate urban patriciate and middle class, (2) the invention of the printing press, (3) the Reformation with its promotion of vernacular translations of the Bible, and (4) the desire of scholars and poets to mould Dutch into a literary language comparable to Latin or Greek. Rather than simply list four factors contributing to the standardization process, however, I would like to argue that the process of urbanization and the emergence of large, relatively literate, politically and economically powerful urban middle and upper classes provided the major impulse for the development of a super-regional standard. The other three factors I have mentioned, the importance of the printing press, the influence of the Calvinist Reformation, and the humanist attempts to mould Dutch into a codified literary language, must be seen as linked to this process of urbanization.

In order to understand the development of the Dutch standard language it is important to realize that the Dutch linguistic area has not had a permanent centre of cultural and economic influence such as Paris in France and London in England. Instead, we see the centre of Dutch culture pass from Brugge/Bruges in Flanders in the late fourteenth century to Antwerp in Brabant, and then from Antwerp to Amsterdam in the province of Holland in 1585. This eastward then northward shift of the cultural and economic centre of gravity in the Low Countries has meant that all of these dialectally diverse areas have made a major contribution to the development of written Dutch. The modern written standard has therefore incorporated both northern and southern elements.

Literary texts and official documents in Middle Dutch do not appear until the second quarter of the thirteenth century. This relatively late appearance of texts in the vernacular is generally attributed to the regular use of French at the Flemish court and to the regular use of Latin or French for local official purposes. It is therefore only when the cities of Brugge/Bruges, Ypres/Ieper, and Ghent achieve by contemporary standards phenomenal growth in the course of the thirteenth century that a need for vernacular literature and official documents seems to arise.[8] The transition from Latin to Dutch in official municipal documents begins in 1236 in Ghent and is followed by Boekhoute in 1249, Ypres/Ieper in 1253, and finally by Brugge/Bruges in 1262.[9] The introduction of Dutch in these documents indicates the development of an urban subgroup that was, on the one hand, literate but, on the other hand, unable, poorly equipped, or unwilling to deal with Latin or French texts.[10] Cities and chanceries in other provinces followed suit, with Middelburg in Holland-Zeeland switching to Dutch in 1254, and the chancery of the Count of Holland in 1267, while Kortenberg, Breda, Mechelen/Malines, and Grimbergen in the province of Brabant all adopted Dutch between 1266 and 1277. It is important to recognize that official and commercial

---

[8] See e.g. de Vries *et al.* (1994: 38). The cities of Brugge/Bruges and Ghent were huge by thirteenth-century standards.

[9] It is worth noting that French remained as the official language in Ypres/Ieper until the fourteenth century, but many documents also appear in Dutch (see de Vries *et al.* 1994: 40).

[10] The necessity of composing official documents in Dutch is probably an indication more of a growth of overall literacy rather than of a decline in the knowledge of Latin or French.

documents in Dutch originating in Holland and Brabant show a strong tendency to suppress local dialect features and to adjust to the 'norm' of the Flanders cities. So strong is this tendency that one is at times hard pressed to find local features in a text originating in Holland or Brabant. In other words, the scribal tradition of Flanders seems to be tacitly accepted as the norm in other provinces. Obviously, the desire to make a document accessible to the widest possible audience proves stronger than any desire to portray a local dialectal variant in writing. The crucial role played by the major urban centres in the increased use of Dutch as a written medium is dramatically underscored by the fact that Flanders' largest city, Brugge/Bruges, an urban giant of its time with roughly 40,000 inhabitants, is the source of nearly half of the 2,000 extant non-literary documents dated prior to 1301 (de Vries *et al.* 1994: 41).

The silting-up of the river Zwin late in the fourteenth century led to the rapid decline of Brugge/Bruges as a centre of trade. The resulting growth of the Antwerp market, the establishment of the first university in the Low Countries at Leuven/Louvain in 1426, and the placement of important governmental functions in Brussels and Mechelen/Malines[11] all led to a shift in the economic, political, and cultural centre of gravity from Flanders to Brabant. As a result, a written language retaining features of the Flanders written tradition but bearing many distinctly Brabant features gains in importance in the fourteenth and fifteenth centuries, and it is now the language of Brabant that exerts a growing influence on texts originating in Holland and Flanders. It is important to emphasize that the incorporation of non-local scribal features in texts of the thirteenth to fifteenth centuries by no means resulted in anything like a consistent or codified standard. Virtually all texts, regardless of their place or date of origin, exhibit idiosyncratic features betraying the dialect of the writer and the general lack of codification. Rather, the conscious elimination of local features, no matter how unsuccessful, must be taken as evidence of a recognition that some sort of super-regional written language was necessary.

Given this transfer of linguistic influence from Flanders to Brabant, it seems clear that the rise and fall in the importance of a given region's written traditions seems to be integrally linked to the fate of that region's cities. It is therefore worth considering exactly why this should be the case and to identify exactly what role urbanization might have on the need for a standard language in the Low Countries. As we have seen, the growth of cities in the thirteenth century can be directly linked to the extension of the use of a written form of the vernacular to domains previously dominated by Latin or French. Furthermore, subsequent development of more complex commercial and legal relationships, and the growth of large-scale industry and trade, result in the expansion of the written language to altogether new uses—in letters of credit, warehouse records,

---

[11] In 1430 Brussels became one of the residences of the Duke of Burgundy, while Mechelen/Malines beccame the seat of the *Hoge Raad* (High Council).

contracts, and the like. If the cities in the Low Countries had existed in relative isolation from one another, as was the case, for example, for many cities in Germany, use of a written language heavily coloured by the local dialect would be unproblematic. But by 1500 the Low Countries were one of the most highly urbanized areas in Europe, and the cities of Holland, Flanders, and Brabant comprised a densely packed and to a large degree interdependent urban network with a rather pressing pragmatic need for a generally acceptable written language. And this need is expressed in all manner of texts—literary, commercial, official, religious, and political—in the course of the sixteenth and early seventeenth centuries.

Because I am emphasizing the crucial role of cities in the standardization process in the Low Countries, I should make clear how unusually urbanized the region was for the time. In the year 1500 there was in all of England only one large city, London, with a population of 40,000. Four other towns, Bristol, Exeter, Newcastle, and Norwich, had approximately 10,000 inhabitants each. The Low Countries, by contrast, packed twenty-three cities of more than 10,000 souls into an area many times smaller. Four of these had 30,000–40,000 inhabitants, and twenty of the twenty-three towns boasted more inhabitants than the second largest city in England. The Low Countries had a total urban population of 445,000 in 1500 compared to 80,000 in England, 385,000 in all of Germany, and 688,000 in France (see de Vries 1984). This figure swells by 25 per cent to 566,000 by 1550.

This degree of urbanization could only be supported with difficulty in the early modern period, given the fact that appalling living conditions in the cities resulted in an urban death rate that far outstripped the birth rate. Without a continual strong influx of new inhabitants, cities were not able to maintain their size, to say nothing of actually growing. The work of modern historical demographers has conclusively shown that massive immigration into the cities of the Low Countries accounts for their size and continued growth. In short, contrary to linguists' traditional preconceived notions of early modern society as relatively static, a large body of data indicates that the pre-industrial population of Europe was highly mobile: large numbers of people of all social classes, urban and rural dwellers 'moved, sometimes repeatedly, in search of spouses, work, skills, and sometimes religious freedom, physical security or sheer survival' (de Vries 1984: 213). Rich as the agricultural hinterland in the Low Countries could be, it was also strictly limited in quantity. Because grown children were generally expected to leave home and establish their own households, migration to the city was often the only option open, given the dearth of arable land. The constantly positive birth-to-death ratio in the countryside ensured a continuing rural population surplus that fuelled the growth of the cities in the Low Countries.

The mobility of the population of the Low Countries exerted a decisive effect both on the development of the spoken language and on the development of super-regional written varieties. Obviously the constant influx of immigrants from rural areas and other cities created an extended period of polydialectalism or polyglossia in the urban centres. While the immigrants may in some instances have been ghettoized, marriage records, which cite place of origin, indicate rapid assimilation of immigrant populations. This rather counter-intuitive development can be attributed to the disproportionally high rate of death for native males, which led to a gender imbalance in the native population, and hence to unions between native women and immigrant men (de Vries 1984). The process of immigration and assimilation had the effect of loosening norm-enforcing traditional, dense social networks and of opening the urban vernaculars to a process of linguistic accommodation, whereby salient dialectal features—features characteristic of only one of the many dialects spoken in a given city—are dropped in favour of variants acceptable to a broader cross-section of the populace. On the other hand, the very mobility of the population and the intensifying commercial and cultural interaction between cities heightened awareness of different dialectal variants and underlined the need for a more universally accessible written language.

While dialect-tinted standardized Dutch had made important inroads by 1500 as a language suitable for certain purposes—municipal and commercial documents, lowbrow literature, and personal letters—the European lingua franca was still Latin, the language of the academy, classical literature, and the Church. Standard histories of Dutch typically cite three factors contributing to the process of standardization in the sixteenth century: the advent of the printing press, the rise of humanism, and the Reformation. The troubling thing about these standard accounts is that it is difficult to assess exactly what effect the efforts of printers, humanist scholars, and Calvinist preachers actually had on the development of the eventual Dutch standard. We cannot draw a direct line between the language of any or all of these subgroups in early sixteenth-century society and the modern standard language. There seems to be a missing link between these alleged sources of the standard language and the eventual product. This apparent difficulty vanishes, however, if we view the various attempts at standardization not as direct sources of the standard language but rather as manifestations of the need for a super-regional written language—a need that is firmly rooted in the demands of Dutch urban society.

Printers had a more practical reason for attempting to achieve some sort of uniformity in the written language: they wanted their products to appeal to the broadest possible market. The largest market for books was in the large cities of Brabant and East Flanders: Antwerp, Ghent, and Brussels. It is, therefore, not surprising that even books printed by the numerous publishers in northern cities such as Utrecht, Gouda, Delft, Leiden, and Haarlem exhibit a language with a distinctively southern flavour (de Vooys 1954: 57). More important was the idiosyncratic nature of each printer's language. While a given house might achieve some internal linguistic consistency, no codified printer's language developed. Therefore, while the advent of the printing press unleashed a flood of printed material, the reader was confronted with wide variation in both usage and orthography from text to text.

The effect of the early Reformation on the standardization process prior to the Dutch Revolt was also minimal. Although the teachings of Luther, but especially Calvin, found a large following in the urban centres of Brabant and Flanders, the Dutch Reformation was not blessed with a leader with Luther's shrewd linguistic insight and skill as a translator. The demand for Bibles in the vernacular resulted in the publication of several translations of the gospels based either on Erasmus' Latin translation or on Luther's High German version. None of these translations, however, proved to be generally acceptable, because the language chosen proved either too local or too super-regional. The Brabander Nicolaus van Winghe admits in the foreword of the third edition of his gospel translation (1553) that readers had complained that earlier editions were incomprehensible unless the reader had been born in Leuven/Louvain. On the opposite end of the spectrum, Jan Utenhove of Ghent tried to produce a translation of the Luther Testament that would be accessible to readers from Dunkirk to Lübeck. The resulting so-called Emden translation (1556) uses a language so heavy with eastern Low German vocabulary and morphology that it found little resonance in the Low Countries. The Antwerp van Liesveldt translation of Luther, with its strongly southern language, became the most widely used translation until the States' Translation supplanted it in the middle of the seventeenth century. But the fact that the southern-dominated Synod of Dordrecht in 1618 commissioned the States' Translation indicates how inadequate the earlier translation had by that time become.

The coincidence of the Dutch Revolt (beginning in 1568) against Spanish Habsburg rule with the appearance of a number of works concerned with the regularization, purification, and expanded use of the Dutch written language provides evidence that the war with Spain spurred intensified interest in the national language. The flurry of interest in the native language was not, however, accompanied by any renewed insight into the nature and function of a written standard—in fact, heightened feelings of nationalism sometimes clouded judgement. The famed scientist and champion of the Dutch language Simon Stevin (*Dialectike ofte Bewyskonst* (1585)) went so far as to claim that Dutch was even more perfect than Latin because of its preponderance of one-syllable words: *kaas*, *angst* versus Latin *caseus*, *anxietas*. Joannes Becanus makes the absurd claim in his *Origines Antwerpiannae* (1569)—written in Latin—that Dutch was the original language of Adam and Eve, as proved by its name, *Duits*, which he explained as a reduced form of *de oudste* (the oldest—as in 'the oldest language').

Histories of the Dutch language rather uniformly describe the grammatical treatises published in the first two decades of the Revolt as 'influential'. But the failure of the ideas put forth in these works to catch on in actual practice leads one to believe that their primary effect was to engender and sustain interest in the entire question of language standardization. Otherwise they seem to have had little effect. Works on regularized orthography were hampered, on the one hand, by over-reliance on the pronunciation of a single dialect—such is the case with Sexagius' *De Orthographia Linguae Belgicae* (1576), while others were based on an idealized pronunciation which no one actually used—for example, Pontus de Heuiter's *Nederduitse Orthographie* (1581). As a result, many competing ideas about the 'best spelling' were current, but actual practice was determined more by tradition, a writer's area of origin, and individual whim. Grammars, the most famous of which is Spieghel's *Twe-spraack vande Nederduitsche Letterkunst* (1584), continue to suffer from the preconceived notion that written Dutch must be a language as heavily inflected as Latin. Spieghel's artificial paradigms, including forms that did not exist in any spoken variety of Dutch, obviously represent a step in the wrong direction if the written language was ever to become generally accessible. The most important lexicon of the period, Kiliaen's famous *Etymologicum Teutonicae* (1574), serves as a rich source of lexical information, with specific information on words that are obsolete or confined to a single dialect, but makes no decision as to which words are to be considered part of the written language and which are to be avoided as archaisms or regionalisms. In short, the lively dialogue regarding the desirability of standardization and the form the standard language should take reflects a broad-based interest in language among merchants, jurists, scholars, and scientists—in the urban middle and upper-middle classes.

Perhaps more important during the first two decades of the Revolt is the increased use of Dutch as a language of science. Medical publications in Dutch such as Carolus Baten's *Medicynboek* (1589) and *Handboek der Chirurgie* (1590) reflect an expanded use of Dutch in domains previously reserved for Latin. In the late 1580s Simon Stevin was the first Professor at the University of Leiden to lecture in Dutch—he was, interestingly enough, training the Prince of Orange's military engineers, whose Latin apparently was not up to the task. In any event, we see a continuation of the expansion of the role of Dutch as a written medium between 1568 and 1585 as well as a flurry of well-meaning but basically ineffectual attempts to codify a Dutch standard, but little real progress has been made—probably because most attempts at codification try to impose idiosyncratic and inorganic prescriptive rules rather than simply regularizing the inherited and naturally evolving written language(s). The written language still shows heavy influence of the unstandardized written tradition, with a greater or lesser degree of dialect-induced variation.

The fall of Antwerp to the Spaniards in 1585 marks a decisive turning point in the history of the Low Countries and in the history of the Dutch language. The loss of most of Flanders, Brabant, and Wallonia results in the permanent split of the Dutch linguistic area as well as the loss of vital centres of commerce and culture. Almost overnight, the cultural, economic, and political centre of the Low Countries shifts to the province of Holland, where Amsterdam has already emerged as the leading city.

The partition of the Netherlands was not, however, a clean break. The Dutch fleet maintained its blockade of the River Scheldt and the Flemish coast, immediately crippling the once flourishing southern economy. The Spanish conquerors in their turn showed an *onverwachte soetichheyd*—an 'unexpected mildness'—towards the rebellious inhabitants of the southern cities, allowing them to emigrate unhindered. Between 1585 and 1620 approximately 100,000 Flemings, Brabanders, and Wallonians chose to move to the United Provinces, some for the sake of religious freedom, very many others to escape the economic desolation of the South.

From an economic standpoint, the stream of immigrants into cities such as Amsterdam, Haarlem, Leiden, and Delft represented a boon: some of the newcomers were wealthy merchants or industrialists who brought with them capital and entire industries (textiles, printing, dyeing, and so on), still others were skilled craftsmen who provided a crucial labour pool for the rapidly expanding northern economy. But a large segment of the immigrant population was desperately poor and contributed to the teeming urban underclass eking out a bare subsistence in the streets and back alleys of Holland's cities. Whatever the lot of the individual immigrant, as a group the southerners made an important contribution—either with their wealth and know-how or with the sweat of their brow—to the burgeoning economic prosperity of the young Republic.

Immigrants were nothing new in the cities of Holland. In fact, at various points equally large numbers arrived from the northern Dutch provinces and from Germany, while smaller numbers of refugees arrived from other countries such as England and France. But the immigrants from Flanders and Brabant were of a different sort. First of all, the majority of southern immigrants had every intention of returning to the South once their lost homeland had been wrested from Spanish control. The indications of this widespread desire to return to the South are many. Escape clauses in contracts closed between southern immigrants and northerners often release the southerner from the terms of the contract if he is repatriated. Documented low rates of intermarriage between southerners and native Hollanders as well as the southerners' decided tendency to remain ghettoized in certain neighbourhoods and to maintain their own cultural institutions (*rederijkerskamers*) reflect their desire to retain their cultural identity. Finally, the much more fanatical desire to prosecute the war with Spain aggressively among the southern immigrants can only be ascribed to their hope of eventually being repatriated. Of course the envisioned recovery of the lost provinces never happened, but the assumption that victory would come in a matter of years effectively postponed the assimilation of the southern immigrants into northern society for more than a generation.

A further source of friction between southern immigrant and Hollander was the question of religion. Prior to 1585 the Calvinist Reformed Church was extremely weak in Holland—congregations in many major northern cities rarely represented more than a tiny percentage of the total population. The sudden arrival of the largely Calvinist southern immigrant population—coupled with the

Reformed Church's status as the only officially recognized church in the Dutch Republic—was a source of considerable friction. In fact the first four decades of the young Republic's history were marked by religious, social, and political upheaval resulting from conflict between predominantly southern orthodox Calvinists and Holland's more liberal and tolerant urban patriciate.

The linguistic effect of this confrontation between southern immigrant and native Hollander has provided historical linguists with some thorny questions. Because many originally southern features persist in the written language of Holland, linguistic histories have tended to minimize the friction between immigrant and native and have claimed that Hollanders even viewed the language of the immigrants as prestigious (whatever that means); influential linguists such as te Winkel (1901) and Kloeke (1927) have argued that contact between Hollanders and Brabanders in the northern cities affected the spoken language as well as the written language, with the native Hollander imitating southern pronunciation. But careful examination of the data pertaining to the development of the spoken language in Holland yields virtually no evidence of any major southern influence whatsoever. As Weijnen (1966) states, 'to the extent that a desire to imitate Brabants ever existed, it existed only on paper'.

But even this statement must be relativized. There is no shortage of contemporary commentary indicating basically particularistic views with respect to the relative value of the differing spoken varieties of Dutch in the seventeenth century. Not surprisingly, Brabanders sing the praises of *Brabants*, while Hollanders such as Bredero (1619) condemn the southern dialects as *misspraek* (bad language). In such an environment, it would seem remarkable that a Hollander would consciously adopt a Brabant variant—in speech or in writing—out of some desire to identify with the immigrant population. So why do a large number of southern lexical items never current in the northern vernacular survive in the written standard? The large-scale northward migration of Flemings and Brabanders and the four-decade-long maintenance of a culturally distinct immigrant community effectively extended the role of southern dialectal influence on the developing written language long beyond the actual partition of the Low Countries. For nearly half a century after the fall of Antwerp we see southern and northern linguistic variants in competition. In virtually every instance this competition is resolved in favour of the northern variant. But we can also observe a clear shift in the perception of many linguistic features as being rooted not in dialectal dichotomies (*Brabants* as against *Hollands*, for example) but in a new dichotomy between spoken language (*spreektaal*) and written language (*schrijftaal*). When the Hollander Bredero condemns Brabant speech as *misspraek* (bad language) in rather formal language in the foreword to his *Spaenschen Brabander*, he employs any number of linguistic elements that are southern in origin—but he has clearly classified them as simply belonging to the written language. It is easy for lexical items to become decoupled from their dialectal origins, given the fact that they do not usually exist in pairs, as do, say, phonological variants such as *paard/peerd* (horse). I would argue that this type of delocalization of originally southern lexical items in the course of the sixteenth and early seventeenth centuries accounts for their continued existence in the northern Dutch written language. There is perhaps no more eloquent testimony to the eventual victory of *Hollands* over *Brabants* than the fact that the South's most prominent literary figure, Joost van den Vondel, edits out a number of southern variants in the latest editions of his works, choosing in each instance the northern variety instead.

Finally, I should mention the last hurrah of southern Dutch in Holland, the States' Translation of the Bible, commissioned in 1619 and completed in 1635. Because this translation became the generally accepted Dutch version of the Bible for Dutch Protestants, linguistic histories have traditionally claimed that the *Statenbijbel*, while exhibiting a definite southern linguistic flavour, has exerted a major influence on the development of the Dutch standard language. Why would a translation of the Bible show a preference for southern forms as late as the third and fourth decades of the seventeenth century? Once again, we have to place the States' Translation in its historical context. First of all, we need to recognize that the Reformed Church was dominated by preachers of southern origin. Furthermore, the Synod of Dordrecht, which commissioned the translation, was also famous for its expulsion of the largely northern Arminian faction (Remonstrants), so that the translation was undertaken at the precise moment that northern influence in the Church hierarchy was at a low ebb. Much is made of the fact that the team of translators was drawn from all provinces of the Netherlands to ensure that a generally comprehensible translation could be obtained. But some provincial representatives for Holland were in fact of southern origin, which hardly made them ideal representatives of northern interests. The choices actually implemented by the translators give us direct access to the linguistic decisions made prior to the beginning of the actual process of translation. Given the general predilection for southern variants among the translators, the preference is most often given to the southern variant at issue—this, in turn, is at variance with the developmental trends in written Dutch at the time. The language of the resulting translation is therefore peculiar, oddly archaic, even as the first edition of the *Statenbijbel* rolls off the presses in 1637 (de Vries *et al.* 1994: 84–6). The language of the States' Bible from the outset leads a sort of parallel existence to the regular written language, much the way the language of the King James version of the Bible does in English. Clearly words and phrases from the States' Bible enter the written language, but its effect on the structure and orthography of the developing standard language is negligible.[12]

---

[12] I should note that many histories of Dutch attribute great significance to the influence of the States' Bible (see Donaldson 1983: 108, van der Horst and Marschall 1989: 67), but elements attributed to the influence of the States' Bible, such as the acceptance of the third person reflexive pronoun *zich*, are demonstrably present in the vernacular decades before the States' Bible was printed (cf. J. B. Hendriks 1997).

The partition of the Netherlands, formalized in 1648, led to the continued development of the Dutch standard language in the North, while Flemish speakers in the South increasingly saw their own native language yield ground to French in most official domains. The Dutch standard language, which might be characterized as a *Hollands* house built on a Flemish and *Brabants* foundation, subsequently continued to develop in the northern Netherlands. The Dutch standard increasingly took on a northern flavour, and today even lexical items that originated in the South but persist in the written standard are seen as words in the 'written language' (*schrijftaal*), not as Flemish/Brabants contributions to the standard language.[13] This cleft between North and South led gradually to a significant linguistic estrangement. In the South, French became *de facto* the language for most public functions, while the use of written Flemish was quite limited. Given the importance of French as a language of administration, many educated Flemings largely abandoned Flemish in favour of French, a situation that persisted into the nineteenth century.

In the course of the seventeenth and eighteenth centuries, therefore, standard Dutch continued to develop without input from or regard for the southern Dutch dialects. As a result, northern Dutch became an increasingly unsuitable written medium for Flemish speakers, although the recognition that both the northern Dutch and the Flemings 'spoke the same language' lived on, a realization made clear by the fact that books written by northern Dutch writers were printed and sold in the South (de Vries *et al.* 1994: 95–6).

The linguistic dominance of French in the South elicited complaints from contemporary seventeenth- and eighteenth-century Flemish commentators (cf. de Vooys 1952: 147; de Vries *et al.* 1994: 95), the most prominent of which are Willem Verhoeven (1780) and J.B.C. Verlooy (1788). Both writers bemoan the fact that French has supplanted Flemish in science, literature, and drama and argue for an end to this *Franschdolheyd* (French craziness). They go on to advocate establishment of a standard pronunciation and codified written language in the South, and Verlooy makes specific reference to the historical unity of the northern and southern Netherlands, stating 'we are indeed the same people, the same in language, character, morals and customs' (de Vooys 1952: 86). Interestingly enough, Verlooy also sets a nationalistic tone when he argues that 'the language of freedom [i.e. Dutch] also finally be the language of the arts'.

6.2.2. *French and Dutch in the Southern Netherlands (modern Belgium)*

The incorporation of the southern Netherlands into the French Republic in 1795 made French the official language of the South. Although French had

---

[13] The separation of 'written language' (*schrijftaal*) from 'spoken language' (*spreektaal*) is particularly sharp in the Netherlands, where many words can generally only be used in one domain or another, eg. written *gans, gaarne* 'whole, gladly' vs. spoken *heel, graag*.

enjoyed *de facto* status as the dominant language for most official public purposes since the seventeenth century, the French annexation of the southern Netherlands virtually eliminated Dutch as a written medium for any public purposes in the South. Even Flemish Dutch-language periodicals had to publish a French translation of each issue. The northern Netherlands was reduced to the status of a French satellite state, and it lost its key position in world trade as a result.

With the eventual defeat of Napoleon, the Congress of Vienna (1815) created a kingdom unifying the northern and southern Netherlands under the Dutch king Willem I. Working under the French Enlightenment principle of 'one land, one language', Willem introduced a radical language policy in 1823 in the Flemish-speaking areas of the South making Dutch the one official language of administration, education, and the legal system. Willem's language policy encountered stiff resistance from the outset. The northern Dutch written language, suddenly the language of all public affairs, had developed for nearly two centuries with virtually no input from the southern vernacular. As a result, it represented a language nearly as foreign to speakers of Flemish as French was, and southerners found it difficult to function in the Dutch bureaucracy and educational system. These linguistic difficulties were exacerbated by social and religious differences between North and South. The Protestant Willem's anticlerical bent aroused the ire of the Catholic clergy and, by extension, of the overwhelmingly Catholic Flemish-speaking populace. Opposition to domination by 'heathen' 'Protestant' Holland and to the imposition of the northern Dutch written language in the South eventually led to open revolt, resulting in the repartition of the Netherlands in 1831 and the creation of the Kingdom of Belgium, where French re-established itself as the dominant language in public domains.

The Belgian revolt against Dutch rule is a salutary example, in the context of this book, of the dangers of overestimating the importance of language in nationalism. In Flemish-speaking Belgium the awareness of a linguistic link with the Netherlands had remained, aided by the presence of some features of southern origin in the standard language, but this did not mean that the Flemish-speaking populace wished to be part of the Dutch nation; religious and social differences from the Netherlands proved stronger than the linguistic bonds.

It is paradoxical that the failed reunification of the Netherlands, doomed in no small part by the resistance to Willem I's linguistic policies, also gave rise to the Flemish movement spearheaded by intellectuals such as Jan Frans Willems, P. M. Blommaert, and Hendrik Conscience. Although this movement to establish Flemish, or Dutch, as the official language of Belgium remained confined to intellectual circles until the second half of the nineteenth century, the very existence of the Flemish Movement from the 1830s onwards foreshadowed the major role that language policy would play in shaping modern Belgium.

6.3. Language and Identity in the Netherlands and Belgium

6.3.1. *The Netherlands*

While it is clear that the Dutch language represents a component in the national identity of the modern Netherlands, language and language policy does not play nearly the central role that it does in Belgium. King Willem I's imposition of Dutch as the official language of his short-lived united Netherlands provides prima facie evidence that the (northern) Dutch standard language was a key element in creating a unified nation. The fact that Dutch is surrounded by three major language areas, French, English, and German, has also led to a sensitivity to extreme cultural influence from abroad. This sensitivity to exaggerated foreign influence on the Dutch language is expressed by purists who have over time reacted to overuse of French, German, and most recently English loanwords. Certainly the storm of protest that greeted Dutch Minister of Education Ritzen's suggestion that English supplant Dutch in some instances at Dutch universities in the early 1990s must also be viewed as evidence that the Dutch language serves as an important constituent of Dutch identity (see de Vries *et al.* 1994: 212). Nonetheless, the long-standing recognition that it is in the best interests of a relatively small trading nation to cultivate knowledge of foreign languages among its populace has led in the Netherlands to a rather modest estimation of the importance of Dutch among the world's languages.

6.3.2. *Frisian in the Netherlands*

The status of the Frisian language in the province of Friesland in the Netherlands has never been the focus of a strong nationalist movement comparable to the Flemish Movement in Belgium. Nevertheless, the influence of the ideas of the Romantic period led to the establishment of organizations devoted to the promotion of Frisian language and culture in the first half of the nineteenth century, the sum of which are often termed the Frisian Movement (*De Fryske Biweging*) (see Pieterson 1969; van der Schaaf 1978). This movement has always primarily promoted cultural awareness rather than political goals, but those Frisians who favour a decentralized, federal government have united in the *Fryske Nasionale Partij*, which has gained modest representation at the local level and in the provincial parliament.

While Frisian enjoys official status in the province of Friesland and fulfils essentially all of the functions of a standard language, virtually all inhabitants of the province speak Dutch as well. In the course of the twentieth century, the immigration of non-Frisian Dutch speakers and the emigration of Frisian speakers to other provinces led to a decline in the percentage of the provincial population with proficiency in the language. Speakers of Frisian nonetheless consider their language to be the strongest marker of their identity, with the vast majority of speakers whose first language is Frisian claiming that 'being Frisian' is more important to them than 'being Dutch'. On the other hand, speakers whose first language is not Frisian overwhelmingly cite 'being Dutch' as more important than 'being Frisian' (Gorter *et al.* 1988: 15, 50). Despite the positive attitudes towards Frisian of those who speak it as a first language (59 per cent of the population in 1980 according to Gorter *et al.* 1988: 30), the general comprehensibility of Dutch and the negative attitude of non-Frisians towards Frisian have led to very limited use of Frisian in the media and in other public domains.

6.3.3. *Dutch in Belgium*

The historically dominant position of French in Belgium has made the status of Flemish and, eventually, of standard Dutch a central question in Belgian identity. While the Flemish Movement gathered strength in the course of the nineteenth century, eventually resulting in laws requiring that all official documents and laws be published both in French and in Dutch, the industrialization of Wallonia lent heavy economic importance to the French-speaking provinces. During the late nineteenth century the Flemish Movement was divided between those who believed in making standard (northern) Dutch the official language of Dutch-speaking Belgium, and the particularists who favoured the development of a standard language based on southern Dutch usage, perhaps best typified by the poet Guido Gezelle (1830–99). Although standard Dutch eventually prevailed, the particularists' concerns about the suitability of the northern standard for Belgium are still reflected by Flemings' frequently ambivalent feelings toward standard Dutch.

While the language laws passed in the late nineteenth and early twentieth centuries helped to gain official status for Dutch in Belgium, it was the broadening of voting rights at the end of the nineteenth century and the establishment of universal suffrage after the First World War that gave the large working-class Flemish-speaking masses the political power to improve their lot. Nevertheless, the dominance of French persisted *de facto*. The massive losses suffered by Flemish units commanded by French-speaking officers in the First World War certainly inflamed the Flemish-speaking populace. In the areas of Belgium occupied by the Germans, a faction of the Flemish Movement collaborated with the occupiers in an effort to further their nationalistic and linguistic aspirations, while still others in the unoccupied areas, especially in the army, agitated for real equality of Dutch versus French in Belgium (Picard 1963: 53 ff.). The sudden collapse of the German army in 1918 left the Flemish Movement tainted with charges of collaboration, weakening subsequent efforts to realize its goals. The same scenario was repeated in the Second World War, though the negative effects of collaboration with the Germans lingered longer after 1945 than after the First World War (Picard 1963: 126–7).

6.3.4. *French in Belgium*

The concept of 'Wallonia' developed only during the last half of the nineteenth century as a reaction to growing Flemish nationalism. The historically local and independent orientation of Belgium's francophone provinces and their inhabitants' strong cultural orientation towards France prevented the development of a concept of Wallonia as a separate national entity until recent times. The Wallonian Movement gathered strength as the dominant position of French was eroded as a result of the language laws passed in the nineteenth and early twentieth centuries. By about 1900 there was strong sentiment favouring union of the Wallonian provinces with France, while other members of the Wallonian Movement favoured administrative separation of Flemish and francophone areas of Belgium on a federal model, complete with separate parliaments. This attitude is graphically illustrated in Jules Destrée's 'Open Letter to the King of Belgium' published in *Revue de Belgique* in 1912: 'your Majesty, permit me to speak the truth, the whole and terrible truth: there is no such thing as a Belgian . . . You reign over two peoples, there are Walloons and there are Flemings, but there are no Belgians' (Ruys 1994: 119).

While a 'Flemish problem' had existed for decades, it did not pose a serious threat to the (francophone) ruling élites in Belgium until the establishment of universal suffrage after the First World War significantly increased the political clout of the Flemish majority. In the first years after the war, the francophone élites responded to the growing Flemish challenge by questioning the loyalty of all proponents of the legislative proposals seeking to strengthen the status of Dutch in administration and education, a programme that was linked to the Flemish 'activists' who had collaborated with the Germans (Sonntag, 1991: 61–3).

In the late 1920s an important division emerged in Belgium's francophone population. Wallonians began to demand official monolingualism for the provinces of Wallonia, while the francophone élite in Brussels and Flanders continued to favour official bilingualism in administration and education, which in turn would protect the use of French in Flanders. Paradoxically, this division brought the goals of the Wallonian Movement into line with those of the Flemish Movement: territorially based monolingualism for Flanders and Wallonia. As a result, three major factions engaged in the resolution of the linguistic situation in Belgium. The administrative and education laws of 1932 set the stage for the eventual tripartite federalism established in the 1960s, with official monolingualism in Flanders and Wallonia and official bilingualism in Brussels (for extensive discussion see Sonntag, 1991: 25–47).

A key point in the programme of the Wallonian Movement was the steadfast rejection of the bilingual administration of the country. In the francophone areas the populace wished to remain under monolingual French-speaking administration. This insistence on monolingual administration set the tone for the development of the eventual Belgian federal structure. After the First World War, the concept of monolingual administration in Flemish areas was appropriated by Dutch speakers as well.

At the end of the Second World War the *Congrès National Wallon* was established as a permanent organ for defending the status of French in Belgium. While there was strong support for union with France in 1945, the leadership of the Wallonian Movement moved away from the concept of secession from Belgium towards a federal structure characterized by monolingual administration.

6.3.5. *Belgium Today*

Nelde's Law states that there 'can be no language contact without language conflict' (Nelde 1996: 294). Resolution of the problem of language conflict in Belgium, therefore, has demanded the official minimization of language contact by establishing the territorial principle, thus satisfying the demands of Wallonians and Flemings, while still protecting the linguistic interests of the francophone minority in Flanders and the large francophone population of Brussels.

In the period from 1963 to 1993 the status of Dutch in Belgium was finally legally settled, with Dutch established as the official language in the provinces of East and West Flanders, Antwerp, Limburg, and northern Brabant and with French as the official language in the provinces of Hainaut, Namur, (Belgian) Luxembourg, Liège, and southern Brabant. Along the linguistic border numerous enclaves are either officially Dutch- or French-speaking, but have official facilities for large linguistic minorities (see de Vries *et al.* 1994: 214). Brussels, the capital, with roughly 10 per cent of the country's population, is officially bilingual, though standard Dutch is making inroads in what was earlier in the twentieth century a primarily French-speaking populace.

Although the legislation of 1962–3 precisely defined the administrative linguistic border between unilingual Flanders and Wallonia, the implementation of the territoriality principle took more than a decade. Since 1971 Belgium has been territorially divided into four Linguistic Regions: Dutch-speaking, French-speaking, bilingual (Brussels), and the small German-speaking region along the eastern border. However, citizens are also recognized as belonging to one of three Linguistic Communities (Dutch-speaking, French-speaking, or German-speaking), regardless of where they live. Nelde (1996: 295) provides a clear typology of the results of Belgian linguistic policy, distinguishing four types of linguistic territories:

1. monolinguistic territories subject to strict unilingualism (Flanders and Wallonia with Dutch and French respectively);
2. bilingual Brussels, where Dutch and French both have their own linguistic infrastructure;
3. monolinguistic territories with special linguistic facilities along the linguistic border to protect Flemish, French, and German minority populations;
4. monolingual territories without special accommodations for linguistic minorities; this situation is limited to German-speaking areas in Belgian Luxembourg, where French serves as the sole administrative language.

While the introduction of this Belgian federalist structure with clearly defined linguistic regulations has taken the edge off the frequently very contentious relations between Flemings and Wallonians, the potential for language conflict resulting from language contact remains in territories of types 2, 3, and 4 above. As a result, the question of language, nationalisms and identity will continue to play a central role in Belgian politics and in the formulation of cultural policy for the foreseeable future.

6.4. Conclusions

The development of Dutch has some interesting lessons for the study of the interrelations of language and nationalism. It reminds us how standardizing processes are influenced by economic and social factors, as well as by political factors such as nationalism.

The role of Dutch in national identity also shows how a shared language is far from being a sufficient condition for the growth of a shared national identity; Netherlanders and Flemings, although both using Dutch, unquestionably belong to different nations.

The Low Countries also provide an interesting contrast with regard to the role of language in national identity. In the Netherlands, early formation of a nation-state assured the primacy of Dutch as an official language. The strong position of Dutch in the North has made it only one of many factors contributing to Dutch national identity. In Belgium, on the other hand, the centuries-long subordination of Flemish to French resulted in the growth of a Flemish national movement whose central demands revolved around linguistic questions.

The situation in Belgium suggests that the resolution of long-standing linguistic conflicts within existing political entities may depend crucially on decentralization of political authority. Only this type of relaxation of central authority affords segments of the population that define themselves in linguistic terms a tolerable degree of control over their own affairs.

While the influence of, say, American culture and the potential homogenizing effect of the EU leave many speakers of Dutch wondering about the future of their language in the face of competition from more powerful languages, its status seems secure. The awareness in both countries of the importance of the Dutch language to the maintenance of cultural and national identity finds expression in the establishment in 1982 of the binational Dutch Linguistic Union (*Nederlandse Taalunie*), whose increasingly vigorous initiatives promote the interests of the Dutch language both in Belgium and the Netherlands and also abroad.

7.

Germany, Austria, Switzerland, Luxembourg: The Total Coincidence of Nations and Speech Communities?

STEPHEN BARBOUR

7.1. The Area

The area under consideration in this chapter corresponds very roughly indeed to the German-speaking area in Europe. More precisely, it corresponds to those states in which the majority of the population has German as its mother tongue.

In the context of a discussion of language and nationalism, even an apparently simple statement like the last one requires extensive qualification. First of all, the states in question represent only those in which a majority of the population are native German-speakers; minorities of German-speakers can be found in numerous other states (see Chapters 3, 5, 6, 8, 9, 10, and 12).

Secondly, there are important differences between the states in the position of German as a majority language. In the case of Germany and Austria (and Liechtenstein[1]), German is a majority language in a straightforward sense; in virtually all communities in these states, exceptions being perhaps a few small isolated communities in the peripheral regions of North Friesland and Lusatia (Germany), and in Burgenland and Carinthia (Austria), a clear majority of the population would consider themselves to be native-speakers of German (*Deutsch*). Even in the peripheral regions mentioned, a clear majority of adults have, objectively, a native command of German, even if they do not consider themselves to be native-speakers. It is important to note, however, that Austria and Germany are certainly not monolingual states; there are substantial minorities, particularly in the larger towns, of native-speakers of other languages. But the subjective perception both within and outside the two states is of monolingual German-speaking territories; German is the only language that plays any role in national identity.

---

[1] Given its small size, there will not be any further explicit discussion of the situation in Liechtenstein; it resembles Austria in most respects in questions of language and nationalism.

In contrast to its status in Germany and Austria, German in Switzerland, although the language with the largest number of speakers, is a majority language only in part of the state, admittedly in the major part. Moreover, in most of the areas where it is not the majority language, other languages—French in the west of the country, and Italian in the canton of Tessin/Ticino—enjoy clear majority status. This is particularly true of French; Italian-speakers at times have felt their language to be under pressure from German. French even enjoys high status among German-speakers, many of them having a good command of it. There is a real sense then in which these non-German-speaking areas of Switzerland belong to French-speaking and Italian-speaking Europe respectively, and not to the German-speaking area; their inclusion in this chapter is justified solely by the fact that German-speakers do constitute a numerical majority in the Swiss state as a whole, and that speakers of French and of Italian do encounter the use of German in Swiss institutions, and can under certain circumstances derive great advantage from a knowledge of the language (see Russ 1987: 94–100; Barbour and Stevenson 1990: 204–12).

German, French, and Italian are all 'national languages' in Switzerland. In contrast to these three, the fourth national language, Romansh, spoken only in the canton of Grisons/Graubünden, has clear minority status in its region; all of its speakers find that they have to acquire a fluent command of German, the major-ity language of the canton (see Billigmeier 1979: *passim*). Given the obvious multi-lingual nature of the Swiss state, German does not play a clear part in Swiss national identity.

The inclusion of Luxembourg in this chapter is problematic; it is justified by the fact that the majority native language, Luxembourgish (*Lëtzebuergesch*) is in a sense closer to German than it is to any other major European language; German dialectology classifies it as a Central Franconian German dialect (see G. Newton 1990). This closeness is recognized by speakers of Luxembourgish, who have generally been prepared to use German in many formal and written registers (see G. Newton 1987); virtually the entire adult native population of Luxembourg has a good passive knowledge of German, and very many have a good active knowl-edge. Luxembourg is then, in a sense, a German-speaking country. The situation is, however, complex; Luxembourgers, unlike the Swiss-Germans, do not refer to their native language as *Deutsch* (even though it is arguably closer to the standard German of Germany than Swiss-German is), and Luxembourg also employs French for very many purposes (see Kloss 1978: 105–16; G. Newton 1987; Barbour and Stevenson 1990: 230–4).

This chapter is then concerned with a group of states that correspond, but only very approximately, to German-speaking Europe.

7.2. The Languages

The major language of the area is, of course, German. However, this statement is deceptive in its simplicity; the German language is, in all kinds of ways, a highly problematic construct. While there is a clear and demonstrable relationship between all the dialects that are described as 'German', in traditional terms they all belong to the West Germanic branch of the Germanic subfamily of the Indo-European language family, they are nevertheless so diverse that communication between speakers of different dialects can be almost impossible (a good picture of the diversity is provided in Russ 1989). At the same time communication in non-technical registers may be easy between speakers of north-western German dialects and speakers of neighbouring Dutch dialects (see Lockwood 1976: 188–9).

Most of the other languages of the area have speakers in other European states, and are treated in the discussion of those states. This category, of course, includes languages of modern immigrant populations; numerically significant are Turkish, Greek, Serbian, Croatian, Italian, Spanish, and Portuguese. Also in this category are languages at the margins of the area that are also spoken in neighbouring states: Danish in Germany; Slovene, Croatian, and Hungarian in Austria. French and Italian in Switzerland can also be placed in this category, but they are, of course, national languages of Switzerland, and majority languages in their areas of Switzerland, and are hence in a fundamentally different position from the languages at the margins of Germany and Austria, which clearly have minority status in every sense. There is a case for saying that Romansh in Switzerland and North Frisian in Germany are languages with speakers in other European states, but the position here is more complex; both of these are related to languages in neighbouring states but not as obviously as Danish, Slovene, Croatian, and Hungarian are. In the Frisian and Romansh cases there is no standard form shared with the varieties across the border, and mutual comprehensibility may be low.

In the Romansh case there is no single standard form within Switzerland, and the related varieties in northern Italy, known as Ladin and Friulian, do not share with it a popular name in any language, though in specialized registers 'Rhaeto-Romance' (German *Rätoromanisch*) is used to designate all of these varieties. Some varieties of Romansh in Switzerland are occasionally referred to as 'Ladin'.

In the North Frisian case the argument that the language has speakers in a neighbouring state, in this case the Netherlands, is even weaker. First, North Frisian itself is highly internally diverse, with low mutual comprehensibility between mainland dialects and the dialects of the islands of Sylt, Föhr, and Amrum, and even within this small area there is no popular shared name for the language among its speakers; while it is known among its speakers on the mainland as Frisian (*Frasch* or similar, German *Friesisch*), on the islands it is referred to by its speakers simply by a local island name—for example, *Sölring* on Sylt. If we look now to the related variety in the Netherlands, West Frisian, we find that mutual comprehensibility between the North Frisian of Germany and West Frisian is very low, but there is a certain sense of shared Frisian identity; however, this is also shared to an extent by the East Frisians of the North Sea coast area of the German province of Lower Saxony (*Niedersachsen*), but their language is not Frisian, Low German and High German having been established here centuries ago, although a Frisian dialect (East Frisian/*Ostfriesisch* or *Saterländisch*) does survive in part of the Oldenburg region just to the south of East Friesland (see Lockwood 1976: 214–34; Feitsma *et al.* 1987).

Although it is related to the neighbouring Polish, and even though some mutual comprehension is possible, the Slavonic language Sorbian, spoken in Lusatia (in the modern provinces of Brandenburg and Saxony), is never considered to be Polish; until 1945 the two languages had been separated for centuries by German-speaking territory, Sorbian-speakers, unlike Polish-speakers, having been under uninterrupted political control by German-speakers since the Middle Ages (see Stone 1972; Barbour and Stevenson, 1998: 282–8).

The separation of minority languages into those with speakers elsewhere and those with no speakers in other states is not a trivial distinction; minority languages with native-speakers elsewhere, particularly where the language has majority status elsewhere, are less vulnerable, since they can receive moral and material support from their other 'homes', and are more likely to have officially recognized standard forms, which increase their prestige, and which can lead to use in a wider range of registers. Minority languages often suffer seriously from the lack of a generally accepted standard, and the minority languages of the German-speaking area are no exception here; while speakers of Danish, Croatian, Slovene, and Hungarian can look to standardized norms for their languages in the neighbouring territories where they have majority status, Sorbian has two written standards, North Frisian has rival standards for four dialect areas (the mainland, Sylt, Föhr, and Amrum), and Romansh no fewer than six. As we have seen, Italian and French in Switzerland are not true minority languages in any case, and moreover reap the benefits of the full standardization, very high prestige, and large numbers of speakers of those languages in Italy and in the French-speaking world respectively.

7.3. The Major Language: German

German is distinguished from most of the other languages of the area by irreducible linguistic differences; the Slavonic languages Sorbian, Croatian, and Slovene, and the Romance languages Romansh, Italian, and French belong to other subfamilies of the Indo-European language family, which means that scholars are able to prove that they share a common origin with German, but this common origin lies so far in the past that the contemporary languages share no striking similarities that are obvious to the layperson. Hungarian is described as belonging to a different language family, Uralic, and exhibits marked and obvious differences from German. All of these languages have, however, been in contact with German for centuries, resulting in lexical borrowings, particularly from Romance languages into German and, to a rather lesser extent, from German into Slavonic languages and Hungarian (there are also words of Slavonic and Hungarian origin in German). These borrowings, and the fact that there is an extensive lexicon of Latin and Greek origin in all of these languages as well as in German, means that speakers of German may understand odd words in all of the languages, but wide divergences in the basic vocabulary, coupled with markedly different morphology and syntax, mean that there is no significant mutual comprehensibility. Romance and Slavonic languages, and Hungarian, are unambiguously foreign languages from the point of view of the German-speaker.

When we turn to the other Germanic languages of the area, Danish and North Frisian, we find a rather different situation; much of the basic vocabulary is clearly related in some sense or other, and there are striking parallels in areas of the morphology (for example, all three have a system of 'strong' verbs, displaying vowel changes between present and past tenses, like the English *sing, sang, sung*); moreover, Danish and North Frisian have been strongly influenced by German, leading to parallels even in more esoteric vocabulary. However, mutual comprehensibility is low between German and these two languages. Despite a very obvious relationship, there are some significant differences even in basic vocabulary, and clear morphological and syntactic differences. Even in related items of vocabulary the differences in sounds are often so great as to impair seriously the possibility of comprehension; we can, for example, compare North Frisian *serk* with German *Kirche* (church) and Danish *to* with German *zwei* (two), where the spelling differences give a fair idea of the scale of the pronunciation differences.

Our task of understanding the pattern of language use in the area would be simpler if, when we turned our attention to the majority language, to German, we were faced by a relatively homogeneous language, whose varieties were clearly mutually comprehensible. We could then state that German was obviously a single language, and that North Frisian and Danish were clearly distinct, though related, from the point of view of the German-speaker, we could then proceed to a straightforward enumeration of the languages of the area, and to a discussion of their roles in national or ethnic identities. Unfortunately things are not so simple. In the case of German we encounter a group of dialects that are generally considered to be a single language, but where certain dialects and dialect groups are considered by some of their speakers to constitute separate languages. We also encounter a group of dialects in which comprehensibility between different dialects is very low in some cases, often lower than it is elsewhere between different languages.[2]

There is nevertheless apparently a majority consensus that this group of dialects is a single language. Why is this so? Looking first at criteria of a linguistic rather than a social nature, we can, of course, say that the dialects in question are related to each other, that there are clear linguistic correspondences, such as a high

---

[2] Mutual intelligibility of language varieties is, of course, in itself a highly complex concept. It is partly dependent on the objective characteristics of the varieties concerned, partly dependent on the willingness of their speakers to understand each other. This may, in turn, depend on whether or not they share ethnic or national identities.

degree of correspondence between lexical items, and that there are morphological and syntactic similarities. However, as we have already seen, this kind of similarity is also found between related but distinct languages; the languages within the Germanic subfamily, such as German, Danish, North Frisian, and even English, resemble each other in these kinds of ways. There is a copious literature on the complex issues involved in collective decisions as to whether a variety is an independent language or a dialect of some more widely spoken language; in the context of Germanic languages the work of Heinz Kloss is highly informative (see Kloss 1967; 1978: esp. 23–89).

Perhaps those dialects that are considered to be German resemble each other more strongly than do dialects which belong to different languages. Sadly this turns out not to be clearly the case. The linguistic similarities between Low German dialects from north-west Germany and Dutch dialects are almost certainly greater than the similarities between Low German dialects and Upper German dialects from South Germany, Austria, and Switzerland. Given this circumstance one could argue either that Low German is a form of Dutch rather than of German, or that Dutch is a form of German. The latter argument does not stand up to close scrutiny (see Chapter 6); although the degree of mutual comprehensibility can be quite high between Dutch and Low German dialects, there are considerable sheer linguistic differences between Dutch and standard German and between Dutch and most German dialects. However, are Low German dialects forms of Dutch? A case can be made for this, since standard Dutch is relatively close to Low German dialects, but political, social, and cultural considerations rule it out; the notion that Low German dialects are dialects of Dutch is almost universally rejected by their speakers. We could, of course, argue that Low German is a language in its own right, and this is indeed the position of some of its speakers, but there is no consensus among scholars that this is so, and until the late twentieth century it was probably true that most sociolinguists regarded it on social and political grounds as a group of German dialects. However, it has now been accorded the status of a regional minority language by the EU. It will be noticed that even here, where I am trying to argue the case for the status of varieties on purely linguistic criteria, the discussion has moved to matters of politics and society; this is highly significant. Continuing to attempt to look at the situation from a purely linguistic point of view, we can see that one reason for describing the German dialects as a single language is that they do form a continuum: that is to say, within the continuous German-speaking area there is a gradual change in traditional dialect from village to village all the way from Schleswig-Holstein on the Danish border to German-speaking South Tyrol in Italy. Frisian and Danish are not part of this continuum: there is an abrupt change in dialects at the border between them and the Low German dialects, a fact that reinforces their status as distinct languages. Unfortunately, however, the existence of the continuum turns out to be no argument for the status of German as a single language, since the dialects of many distinct languages form continua.[3] This is true of the continuous area of Slavonic speech including Polish, Czech, Slovak, Belorussian, Ukrainian, and Russian, and of the continuous Romance area including French, Occitan, Italian, Catalan, Castilian Spanish, and Portuguese, which is certainly not a candidate for consideration as a single language. In the German case, the continuum includes Dutch, and so its existence does not strengthen the case for considering the German dialects to be one language.

It turns out in fact to be extremely difficult to argue the case for the existence of a single German language, subsuming all the German dialects, on purely linguistic criteria, and indeed the notion of 'purely linguistic criteria' is itself open to serious question. We therefore now turn to social and political criteria. The first criterion for regarding the German dialects as a single language is the existence alongside all of them of a single standard language, which is regarded by speakers of all the dialects as, in some sense 'the same language' as their native dialect. The coexistence of a standard language and dialects does influence the linguistic characteristics of the dialects (here we see the impossibility of separating social and political criteria from linguistic ones); over time dialects will usually receive a great deal of linguistic influence from the standard language and indeed may be replaced by forms that can be regarded either as standard or as intermediate between dialect and standard. This process is far advanced in much of the German-speaking area (see Barbour and Stevenson 1990: 133–80). In contrast, the minority languages of the area are clearly regarded by their speakers, even where they are proficient in standard German, to be languages distinct from standard German; this even applies to the Germanic languages North Frisian and Danish. However, it also applies, though not quite so clearly, to Luxembourgish, Swiss-German, and, for some of its speakers, Low German. The contemporary attitude of Luxembourgers to standard German, even to the characteristic Luxembourg variety of standard German, which differs a little from the standard German of Germany, seems to be that it is in some ill-defined sense foreign. Moreover, Luxembourgish does possess its own rival codified standard written form, and to a certain extent a standard spoken form, even though the uses of this are rather restricted (see G. Newton 1987).

Although there is dialect writing, German-speaking Switzerland, in contrast to Luxembourg, lacks a codified standard form that is clearly and unambiguously separate from the standard used in Germany. Because of its fairly clear lexical characteristics, the written standard German of Switzerland can usually be fairly easily recognized as a Swiss variety, but its users (and it is their only widespread written medium) nevertheless perceive it in some sense as 'German'—that is, as not Swiss. Spoken standard Swiss-German is even more clearly recognizable as Swiss and yet its users feel it to be foreign, or German, in some sense; this feeling

---

[3] In some of the cases cited continua may in recent centuries have become disrupted at political borders where dialects have been influenced by the respective standard languages.

is so strong that its use is now more or less restricted to communications with Germans and Austrians, or to certain learned or specialized registers. Its use in an informal conversation between Swiss-Germans would be held to show disloyalty to Switzerland (see Barbour and Stevenson 1990: 204–17; Russ 1987).[4]

In purely linguistic terms Low German dialects differ very substantially from standard German, and it is partly for this reason that at least some of their speakers consider them to represent a distinct language (see above). However, their use is very much more limited than that of Swiss-German and Luxembourgish, being largely confined to informal spoken registers (though some writing and broadcasting are to be found), and they very clearly coexist with standard German; indeed, the most prestigious variety of standard German is found in the same geographical regions as Low German, and there is no sense in which speakers of Low German dialects regard standard German as foreign.

To sum up, the limits of German can actually be described as vague, although the very diverse central and southern dialects of German in Germany and Austria are unambiguously a single language. Swiss-German, Luxembourgish, and Low German, particularly Luxembourgish, have some, but not all, of the characteristics of independent languages. Dutch, linguistically close to Low German, has the clear social, political, and cultural characteristics of an independent language, and North Frisian, while existing alongside standard German, is linguistically relatively remote from it, and not part of the German dialect continuum. Danish is, on grounds of linguistic distinctness, separateness from the dialect continuum, and independent standardization, clearly a distinct language from German.

7.4. Language and Identity in German-Speaking Europe

7.4.1. *The Interdependence of Language and Identity*

Given the extreme diversity of German dialects, the acceptance of a single standard language by their speakers, and the concomitant acceptance that all of these dialects are 'German', can be explained only by some sense of shared identity on the part of the speakers of those dialects. Elsewhere much less diverse dialects—for example, Scandinavian dialects—are considered to be a number of languages (see Chapter 5). What, however, is the nature of this shared identity? Is it quite simply a national identity? The case for a national identity shared by all speakers of German is not easy to make. Today people who share a national identity generally aspire to be citizens of a single nation-state, but this does not apply to all German-speakers. To an extent Germany sees itself as a kind of homeland for all German-speakers—it is to Germany rather than to Austria that the vast majority of 'Germans' have 'returned' from central and eastern Europe and the former Soviet Union in recent years—but a policy of uniting all German-speakers into a

---

[4] For a very detailed account of attitudes to dialects and the standard language, and of the complex differences in such attitudes between the German-speaking countries, see Ammon (1995).

single state is not advocated by any mainstream political party in Germany. While speakers of German or of German dialects in some other European states do share a sense of German identity, which has expressed itself as a desire to be citizens of a German state, this is very variable. It has often been true to the east of the main German-speaking area, but in the south, west, and north it has been weak or non-existent in the last few decades. Until the 1970s German-speakers in South Tyrol in Italy often expressed a desire to be united with Austria (not Germany), but speakers of German in Alsace-Lorraine in France have often shown strong anti-German sentiments in the last hundred years, and displayed resentment at their incorporation into the German Reich in 1871 (see Schieder 1992: esp. 201–3). Despite using dialects or languages that are German, or at least very close to German, Luxembourgers and Swiss-Germans do not now share a German identity.

Austrian identity is, in contrast, clearly 'German' in some sense or other; Austria is, and sees itself as, a German-speaking country, and yet, since the Second World War, a majority of Austrians have come to accept a distinct Austrian identity, distinct from that of Germany (for discussion of the complexities of Austrian identity, see Pelinka 1990).

The fact that there has never been a state uniting all German-speakers, and that many of them in the past and in the present have not desired such a state, makes the case for postulating a common national identity linking speakers of the language difficult to argue. In Germany itself this has led to considerable currency for the concept of the *Kulturnation*, the nation united only by a common culture, as distinct from the *Staatsnation*, the nation united by a state; many nations of Eastern Europe, such as Poland or Romania, defined by a common culture in the absence, until 1918, of political independence, would be examples of the former, while west European nations, such as France or Britain, in which national identities were arguably forged in considerable measure by the state's institutions, would be examples of the latter. In this line of argument, the German-speaking area can be seen as an example of the *Kulturnation* (see e.g. Dann, 1993: 36–8).

Postulating that the German-speaking area represents a *Kulturnation* does not, however, solve the problem as to why German is considered to be a single language. The argument becomes circular: German is a single language because its speakers share a single national identity; they share a single national identity because they belong to a single *Kulturnation*; they belong to a single *Kulturnation* because they share cultural characteristics; the most noticeable shared cultural characteristic is the shared language. In fact, other than the language, shared cultural characteristics, which are not also shared by other Central European populations, are very hard to establish, in the absence, for example, of a shared religious identity.

In German-speaking Europe, we hence find the highly complex phenomenon of a national identity defined in large measure by a shared language, while, at the same time, that shared language is demarcated from other languages—Dutch, the 'partly German' Luxembourgish and Swiss-German—by differing national identities. The high degree to which the notion of a German language and German national identity depend on each other is not clearly paralleled elsewhere; other languages that have defined nations (*Kulturnationen*) in the absence of political independence tend to be either more homogeneous than German (Polish, for example) or more clearly demarcated from neighbouring languages (Hungarian or Romanian are good examples here). Other nations that are highly linguistically or culturally diverse (with either a number of different languages, or dialectally fragmented major languages) are more clearly separated from other nations by the simple facts of physical geography; the sea and the Alps separate Italy rather well from its neighbours, and Spain is separated by the sea and the Pyrenees from all neighbours but Portugal, although these two cases do, of course, display complexities of their own (see Chapters 4 and 8). As I have argued elsewhere (see Barbour 1991, 1992, 1993), the great importance of the German language as a mark of national identity possibly reflects the fact that a Continental West Germanic ethnic group emerged during the Middle Ages demarcated by language, but demarcated in a rather negative way as those inhabitants of the Holy Roman Empire (*Heiliges römisches Reich deutscher Nation*) who did not speak Romance or Slavonic languages. A rather negative definition was possible since the élite of this ethnic group was held together by a common interest as, in a sense, the ruling group in the Empire, and also since the non-Germanic groups, particularly Romance-speakers in Italy and Slavonic-speakers in Bohemia, developed strong non-German ethnic and local identities. The Continental West Germanic ethnic group was very large compared to others, and it could well have given rise to several smaller ethnic groups, which would have been comparable in size to, say, the neighbouring Slavonic-speaking ethnic groups such as the Poles and the Czechs. Given the high diversity of its language, and the group's increasing cultural and political fragmentation, it is indeed surprising that it did not develop into a number of different ethnic groups, speaking what would have been considered to be a number of different languages, which then, with the modern development of the nation, would have become a number of different nations. What has in fact happened has varied greatly between different parts of the area. Non-Germanic languages in the old territory of the Holy Roman Empire are obviously considered distinct from German, and have become part of the basis for clearly distinct nations, the Czechs and the Italians, with Romance dialects to the west of Germanic being considered French dialects, and their speakers becoming part of the French nation, or the complex Belgian nation (see Chapter 6). Non-Germanic languages with a very small number of speakers, Romansh and Sorbian, contributed to the distinctiveness of small ethnic groups, whose modern status as nations can be argued—and sometimes is (see e.g. Stone 1972).

Within the area of Continental West Germanic speech, one area became clearly distinct in both language and national identity: the Netherlands. In my view the Netherlands represents the typical European development of a modern nation, both in terms of its size and its partly linguistic basis; its much larger German neighbour is untypical in its size and its linguistic heterogeneity.

7.4.2. *Frisian Language and Identity*

Another Continental West Germanic region, now split into three smaller areas, the Frisian dialect areas, retained or developed a sense of distinctiveness, and its speech is indeed often not considered part of Continental West Germanic. The authority of the Holy Roman Empire seems to have been weak here for long periods, and the feudal system seems to have been incompletely imposed, resulting in the growth of semi-independent peasant republics (see Feitsma *et al.* 1987). A political border, greatly fostered by the isolation and remoteness of the area from the centres of princely and imperial power, hence developed between Frisian dialects and neighbouring Dutch or Low German dialects, which reinforced and maintained existing linguistic differences. The Frisian dialects hence gave rise to what is considered a distinct West Germanic language (or languages). In Germany the North Frisian area came under Danish political control for a period, and the language was influenced by Danish, which reinforced its distinctness from the rest of Continental West Germanic. The question of North Frisian national or ethnic identity is complex. It has generally been considered that, despite speaking a distinct language, Frisian-speakers share a German identity; but now Frisian-speakers will refer to non-Frisian-speakers as *Deutsche* (Germans), with the converse implication that Frisian-speakers are not *Deutsche* (Alastair Walker, personal communication).

7.4.3. *Identity and Language in Switzerland*

Another area that, in the Middle Ages, was peripheral and remote, that escaped the imposition of classic forms of feudalism, and that was rather similarly organized into independent peasant republics, was the core area of what is now German-speaking Switzerland. While the Frisian dialect area ultimately lost its political independence, being absorbed by the Netherlands or by German principalities, in German-speaking Switzerland political independence was maintained, and the Swiss state expanded to absorb non-German-speaking areas (see Russ 1987). Unlike Friesland, it was not at the outset linguistically very different from neighbouring German-speaking areas, and its people did not in the Middle Ages have a sense of speaking a distinct language. When, in the nineteenth century, language became regarded as a prime symbol of national identity, Switzerland might have developed a sense of clear linguistic distinctiveness, but a number of factors militated against this. First, standard German was already established as the written language (albeit a Swiss variant of this), and until German unification in 1871 did not represent the language of a distinctively different and potentially threatening neighbouring state; it was, rather, the language of a highly diverse area, being used by a whole host of different German-speaking states. Also by the nineteenth century Switzerland was a multilingual state, and hence had no motivation to promote its variety of

German as a distinct Swiss language. In the twentieth century, however, particularly since the Nazi period and the Second World War, a German identity was seen as undesirable for the Swiss, and this led, as we have seen, to Swiss-German acquiring many, but not all, of the characteristics of an independent language. German-speaking Swiss now potentially enjoy at least two kinds of identity: a multilingual pan-Swiss national identity, linked to the state and its institutions, and to an Alpine way of life, and a Swiss-German identity, which often has more of a local or cantonal focus, linked to the use of Swiss-German dialect. The use of standard German is a matter of convenience rather than identity, although there is a vaguer kind of loyalty to the German-speaking literary culture on the part of the intelligentsia (see Ammon 1995: *passim*, esp. 229–316).

7.4.4. *Language and Identity in Luxembourg*

Until the nineteenth century Luxembourg was one of the many German-speaking principalities, although it bordered on French-speaking territory, and hence the aristocratic use of French, common throughout the German-speaking world, probably extended further into other strata in society. For complex dynastic reasons it did not form part of the united Germany of 1871, but acquired and maintained the status of an independent state. This political independence, coupled with the continuing use of French in certain formal registers, has maintained its linguistic distinctiveness, but this was undoubtedly fostered by anti-German feeling. Although standard German, again in a local form, is used for many purposes in Luxembourg, the Luxembourgers' modern insistence that their native speech is a distinct language, and the independent standardization of the language, owe much to the animosity generated by the invading Germans in both world wars, who simply insisted that Luxembourgish was a German dialect, and that Luxembourgers must use German for all official purposes. Luxembourg's national identity is linked to the use of Luxembourgish, the use of standard German being, as in the Swiss case, a matter of convenience and not identity (see G. Newton 1987). Those for whom a literary culture has a significance for identity share in both French and German traditions.

7.4.5. *Language and Identity in Germany and Austria*

Only after the battle of Königgrätz between Prussia and Austria in 1866 did the establishment of a clearly non-German Austrian identity begin. Until then Austria was simply one of the many German-speaking states, though it did have a special position in controlling much more non-German-speaking territory than any other German state, making it perhaps in a sense less German than other states. Yet, on the other hand, until the dissolution of the Holy Roman Empire in 1806, the Austrian archdukes had simultaneously been Holy Roman Emperors for 500 years. Given that the clear separation between Germany and Austria is a relatively recent development, there is, not surprisingly, a considerable amount of common ground between the two states in matters of language and identity. As we have seen above, the area covered by modern Germany and Austria is remarkable in that, at least until the latter part of the nineteenth century, there was only one ethnic or national identity shared by all of the German-speaking population of this vast area, much larger than almost all other language areas in Europe, despite the lack of other common cultural characteristics apart from the language, and despite the enormous diversity of the language, considerably greater than the diversity of what, elsewhere, are considered to be groups of related but distinct languages. It is not easy to determine why distinct languages and distinct national identities failed to develop within the area. Perhaps the most one can say was that such a development was hindered by the persistence until the early nineteenth century of a single state of a kind, the Holy Roman Empire, and by the fact that alternative, smaller political units failed to develop distinctive cultural character-istics, or were simply too small, and too mutually dependent, to develop a sense of distinctiveness.

A crucial factor was the development from the fifteenth to the seventeenth centuries of a single standard language covering the entire area. The standard developed at a time when the common political unit, the Empire, was still reason-ably effective, and, crucially, it took hold most firmly in those areas that were Protestant in religion, which included most of the area where Low German dialects, the dialects linguistically furthest from the standard, were spoken. Some of the German states could have been, in terms of size and population, candidates to become distinct nations; Prussia and Austria certainly fall into this category, Saxony and Bavaria almost certainly, and possibly also Hanover. However, Prussia and Hanover had a great deal in common, being Protestant and largely using Low German dialects; they both adopted the standard language early (the contempo-rary standard is close to middle-class Hanoverian speech), despite the fact that linguistically the standard owed much to the speech of a third largely Protestant state, Saxony, where the dialects were High German. The standard, however, also displayed many Bavarian and Austrian characteristics, although Catholic Bavaria was slower to adopt it, and non-standard dialects even today enjoy higher prestige in Bavaria and elsewhere in the South than they do in the North. Linguistically Austria is relatively close to Bavaria, and is also Catholic, and the pattern of adop-tion of the standard was similar here (see Barbour and Stevenson 1990: 36–51). To sum up, none of the major candidates for the development of distinct linguistic, ethnic, and national status was sufficiently different from all of the others for this to happen.

In the nineteenth century a consensus developed that none of the German states was a distinct nation, and that national identity resided on the level of the entire German-speaking area, and ultimately a united state was established in 1871 based on a pan-German identity. However, there were certainly strong loyalties to the smaller predecessor states, and, since the German Empire of 1871 excluded Austria, it had a conscious policy of fostering loyalty to its state institutions, to its own *Staatsnation*, rather than to the *Kulturnation* of the entire German-speaking world (for an interesting account of the conflicts that this presented, see Dann 1992). Although the German Empire aspired to be a *Staatsnation*, its ultimate political legitimacy rested on its being a federation of states sharing a language. This implied a fundamental contradiction in its relationship with Austria; on the one hand, the German Empire's ethnic–linguistic basis dictated that it should include the German-speaking area of Austria; on the other hand, the unwillingness of the Austrian ruling house to relinquish its vast non-German-speaking territories would have meant that a German state incorporating all of Austria's possessions would have been virtually deprived of its ethnic-linguistic basis: it would have included millions of speakers of other languages. In view of this insoluble dilemma, the Prussian government under Bismarck adopted the *kleindeutsche Lösung*, the solution of a 'small' Germany (still larger than almost any other European state) under Prussian leadership and excluding Austria.

Since 1871 there has been a continued tension between political movements that have attempted to foster national identities focused on the various different Germanspeaking states, and movements stressing the unity of all German-speakers.

The political leadership of Austria has, since the Second World War, successfully promoted a distinct Austrian national identity, with some of its basis being provided by loyalty to distinct Austrian forms of German. There has, however, been no serious attempt to promote the notion of a distinct Austrian language, although for a while after the establishment of the modern Republic the native language classes in school were labelled *Muttersprache* (native language), rather than *Deutsch* (German). The nature of modern Austrian identity is complex. On the one hand, apart from sections of the extreme right—for example, in the Freedom Party of Austria (*Freiheitspartei Österreichs*)—there is no significant desire for political unification with Germany, and the German state and its inhabitants can arouse quite negative responses from Austrians. On the other hand, as well as identification with the state and its institutions, Austrians do often see a strong link between their Austrian national identity and their status as nativespeakers of German; this is witnessed by often strongly negative attitudes to speakers of other languages, such as the Slovene-speaking minority in Carinthia. At the linguistic level, there is even some sort of contradictory and ambivalent acceptance that the German of Germany represents a kind of norm, to which Austrians should aspire (see Clyne 1995: 31–41).[5]

In the German Empire and its successor state the Weimar Republic, between 1871 and 1933, governments were generally concerned to foster national identification based on loyalty to the state and its institutions; on the other hand, there was an awareness that a common language and a common culture were the most important bonds uniting the nation, and there was a considerable political concern with language. This often took the form of purism, of a desire to remove supposedly 'foreign' words from the language (see Ameri 1991), a sometimes futile

---

[5] For a detailed account of Austrian attitudes to German, see Ammon (1995: passim, esp. 117–227).

activity, and one with a highly questionable theoretical basis, as Alan Kirkness has often demonstrated (see e.g. in Kirkness 1984, 1993).

The Nazi regime from 1933 to 1945 represented, in a sense, the total victory of a cultural and linguistic nationalism; it was the first state with the political unification of all Germans as its express aim, an aim that it almost achieved. While 'Germans' in the sense that it intended can be defined only in terms of culture and language, the German language and German culture are highly nebulous entities (even more debate is possible about the characteristics of German culture than about the nature of the language), and could not well serve the purposes of a populist authoritarian movement. It therefore bolstered, even eclipsed, the factors of culture and language with appeals to 'race' and 'blood', unifying factors of highly questionable validity, which nevertheless have a strongly emotive appeal, and it turned from purging foreign words from the language, to expelling, imprisoning, and exterminating people of supposedly alien race.

In the two post-war German states fundamentally new attitudes to national identity emerged. In the Federal Republic outside observers, such as the present author, detected, particularly among the liberal intelligentsia, a strong internationalism, and an identification with West Germany based upon a pride, albeit often highly critical, in its efficiency, both political and economic. I have, however, heard from members of this social group themselves the view that the Federal Republic lacked an identity. The government had great difficulties with identity questions as shown, for example, by the interesting group of essays published under its auspices with the title *Die Identität der Deutschen* ('German Identity') (Weidenfeld 1983). The government faced the dilemma that it could not base its view of German identity on race, as this was utterly discredited, nor on language, as this could imply a claim to incorporate Austria. However, it could not identify itself too closely with the territory of the Federal Republic, since it was bound to claim that the citizens of the GDR were also Germans. The dilemma was never resolved, and created a number of enduring problems. For instance, the state had little option but to recognize as Germans those who considered themselves to be Germans, with the result that thousands of ethnic Germans from Eastern Europe and the former Soviet Union have the right to German citizenship, even though many of them have little knowledge of the German language (see e.g. Hoffmann, 1991). This results in tensions between these people and sections of the indigenous population of Germany, who still see Germanness as expressed primarily in native-level proficiency in the language.

The GDR attempted a more radical solution: the creation of an entirely new 'socialist identity' based upon loyalty to a socialist society and its state in the *sozialistisches Vaterland* (socialist fatherland). We are too close to the collapse of the GDR to see precisely why this failed rather spectacularly; it does, however, seem that these ideals simply did not convince many of the population, who, rather than developing a new kind of identity, as many did in the West, retained a strong cultural and linguistic form of German nationalism.

Given that language and culture had always played such a large part in German identity, there was an assumption during the period of the post-war division that a division of the nation would result in a division of the language. In the Federal Republic this assumption at first produced a concern that the Communist regime in the East under Soviet influence was deliberately changing the language to help perpetuate the political division, and in the 1950s and early 1960s Western observers, perhaps partly politically motivated, considered that they had difficulty in understanding eastern German. This ignored two factors; first, changes in the language were largely restricted to the lexicon, particularly to political and economic vocabulary linked to a socialist state and a planned economy. Secondly, any change in the East was paralleled by a change in the West under Anglo-American influence. Indeed, changes in the West were arguably more thorough-going, since American influence massively permeated the popular culture, in a way that Russian influence certainly did not in the East.

From around 1970 it came to be accepted on both sides that comprehension between East and West Germans in the vast majority of contexts was not seriously impaired. Now, with unification, a more dispassionate view of the differences is being developed. Political and economic vocabulary is an obvious area of differ-ence, but some vocabulary relating to relatively modern technological develop-ments, and to new habits of consumption, shows differences: for example, eastern *Plaste* corresponds to western *Plastik*, eastern *Speisegaststätte* to western *Restaurant*. There are also appreciable sociolinguistic and pragmatic differences, with, for example, a higher status for non-standard speech in East Berlin compared to West Berlin, or more overt friendliness on the part of Westerners who will wish complete strangers *einen schönen Tag* (=American 'have a nice day'), which Easterners find insincere (a succinct account of the differences is D. Bauer 1993). It is indicative of the importance of language to German nationalism that anxiety about linguistic differences played such a prominent part in thinking about the division.

In the new Federal Republic united in 1990 the ingredients of a number of different kinds of nationalism are present, and it is impossible to say at the time of writing whether any one will become dominant, or whether they will coexist in uneasy or stable equilibrium. They range from the virulently racist nationalism of the extreme right, to the internationalism of the liberal left; many people still see language as the prime marker of German identity, others have a greater loyalty to a modern German efficiency, in the best sense of the word.

7.5. Conclusions

There is possibly no area in which language and national identity are more closely linked than in German-speaking Europe; indeed some of the clearest and earliest formulations of this link are found in the work of German-speaking scholars such as Herder and Fichte (see Johnston 1990: 47–64; Barbour 1993).

However, this link presents problems specifically in the German-speaking area; the German language is highly diverse, and is probably considered to be a single language only because its speakers share a sense of German identity, but the bases of that identity, apart from language, are far from obvious. At another level, a highly diverse language is not a particularly satisfactory basis for national identity, and the German-speaking area has hence seen attempts to find additional bases, which have been problematic, particularly the virulently racist and destructive nationalist ideology of the National Socialists.

Modern nationalist movements typically strive to create a nation-state to encompass all members of the nation, but again this has been highly problematic in the German-speaking area; the only political unit that did encompass virtually all German-speakers in Europe was the Nazi state from its incorporation of Austria in 1938 until its defeat in 1945. Given the nature of that state, the idea of a pan-German state is thoroughly discredited, except on the extreme political right.

Given the problems that the nationalism of German-speaking Europe produced in the twentieth century, there is now a consensus, not necessarily particularly clearly articulated, in the political mainstream in the area that German-speakers' need to identify with a political unit should be satisfied at a regional and at an international level, with less emphasis on the nation. Regional identification finds expression in the federal constitutions of both Germany and Austria, and incidentally also of Switzerland, and the internationalist dimension is seen in the strong commitment of Germany's political élite to European integration.

8.

Language and Nationalism in Italy: Language as a Weak Marker of Identity

CARLO RUZZA

8.1. Introduction

Languages are among the most powerful symbols of national identity. Both historically and in the recent past, the feeling of common belonging that sustains nationalism has often been enhanced by a common language, which has, therefore, frequently been used as a means of identifying the community in question. Together with anthems, flags, oath-swearing ceremonies, and the vast array of symbols and historical myths that sustain national identity, languages are often the marker that communities utilize to differentiate insiders from outsiders (Edelman 1977). This is particularly the case where the nation and the language community largely coincide. However, in Italy, I will argue, language is a relatively weak indicator of national identity, despite the substantial coincidence of linguistic, national, and state boundaries. In order to explain this seeming anomaly, I will review the emergence of the Italian language, showing how the difficult gestation and late development of the standard language reduced its relevance as a marker of national identity. Only in recent times, with the advent of mass literacy and mass-media consumption, has a standard language become prevalent, while for substantial minorities mutually incomprehensible dialects are still the language of choice.

The weak institutionalization of standard Italian in civil society has in the last few decades been threatened still further in some areas by regionalist movements that utilize local dialects as a basis for resurgent ethno-nationalist sentiments. This has occurred most notably in areas where economic grievances supported separatist sentiments, such as in the north and north-east, and also in Sardinia, where there are prominent independence movements based on long-standing cultural and linguistic diversity, and isolation. In other areas, it has happened too, but less markedly. In all of these areas, local linguistic varieties channel feelings of identity and thereby make up, to some extent, for a weak 'Italian' national identity.

With reference to the crucial case of the northern Italian separatist movement, the Lombardy League (*Lega*), [1] I will argue in this chapter that in recent years two features of the Italian language contributed to a distinctive form of 'identity politics' that were utilized to sustain ethno-nationalist sentiments. First, Italian dialects are mutually intelligible only within territorially circumscribed areas, creating the possibility of distinctive identities within areas encompassing 'families of dialects'. Secondly, the sociolinguistic evolution of Italian has clearly differentiated everyday spoken language from a formal standard language—the latter used originally almost exclusively in writing, but now also possessing an oral variant used by, among others, the Italian political establishment.

I will argue that these two features have formed the basis of alternative strategies for rallying mass support for the League's efforts to instil ethno-nationalist sentiments. In an earlier period, the use of dialect constituted an exclusionary device to deny access to the movement to anyone other than indigenous northern Italians. In a later period, this exclusionary strategy was replaced by the adoption of a popular colloquial variant of Italian. This linguistic strategy served the purpose of redefining 'the enemy' by including first- and second-generation southern migrants as potential movement supporters, and excluding a political class perceived as corrupt and Byzantine, a class that, in the League's mythology, had its base in Rome, a southern city, which symbolizes 'otherness' from the *Lega* 'homeland'—a conceptual operation easy to accomplish as Rome has frequently symbolized the nature of the Italian state, a state born late from the forced Piedmontese conquest of the greater part of the Italian territory. For many southern Italian peasants Rome has historically represented a distant, unpredictable, corrupt, and hostile state as Levi's powerful depiction of a southern village illustrates (see Levi 1982: esp. chs. 13, 14). In both cases—the 'we as an oppressed linguistic community' and the 'we as the people oppressed by a class of state officials and bureaucrats'—the territorial claim to self-determination could be sustained and grounded linguistically, but, as I will show, the political implications were rather different.

In the next section, I will briefly outline variation in the Italian language and examine the historical background to its emergence. I will then consider how language issues have figured in the efforts, to date only partly successful, to develop an Italian national identity.

8.2. The Italian Language

8.2.1. *A Linguistic Sketch of Italy*

The standard Italian language today is the product of the influence of a variety of local dialects on a dominant Tuscan dialect. Almost all of the indigenous speech

---

[1] This movement has over time contributed to the foundation or the support of similar movements in other northern Italian regions, which have been appropriately labelled with different regional names. The overall movement, led by the *Lega Lombarda*, is called *Lega Nord*. I will use *Lega* to refer broadly to the overall movement.

of Italy consists of Romance or neo-Latin dialects, and most, but not all, of these dialects are considered to be variants of a single Italian language.[2] Among these dialects, the Florentine variety gained the greatest prominence. Each dialect has a restricted area of use. The main isogloss (dividing line) demarcates northern varieties, characterized by Celtic influences, from more southerly varieties in which the speech of ancient Rome has evolved with less obvious influence from other major language groups. The more southerly dialects can be divided into those used in the south, the centre-south, Umbria, and Tuscany. Northern dialects can be divided into Gallo-Italian and Venetian. Many dialects have remained relatively distinct over the centuries, maintaining much of their integrity and in several cases a variety of registers. They have often produced valuable literatures and poetry. For instance, one might consider the works of Goldoni in the Venetian dialect of the eighteenth century, of Porta in the Milanese dialect of the nineteenth century, and of De Filippo in the Neapolitan dialect of the twentieth century. As Maiden (1995: 3) points out, it is important to stress that the Italian dialects did not develop out of the standard language:

The Italian dialects are not 'dialects of Italian'. And they are not 'daughters' of Italian, in the sense of being regional variants of Italian historically descended from the Italian language. Rather, Italian has its roots in one of the speech varieties that emerged from Latin in the Italy of the first millennium AD, namely that of Tuscany, and more precisely the kind of Tuscan spoken in Florence. Historically, then, the Italian language is simply a 'sister' of the other dialects of Italy.[3]

Although the Tuscan dialect provided the chief basis for the standard language, it failed to provide a symbol for a sense of national identity in the same way that, for instance, the French standard language did (see Section 3.3.6). Because of the low level of literacy in Italy, the standard variety has influenced the sense of national identity to only a limited extent. Indeed, if the label 'language' is essentially one that acknowledges political and cultural prestige, then many of these dialects could claim it, or could have claimed it in an earlier time. However, this is no longer the case, since only standard Italian has been taken as a means of communication by the media, a situation different, for instance, from that in Italian-speaking Switzerland, where a variety of dialects largely similar to those spoken in Lombardy are currently often used in television and radio programming.

The relationship between the evolution of language and the development of national identity is a complex one. In Europe, the two processes often unfolded gradually and simultaneously, but one process can also advance independently of

---

[2] In the writings of Italian linguists, and in works in English on the Italian language, such as Maiden (1995), Italian/*italiano* may refer to the standard language only. This contrasts with usage in works on many other languages, where the name of the language, such as English or German/*Deutsch*, refers to both the standard language and the non-standard dialects.

[3] See n. 2.

the other. In France and Spain, for example, the language of the court gained dominance through its use by state administration (see Chapters 3 and 4). In Italy, however, cultural factors, such as the prestige of the works of Dante, Petrarch, and Boccaccio, contributed to the dominance of the Florentine dialect of the four-teenth century. However, this prestige and the related adoption of the language was limited to a class of *literati*. This situation has persisted over time, with stan-dard, or near-standard Italian remaining until recently a literary language only, or a lingua franca for travellers and migrants.

Even today, in addition to standard Italian, the majority of Italians can speak a dialect of Italian that has roots in late Latin, but that has since been transformed along with the evolution of the culture in the different small regions of this state. Like many European states, Italy encompasses a variety of distinct indigenous languages, and linguistic differences between the dialect groups divide the coun-try; these differences are usually quite substantial. The dialects of Sardinia are considered to constitute a distinct Romance language, related to Italian, but not readily comprehensible to mainland Italians; today it is largely confined to the interior of the island. There is an enclave of Catalan, a distinct Romance language, at Alghero in Sardinia. The Romance dialects of Valle d'Aosta/Val d'Aoste are considered to be varieties of Franco-Provençal (see Chapter 3) rather than Italian, and in this region French functions as an official language alongside Italian. In the Friuli region there are many bilingual or even trilingual individuals and families. The languages in question are (near) standard Italian, German dialects, and local Romance dialects that their speakers consider to represent a distinct Romance language, Friulian, but that Italian linguists often consider to be Italian dialects. Friulian is close to the Romansh speech of Switzerland, and can be viewed as constituting a single Rhaeto-Romance language along with Romansh and with the Ladin dialects of Alto Adige (see Haiman 1988: 351–90). The territory of Alto Adige/South Tyrol on the north-east border, which Italy acquired during the twentieth century, includes many German-speakers, and is officially designated as bilingual. The relatively privileged position of German-speakers in this region has weakened demands, common in the 1960s and 1970s, for its separation from Italy and unification with Austria (see Barbour and Stevenson 1990: 237–42). There are other small indigenous linguistic minorities—speakers of Slovene in the north-east, Albanian and so-called Italiot Greek in the south—but these have made few political demands that might be termed 'nationalist', although there are Slovene activists in Trieste who generally want to raise the profile of their language in public life.

While Italians may have little difficulty understanding people speaking a dialect of a neighbouring region, speakers of dialects from the north and the south of the country often find each other's speech unintelligible. Nevertheless, while language issues have surfaced during the political project of nurturing a sense of being Italian over the last two centuries, for most people living in Italy, language politics have been of secondary importance until recently, a secondary marker of a political identity, rather than a source of identity in its own right. This is significantly different from several other European countries, where language development and state building went hand in hand. It is, therefore, useful to trace in some detail the historical development of the language to account for this difference.

8.2.2. *The Development of Standard Italian*

Italy's political fragmentation from the Middle Ages until the nineteenth century resulted from several factors, which included the presence of a papacy that deferred to strong foreign powers, and the emergence of rival city states; political fragmentation contributed to Italian linguistic fragmentation. The medieval city states constituted linguistic models imitated in surrounding areas, with widespread linguistic diversity as the result. The prominence of the Tuscan dialect resulted in cultural terms from the literary prestige of Florentine authors of the Renaissance. However, in political and bureaucratic transactions, Latin remained a viable language for centuries. By the early sixteenth century, however, there emerged a feeling that some form of *volgare*, or ordinary language, should supplant it, opening a long discussion that continued well into the nineteenth century (Maiden 1995: 7). Crucially for the evolution of standard Italian, the adoption of Florentine took place from the beginning in its literary form, a form that was already obsolete in speech in the 1500s, being modelled on the Florentine of Dante and Petrarch of two centuries before. Hence, standard Italian was born as a literary language, a language that, because it was not rooted in common usage, had from the start little chance to adapt and change, the better to reflect a wide variety of uses. The legacy of its noble birth was to hinder for centuries its viability as an effective, flexible, and accepted tool. In principle, however, this does not explain why national sentiments were never particularly bound up with the language. It is better explained by Italian history during and after state formation.

8.3. The Language in Political History

8.3.1. *Italian Nation-Building and Language*

The political implications of the importance of nationalism, and, in this context, of the importance of language during nation-building, have been clear for a long time. Nationalism has been a prominent force in Europe since the French Revolution, and within that upheaval the importance of specific language codes that differentiated groups of the population (Hunt 1984). The Revolution made governments aware of what could happen in the name of 'the nation'. It showed that, as a doctrine, nationalism can spread, that in its name massive social and cultural change is possible, that nations can be independent of states. In Europe, whilst revolutionary zeal subsided, nationalism gained strength in localized contexts. As the educated classes grew in the 1830s, they began to use national languages instead of foreign languages (Czech, Romanian, Hungarian, and so on emerged as languages with textbooks) and to tie their nationalist sentiments to specific languages.

At its inception, nationalism was essentially a middle-class issue and had as its aims national reunification and cultural unity. Hence its attitude towards language was one of minimizing internal linguistic difference in the community in question, formalizing language in a way that would empower intellectual classes, and emphasizing external linguistic difference. These processes also typically occurred in the Italian *Risorgimento*. Even more than in other countries, however, they were the concern of a small élite. The majority of Italians were never particularly interested in the process of national unification, or in the creation of a national language.

De Mauro (1963) estimates that, in 1861, the year of Italian unification, only 2.5 per cent of the total population spoke a language called 'Italian/*italiano*', a term then as now reserved for forms relatively close to the standard. This reflects the fact that it was not the actual use of the language that provided identity, because 'Italian' merely served as a weak marker of a common heritage. Instead, the push for nationalism emerged from the contempt the educated classes in cities had for foreign occupiers, whose colonialism had severely hampered the aspirations of these élites. This resentment is well represented in many literary works of the *Risorgimento*. Pursuit of an Italian identity became a political project that mobilized élites to participate in radical forms of social activism, and sustained a romanticized vision of community. The philosopher Benedetto Croce described these movements as the 'heroic minority'. No mass movement developed to support the élite's dream. On the contrary, in the south there were episodes of popular rebellion against the unifying Italian Savoyard rulers and their troops. D'Azeglio, one of the leading intellectuals in post-unification Italy, characterized the difficulty of infusing the sense of identity developed by the educated classes into popular culture as follows: 'Italy has been created, now it is the Italians who are to be made.'

The national movements of that time did not wholly succeed in making 'the Italians'. Instead, Italy remained a collection of local élites negotiating and exchanging favours. Piedmont emerged as the most influential region in defining the emerging nation-state and its élites held the monopoly of power. Over time they established alliances with southern élites. The ultimate organization of the state emerged from compromises between the different interests of the northern and southern power élites, a fact that some historians see as the cause for the dual development of the country. The northern industrial classes gained access to a large market for their goods in exchange for the legitimization and political power granted to the southern landed aristocracy. This division of roles supported an entrepreneurial culture in one part of the country and a subsidized political class in the other, and engendered long-lasting cultural differences. This fact explains the roots of a lasting territorial fragmentation that subsequent policies never effectively suppressed, and that still limits the viability of an overarching Italian identity (Allum 1973: 3). Meanwhile, until the 1930s the very low literacy rate denied access to the standard Italian language—as previously mentioned, a literary language—to all but an élite. It was with improved literacy that standard Italian began to permeate the wider population. In 1911, for instance, 38 per cent of the population was still illiterate (with wide differences across regions).[4]

8.3.2. *Fascism and the Language*

It was with Fascism that the combined influence of propaganda and films enabled the Italian standard language to reach many citizens for the first time (Clark 1984: 244). With Fascism, primary education became well-nigh universal, diffusing knowledge of the standard language among peasants and the urban poor. In addition, the Fascist emphasis on the nation, its history and power, implied a new emphasis on, and suggested a new pride in, the use of standard Italian as a means of communication. Fascist associationism in organizations such as the *Dopolavoro* (After-Work Clubs), the *Gioventù Italiana del Littorio* (Italian Youth) and the *Gioventù Universitaria Fascista* (Fascist University Youth), stimulated the use of the standard Italian language. A new attention to the language was emerging—one that required that the language should reflect the revolutionary zeal of the Fascists. A number of prescriptions was enforced, such as that requiring the substitution of the less formal *Voi* for *Lei*, the formal second person mode of address, or that preventing use of words of obvious foreign origin. For instance, the commonly used English word 'cocktail'—meaning a mixed alcoholic drink—was forbidden, and the use in its place of the literal translation *Coda di Gallo* enjoined (Clark 1984: 243). Similarly, a taxi was to be renamed *autopubblica*, and so on. The Fascists' ultra-nationalist agenda also led to sustained attempts to suppress minority languages, such as German, Croatian, and Slovene, in South Tyrol, Venezia Tridentina, and Venezia Giulia. There, the use of Italian was enforced in primary schools and public offices, provoking much resentment (Clark 1984: 252). Migrations from other parts of Italy were encouraged, and there was even enforced replacement of German, Slovene, and Croatian surnames with Italian names, extending as far as the alteration of inscriptions on tombstones. But there was resistance to these changes, seen, for example, in the private funding of secret schools.

With the demise of Fascism, much of its cultural baggage lost prestige, and that included the emphasis on nationalist sentiments, and the overarching desire to 'make the Italians' in a variety of areas, including, prominently, language use. Thus the Fascists' ideological path to linguistic uniformity was unsuccessful, and left little legacy. The doctrines that gained momentum in post-war Italy—Catholicism and Marxism—were in principle internationalist. Their cultural agendas were different, and emphasis on the nation was replaced by different principles of solidarity, in which language has little relevance.

---

[4] Data elaborated from Italian annual statistics by Martin Clark and reported in Clark (1984: 36).

In general, the linguistic policies of Fascism met with resistance in a country where limited media consumption and limited geographical mobility reduced their effectiveness. Just as literacy was the decisive factor in spreading standard Italian in the first part of the century, market dynamics—in the form of media diffusion and mass migrations—would be more important than ideological zeal in altering the situation significantly in the second part of the century.

8.3.3. *Literacy, the Media, and the 'Economic Boom'*

The economic and cultural situation changed radically in the post-war period. Italy experienced an economic boom in the 1950s, the consumer economy expanded rapidly in this period, and people began migrating in large numbers to areas with growing industrial employment, particularly from the south to the north. These economic trends required a certain degree of linguistic homogenization to facilitate communication in the workplace and marketplace. The postwar generation, which grew up in a relatively affluent society, enjoyed wider access to formal education. Additionally, from the 1950s, mass culture, most prominently promoted by the media, and by television in particular—regular broadcasts began in 1956—led to the spread of a relatively uniform national spoken norm. Throughout the country instruments of political mobilization, such as political parties, trade unions, and other social movements, gained prominence throughout civil society, and also acted as instruments of linguistic homogenization, especially after a new politically active industrial proletariat of varied regional origin was formed in northern cities.

As a result of all these changes, in many regions a new standard spoken Italian, not identical to the old literary norm, took on unprecedented prestige and relevance, and began to supplant local dialects for an increasingly large portion of the population. This transition brought standard Italian out of the narrow confines of the educated élite. De Mauro (1992: 47) summarizes the transition thus 'Until the end of the Fifties only in Tuscany, and to a lesser extent in Rome was Italian[5] learned in the family and in daily life. Elsewhere, out of the limited social strata of university life (and not always even there) in families and daily life the use of dialects dominated.' But during the 1960s and 1970s, the proportion of habitual speakers of standard or near-standard varieties grew significantly. In the mid-1970s a quarter of the population used standard Italian regularly (De Mauro 1992: 49) and 32 per cent could alternate between standard and dialect. Hence we can characterize the Italian population of this period as in general bilingual or diglossic (Berruto 1974: 80).

There is every reason to believe that in the last two decades of the twentieth century this proportion increased still further. However, in comparison to some other European countries, the proportion of exclusively standard language speakers is still limited. Dialects have maintained a primacy, especially in informal

[5] See n. 2.

contexts, that is probably paralleled in western Europe only in Norway and Italian-speaking Switzerland.[6] In 1989 33 per cent of Italians used dialects outside home contexts (De Mauro 1992: 191), and the proportion using them at home was probably much higher.

Italy retains what is in effect a form of widespread diglossia. The switch from dialect to standard language depends upon situational factors that include knowledge of the linguistic background of the other speakers, the perceived social status of other speakers, the degree of intimacy with the speakers, and the selection of topics of conversation. For instance, topics having a political content can trigger use of the language of the media; topics with a heavy technological content, which require use of an educated vocabulary, might also trigger a switch to standard Italian. Similarly, people who principally use a regional dialect will often switch to standard Italian when dealing with the state bureaucracies, since Italians recognize that a bureaucrat is likely to come from a different region. In some regions, however, dialect remains the acceptable medium of communication even in situations perceived as 'educated', such as those encountered in pharmacies, for example, despite the general perception that pharmacists belong to an élite. An intermediate linguistic form between dialect and standard Italian might also be adopted in such cases.

Nevertheless, in comparison to some other countries, such as German-speaking Switzerland, diglossia is relatively rare among the educated classes. I believe that this is the case because the usage of standard Italian has traditionally indicated an aspiration towards upward social mobility for the middle classes. In a country where mass education is relatively recent, speakers are often keen to symbolize a decisive break with what could be perceived as a membership of a peasant subculture. In other words, diglossia is relatively rare in the upper strata of the population because educated Italians identify with the dominant national culture more than the rest of the population, a culture distinct and in many ways ideologically opposed to all forms of regionalism. One needs to bear in mind that Italian linguistic unification was predicated upon perceived Florentine literary supremacy, which somehow led to a devaluation of other dialects. When Machiavelli referred to 'Italy' he probably meant 'greater Florence'—a land to which the civilized ways and speech of Florence had to be exported. It is thus a process parallel to the one described by Eugen Weber in *Peasants into Frenchmen* (1977) but much delayed by the ineffectiveness and relative lack of prestige of the state. The 'trickling down' of the prestige of standard language usage has been slower, not only because of the more limited appeal of a national identity, but also because the proportion of the Italian population with higher education is still relatively low, and because there has in the meanwhile been a revival of folk culture. Yet the impact of geographical mobility and the media is now substantial.

---

[6] The degree of dialect use in German-speaking Switzerland is undoubtedly greater (see Chapter 7).

Dialects remain generally viable, but they are nonetheless gradually losing their distinctiveness.

The economic changes and rise of mass culture in recent decades have produced dialect levelling. In other words, the prevalence of standard Italian has become such an important currency in Italian society that people have begun to speak forms that represent, in their lexicon and grammar, a compromise between standard Italian and the regional dialects. The resulting levelling of the dialects has reduced the scale of linguistic diversity in the state. But, just as standard Italian has influenced and modified the regional dialects, regional dialects have also influenced the standard language. Clearly, this mixing of linguistic codes has substantially modified standard Italian and has traditionally led pundits to complain about low or even declining standards of language proficiency. In the national newspaper, *Il Corriere della Sera*, for example, an editorial writer complains that the increasing difficulty teachers have experienced working with students reflects the degree of discrepancy between students' home dialects and the vocabulary and syntax of standard Italian, especially in its written and spoken academic versions (see Isotta 1994). It should be noted, however, that problems do not really arise through some kind of 'corruption' of the standard language; much more serious is the development of specialized registers that are simply not sufficiently familiar to the majority of the speakers. This situation is not too different from the one analysed by Weber (1977: 94) at the beginning of the century in France:

Language is one technique for mastering reality. Local dialects had mastered the everyday world of the peasants' experience, personified it in its details, coped with it. As urban speech edged those dialects out, the familiar became alien. New speech, new words, new forms did not permit the same easy, immediate participation in situations that time and habit had made familiar and the words had, so to speak, to domesticate too. The new words were more abstract. The values and ideas they reflected were more distant.

But this distance is exacerbated in Italy by the particularly convoluted language that 'high culture' makes use of there, and also by the wide gulf between the registers employed by different sectors of the cultural and political establishment.

A common complaint in Italy is that academics, politicians, and journalists use strikingly different variants of standard Italian, placing the existence of a unified Italian in doubt. In other words, just as Italian was once only a literary language, today it is to an extent a set of disparate codes used by politicians, academics, bureaucrats, and so on, but with such differentiation as to call into question the unity of the language.

Recently, there has in effect been a public reaction against these highly specialized registers within standard Italian. Many Italians see the development of a bureaucratic variant of the language as a move towards cultural domination by a baroque and jargonistic intelligentsia that utilizes esoteric linguistic codes to retain and symbolize their social power. As previously mentioned, one ethno-territorial movement, the *Lega Lombarda*, has expressed this sentiment particularly vociferously. This chapter now turns to the recent period and the test case of the language politics of the *Lega*.

8.3.4. *Language and Politics Today: The* Lega

A process that is in some ways similar to the nationalism-driven language codification of the 1830s is re-emerging today as an important characteristic contemporary ethno-nationalism, which is mainly divisive in character. In an era of cultural globalization, language issues are central to nationalist groups in such disparate places as the Basque country, Catalonia, Quebec, Wales, and Sardinia. However, the political relationship between the language of the aspiring separate community and the language of the respective nation-states varies significantly, and this affects the possible strategies for language politics. One can, for instance, consider the different relations of Spanish to the Basque language, on the one hand, and Catalan, on the other (see Chapter 4). In both cases, language plays an important role in the cultural construction of difference, and requests for separate language provision are commonly made. But the difficulty of the Basque language for Spanish-speakers, and its long historical decline, militate against a strong revival; similar factors apply to the indigenous minority languages of Britain and Ireland (see Chapter 2). Hence, insistence on the centrality of language can limit a nationalist constituency. Conversely, for Catalans, the language can be more easily adopted as a marker associated with nationalism. Identifying the language as a crucial identity-building factor is in part determined by the strategies of nationalists and in part rooted in linguistic factors related to the strength of the languages themselves.

The relationship between linguistic and political factors is well exemplified by the political history of the *Lega Lombarda*. The *Lega* arose as a social movement and political party representing people from the north of Italy, and originally promoted a xenophobic and anti-southern agenda, though more recently it has alternately toned down its rhetoric to broaden its political support, or emphasized it to appeal to its activist hard core, according to variations in its political opportunities (Ruzza and Schmidtke 1996).

The rise of the League to national prominence was rapid and unexpected, posing the question as to why some areas are more prone than others to regionalist or ethno-nationalist movements (see Pileri *et al.* 1994; Ruzza 1996; Ruzza and Schmidtke 1996). In contrast to the nineteenth century, when mainly integrating nationalisms emerged, in the twentieth century one can identify two kinds of nationalisms in Western Europe, both of which are, in principle, separatist. One is based on a reaction to perceived forced assimilation of what remains of traditional small nations embedded in large nation-states, often in marginal areas. These are areas with long-standing and distinctly different cultural and linguistic traditions. In Italy, one can think of Sardinia as the most prominent example.

The second kind of nationalism is to be found in wealthy areas, whose regionalism is as much related to economic grievances rooted in the redistributive policies of nation-states as to embryonic cultural and linguistic difference. In both cases the ethno-territorial difference is a construct that a politically active body, such as a party or a movement, promotes, more or less successfully, on the basis of exploiting political opportunities. A typology of the political opportunities that affect ethno-nationalist movements is not possible here. I can only note briefly that it is possible to identify both common and different factors in the two types of movements. Among the common factors, it is significant that Rome and its government and state are perceived as remote and hostile. As previously mentioned, Levi's peasants feel little sympathy for Rome. 'What had the peasants to do with Power, Government and the State? The state, whatever form it might take, meant "the fellows in Rome". "Everyone knows", they said, "that the fellows in Rome don't want us to live like human beings. There are hailstorms, landslides, droughts, malaria, and . . . the state" ' (Levi 1982: 77–8).[7]

But the new regionalism of Lombardy and other northern Italian regions has an added ingredient beyond the reaction against a form of internal colonialism by a centralized state. This further ingredient is the sense of grievance of a relatively rich region, also seen in the regionalism of places like Baden-Württemberg in Germany and Catalonia (although ethnically and linguistically based nationalism is highly important in the Catalan case).

Certainly, in the case of the League, what contributed to its viability as a relevant political actor are a set of factors connected to the wealth of the area where the League has emerged, notably feelings of exploitation, pride in the ability to produce and retain wealth, pride in hard work as a sacralized character trait, and so on.

From its formation in the early 1980s, the members of the *Lega* have perceived language as a carrier of social identity. The *Lega*'s early autonomist and separatist political platform included a pledge to revive the northern dialects and to elevate these dialects to the status of *bona fide* languages. In the early years, *Lega* activists utilized the local dialects extensively, redefining these dialects as 'the language of the Lombard Nation'. Dialects thus served as boundary-defining devices. At night, activists rewrote street signs in the local spelling, sometimes creating problems for non-natives. Since the Lombard dialects generally lack the word-final vowels of standard Italian, in many cases it was sufficient to efface a single letter from street signs with spray paint to make a political statement. Such actions provided a fast and effective way of gaining exposure without requiring commitment to specific policy programmes.

However, over-reliance on dialect politics proved counterproductive for the *Lega*. Many educated young people had not mastered the dialects, which varied significantly between small areas, or, alternatively, they were proud of a newly

---

[7] For references to Rome, see also Levi (1982: 121, 131, 133).

acquired familiarity with standard Italian and reluctant to abandon it. There was a risk of creating barriers within the movement instead of enhancing solidarity. In addition, using dialects had an alienating effect on those potential members born in the north but having one or both parents from the south. Furthermore, members of other parties have perceived the emphasis on dialect as a parochial strategy that lent itself to ridicule. For instance, in city-hall meetings a working-class communist mayor could tease a young *Lega* city councillor about an imperfect understanding of the dialect. This problem acquired even wider dimensions after the *Lega* decided to propose an alliance with other northern leagues, and create a larger political unit called *Lega Nord.* For these reasons, the *Lega* has more recently reduced its reliance on the politics of dialect.

A new linguistic strategy, taking a linguistic code directly from the street and importing it into the political arena, has increasingly replaced the use of dialect. The public speeches of the *Lega* rely heavily on metaphors, catchphrases, and other elements of everyday language, and reinterpret these elements in political terms. For instance, a *Lega* billboard poster reads 'The *Lega* cleans the engine [of politics]'. It is a simple message, taken directly from advertising and expressed in ordinary language.

This strategy has particular potency in Italy against the background of the extremely convoluted and baroque political jargon developed by the former mainstream political parties over the years, which sounds obscure to most Italians. The dominant language of politics assumed an insider's knowledge of political affairs, and the ability to 'read between the lines'. Presenting itself as an anti-system movement, the *Lega* has chosen a language that, as an activist says, seeks to bring politics 'down to the level of common people', and thus desacralizes politics. This becomes evident if one considers that one of the most common slogans is a simple affirmation of masculine sexual prowess, in crude language: 'La Lega ce l'ha duro' (The League has a hard-on). It is a sentence used as a disingenuous reaction to complicated questions or comments by political opponents. It does not make sense, but it creates embarrassment and anger in political circles. It provokes hilarity and great satisfaction among activists, and conveys the anti-system component of the *Lega.* Vulgarity is raised to the status of a virtue because it possesses a simplicity and directness that is felt to be lacking elsewhere.

Not surprisingly, with so much 'machismo' in its language, proportionately few women number among the activists. However, to a part of the Italian public this emphasis on simplicity appears refreshing, and comprehensible. The *Lega* uses a language that can convey the views and the anger of working people. It seems more difficult to lie, cheat, and embezzle in such simple language than in the convoluted speeches of many professional politicians. A similar device was adopted by new social movements in the early 1980s. Groups of activists would disrupt complicated and unconvincing speeches of political opponents by chanting *scemo, scemo* (stupid, stupid) in a tone children use to tease each other.

The choice of popular lexicon goes together with the utilization of simple and at times clearly non-standard syntactic structures, borrowed from the dialect. It is intended to be a statement about the personal background of *Lega* voters, an electorate of prosperous artisans, small business people, and shopkeepers. Thus it has almost the same identity-forming result as using dialect, without the comprehensibility problems mentioned previously. In addition, it enables complex problems to be expressed in accessible language, and offers an opportunity for supporters with little education to be active.

The success of the *Lega* in Lombardy testifies to the value of these strategies and to the strength of regionalist sentiments.

8.4. Italian Nationalism Today

I have reviewed the historical reasons for the relatively weak institutionalization of Italian nationalism, but here one might ask whether political and cultural developments are altering this situation. If one simply reviewed the names of the prominent parties in Italian politics at the end of the twentieth century, one would be led to believe that the politics of territorial and ethnic nationalism was alive and well. The Berlusconi-led party, *Forza Italia* (Go Italy!) clearly intends, as its name suggests, to appropriate the nationalist banner. So does the right-wing coalition *Alleanza Nazionale* (National Alliance). In addition, as already discussed, the *Lega Nord*, which encompasses a number of regional leagues, can be seen as representing an alternative kind of regional chauvinism. Of course, there still remains the left coalition, which has no specific claims to be a standard-bearer of the nation.

Looking at opinion-poll data (see Diamanti and Segatti 1994), there seems to be a resurgence of both nationalist and regionalist sentiments. But also one can probably still identify a sense of self-contempt (Romano 1994) rooted in shame arising out of losing the war, as well as from a number of national ills, such as the Mafia, bureaucratic chaos, and lack of economic success. Romano (1994: 163) says: 'A country of which you cannot speak with pride, and which forces you to lie, becomes despicable or ridiculous. The suppression of national sentiments has had the effect of encouraging many Italians to find refuge in municipalism, in localism, in village-pride.' Clearly, this situation has an impact on language as well. Many people take more pride in mastering their dialect than the national language, even when the transition to standard Italian is a *fait accompli* for many belonging to younger generations.

8.5. Conclusions

This chapter has pointed out the clear connection between linguistic, political, and cultural factors in determining the features of Italian nationalism, and has emphasized the relative weakness of the linguistic element.

Cultural factors have limited the viability of the Italian state as an economic actor, something that, over time, negatively affected Italian identity and indirectly reduced the desirability of a common language and the possibility of pride in a common language. Slightly ashamed of the relative backwardness of their state, many Italians retained other identities that did not force them to compare themselves with apparently more successful nations. Instead, Italians were more likely to associate themselves with a group aspiring for global appeal, such as the Communists, sharing an ideological identity, or the Catholics, sharing a religious identity. Similarly, regional identities maintained a viability that might have diminished in other national contexts.

It is only recently, notably after the sea change in world politics after 1989, that these ideological identities have declined in Italy. The resurgence of older and probably previously submerged local territorial identities have brought the language issue to the fore. The linguistic landscape today is one of re-emerging dialects and pride in regional accents. Cities' cultural associations (*pro-loco*) are valuing dialects, schoolchildren are invited to learn them, and this is ironically happening at a time when the proportion of mother-tongue dialect speakers is at least in some regions in terminal decline.

As standard Italian has become predominant, it has also gradually lost its literary character. The *Lega* glorification of popular Italian might then be the acknowledgement that, for the first time, a truly viable common Italian language has emerged that can replace the myriad dialects.

9.

Contrasting Ethnic Nationalisms: Eastern Central Europe

BARBARA TÖRNQUIST-PLEWA

9.1. Introduction

In this chapter, perhaps more clearly than in some others, 'nation' is understood as a community based on cultural communication, delimited and kept together by means of a cultural identity (see Johansson, 1993a: 18). During the process of nation-building, this cultural identity receives a political dimension, which is the basis for the group's demands for political autonomy or sovereignty. It is precisely this political aspect that is decisive and distinguishes national identity from other kinds of identities—for instance, ethnic identity. This national identity varies greatly between nations for historic reasons, making it difficult to point to any universal components of national identity.

National identity consists of a number of components that are integrated and interacting. These identity-forming elements are: territory, common institutions and laws, common history, ethnicity and/or an idea of common origin, culture, language, and religion—the last mentioned often important in the earliest phase of nation-building (see Enloe 1980: 366).

Language is supremely important for a group's cultural identity. It delimits, identifies, and integrates. Language has an impact on the collective consciousness of the community.[1] This collective heritage can then be transmitted from one generation to the next by means of language. Thus language becomes an important prerequisite for cultural continuity. Although language, presented in this way, may appear to be a basic element of the cultural heritage and thus an important component of national identity, there is no indication that it must automatically become the object of ideologization or politicization. It does, however, become politicized when there is a crucial role for language in national mobilization and in nationalism, understood as an ideological movement for the acquisition and preservation of the political autonomy, unity, and identity of a population, which

---

[1] It is not necessarily an active causative factor, as Sapir and Whorf would have it, but rather a reflective factor (see Fishman 1980: 90).

at least some of its members consider to be a nation.[2] From the point of view adopted here, language is seen as one of many variables of national identity and not as its basis. Other markers of collective cultural identity can become politicized and constitute equally important or even more important instruments for mobilization of a national movement.

The role of language in national mobilization may vary not only from one nation to the next but also between different phases in the history of the same nation. The four countries of eastern central Europe under consideration in this chapter are usually described as ethnic nations, with language and culture as the most important integrating factors, in contrast to so-called state-nations or civic nations—supra-ethnic communities integrated by means of a shared state (see Chlebowczyk 1980; Sugar 1980). On the basis of this general typology, initially formulated by Meinecke and derived from the philosophy of the Enlightenment and of Romanticism, and further developed by Kohn and others, I shall isolate and examine the role of language in eastern central Europe, concentrating in particular on the period since the late eighteenth century. In the discussion as to whether nations and nationalism are modern phenomena (as argued, for example, by Hobsbawm, Gellner, Hechter, Hroch, and Anderson) or whether they existed earlier and may even have been primordial (as argued by van den Berghe and others) I occupy an intermediate position. Nationalism as a mass movement, and the nation as the idea of a community accepted by all social strata of a given population, must be viewed as relatively late phenomena, since their appearance was not possible without fundamental economic, social, and political prerequisites. Political emancipation of the lowest classes and their participation in a culture shared with other classes, a significant degree of social mobility, and technological progress enabling mass diffusion of the idea of a nation—all this has been possible only in modern societies. Various factors contributed towards the emergence of modern nations: economic factors (industrialization, the struggle for a fair distribution of resources), social (the dismantling of feudalism, the metamorphosis of the entire social structure), and cultural (the ideas of the Enlightenment and of Romanticism) as well as political (the action of individual actors and the 'demonstration effect' of various nationalisms) (see Johansson 1993*b*: 30). In my view none of these factors alone played a crucial or exclusive role in the formation of nations; they were linked together in a chain of cause and effect with reciprocal impact.

These factors first appeared during the modern period; however, one cannot disregard the fact that the ideas referred to in our definition of nationalism can be found much earlier, with the difference that they cannot be viewed as mass phenomena. This 'proto-nationalism' (the term is used by Johansson 1993*a*: 25), most often connected with early territorial state formation, will also be discussed, since it played a part in nation-building in the countries discussed here. The rele-

---

[2] The definition of nationalism used here is the one presented by A. D. Smith (1991: 73).

vance I grant to pre-modern history in the process of nation-building will also be reflected in the typology I have applied in my analysis, distinguishing between so-called 'historic' and 'non-historic' nations.[3]

By 'historic nations' I mean those nations that entered the decisive phase of nation-building with their own national upper class and a tradition of independent political structure dating from pre-modern times. The 'non-historic nations', on the other hand, are characterized by the lack of both of these features.[4] Thus the Hungarians and the Poles represent the putative 'historic nations', while the Slovaks represent the 'non-historic'. In my view the Czechs constitute an intermediate case, since, at the beginning of the nineteenth century, they did not have their own national upper class (there was a Bohemian but not a Czech nobility); on the other hand, they had a tradition of an earlier independent political structure.[5] This distinction is relevant also for the analysis of the role of language in the national movements in eastern central Europe.

9.2. Hungary

9.2.1. *Hungarian Proto-Nationalism*

At the end of the ninth century a nomadic people, the Magyars, conquered areas along the middle Danube. They spoke a distinct language belonging to the Finno-Ugrian branch of the Uralic family. Around the year 1000 this population converted to Christianity and Stephen I (997–1038) became its first formally crowned king.

A Hungarian state then flourished for several centuries and extended from an area around the middle Danube (including the Slovakia of today) to Transylvania and Croatia; these territories were referred to as belonging to 'the Crown of Saint Stephen' and later as 'historic Hungary'.

After the Ottoman invasion in 1526 a third of the territory came under the Sultan's rule, while Transylvania gained the status of an independent duchy. The remaining territories became, through a personal union, part of the Habsburg Monarchy. In 1699 the Ottomans were forced to relinquish the occupied Hungarian territories, and these, together with the rest of Hungary, were incorporated into the Habsburg Monarchy—a union that was to last until the end of the First World War. However, after 1867, as a result of the so-called *Ausgleich*, this

---

[3] This typology dates from Hegel and was later discussed by Engels, but was developed by Otto Bauer, who attempted to rid it of its evaluative, non-scientific overtones (see O. Bauer 1924).

[4] As a social-democratic ideologue, Otto Bauer viewed the difference between the social structures of nations as crucial. In my opinion the tradition of independent political structure is just as important, as I show in this chapter.

[5] Otto Bauer counts the Czechs among 'non-historic' nations, since he gives priority to the social structure. Robert Kann, on the other hand, sees them as a 'historic nation', since historic consciousness is for him crucial when he uses Bauer's model as the basic organizing principle in his book *The Multinational Empire* (1950).

union acquired the form of a partnership within the Austro-Hungarian Empire. Thus the Hungarians never completely lost their own state (which was the fate of the Poles), even if its sovereignty was for some time very limited. The *Regnum Hungariae* maintained its separate status within the Habsburg Monarchy, and also some separate institutions, such as a Hungarian Catholic Church under its own primate (*Primas Hungariae*), and a Hungarian Parliament (*Dieta*), although the latter was not a permanent one. Habsburg emperors were crowned kings of Hungary and had to pledge respect for the rights of the Hungarian estates (the nobility and the towns).

An important bearer of the idea of the Hungarian state was the numerous nobility (about 10 per cent of the population), which enjoyed special privileges, laid down in the Golden Bull of 1222. One important privilege, *ius resistendi*, allowed them to oppose decisions taken by the central power. This right was frequently used in their struggle against the Habsburgs in a series of uprisings in the sixteenth and seventeenth centuries led by Bocskay, Bethlen, Thököly, and Rákóczi. These uprisings had first and foremost the character of a feudal or religious struggle between the nobility and the absolute ruler, but the nobility affirmed in this conflict the independence of the Hungarian monarchy from the Habsburg Monarchy. Slogans such as *pro patriae et libertate* and ideas about separating the Hungarian state from the Empire circulated. This proto-nationalism created a number of historical myths, which formed an important integrating role in the mobilization of Hungarians in the nineteenth century. These 'wars of independence' (as they are known in Hungarian historiography) ended in every case in compromises between the Hungarian nobility and the Habsburgs—for example, concerning the rights of Hungarian Protestants in 1621.[6] The emperors never crushed the Hungarian nobility, as they did the Czech nobility in 1620. A political upper class that was the bearer of the idea of a Hungarian state therefore continued to exist, with some state institutions of its own and a rich history of self-affirmation and struggle, which could be reinterpreted as national history.

The Hungarian nobility had a variety of ethnic origins. The expression *Natio Hungarica*, in use during the pre-modern period, referred only to the nobility—that is, the members of the ruling estate—but did not designate speakers of any particular language. *Hungarus* or *Hungaricus* was not identical to *Magyar*, which had a clear linguistic and ethnic reference. In public life, members of *Natio Hungarica* used Latin. By the end of the eighteenth century, modernization brought about socio-economic changes in Hungarian society. As a consequence, and also because of the influence of the ideas of the Enlightenment and the French Revolution, which spoke of the right of the whole nation, not only of the

---

[6] For an analysis of the character of these uprisings, see Szücs (1981: 125–30) and Péter (1990: 100–21).

upper strata, to be political actors, the socially limited notion of *Natio Hungarica* was questioned.[7]

9.2.2. *The Nineteenth Century: Language in Modern Hungarian Nationalism*

The nineteenth century saw the disappearance of *Natio Hungarica* in its old sense. A new Hungarian term for the idea of the nation emerges—*magyar nemzet*, which is understood as referring both to all inhabitants of the *Regnum Hungariae*, regardless of their mother tongue, and, in the spirit of Herder, to the linguistic and ethnic Hungarians—that is the Magyars. The fact that the Hungarian language at this stage did not make distinctions between a 'Hungarian' nation (in the territorial and political sense) and a 'Magyar' nation (in the linguistic and ethnic sense) reveals the dualism in the understanding of the term 'nation' by the Hungarian élite.

This dualism arose from the attempts to define the Hungarian nation by means of two markers of identity, which in Hungary were irreconcilable: the political–historical heritage, and the language. National mobilization needed both markers, depending on the aim. In order to maintain loyalty towards the Hungarian state from the multilingual population that inhabited the lands belonging to 'the Crown of Saint Stephen', the historical heritage was invoked. On the other hand, if the goal was to affirm a distance from the German-speaking Habsburgs, an identity based on the Hungarian language was fostered.

Hungarian was, however, not the mother tongue of the majority of the population in historic Hungary. Within the borders of historic Hungary there were Germans,[8] Romanians, German-speaking, Hungarian-speaking, and Yiddish-speaking Jews, and peoples speaking various Slavonic languages: South Slavs (Serbs, Croats, and Slovenes), West Slavs (Slovaks), and East Slavs (Ruthenians). The last-named group, also called here Rusyns or Carpatho-Rusyns (see Udvari 1993), spoke a number of East Slavonic dialects, which are generally classified today as Ukrainian, but they wrote in Russian, or in Ukrainian (after the emergence of the Ukrainian literary language), or, for those who were trying to establish their own literary Rusyn language, in a written form based on popular speech.[9]

This multi-ethnic composition was perceived as a problem only when Latin was abolished as the official language in 1790. It was replaced first by German, and

---

[7] The social delimitation of the concept was questioned by e.g. Széchenyi in his work *Világ* (*The Light*) (see Barany 1990: 193).

[8] Throughout this chapter, 'German', referring to people, is used in the sense of 'German-speakers' or 'ethnic Germans', and not in the sense of 'citizens of the state of Germany'.

[9] The Carpatho-Rusyns were recognized as a separate ethnic and later (in inter-war Czechoslovakia) even national group until the mid-twentieth century. After the Second World War, when 'Subcarpathian Rus' was incorporated in the Soviet Ukrainian Republic, Ukrainian nationality was administratively imposed on them. In the 1990s, after the fall of the Soviet Union, the revival of a Rusyn identity and the Rusyn language could be observed (R. A. Smith 1997). For further detail about the Carpatho-Rusyns, see Magocsi (1978).

then by Hungarian, first in 1830, and then definitively in 1844. The decision by Emperor Josef II to introduce German as the official language was motivated by the need to modernize and rationalize the state bureaucracy. The Hungarian nobility, however, saw it as an attack on the separate status of Hungary, an attempt to bind the country even more firmly to the Austrian Empire. The Hungarian language was seen by the nobility as the only possible alternative to Latin. This meant a linking of the birth and the history of the Hungarian state to a Magyar identity. The majority of the nobility had Magyar roots (even if they sometimes were not themselves proficient in Hungarian) and they were convinced of the superiority of Magyar culture compared to the cultures of the other populations of Hungary. These populations were handicapped by the fact that they did not have their own nobility that could plead their cause (the Croats were an exception).

The superiority complex of the Magyar aristocracy was later transmitted to part of the bourgeoisie and intelligentsia and thus they had little understanding (with the exception of liberals such as Martinovics, Rát, Kovachich, Eötvös, Deák, Jászi) for the aspirations of the various nationalities (see also Barany 1990:193). The Hungarian bourgeoisie and intelligentsia saw the struggle for the language as a step towards the democratization of society. All Hungarian-speakers of all social classes were to be integrated into one nation. The most important goal of the Hungarian liberals was the equality of individuals before the law, not the equality of nationalities. A number of these liberals (with Kossuth as their leader) saw a combination of Magyarism and liberalism as a means of advancing the prosperity of all the inhabitants of Hungary.[10] An awakening from this simplistic and naïve vision came in 1848 during the Hungarian uprising, when Slovaks, Croats, and Romanians, alienated by the Hungarians' attempts at Magyarization, assisted the Habsburg emperor in defeating the Hungarian insurgents.

If Hungarian was to compete with German as a language of administration and education, it needed to be standardized and modernized. At the end of the eighteenth century its vocabulary and stylistic resources were insufficiently developed for it to function as a means of communication in a modern community. Besides, its status, until 1790, was low. Certainly, progress had been made towards the standardization of Hungarian during the Reformation and even during the Counter-Reformation (owing to the great stylistic talent of Peter Pázmany), but this was followed by a long period of stagnation, when the standardization of the language lagged behind other developments in society.

By the end of the eighteenth century a huge reform movement for modernizing the language began, in which the main figures were, among others, Ferenc Kazinczy and Miklós Révai. It was accompanied by a flowering of literature in Hungarian (e.g. Vitéz, Vörösmarty, later Petöfi and others). This literature was important in disseminating nationalist ideas. The beginning of the nineteenth

---

[10] For discussion of Kossuth's attitude on this issue, see Kann (1950: i. 120–32).

century saw the opening of a national theatre and of the Hungarian Academy of Sciences. One of its preoccupations was the language issue. Hungarian was standardized on the basis of the north-eastern dialects (from the areas that were the strongholds of the Reformed churches), with many additions from the central dialects. Scientific, administrative, and technological terminology was created by means of neologisms. Borrowings from other languages, especially from German, were shunned (Benkö and Imre 1972: 287). Even borrowings from Latin were avoided; 'university', for instance, was rendered by the calque *egyetem*.

Another example of how nationalistic tendencies were expressed in linguistics is the fact that Hungarian language historians were fierce advocates of the so-called Ural-Altaic hypothesis. According to this, Uralic languages (Hungarian, Finnish, Estonian, and the Samoyedic languages) were related to the Altaic group, consisting of Turkish, Mongolian, and Tungusic languages (sometimes even thought to include Japanese and Korean). The kinship with peoples, such as the Mongols and the Turks, who had once been powerful warriors was flattering for the national spirit and seemed a compensation for those who felt embarrassment because of the relationship of the Magyar language to the speech of nomadic peoples in Siberia, like the Samoyedic languages. This hypothesis, popular in the nineteenth century, was typical of a trend among national movements in Europe at that time: glorifying the past of one's own people and searching to prove the ancient character of one's culture, its excellence and uniqueness. Philologists, historians, and writers were actively involved in this pursuit and thus shaped the historical consciousness of their kinsmen.[11]

The first decades of the nineteenth century saw an extremely intensive development of the Hungarian standard language. During a short period some 10,000 new words were integrated into the language, raising its vocabulary to such a level that it could serve as an adequate means of conveying a modern culture (Benkö and Imre 1972: 280–1). The linguistic reforms, carried out with exceptional speed, were met with some resistance by the conservative nobility, who, however, accepted them in the end, because their ultimate goal was the same as that of the advocates of the reforms—a greater independence of the country from centralized Habsburg power. Characteristic of the formation of the Hungarian nation was that the struggle for the language and for a national culture went hand in hand with political mobilization. It did not precede it, as was the case in the small non-historic nations of eastern central Europe.[12]

The language was an important instrument of mobilization for national goals.

[11] The notion 'historical consciousness' signifies here so-called 'living history'—i.e. history that is politically and ideologically relevant for the community. It consists both of historical facts (which may be interpreted in various ways) and collective myths.
[12] M. Hroch, who studied the formation of 'small, oppressed nations' (his expression), claimed that it could be divided into three phases: (1) the phase of the awakened interest of the élite in the national language and culture, (2) the phase of patriotic agitation, and (3) the rise of a national mass movement (see Hroch 1985: 23).

Just as important was the historical tradition of a Hungarian state, which was gradually transmitted by the nobility to other social strata. This resulted in a notion, which from the beginning of the nineteenth century onwards became prevalent, that all other peoples who inhabited historic Hungary should be included in Hungarian culture and learn the Hungarian language because they were members of the Hungarian nation (*magyar nemzet*). The latter concept was in turn interpreted in two ways. Those with the most liberal views (such as Széchenyi, Wesselényi, Eötvös, Déak) understood it as a supra-ethnic community, political, territorial and national, whose members would be entitled to develop their languages and cultures albeit within the framework of the Hungarian state.[13]

The majority of the Hungarian political establishment, however, espoused the linguistic and ethnic understanding of the concept of nation, while they at the same time wished to maintain the territorial unity of Hungary. This led to the attempt, after the *Ausgleich* of 1867, to realize their ideal of a nation-state and the consequent policy of Magyarization.

This equivocal Hungarian understanding of the concept of the nation was expressed in the Law on Nationalities of 1867. The law stipulated that all citizens in Hungary, regardless of ethnic origin, belonged to a united Hungarian nation (*magyar nemzet*). Hungarian would become the official language of the country, but the use of languages of other nationalities would be allowed at lower administrative levels. This was in line with the liberals' view of a Hungarian territorial state-nation. In practice, however, the interpretation of the ethno-nationalists prevailed. After the *Ausgleich*, the Hungarian state became totally Magyar in its character, with only Hungarian used in administration and almost entirely dominant in education. Language became an instrument of discrimination, a means of maintaining Magyar hegemony in political and cultural life.[14]

Hungary did not succeed in building a supra-ethnic Hungarian state-national identity for all its inhabitants. There is a string of probable reasons for this failure. A state-nation in a country with such a great ethnic diversity as Hungary would have needed a strong state power keeping the nation together, creating loyalty, and active from the outset of state formation. This Hungary lacked. Ever since 1526, the Hungarian people had owed loyalty firstly to the Habsburg emperor, who had no interest in creating a Hungarian state-nation. By the time the ideal of a Hungarian nation had become a mass phenomenon, the various different nationalities in historic Hungary had already begun their own processes of nation-building, and Hungarian nationalism precipitated this rather than slowing it down. In such a situation the acknowledgement of rights of nationalities and the achievement of

[13] There was hardly any talk of federative solutions. Such proposals were made by the most liberal circles (e.g. Oskar Jászi), but only at the end of the First World War, when the fate of Hungary was largely sealed. See Pearson (1983: 170).

[14] According to Kann (1950: i. 110), the Magyars accounted for about 96% of civil servants, about 93% of university lecturers, and about 92% of grammar-school teachers before the First World War, whereas they constituted less than 50% of the total population at that time.

social and political reforms were probably the only way of winning the loyalty of the non-Magyars towards the Hungarian state.

This, however, was never carried through, because the nobility, who held the leading positions, were mainly concerned with preserving their own privileged status. Since national differences were to a great extent accompanied by social cleavages (for example, the nobility were almost all Magyars or Magyarized; speakers of Slavonic languages or of Romanian were largely peasants), discrimination against other nationalities lay in the socio-economic interest of the nobility. It allowed them to maintain their domination over the non-Magyar population and simultaneously gave the lowest Magyar classes social and psychological advantages, which made it easier for them to accept the non-democratic social and political system.[15] Another aspect of the parallelism of linguistic and ethnic differences with social ones was that the national aspirations of the oppressed peoples were allied to the struggle for the emancipation of the lowest classes, which gave force to the national movements. The Habsburg emperors also learned to use these conflicts between Magyars and non-Magyars to their own advantage in order to control all the nationalities in the empire. Not infrequently they acted according to the principle of divide and rule.

Last but not least, a reason for the failure of the Hungarian project of a state-nation can be seen in the demographic factor and its emotional consequences. In the nineteenth century, Hungarian-speakers constituted less than 50 per cent of the population of Hungary. The fear of 'drowning in a Slavonic sea', which Herder gave expression to, the feeling of being 'a fortress under siege', created emotionally defensive reactions, which influenced politics in the direction of Magyarization (see Barany 1990: 180). This policy in the end led to the alienation of all non-Magyar nationalities from the Hungarian state, and they sought to leave it, when, as part of Austria-Hungary, it was defeated in the First World War.

9.2.3. *Hungary since the First World War*

The implementation of the Treaty of Trianon in 1920 meant that Hungary was reduced to 32.7 per cent of its previous territory and kept only 41.6 per cent of its population. The Slovaks formed a state together with the Czechs, the Croats became part of Yugoslavia, and Transylvania with its Romanian majority was incorporated into Romania. The new Hungary was ethnically relatively homogeneous. About 10 per cent were minorities: Germans, Slovaks, Croats, Romanians, Roma.[16] The problem, however, was that 32 per cent of the Magyars of historic Hungary found themselves in new states and divided by new borders drawn in an arbitrary way by the great powers. Thus Hungary could use the linguistic princi-

---

[15] Kann discusses the significance of this factor for Magyar nationalism and compares the situation of the Magyar peasant in Hungary to that of the poor British worker in a British colony. Both could use the inferior position of the poor of other nationalities to their advantage (see Kann 1950, i. 113).

[16] Since the classification was based on mother tongue, these statistics give no indication of the number of Jews in the Hungarian state (see Pearson 1983: 172–3; cf. Horak 1985: 2).

ple to legitimate its revisionist claims upon territories inhabited by Hungarians that had been incorporated into other states—for instance, Czechoslovakia or Romania.

In 1939–40 Hungary, with the support of Nazi Germany, annexed parts of these states. Since 1945, Hungarian borders have been more or less the same as set down in the Treaty of Trianon, and, because of Magyarization, Hungary became in the second half of the twentieth century by and large an ethnically homogeneous state. The minorities form only 1.5 per cent of the total population (Horak 1985: 2).This uniformity largely contributes to the fact that the linguistic and ethnic principle now determines national identity.

However, the Hungarian minorities in the neighbouring countries remain, and, if antagonized, they may cause a conflict in which Hungarian nationalists could make use both of linguistic and ethnic arguments, as well as historic claims.

9.3. Poland

9.3.1. *Polish Proto-Nationalism*

The date for Poland's entry onto the historic arena of Europe is usually set at 966, the year when the country was converted to Christianity. Linguistically Poland was probably a rather homogeneous country at that time: its inhabitants spoke a Slavonic language, which, as a result of the drawing of political borders, was called Polish, although during the Middle Ages it did not greatly differ from the neighbouring West Slavonic languages, such as Czech or Slovak. The territory of all of these languages (apart from the isolated Sorbian) was, and still is, a dialect continuum—that is, the dialect speech of each locality is comprehensible in the next locality throughout a large territory, though dialects at the ends of a chain of localities may not be mutually comprehensible (see Marti 1993: 290–1). This continuum was in time weakened through political divisions into separate states. These divisions entailed cultural differences and the gradual emergence of distinct standard languages.

From the eleventh to the fifteenth century, due perhaps to the fact that Christianity had come to Poland via Bohemia, the Polish literary language developed under the influence of Czech. However, during the same period, a series of linguistic changes took place that tended to separate the two languages, such as the loss of nasal vowels in Czech, and the loss of vowel-length distinctions in Polish (see Lehr-Spławiński *et al.* 1947: 10–12). The languages went their own ways, and, in spite of a linguistic kinship, there is no doubt today that Polish and Czech are two distinct languages.

With the exception of Jewish and German settlements in the towns, medieval Poland was linguistically relatively homogeneous, and this uniformity was a source of ethnic unity, particularly pronounced during the wars against German neighbours recorded in medieval chronicles by Gallus Anonymus and others. The etymology of the Polish word *Niemiec* (German) is, as its counterparts in all other Slavonic languages, derived from the word meaning 'the mute', 'the one who cannot speak'. In other words, language was here an important dividing line between two different ethnic identities: Slavonic, on the one hand; German, on the other. The divisions within the Slavonic-speaking peoples were based on loyalty to different rulers and on different religions, which left an impact on the languages. The languages of the Slavs who belonged to Western Christianity were influenced by Latin (for example, the Latin alphabet was used, there were loan-words from Latin), and the languages of those who belonged to the Eastern Orthodox Church were influenced by Church Slavonic, the liturgical and literary language of Slavs belonging to the Eastern Orthodox Church, and the Byzantine heritage (for example, the Cyrillic alphabet was used).

In 1385 Poland formed a personal union with Lithuania, which led to the emergence of a vast, multi-ethnic empire. The Polish–Lithuanian state was inhabited by Poles, Lithuanians, Ruthenians, Germans, Jews, and smaller minorities such as Armenians and Tatars, each of them speaking their own language. Lithuanian, as a language belonging to the distinct Baltic subgroup of Indo-European, was clearly different from Polish, although in time, because of the close contact between the languages, its vocabulary was affected by Polish and Ruthenian. 'Ruthenians' (from Latin *Rutheni*) is the name given to those Orthodox East Slavs who were ruled by non-Orthodox sovereigns. Since its speakers were Orthodox Christians, the Ruthenian language was influenced by Church Slavonic. It was spoken in the territory of contemporary Belarus and Ukraine, and is the precursor of the modern Belorussian and Ukrainian languages, as well as modern Rusyn (see Section 9.2.2).[17]

The large Jewish population in Poland were so-called Ashkenazic Jews who had Yiddish as their mother tongue. Yiddish was originally a Jewish variety of Middle High German, influenced by Hebrew, and later by Slavonic languages. The Jews' position in Polish–Lithuanian society until the end of the eighteenth century can be compared to that of a caste. They had an established role in the economy, but they lived a totally separate social life and very few assimilated to their Christian surroundings.

The language of administration in the multi-ethnic Polish–Lithuanian state was Latin. From the end of the fifteenth century, however, Polish gained in importance. This was due partly to the development of a Polish literary language under the influence of the Reformation, partly to the political emancipation of the Polish nobility. In a gradual process, crowned by a special law, *Nihil Novi* in 1505,

---

[17] The Latin term *Rutheni* delimited them from the other Orthodox East Slavs called *Moscovitae*. However, the Ruthenians called themselves *ruskije* in their own language, the same name as the *Moscovitae* also gave to themselves. Both groups inherited this name from the period when they were united within Kievan Rus between 800 and 1240 (see 12.1.2). The Ruthenian ethnic community split up during the nineteenth century into different national groups: Ukrainians, Belorussians, and Rusyns (see above, n. 9). For more about the Ruthenian language, see Moser (1995: 117–23).

the nobility gained control over the state. The power of the king was severely curtailed to the advantage of the *Sejm*—the parliament of the nobility. In 1539 the *Sejm* decided that all legislation was to be published in Polish, with summaries in Latin. This added significantly to the status of the Polish language. In 1569 the Polish–Lithuanian personal union became a constitutional union. The institutions, which had until then functioned separately in Poland and Lithuania, were now the same for Poland, Lithuania, and part of Little Russia (Ukraine). The noblemen who were speakers of Polish, Lithuanian, or Ruthenian sat together in the *Sejm* and decided on all important affairs of the state. They used Latin as a means of communication, but learning Polish became more and more attractive for Lithuanian and Ruthenian noblemen, and also for the townspeople in those territories. Polish was at that time a well-developed literary language and the Polish parts of the country held the most important centres of culture and learning. Not without importance was the fact that Latin was particularly alien to the Ruthenian nobility, who belonged to the cultural sphere of the Eastern Orthodox Church. The nobility of the *Rzeczpospolita* (this name is a translation of Latin *res publica* (republic), and refers to that particular political system, the democracy of the nobility) was numerous (more than 9 per cent of the entire population) and considered equal before the law. Neither in Poland nor in Hungary, however, was a title accompanied by a granting of land. Therefore, the material status of the nobility varied greatly and some noblemen were as poor as peasants. By speaking Polish, the Lithuanian and Ruthenian nobility could affirm their social position in relation to Lithuanian and Ruthenian peasants.

In the seventeenth century, Polish became, besides Latin, which still retained an important position, the cultural language of the Lithuanian and Ruthenian nobility. In 1697 Ruthenian was abolished as the language of the Lithuanian ducal court and replaced with Polish. In spite of this tendency towards Polonization, it must be noted that the notion of *Polonus* (Pole) did not, at that time, have an ethnic or linguistic dimension. *Natio Polonica* signified all the nobility, and only the nobility, in the Polish–Lithuanian state, regardless of ethnic origin. In this respect *Natio Polonica* was a phenomenon parallel to *Natio Hungarica*, described earlier. *Natione Polonus, gente Ruthenus, origine Judaeus* (Polish by nationality, of the Ruthenian people, and of Jewish origin) is a frequently quoted example of how noblemen in the *Rzeczpospolita* could describe their identity.[18] The affiliation to *Natio Polonica* was founded on loyalty towards the state, its political institutions, the political system and the territory, but not necessarily towards the king, whom the nobility often defied. Moreover, it was important to be part of a cultural community, constituted by the values, traditions, attitudes, and so on shared by all the nobility in the *Rzeczpospolita*.

---

[18] Davies (1981: i. 12). Davies compares the significance of 'Polish' at that time to 'British'. Both refer to the affiliation to a state and do not exclude the affiliation to an ethnically defined nation, e.g. Lithuanian or Scottish. See also Davies (1981: i. 119–20).

The limitation of the notion *Natio Polonica* to the nobility was not questioned until the second half of the eighteenth century. Because of the influence of the ideas of the Enlightenment and the French Revolution, discussions began about the necessity to extend the notion to the members of all estates (see Walicki 1990). The majority of the nobility wanted to safeguard their particular position and opposed this idea. Still, a huge step was taken in this direction by the adoption of the Constitution of 3 May 1791. It was never more than a piece of paper, however, since Poland ceased to exist politically in 1795 as a result of the Third Partition of the state between Russia, Prussia, and Austria. The fact that the idea of a nation encompassing all social strata found a breeding ground among part of the population is confirmed by the events of 1794, when some of the peasantry and poor urban population joined the Kościuszko uprising. The aim of this defeated revolt was to defend the Constitution of 3 May and the remnants of independence the state still enjoyed.

9.3.2. *Poland in the Nineteenth Century: The Period of the Partitions*

The Polish–Lithuanian state disappeared and its territory and population were incorporated into the three neighbouring states: Russia, Prussia, and Austria. The Polish nobility remained the most important bearer of the idea of a Polish state and claimed that there still existed a Polish nation with a right to its own state. This claim was voiced during the 123 years of Polish absence from the map of Europe; it was expressed both in diplomatic endeavours and in armed struggle (1797–1813, 1830, 1846, 1863, 1918). During this entire period, the nobility and later also the Polish intelligentsia preached the need to defend Polish national identity.

In time, however, the content of this notion changed. During the first half of the nineteenth century, Polishness was defined mainly on historical and territorial grounds. All peoples who inhabited the territory of the old *Rzeczpospolita* were understood to belong to the Polish nation. This was a political definition of national identity, inherited from the Republic of the Nobility, but more democratic. The great Polish national poet of the Romantic era, Adam Mickiewicz, saw no contradiction in writing in Polish and praising Lithuania as his homeland. Members of the Lithuanian nobility were also active in the Polish liberation movement of the Romantic period. Future Poland was to be, according to the politicians of Polish Romanticism, a multi-ethnic state, in which all nationalities had the right to develop their languages and cultures (even federal models were discussed). Polish would be the official language (Ruthenian was also mentioned (see Walicki 1982: 69–74)) but, in contrast to developments in Hungary, any programme of assimilation to the (Polish) majority met with opposition.

In the course of time, this political definition of the Polish nation could not be maintained. Historical memories could not, in the absence of a state, create unity among a multi-ethnic population. Moreover, the emancipation of peasants who did not speak Polish (Ukrainians, Belorussians, Lithuanians) led to an awakening of their own national aspirations, in which they particularly identified Polishness with their social and economic opponents, the nobility. The élites that emerged from these populations advocated their own ideas of a nation, based on language, ethnic origin, sometimes also religion. Polish territorial nationalism, which had no support from a state power, could not assert itself in the confrontation with these ethnic nationalisms. Instead, Polish nationalism gradually also acquired a linguistic and ethnic character.

Moreover, the historical memories of a dismantled state did not suffice to mobilize the Polish masses, especially the peasants, towards national goals. Other components of the collective identity had to be employed: language and religion served well. In the *Rzeczpospolita*, Polish had never succeeded in superseding Latin in official use. That had been the goal of some of the Polish reformers of the Enlightenment. The Commission for National Education (*Komisja Edukacji Narodowej*), founded in 1773, had advocated Polish as the language of instruction in all schools, developed Polish scientific terminology, and codified the language in the first Polish grammar for schools, which was the contribution of Onufry Konopczyński. All these endeavours bore fruit later, during the period of the partitions. The partitioning powers abolished Latin and introduced Russian and German respectively as the languages of administration and education. The policy of Russification and Germanization was at times very harsh. However, the Polish language resisted the pressure, was developed and modernized. This was due to the existence of a nationally conscious nobility, and, more important still, of an intelligentsia, first stemming from the lower nobility, later also of lower-class origin. These groups saw in language the foundation of national identity—a perception at least partly due to German Romantic philosophy and the German model of a nation that maintains its identity through culture and language, while not united within a single state. The language united the Poles of all three partition regions; it was the key to Polish literature that played an enormous part in spreading national ideas and historical consciousness. The language also united the nobility with the peasants, which was important for the formation of a Polish nation in the modern sense, one encompassing all social strata.

Another unifying factor was the Catholic Church, not least because the Poles now found themselves as minorities among an Orthodox majority in the Russian Empire and a Protestant majority in Prussia (Austria was Catholic). The Church also represented the continuity of the vanished state, since it was the only Polish institution that had survived the state's fall. It cultivated the Polish language; priests of lower rank joined in the struggle for liberation. Moreover, the connection between Polishness and Catholicism had its roots in the Nobility Republic of the seventeenth century, when the Counter-Reformation had its heyday. At that time, Poland had fought wars with neighbours of other creeds: Protestant Swedes, Orthodox Russians, Muslim Turks. Poland adopted the role of 'the bulwark of Christianity'. National (in the meaning of that time) and religious goals were linked and that resulted, among other things, in a number of myths and symbols of national-cum-religious character, such as the icon of the Virgin Mary of

Częstochowa, known as 'the Black Madonna' and 'the Queen of Poland', which were spread by the Church and later also by literature. In the process of nation-building these myths and symbols became part of Polish national identity. They had a mobilizing and integrating function.[19] The Catholic faith itself was an iden-tity-marker first and foremost among those peasants who lived in the ethnically mixed border territories. Catholic peasants were then treated as Poles in opposi-tion to peasants belonging to the Orthodox or Uniate churches.[20] These were regarded as Ruthenians or later, after the emergence of the Ukrainian and Belorussian national movements, as either Ukrainians or Belorussians; in other words, they were defined, and they defined themselves, as belonging to different ethnic or national communities, even in cases where they all (Catholics, Orthodox, Uniates) spoke the same dialect. In the ethnically more homogeneous territories, and among the nobility and the intelligentsia, religion was, alongside the language, an important marker of identity for Poles in Orthodox Russia and Protestant Prussia, but less important in the Catholic Habsburg Monarchy.

Both language and religion became foundations of the modern national ideol-ogy that was formulated in Poland at the end of the nineteenth century and advo-cated by a political party called *Endecja* (National Democracy) with Roman Dmowski as its leader. The advocates of this ideology repudiated the Romantic notion of the Polish nation as a historic, political, and multi-ethnic community. In opposition to it they formulated the concept of a nation based on ethnicity, language, and religion. The Polish nation was to include those that had Polish as their mother tongue and preferably were Catholics. Such an interpretation of the concept of nation left outside the Polish community not only those who did not speak Polish but even Polish-speaking groups who did not want to give up their separate religious identities. This was the case with some Jews, who had just started to be assimilated into Polish society. However, national ideology thus formulated gained the support of the Polish peasantry. They could be mobilized to defend their language and faith, which were threatened by the powers of which they were subjects. In a widely known patriotic song dated 1908, '*Rota*' ('The Vow'), written for the peasants who fought Germanization, the following phrases recur: 'We shall not abandon our tongue . . . we shall not abandon our faith . . . we shall not abandon our land . . .'. Language, religion, and territory are thus viewed as the backbone of Polish national identity.

9.3.3. *Poland since the First World War*

Polish political nationalism, a form of state nationalism that grew out of the old

---

[19] On the role of national myths in Poland, see Törnquist-Plewa (1992). On the significance of myths for national identity in general, see A. D. Smith (1986: 2).

[20] The Uniate Church, known also as the 'Greek-Catholic confession of the Slavonic Rite', came into existence in 1596 when a section of the Orthodox Church in Poland accepted a union with Rome. It recognized the supremacy of the Pope, but was allowed to keep its Slavonic liturgy and its traditional practices (such as married clergy).

Polish–Lithuanian state, could not be transferred to the broad strata of the popu-lation when that state ceased to exist. Ethno-nationalism gained more and more ground in the nineteenth century and became the truly active force in the build-ing of the modern Polish nation at the end of that century.

Nevertheless, the ideas of political nationalism were not totally forgotten. At the end of the First World War, when the Polish state was reborn, they were taken up again by part of the political élite, with Józef Piłsudski at its head. Piłsudski's plans for a federation of Poland, Lithuania, Belarus, and Ukraine ended in Poland annexing, after a war with the Soviet Union, the western part of Ukraine and Belarus as well as the town of Vilnius in Lithuania, against the wishes of its Lithuanian population.

Large minorities found themselves within the borders of the Polish state: Ukrainians (10.5%), Ruthenians (4%), Jews (8.5%), Belorussians (3.1%), Germans (2.3%). Putting into practice the idea of a political nation including all these peoples, who already had their own national movements on ethno-nationalistic principles and often with the support of neighbouring states, was by and large impossible, especially as the Poles themselves, as the dominant nation, were ethno-nationalists and a great many of them dreamt of an ethnically based state. This could not lead to anything other than attempts at Polonizing the minorities and rejecting their claims for autonomy, which also happened during the years between the world wars.

Events during and after the Second World War—the Nazi extermination of the Jews, a new drawing of borders, population transfers (mainly Germans and Ukrainians)—all contributed to a relatively homogeneous population in post-war Poland. This fortified the role of language in national identity. However, sociolin-guistic research in Poland shows that the position of language as a marker of national identity is evaluated differently depending on the level of education of the persons questioned. The intelligentsia ranks language as the most important, primary factor, while peasants and people with less schooling consider the complex culture–tradition–religion to be just as important, as well as ethnic origin (see Bartol-Jarosińska 1991). The principle of 'ethnic origin' was applied in Poland by the Communist authorities against Jews in 1968; more than 40,000 totally assimilated Jews were forced to leave Poland at that time (Kersten 1992: 160).

Catholic religion as a marker of nationality gradually diminished in impor-tance during the twentieth century, even though the position of the Catholic Church in Polish society was fortified during the years of Communist persecu-tion. However, it is not the Catholic faith itself, but Catholic tradition, entwined with the national element in the Polish cultural heritage, that is relevant for Polish national identification. It is the internalization of this cultural code (including myths, customs, attitudes) and not affiliation to the Catholic Church, that today is significant for one's national identity in Poland.

Today there are minorities who declare themselves to belong to other nations.[21] There are Ukrainians, Belorussians, and Lithuanians, who define themselves thus on the basis of their mother tongue. Since 1989, the year of the collapse of the Soviet system, there are also a growing number of inhabitants of Upper and Lower Silesia who declare themselves to be Germans, although a large part of them do not speak German. They base their Germanness on blood ties, on their origin. After the Second World War those who declared themselves to be Germans were forced to leave Poland, according to the provisions in the Potsdam Treaty. Those who for various reasons were allowed to stay concealed their origin. The families were Polonized, but today they want to reassert their German nationality and they are accordingly regarded by Germany as a German minority, on the basis of the ethnic (but not the linguistic) principle.

Apart from national minorities in Poland, there are various ethnic groups, such as Lemkos (who most often declare themselves to be Ruthenians), Roma, and Kashubians. The status of Kashubians is controversial. They are seen (and considered themselves) as either an ethnic or a linguistic group, depending on the view of the Kashubian language as either a distinct Western Slavonic language or a Polish dialect. The status of Kashubian has been the subject of prolonged disputes among linguists and can serve as an illustration of how nationalistic thinking can distort the perception of a language. From the diachronic point of view of historical linguistics, Kashubian, together with Polish and the extinct Slovincian and the extinct Polabian, constitute the so-called Lechitic subgroup within the West Slavonic languages. Kashubian underwent by and large the same linguistic processes as Polish, but maintained a series of archaic features, some of which were also present in Polabian and some in Old Polish. To this were later added a few phonetic and morphemic changes, typical only of Kashubian. The vocabulary, on the other hand, was influenced by both Polish and German.[22] Kashubian has several dialectal varieties that differ significantly from each other, and it is not possible to speak of a Kashubian standard language, even though attempts at standardization have been made (see Topolińska 1980: 183). From a synchronic point of view, Polish linguists therefore view Kashubian as a Polish dialect. This is refuted by those non-Polish linguists who in their analyses assume the diachronic perspective, such as Brozović (1965: 245–54) or allow the degree of mutual comprehensibility between Kashubian and Polish to be decisive, such as Kloss (1969: 146–55). As is always the case with a division of a dialect continuum into separate languages, there is scope here for manipulation. Since both Poles and Germans have in the course of history made claims on the territory that is inhab-

---

[21] There are no official data concerning the number of national minorities published by the Polish statistical yearbooks. According to estimations made by the Department of Minorities and Ethinic Groups in the Ministry of Culture and Art in Warsaw (Nov. 1993), there were about 500,000 Germans, 350,000 Ukrainians, 300,000 Belorussians, 25,000 Lithuanians, 25,000 Slovaks, and 20,000 others (see Gwiazda 1994: 442).

[22] For a more detailed account, see Baudouin de Courtenay (1983). See also Topolińska (1980) and Popowska-Taborska (1980).

ited by Kashubians, the Poles were eager to prove that the Kashubians belonged to Poland, while the Germans wanted arguments for the opposite. The Kashubians themselves have been divided about the issue of the status of their language. However, because of political and social changes in Poland during the 1990s, a movement has arisen that aims to upgrade the social and linguistic status of Kashubian. A growing consensus that Kashubian is a distinct Slavonic language can be witnessed. In 1999 Kashubian was taught in some schools in northern Poland, and at the University of Gdansk. There are no statistics about speakers of Kashubian, but it is estimated that they number about 330,000.[23]

9.4. Slovakia

9.4.1. *Slovakia before the Nineteenth Century*

In contrast to the nations of Poland and Hungary, Slovakia is an example of what we here call a 'non-historic nation'. From the time of the invasion of the Magyars (903–7), and their destruction of the Slavonic state of Greater Moravia, until 1918, the areas along the crescent of the Carpathian mountains inhabited by Slovaks were part of the Hungarian state.

During the Ottoman period (1526–1699), the Slovak part (Upper Hungary) was the core of what remained of the old Hungarian state. The nobility of Slovak origin became part of *Natio Hungarica* and was with time Magyarized. By the end of the eighteenth century, at the time when modern nations began to form, the Slovaks had for this reason no nationally conscious nobility of their own. The bearers of national ideas were the intelligentsia, including the clergy, and to some degree the bourgeoisie (see Hroch 1985: 44–61).

Politically and, to a considerable degree, culturally, the Slovaks were integrated into the Hungarian state. One reason for this was the unifying Catholic tradition in its Hungarian version (with *Primas Hungariae* as the head of the Church, Hungarian kings as saints, and so on). The separating factor, which determined the distinct ethnic identity of the Slovaks inside the Hungarian state, was the language. This language, or, more precisely, three different Western Slavonic dialects that were spoken by the Slovaks before the codification of a standard language, was the basis for their affiliation with their Slavonic neighbours, the Czechs. From the eleventh century Czechs and Slovaks belonged to two different political units, which led to the development of different cultural identities. The borders between the Czech and Slovak language areas have always been difficult to trace. We can here speak of a dialect continuum with a broad transitional area in Moravia (see Marti 1993: 298–9). Mutual intelligibility has always been high, which led to the development of close cultural contacts. In the fifteenth and sixteenth centuries many Slovaks studied at the university in Prague. There they

---

[23] On the Kashubians, see Gustavsson (1990: 74), Majewicz (1996).

came into contact with the Czech literary language, which they used as their own written language as an alternative to the universally used Latin. This was particularly attractive to the advocates of the Lutheran Reformation. For Slovak Lutherans, Czech was the language of worship and also the language of culture (Ďurovič 1980: 212).

Catholic Counter-Reformers could not, therefore, avoid using Czech as their written language, but, in order to mark a difference from their religious opponents and reach the broad masses of the faithful, they used a version of Czech with Slovak influence, the so-called *jezuitská slovenčina*. Czech maintained its strong position in Slovakia during the entire seventeenth century, owing among other factors to an influx of Czech Protestant emigrants who had fled persecution in Bohemia, where the Habsburgs began a harsh Counter-Reformation campaign after 1620. In the Hungarian crown lands they were protected by the separate laws of Old Hungary (the Golden Bull of 1222, Tripartitum of 1517), which the Habsburgs respected. The Czech Protestants soon merged into their Lutheran Slovak surroundings, and contributed to the strengthening of ties between Lutheran Slovaks and Czech culture. These ties, and the strong linguistic consciousness of the Lutheran Slovaks, made them especially aware of the separate identity of the Slovaks among the peoples of Hungary and of the linguistic community they formed with the Czechs. Grammars written by Lutheran Slovaks with the purpose of codifying their language, which they called *lingua Slavonico-Bohemica*, reinforced these links.[24]

The ties of the Catholic Slovaks with the Czechs were weaker than those of their Lutheran compatriots and their affiliation to Hungary was much stronger, mainly because of the common Catholic Church and tradition. These differences turned out to be important when the Slovaks at the end of the eighteenth century needed to assert their language against first German, which had been introduced as the language of administration in the Habsburg Monarchy, and later against Hungarian. The Slovak Catholics rejected Czech as their written language. Instead they attempted to create their own literary language. In 1790 Anton Bernolák published a first grammar of the Slovak literary language, based mainly on Western Slovak dialects; Western Slovakia was an important cultural centre. The language of Bernolák was not generally accepted. It was rejected by the Lutheran intellectual élite, which held an important place in Slovak cultural life. Nor was his linguistic reform accompanied by a national political programme. In the introduction to his grammar he declared his loyalty to Hungary, which he called his homeland (Niederhauser 1982: 226). Besides, the variety of Slovak that he proposed was too remote from other Slovak dialects to be readily accepted in all regions.

---

[24] Ďurovič presents evidence of the links from the grammar books of Krman of 1704 and Doležal of 1746. See Ďurovič (1992: 180, *passim*). See also Ďurovič (1993: 96–7).

9.4.2. Slovakia in the Nineteenth Century

In 1843 there was another proposal for codification of the Slovak literary language, this time from the Lutherans.[25] Ludovit Stúr and his friends Jozef Miloslav Hurban and Michal Miloslav Hodža from the Lutheran College in Bratislava based their variety of the literary language on the speech of the towns of central Slovakia, which meant that it was further removed from Czech than in Bernolák's case. The differences were especially manifest in phonology and morphology. As for vocabulary, Stúr was eager to maintain common ground with Czech as far as possible (Ďurovič 1980: 216).

Stúr's language reform was an important step in the formation of Slovak national identity. Along with the definitive rejection of Czech as the literary language went the rejection of the idea that the Slovaks were part of the Czech nation because of the language and some shared cultural traditions. That idea had prevailed within the Czech national movement (e.g. Palacký) and also among some Slovak Lutherans (e.g. Kollár, Palkovič). By developing their own literary language, the Slovaks at the same time initiated the struggle against Magyarization and the political domination of the Magyars. They refuted the idea that they were part of the Hungarian state-nation.

This linguistic and cultural programme was followed up by a political one. In 1848 the Slovak national élite, led by Stúr, demanded Slovak autonomy within the Habsburg Monarchy. In the same year the Slovaks took part on the Austrian side in the suppression of the Hungarian Revolt. The political alignment of Stúr and his circle contributed to the acceptance of his reform among both the Lutherans (not without harsh criticism) and Catholics; after some adjustments there was a Lutheran–Catholic compromise in 1851.

The development of the language and the national culture for which it laid the basis (literature, science, theatre, education) remained until 1918 the most important goals of the Slovak national movement. Political demands were but feebly articulated. Nationalism was expressed in the struggle for the status of the national language and culture, for instance in national myths connected with the Slavonic Greater Moravia or in pan-Slavonic ideals that looked for support towards the mighty Russia. The struggle for language was first and foremost directed against Hungarian, but the separate status of Slovak versus Czech was also asserted. One example of this was the linguistic theories of Sumo Czambel, who wished to prove that Slovak was in fact part of the South Slavonic and not the West Slavonic language group. Disagreement among the Slovak intelligentsia about political loyalty towards the Hungarian state was the main reason why the Slovak national movement lacked a strong political programme. The lack of such

---

[25] According to Niederhauser, one of the factors that speeded up language reform was the Hungarian proposal to unite the Lutheran and Calvinist church organizations, which would have meant a Hungarian predominance in the Protestant churches. Opposing this project, the Lutheran Slovaks needed the support of Catholic Slovaks. See Niederhauser (1982: 230–1).

a programme and weak support for the Slovak national idea among the masses, especially the peasants, jeopardized the further development and perhaps the very existence of the Slovak nation when harsh policies of Magyarization set in after the Austro-Hungarian *Ausgleich* in 1867. Practically no Slovak schools were left. Because of persecution, nearly all political activity ceased.

9.4.3. *Twentieth-Century Slovakia*

The dissolution of Austria-Hungary at the end of the First World War meant a new chance for the Slovak nation. However, there was no national mass movement. A group of active Slovak politicians (Hlasists and later the Slovak National Party) shared Tomáš Masaryk's idea of one Czech and Slovak state. This idea had its main supporters among the Slovak and Czech émigré community in the USA, who produced the so-called Pittsburgh Agreement on 30 May 1918. The issue was not put to a referendum either during or after the war. Instead, Slovak politicians declared on 30 October 1918 their will to be unified with the Czechs in one Czechoslovakia, two days after the Czechoslovak Republic had already been proclaimed under the leadership of a provisional government. In general, the Slovak population stayed passive also during the armed struggle for the control of those Slovak territories that were in Magyar hands. These would have remained so, had it not been for the Czech army supported by France.[26]

It was not until after the foundation of the Czechoslovak Republic that the Slovak national idea gained popularity among the masses. This became possible because of the democratic constitution, which guaranteed the Slovaks access to education in their own language and freedom to develop their culture and create their own national political parties and organizations. However, Slovak nationalism gradually took a turn that opposed the fundamental idea of the republic, of the existence, proclaimed in the constitution of 29 February 1920, of a single Czechoslovak nation. The Czechoslovak idea had broad support among Slovak Lutherans, who traditionally were more attached to Czech culture, and liberals, who in the further existence of the Czechoslovak Republic saw a guarantee of the maintenance of democracy in Slovakia. The emergence of nationalistic and fascist regimes in several European countries dampened their enthusiasm for Slovak independence, especially as such right-wing tendencies could be seen in the Slovak nationalism of the time. Nevertheless, the anti-Czechoslovak atmosphere grew stronger during the period between the wars and was fully expressed in the separatist demands of Andrej Hlinka's clerical Slovak People's Party. The background to these tendencies is extremely complex and here we can mention only a few factors.

Already when the state was formed, the Czech part was much stronger economically and culturally. Thus the Slovaks occupied a secondary position from the outset. This was in contrast to their earlier relative economic strength, which

---

[26] The Slovak National Committee asked the Czechs for military assistance (see Horak 1985: 111–12).

had been high compared to the rest of Hungary. The Czechs assumed the role of bearers of modernization and civilization (*Kulturträger*), sometimes resulting in a barely concealed arrogance, which upset the national feelings of the Slovaks. The large influx of educated Czechs into Slovakia, motivated by the lack of a qualified workforce, was seen by many Slovaks, especially the emerging Slovak intelligentsia, as some kind of colonization, and as an attempt to monopolize the most attractive jobs. Conflicts of mentality and cultures also appeared. Catholic Slovaks were alienated by the atheist or religiously indifferent attitudes of the Czechs, who in turn saw Slovak Catholicism as a sign of backwardness. This led to Catholicism becoming a marker of an anti-Czechoslovak attitude. Devout Catholics even wanted Catholicism to become a new marker of Slovak national identity, which was naturally unacceptable to Slovak Lutherans. Next to language, religion was particularly important for Catholic peasants, who now massively joined the national movement for the first time. They also gave their support to Hlinka's nationalistic party. Nationalism found expression both in political activities and in linguistic campaigns. The background to this was the proclamation in the Czechoslovak constitution not only that Czechs and Slovaks formed a single nation, but also that they shared a single Czechoslovak language in two varieties: Czech and Slovak. The idea of a Czechoslovak language had its roots in the earlier tradition I have described, but it was unacceptable to many of those who wanted to assert the separate status of the Slovak nation. Thus the language issue again became extremely sensitive for the Slovaks. During the whole period between the wars, Slovak purists fought against everything they perceived as attempts to bring the two languages closer; for instance, where there were lexical and morphological doublets, one of which was close to its Czech counterpart, the normative handbook and the dictionary *Pravidlá slovenského pravopisu* of 1931 favoured the more distinctly Slovak alternatives (Ďurovič, 1980: 223). However, the anti-purist and pro-Czech side often had the upper hand because of its significant role at the University of Bratislava.

In the 1930s nationalist groups in Slovakia gained power, which in turn led to Slovakia leaving the crumbling republic in 1939 and setting up a Slovak state under German protection, a puppet republic steered by Nazi Germany.

In 1944 a national uprising proclaimed the restoration of Czechoslovakia. In the so-called *Košice* programme of 1945, elaborated by the Slovak resistance movement and the Czechoslovak government in exile, the conditions for coexistence in the common state were laid down. The Slovaks were allowed to form their own government and their own parliament, and there were to be analogous Czech organs—a so-called symmetrical model. The Czech organs were, however, not established; instead of corresponding Czech authorities, Prague was home to the state apparatus of the entire country. An asymmetrical model replaced the promised one, to the dissatisfaction of the Slovaks. However, the national issue was soon eclipsed by the struggle for power between Communists and the right-wing parties.

After the seizure of power by the Communists in 1948, the national apparatus of Slovakia became a pure formality in a centrally governed state, where all power was held by a single party with its headquarters in Prague. On top of all this the Communist party launched, in the 1960s, a struggle against so-called 'bourgeois nationalism', which the regime turned exclusively against the Slovaks (Kuhn 1982: 103). Similarly, the Slovaks were the hardest hit by the atheist programme of the Communists, since religion was firmly rooted in Slovakia. The involvement of Czech Communists in the anti-religious campaign fortified in Slovak eyes the negative stereotype, already familiar from the period between the wars, of the Czechs as enemies of religion. Thus religion again became important for Slovak peasants as a marker of national identity. All this left profound traces in the collective memory of the Slovaks and could later be used by the advocates of a separation of Czechs and Slovaks.

The Czechoslovak state became federalized only through the reforms of 1968, during the 'Prague Spring'. The federation law of 1968 proclaimed the coexistence of two equal socialist republics—the Czech and the Slovak—within the framework of one state (the symmetrical principle). Autonomy within a strictly centralized Communist state was in practice impossible, but federalization implied, among other things, the observation of national balance in the appointment of holders of important posts in the administration, and in the distribution of investment. This favoured Slovakia, which received 50 per cent of investments in spite of a smaller population (Slovaks 4.6 million, Czechs 9.8 million in 1980). The gap that, despite decades of coexistence, had formed between these two nations could, however, not be overcome by economic advantages.

After the fall of Communism in 1989 and the introduction of democracy, the Slovaks chose to go their own way.[27] The year 1993 saw the emergence of the independent Slovak Republic with a considerable Hungarian minority on its territory of about 580,000 or roughly 10 per cent of the population. Because of the linguistic and ethnic character of Slovak nationalism, this population, as well as other minority populations such as Roma, may come under severe pressure. The anxiety of Hungarian-speakers in Slovakia is based on earlier experience from the years immediately following the Second World War (see Lékó 1992: 84–6). At that time, an expulsion of the Hungarian minority to Hungary had been planned, but it was prevented by the great powers and ended only in a limited 'population exchange'. Attempts were also made at 're-Slovakizing' those Hungarians who declared or were made to declare that they had Slovak ancestors. Thus the linguistic definition of nationality was discarded in favour of the principle of 'ethnic origin' or 'blood ties', a practice known from other ethno-nationalisms—for instance, German nationalism—applied in Silesia, or Polish nationalism, directed against Jews in 1968.

---

[27] For the circumstances and the discussion surrounding the separation of the republics, see, *inter alia, Röster från Tjeckoslovakien (Tjecker och Slovaker går skilda vägar)*, 30–1 (Stockholm, 1992). The review contains a selection of articles from Czechoslovak papers. For references in English on this subject, see Innes (1995) and Leff Skalnik (1997).

As for the status of Slovak in socialist Czechoslovakia, the idea of a Czechoslovak language was not taken up again. Nevertheless, Slovak was under the influence of Czech, since the most important centres of power lay within the Czech part of the state. Some Slovaks, sensitive to the language issue, saw the remains of the Czechoslovak ideology in the activity of the joint commission for terminology, or in the Slovak dictionary, published in the 1960s. The Czech language remained the most important source for loan words in spite of the purists' endeavours.

The Slovak literary language has very strict norms, with an enormous intolerance against foreign words and even words from Slovak dialects. This is due to the fact that the language has become the most important marker of Slovak national identity. The language was used to compensate both for the lack of an independent state and for the lack of a historical tradition of a Slovak political entity. The importance of the language also arose from the fact that the intelligentsia was for a long time the sole bearer of the Slovak national idea. In a nation-state, such as Hungary after 1867, which forced a single language upon all inhabitants, the intelligentsia of the minority had, in order to advance socially, either to assimilate or to fight for the status of their language, a struggle often combined with politically nationalist goals.

There are cases when a distinct language constitutes a basis for separation of a group and creation of a nation, and cases when a nation creates a national language with the very aim of separating itself from others. In the Slovak case both kinds of development can be seen to apply. Their Slavonic language separated the Slovaks from the Magyars, in spite of their historic unity. Their separate identity was the basis for the next step, the creation of their own written language, which was shared with the Czechs before the reforms of Štúr. The Slovak case shows that language as an identity-marker in itself is important as a delimiting factor in the process of separation between nations. Language, on the other hand, is insufficient to create unity if it is not accompanied by historical, cultural, or religious affiliation or at least by strong shared economic interests.

9.5. The Czech Lands

9.5.1. *Bohemia before the Nineteenth Century*

The independent Czech state is usually dated back to the tenth century when a feudal duchy was formed. In 1212 it became a kingdom consisting of two Crown lands: Bohemia (*Čechy*) and Moravia (*Morava*). At times, Silesia and Lusatia were also part of this state. It was often referred to as 'the Lands of the Crown of Saint Wenceslas', so named after the legendary ruler of the Premyslid dynasty and an important figure in Czech national tradition. In 962 the Czech Crown lands became part of the Holy Roman Empire and came under its cultural influence.[28]

---

[28] Henceforth I will call the Czech Lands, Bohemia and Moravia, 'Bohemia', following the practice

The country maintained its independence in all domestic affairs. Until the thirteenth century the majority of the population were Czech-speaking Slavs. Then significant German colonization took place, encouraged by the Czech kings. This radically changed the linguistic and ethnic structure. From then on, Bohemia was a country inhabited by two peoples with two languages. The culture of medieval Bohemia was an amalgam of Czech, German, and Latin–Christian elements. However, the coexistence of Czechs and Germans in the Czech Lands was not without problems. Medieval chronicles speak of ethnic conflicts, which stemmed from rivalry for power in the administration and at the royal court, as well as in the economy, mainly in the towns. There was no linguistic conflict, since Latin worked well for communication.

Still, language was stressed as an important separating and identifying factor between Czechs and Germans. The Czech *Dalimil* chronicle of the fourteenth century encourages the Czech nobility to cultivate their language and refrain from marriage with German women, who 'will teach their children German and alien customs'. This shows that some of the Czechs of that time had a clear ethnic identity, which was based mainly on the language. The emphasis the Czechs put on language as an identity-marker is explained by some scholars—for example, Roman Jakobson (1968: 585–97)—by the so-called Cyril (or Constantine)–Methodius heritage. Cyril and Methodius were two missionaries from Byzantium who came to Greater Moravia (of which Bohemia was part) in the ninth century and there introduced the first Slavonic written language, Old Church Slavonic. This language later had a considerable influence on several written Slavonic languages, Czech among them. An important part in the Cyril–Methodius heritage was the idea that the language of a people has the same value as Latin or Greek, and that 'God's word' ought to be preached in the vernacular. This was taken up in Bohemia in the fourteenth century (examples can be found in the translation of the Bible of the 1360s, the Slavonic liturgy in the Emaus monastery, and the ideas of Štitný) and became an important idea in the so-called Hussite movement at the beginning of the fifteenth century, one of the first reformation movements within Western Christianity, led by the Czech Jan Hus. An important demand of this early Czech reformation movement was precisely the availability of religious texts in the vernacular.[29]

The Czech literary language was based on central dialects from the Prague area, without any regional rivals. It progressed considerably in the fourteenth and fifteenth centuries. During the reign of Charles IV, Czech was introduced into education and partly into administration beside Latin. Its status was further fortified during the Hussite period, when it developed, was reformed (through Hus's

---

in many historical writings about this area. I will differentiate Moravia only when this is relevant for my argumentation.

[29] There had been translations of the Gospels and the Book of Psalms for centuries. These consisted of early translations into Church Slavonic, and later ones into Czech. In the 1360s came a complete translation of the Bible (see Ďurovič, 1986: 9–10).

spelling reform), and given more functions. In the middle of the fifteenth century Czech became a normalized and well-established standard language, used from 1495 as an official language in Bohemia (see Auty 1980: 170). The climax of its development during this period was a new translation of the Bible at the end of the sixteenth century by members of the Czech Brethren (*Jednota bratrská*). It was named the Kralice Bible, after the town of Kralice where it was printed.

During the Hussite reformation the balance of power between Czechs and Germans in Bohemia tipped in favour of the Czechs. The Germans repudiated Hus's teachings (for example, in the conflict on Wycliffe in 1409) and left Prague University and towns dominated by Hussites. The Czechs, on the other hand, largely supported Hus. Thus an ethnic dimension was added to the Hussite conflict, which was both religious and social, aligning petty nobility, poor peasants, and artisans against the established church and wealthy German burghers. Nineteenth-century Czech historians, beginning with Palacký, interpreted Hussitism as a national anti-German movement, a mass movement that united the Czech population of Bohemia in religious, social, and anti-German resistance. Hussitism is an example of the kind of 'proto-nationalism' that in the 19th century created a historical legitimacy for the modern national movement.

In spite of the Czech–German conflicts during the Hussite Wars (1419–34), the Germans remained an organic part of Bohemian culture. Nor did Bohemia dissociate itself from the Holy Roman Empire. In 1526 the Bohemian nobility elected a German–speaking ruler from the Habsburg dynasty. In the course of the sixteenth century the large part of the nobility adopted Lutheran Protestantism, which caused conflict with the Catholic Habsburg emperor, leading to the armed struggle of 1618–20. This had, however, a religious and not a national basis.

After the defeat of the Bohemian nobility by the Catholic Habsburg army at the Battle of the White Mountain (1620), Protestantism was forbidden by law, the Protestant Bohemian nobility emigrated *en masse*, and their estates were confiscated. A side effect of these measures was a strong Germanization; the Czechs had lost their cultural and political élite, while the Habsburg emperor accorded new titles and lands to outsiders, mainly Germans, who pledged loyalty to him. In 1627 the Habsburgs proclaimed their right to inherit the throne of Bohemia and power was centralized in Vienna. In the nineteenth century the Habsburgs were no longer crowned kings of Bohemia and Bohemia's legal status as a state was thus severely weakened.

The process of replacement of the Czech language by German began in the seventeenth century, and in 1784 German was proclaimed the only official language. Czech as an official language fell into disuse because the élite was either of German origin or voluntarily Germanized. A large part of the population with Czech ethnic roots was bilingual, using German in official situations and Czech in private life. The Czech written language stagnated and Czech was influenced by German. The lowest social classes often used a variety of Czech that was very heavily influenced indeed by German, so-called *Küchelböhmisch* (Kren, 1990: 45).

Thus the range of situations in which Czech was used was, until the nineteenth century, greatly restricted.

9.5.2. *The Czech Lands in the Nineteenth Century*

The end of the eighteenth century saw a renewed interest in the Czech language among intellectuals in Bohemia. Dobrovský (1753–1829), who assumed the task of describing the language as it had been in its time of glory at the end of the sixteenth century, considered it a historical relic that survived here and there in the Bohemian lands but did not stand a chance of becoming once again a living language of culture. His followers, both Czechs (Jungmann, Palacký, and Hanka) and Slovaks (Kollár and Šafárik), had a wholly different view. They considered that Czech ought to develop and become the most important instrument in the process they called 'the national revival'. In fact, this process was to be the formation of a new, modern nation, a complicated process with many interacting factors. The national fervour of the Czech intelligentsia was one of many facets of the forces opposing centralization that shook the authoritarian Habsburg Monarchy at the beginning of the nineteenth century. In Bohemia three such forces came to the fore, first Bohemian *Landespatriotismus* (a kind of state nationalism), which aimed to promote the special status of the whole of Bohemia within the empire, secondly German nationalism, and thirdly Czech nationalism.

Bohemian *Landespatriotismus* did not win wide acceptance, while the other two gained considerable support and led to the division of the Bohemian population into two linked and fiercely competing nations: Czech and German.

Czech nationalism developed to a considerable degree under the impact of German nationalism, which grew strong after the Napoleonic Wars. The Czechs, like other eastern Central European nations, were inspired by the German concept of nation, defined by culture and language. The Czech intelligentsia was also influenced by the national struggles of other central European peoples, such as the Hungarians and Poles (see Tarajło-Lipowska 1994). Another important factor was the idea of a Slavonic community, which developed among Czechs and Slovaks. It had its roots in the theories of Herder, which assumed that related languages implied related nations. This notion then gave inspiration in the twentieth century to the advocates of the ideal of a single Czechoslovak nation.

The Czech nationalism that grew in the nineteenth century also had a social dimension. It fed upon the socio-economic conflict between Czech peasants and German landed gentry and in a rivalry between the growing new bourgeoisie of Czech origin and the well-established German middle class (see Chlebowczyk 1980: 176–8; also Waldenberg 1992: 46). The Czech-speaking intelligentsia appointed themselves the spokesmen for this social and national struggle for emancipation. The Czech language became the most important mobilizing and integrating instrument in the formation of the modern Czech nation. Jungmann (1773–1847), a leading figure in the Czech 'national revival' proclaimed in his works that 'our nationality is in the language' (Bugge 1994: 26–7). Those who did not speak Czech could not call themselves Czechs. He claimed that there were two nations living in Bohemia. The task of the Czechs was to defend themselves against Germanization and be loyal towards their own nation.

Although there was in Bohemia an earlier historical tradition of an independent state, it could not readily be used in the creation of Czech national identity, since it was easier to use as an argument for a *Bohemian* identity, uniting Czech-speakers and German-speakers. History thus had to be reinterpreted on the basis of linguistic and national criteria. This was done in the most important historical work of the 'Czech national revival', *History of the Czech Nation* by F. Palacký. Palacký's work may be described as the history of the life of the Czech language in Bohemia. German–Czech relations since the thirteenth century were presented according to a contact-conflict model and showed the German-speakers as a permanent alien element (Bugge 1994: 51–3). Palacký himself was not anti-German, but his writings were later used in nationalist ideology and contributed to widening the gap between the Germans and the Czechs. Palacký's interpretation of Hussitism as the climax of the history of the Czech nation also had an important impact. It was a legitimating historical argument in national mobilization. However, it also led to a kind of religious schizophrenia (Czech Catholics had to be in favour of the Hussite reformation) and later to a widespread religious indifference. As I argued earlier, it had a negative impact on the relations between Czechs and the Catholic Slovaks.

In order to make the Czech language an integrating and mobilizing instrument for the national movement, its status had to be raised: it had to be standardized and developed into a fully fledged means of communication for a modern society. Jungmann and his generation of intellectuals, who were mobilized in the national cause, viewed this as their main task. However, as the model for the modern written literary language, they chose not the living language of that time, but the older written language in the form that had been codified in the Kralice Bible and described by Dobrovský. Phonologically and morphologically this language differed considerably from the Czech spoken at the time of the national revival. However, this choice was motivated partly by the low social status of spoken Czech and its considerable regional differentiation, and partly by the special historical legitimacy and authority of the older language, a fact that greatly facilitated its propagation (see Auty 1980: 175; Tarajło-Lipowska 1994). This older variety of the language was linked to the most glorious era in the history of the Czech people, the sixteenth century, to the time when the Czech Lands were an independent political entity, with Czech supremacy. The tradition of this state, together with the language, was to legitimize national aspirations. Besides, this language constituted a link with the old state's cultural heritage, the continuity of which had been disrupted after 1620. Linguistic continuity with the old Czech tradition was represented only clearly by Czech emigrants in Saxony, at Zittau, and Slovak Lutherans who in their churches used the Czech Kralice Bible, which also constituted a norm for their written language. Thus the old Czech language formed a cultural link between Czechs and some Slovaks. The next step in the language-planning undertaken by Jungmann and his followers was the extension and modernization of the vocabulary. The most important sources for new words were old Czech writings, dialects, and other Slavonic languages. Borrowings from non-Slavonic languages, especially German, were avoided. Neologisms were the preferred means of vocabulary extension. By the middle of the nineteenth century, Czech was already an established literary language with a variety of functions.

However, it was not entirely satisfactory for those who wanted to see the language as the bearer of Czech national identity, as the very essence of what was Czech. They considered that Czech ought to be purified from all traces of foreign influence. Intensive puristic activity (for example, the pamphlet *Brus jazyka českćho* of 1877 or the review *Naše řeč* of 1917) took place between the end of the nineteenth century and the First World War. All Germanisms were banned, even those that were common in many languages—so-called internationalisms; for example, *tyátr* (theatre) was replaced by *divadlo*. Alternative grammatical forms, taken from the spoken language and dialects, were eliminated as well. The historical model was to be followed in all situations, even if it made the written language seem archaic.

Criticism of this historical and puristic attitude came only in the 1930s, from the Prague linguistic circle, and slowly the prevailing trend was abandoned. Purism directed at elements of German origin disappeared after the Second World War when the Czechs found themselves beyond the influence of German culture (see Auty 1980: 181–2). Since 1989 the influence of English has increased.

The choice of the historic variety as a basis for the codification of the written language, followed by language-planning, led to a considerable gap between the written and the spoken languages. This gap is still present and the linguistic situation in the Czech Republic could be described as 'diglossia'. Within the same language there are two different codes used in different situations: the literary language (*spisovná čeština*) is used in all official situations (administration, education, and so on) and in writing, while the other variety (*obecná čeština*) is used in private life as the spoken language.[30]

Czech nation-building, initiated in the nineteenth century, made rapid progress. After the first phase of exclusively cultural character came, in 1848, political demands for autonomy within the empire. The national movement became a mass movement during the second half of the nineteenth century.[31] The national idea gained support among the lowest social classes much more quickly than in Hungary, Poland, or Slovakia. This had a number of reasons: the lands inhabited by the Czechs were among the most industrialized regions of the Habsburg Monarchy,

[30] For more on this, see Auty (1980), Townsend (1990: 1–14), and Tarajło-Lipowska (1994).

[31] The popularity enjoyed by the national organization *Sokol*, or the active participation of the masses in national festivals so-called 'tabors' (named after the town of Tabor, an important Hussite centre), in the years 1868–71, are instances of this. See Waldenberg (1992: 41).

which led to significant social mobility and a relatively high level of education, facilitating the spread of nationalist propaganda and contributing to intense cultural activity.[32] To this was added the need for incessant competition with growing German nationalism and its organizational structure.[33] Considering the force of the Czech national movement, its political aspirations were modest. Their furthest-reaching claims were made after the *Ausgleich* between Austria and Hungary in 1867, when they demanded the same status within the monarchy as the Hungarians. They argued from historical facts, demanding the right to a state for lands belonging to 'the Crown of Saint Wenceslas' (that is, Bohemia, Moravia, Silesia). These demands were never met. The frustrated Czechs then concentrated their political activities on promoting the status of the Czech language and putting it on an equal footing with German. Czech nationalism was mainly expressed in the struggle for the language and for Czech economic and cultural institutions, but not for political sovereignty. The latter was considered inappropriate, mostly because of the geographical and demographic situation of Bohemia. The numerous German population in Bohemia (about 3 million Germans versus 7 million Czechs in 1918), and the fact that there was a long border with the German Empire that aspired to unite within its territory all German-speakers, created a serious danger that Bohemia, separated from Austria, would be engulfed by the German state. The fear of absorption by Germany was expressed in Palacký's Austroslavism and later in the arguments of Masaryk. The large German minority was also an important reason why the Czechs sought unity with the Slovaks in one state. It was hoped that two million Slovaks would diminish the political importance of the Germans in the Czechoslovak state created in 1918.

9.5.3. *The Czech Lands in the Twentieth Century*

Czechoslovakia between the two world wars was a multi-ethnic state; in 1930, Czechs and Slovaks made up 64.1 per cent of the population, Germans 22.5 per cent, Hungarians 4.9 per cent, Ruthenians 3.9 per cent, Jews 1.4 per cent, Poles 0.7 per cent and others, including Roma, 4 per cent (see Pearson 1983: 152).

Its constitution was democratic and liberal, and guaranteed all citizens their rights. However, none of the minorities within the Czechoslovak borders was granted the autonomy that had been vaguely promised to the Slovaks (in the Pittsburgh Agreement) and to the Ruthenians (in the Philadelphia Agreement), and that the Germans demanded. This led to antagonisms. Particularly antagonized were the Germans and the Hungarians, whose position had been reduced

---

[32] Horizontal and vertical social mobility is viewed as an important factor for national mobilization and the process of nation-building (see Hroch 1985: 181–91). Among Czechs over the age of 6 only 4.26 % were illiterate, according to statistics from 1900 (see Waldenberg 1992: 41). For the connection between level of education, communication, and nationalism, see Deutsch (1966: 86–106).

[33] Some researchers see a clear parallel between the Czech and the German cultural organizations and institutions of that time, such as theatres, and mass cultural movements, and so on. See Bugge (1994: 28).

from leading nations within Austria-Hungary to minorities in a Slavonic state. Among them irredentism and nationalist tendencies were not unusual, particularly as they were fomented by the neighbouring states of Germany and Hungary.[34] The Polish minority was involved in the conflict between Poland and Czechoslovakia about the Teschen region. The Jews were integrated into the community and enjoyed a better situation than in the neighbouring countries, but there was still a pent-up popular anti-Semitism, fanned by the fact that in the nineteenth century Jews had generally been pro-German. The situation was not helped by the fact that there was both Czech and Slovak nationalism, both ethnic nationalisms, plus an official Czechoslovak state nationalism. The latter saw Czechoslovakia as a nation-state of Czechs and Slovaks, with a mission to render the Germans powerless, in spite of the fact that there were more Germans than Slovaks in the new state (3.2 million as opposed to 2.3 million (see Horak 1985: 117)). If the Slovaks' demands for autonomy were met, it would be difficult to deny the Germans the same. Instead, claims were made that Czechs and Slovaks formed one nation because of linguistic and ethnic kinship. The future showed how artificial and brittle this national construction was (see Section 9.4).

The polarization of Czechs and Germans in the nineteenth century, due among other things to the fact that the Czechs (and, to a considerable extent, also the Germans) adopted the concept of a nation based on language, made it impossible for the Czechs to conceive of a common Czech–German state founded on historic community and the cultural heritage of Bohemia. The Germans were excluded by definition from the historic community. Even Tomáš Masaryk, a politician and intellectual of high moral standards, could not reach beyond this ethnic and linguistic idea of the nation. In his inaugural address as president he emphasized that it was the Czechs who would decide on the status of the Germans, and that the Germans had originally come to Bohemia as immigrants and colonists (see Horak 1985: 111).

From the outset the Germans felt alienated in the Czechoslovak state. After a few years their parties were indeed represented in coalition governments, but they never acquired the status of a state-bearing nation, as did the Slovaks and the Czechs. To this day, Czech and German historians argue whether the Czechoslovak state did enough to win the loyalty of the Germans. One can wonder if this could ever have been possible, because of the strong antagonism that was present from the start. Apart from the shared territory, the only thing Germans and Czechs had in common during the period between the wars were economic interests. When these interests were threatened during the Depression, the Germans became receptive to nationalistic propaganda from Nazi Germany and demanded to be included in the Third Reich.

---

[34] Irredentism signifies here the idea of implementing the right of self-determination by breaking the existing political state structures and building (or uniting with) a new state organization based on the principle of an ethnic-national community.

Inter-war Czechoslovakia neither inspired a loyalty to the state in its minorities, nor created a Czechoslovak nation. In 1938, when the country was threatened by Germany and made to relinquish the Sudetenland, the republic collapsed like a house of cards: Hungary took parts of Slovakia and Ruthenia, Poland occupied the Teschen region, and in 1939 Slovakia, with German support, proclaimed its independence. This sudden collapse cannot be explained merely by outside pressure and the difficult geopolitical situation. The cause also has to be found in the concept of the nation on which the Czechoslovak state was constructed.

After the Second World War this concept of the nation became the subject of revision in the reborn Czechoslovakia. The separate national identity of the Slovaks was recognized, but Germans and Hungarians (in the Slovak part) were regarded as foreign elements, 'traitors' to the First Republic. In 1945, following on from President Beneš's decree, which invoked collective German guilt, the Germans were expelled from Czechoslovakia. According to the census of 1950, there were only 165,117 Germans left. Those who were allowed to stay were anti-fascists, indispensable specialists, and spouses of Czechs. They were not recognized as a 'culturally protected minority', and it was only after 1968 that they were allowed to cultivate their language and create their own organizations (see Kuhn 1982: 108). After 1945 official policy was to erase traces of the presence of Germans and German-speaking Jews, such as Franz Kafka, Max Brod, and others, in Bohemia, and their contribution to Bohemian culture. Linguistic nationalist criteria dominated the writing of history, and the history of Bohemia was interpreted as only that of Czech-speakers. Historical myths of the 'pure' Czech past before the arrival of German immigrants were invoked. This was a sequel to the linguistic vision of nationalism that had been invoked in the nineteenth century.

A gradual change of attitudes towards the place of Germans in the history and culture of the Czech Lands appeared only after 1968—however, not among the Czech public, but only among the intellectuals of Charta 77 and those in exile. Since the fall of Communism in 1989, these issues can be discussed openly, which inspires hope that parts of Czech history long suppressed will be brought back to the collective memory of the Czechs.

After the division of Czechoslovakia in 1993 the Czech Republic was created, which is extremely homogeneous in its ethnic composition. Minorities (mainly Roma and a small number of Germans and Poles) make up only a few per cent of the population. The 1991 census applied generous rules for stating one's national identity. The inhabitants were even allowed to declare a Moravian or Silesian nationality. It turned out that more than 32 per cent had declared a Moravian identity and more than 1 per cent a Silesian identity.[35] These declarations are based on the existence of particular regional identity, which has historical roots. Moravia was the core of the early medieval Greater Moravia. In both Slovak and

---

[35] The figures are from the article 'Från Karpaterna till Hanás stränder', *Röster från Tjeckoslovakien* (see n. 27 above).

Czech mythology, this state holds an important place. Later Moravia and Bohemia plus Silesia were part of the Czech state, but Moravia maintained formal autonomy until modern times. This was important for the regional identity of the Moravians, their delimitation from Bohemian Czechs. There are some cultural differences between Moravia and Bohemia, as well as a few differences in the spoken language. The Czech literary language and a common history are the strong unifying factors for the peoples of Bohemia and Moravia. Silesia is a distinct region historically connected with Poland, Bohemia, and Germany. There is only a small part of Silesia within the Czech borders. The main part of the region now belongs to Poland. Silesians (and particularly Polish Silesians) demonstrate a typical borderland identity with relatively unclear and changing national identifications (Polish, German, Czech, or Silesian). They have their own dialect (classified as a Czech dialect in the Czech part and as Polish in Poland) with strong German influences. However, there has never been a serious attempt to create a standard Silesian language on the basis of this dialect.

At the beginning of the twenty-first century there is no Moravian or Silesian national movement in the Czech Republic, but there is a movement that demands the reintroduction of autonomy for Moravia and Silesia, which was abolished by the Communist regime in 1948. In Polish Silesia the movement for regional autonomy is even stronger, and in 1997 there emerged a small Silesian national party— Związek Ludności Narodowości Śląskiej (ZLNS). The future will tell how deeply rooted the autonomy demands are in the Moravian and Silesian population.[36]

9.6. Conclusions: Language and Nationalism in Eastern Central Europe

The part of Europe described here displays a great linguistic, cultural, and ethnic diversity. It has for centuries been a meeting place for Germans, Jews, Poles, Czechs, Roma, Slovaks, Hungarians, Ruthenians, and other peoples. Independent, strong states with deep historical roots and rulers regarded as legitimate would have been necessary for the integration of such an ethnically mixed population into supra-ethnic state-nations. In these areas no such states emerged. After nationalism became increasingly important in the nineteenth century, all the national or ethnic groups described here questioned the legitimacy of the state powers they were subject to—the Habsburg Monarchy, the Russian Empire, the Kingdom of Prussia.

Another important factor was that this linguistic and ethnic differentiation largely coincided with social differences. With industrialization, democratization, the abolition of serfdom, and growing mobility, the linguistic issue became relevant for the lower social classes, since linguistic differences became a barrier to social emancipation. In order to advance socially, Slovaks, Czechs, and also, by the

---

[36] For more on Moravia and Czech Silesia, see Foret (1991), Trefulka (1991), and Macháček (1993a,b).

end of the nineteenth century, Poles in Russia and Prussia had to master the language of the dominant ethnic group, who had a lead in the competition for prosperity and status in the community.[37] In order to compete in the labour market on approximately the same terms, the subservient ethnic group had to choose: they could either assimilate or assert their own language at least in certain fields. Thus the awareness of language both as a means of communication, the key to education and a career, and as a uniting link, a marker of group affiliation, grew.

The Enlightenment had spread throughout Europe the ideas of the equality of all humans and of their right to participate in the exercise of power—which created the ideological basis for the development of nationalisms. Then, however, German Romanticism brought ideas of the special mission of every people and the expression of its individuality in language and culture. The educated classes in the German, Hungarian, Czech, Slovak, and Polish communities were inspired by these thoughts and sought to define their people's individuality by nurturing and developing the national language and culture. They also assumed the task of spreading these ideas among the masses and making them nationally conscious. In the nineteenth century, these new national ideologies fell on fertile social ground. National ideologies, with the struggle for language as one of the most important aims, coincided well with the social and political ambitions of the lower social classes. Language, origin, and religion were especially important for the peasants, since they had to do with their social advancement, and they fitted their values, world view, and mentality (religious feelings, traditionalism and ethnocentrism).[38] In contrast to many Western European countries, where national mobilization was carried out from above, through the bureaucratic apparatus of the state, through schools and other institutions, the populations of eastern Central Europe were generally mobilized from below.[39] In their propaganda, the national movements had to rely on those elements of cultural identity that the lower classes viewed as decisive, such as religion and language.

In many aspects Hungary offers a different picture. For the Magyars, there was no linguistic barrier linking national and social emancipation. The linguistic issue became important for political reasons—in the struggle against the Habsburgs for the greatest possible independence of Hungarian institutions. The Hungarian language became a marker of this independence.

The obsession of the Magyars with language was also due to their demographic weakness and thence the fear of losing their dominating position. This feeling was

---

[37] The significance of language for the competition of various national groups on the labour market during the development of capitalism and industrialism is discussed by Chlebowczyk (1980), Gellner (1983), and Hroch (1985).

[38] Ethnocentrism may be defined as an inclination to judge and interpret other cultures from the point of view of one's own, often with xenophobic tendencies. On the ethnocentrism of the peasant communities in Eastern and Central Europe, see Chlebowczyk (1980: 56–7).

[39] See A. D. Smith (1991: 68). Smith distinguishes two types of community: vertical, which is mobilized nationally from below, and lateral, which is mobilized nationally from above.

also manifest among Germans in Bohemia, who, like the Magyars in nineteenth century Hungary, were a dominant group, but numerically weak. It seems that the stronger the cultural and political claims of the oppressed nations, the stronger the defensive nationalist reactions from the dominant nations. These in turn caused an even greater need for self-assertion among the dominated peoples (see Chlebowczyk 1980: 128–30; Waldenberg 1992: 46). Nationalisms stimulated each other in this way in a chain of action and reaction. More or less well-founded feelings of oppression and threat were aroused and became important in national propaganda and in political life. The model set by successful nationalisms, such as German nationalism, which emphasized the importance of language for national identity, also had a mobilizing effect.

The rise of ethno-nationalism in Central Europe hampered a process of assimilation of different ethnic groups into bigger national entities. The case of central European Jews illustrates this well. At the beginning of the nineteenth century the emancipation of the Jews began. They left their isolated community life and many of them became German-, Hungarian- or Polish-speaking. The language shift did not in itself signify assimilation if they maintained their religion, since Judaism was the most important marker of Jewish identity at this time. Those who gave up their religion were able to assimilate to other ethnic and national groups. However, at the end of the nineteenth century, the ethno-nationalists started to accentuate the importance of 'origin' for national identity. Giving priority to origin before language meant the exclusion of the Jews from the Hungarian, Polish, and German nations with all its tragic consequences in the twentieth century.

After the First World War a series of states emerged in Central Europe that housed the nations mobilized on a linguistic and ethnic basis. Often several such nations found themselves within the framework of one state. This paved the way for conflict, and only strong democracies could perhaps have created state-national identifications in this part of Europe, if they had had enough time. None of this was to happen: neither time, nor stable democratic development, with the exception of Czechoslovak democracy. Both Poland and Czechoslovakia spent much of the time preceding the Second World War in endeavours to defend their territorial integrity against external and internal enemies. After the short period of independence they became the victims of the military expansion of neighbouring powers. During the same period the Hungarians suffered from trauma after the Treaty of Trianon and were oppressed by dictatorial regimes, both Communist and Fascist.

After the Second World War Communist regimes, widely seen as lacking legitimacy, were installed. Large parts of the population in Poland, Czechoslovakia, and Hungary could not readily identify with them. Codes of law and institutions, often viewed as illegitimate and even hostile to the nation, could not become components of their national identities. Markers of linguistic and ethnic identity were still important, and were even strengthened after population transfers generated greater uniformity. As a reaction to the oppression of the Church by the regimes, the role of religion increased, especially in Poland and Slovakia. During great social conflicts—Hungary 1956, Czechoslovakia 1968, Poland 1980—the masses were mobilized against the state power by means of nationalistic slogans. National culture, history, and religion were frequently used components of national identity in the struggle against Sovietization. Because of this development, ethno-nationalism mobilized from below remained an active force.

The fall of Communist regimes was followed by a relative ideological vacuum into which ethno-nationalism rushed. The democratic developments initiated in Poland, Hungary, the Czech Republic, and Slovakia after 1989 gave them a chance of building national identities where the state and its institutions play an important integrating part and where there is less need for mobilization from below.

Language and ethnic origin are today crucial for national identification in all the countries described here. However, historical analysis shows that development toward ethno-nationalism has varied, explained to a great extent by the differences between historic and non-historic nations. Historic nations such as Hungary, Poland, and the Czechs (the intermediate case) began their nation-building in the nineteenth century with a tradition of independent political structure, a state formation of their own. This tradition constituted a basis for potential development of state-national (Hungarian, Polish, Bohemian) identities and in fact state nationalism existed in Hungary, Poland and Bohemia in the nineteenth century. In Bohemia state nationalism turned out to be weak, and, in contrast to the situation in Hungary and Poland, its role in Czech nation-building was secondary. The Czech development was thus more in line with non-historic nations. The state nationalism among Poles and Hungarians was, however, alive until the end of the nineteenth century and at first gave way only gradually to ethno-nationalism. In this process the tradition of the earlier existence of a Polish or a Hungarian state was reinterpreted along ethno-linguistic lines, in order to give legitimacy to new ethno-national identities. This division into two phases— first cultural and then political mobilization—so typical for Czech and Slovak nation-building, was not present in the formation process of the historic nations, Poland and Hungary, where political and cultural mobilization went hand in hand. The institutional, political forms of national life were from the outset as important as culture. Because they had been independent states, the historic nations had a political legitimacy and did not need to prove to the world their right to independent existence.

Non-historic nations, such as the Slovaks, who had no tradition of independent political structure had only their own language and ethnic origin ('natural right') to fall back on, in order to justify their separate national existence. Therefore the linguistic issue was from the outset of crucial importance. Political mobilization on a larger scale came later. The national aspirations of those peoples for whom language was a crucial component of their identity influenced the development of their national languages. This was the result of those particular goals that guided national activists and language reformers when they developed the language and fought for it. First and foremost, they wanted to develop their language into a functional means of communication, used in all contexts and equal in status to the languages of other nations. Secondly, language was to have a unifying, delimiting, and identifying role. Thirdly, it was to express the essence and strength of the nation—that is, to be free from alien influence as far as possible. These goals could not be fulfilled by just any dialect spoken by the population with national aspirations, but only by a standardized, codified language that was ascribed the status of a national language.

When nations began to form at the end of the eighteenth century, Poland was the only one of the four nations with a standardized, well-developed literary language in use. In the remaining cases the national standard languages were created or resuscitated (Czech) in the course of nation-building by the intelligentsia involved in national issues. The choice of a base for the national standard language could be the result of practical considerations and earlier evolution (the case of Hungary) or could be directly steered by national aims. The choice of the dialect of central Slovakia as the basis for the literary language was aimed at emphasizing the independent status of the Slovaks against the Czechs. The Czechs chose the sixteenth-century literary language for their modern standard language in order to give their language a prestige by linking it to their past. Uniform and standardized, language would become a unifying and integrating element.

The next step was the struggle for the use of the language in education and other official contexts. One important task was vocabulary extension. In the older literary languages, such as Polish, this process was gradual and evolutionary, but in the younger ones (Hungarian, Czech, Slovak) this was the work of one or two generations of nationally minded intellectuals. Their nationalistic zeal left its traces in the language, first and foremost in the vocabulary, which in these languages is characterized by their preference for neologisms formed from native roots. Neologisms were used not only for new concepts, but also to replace old well-established loanwords (Latin loanwords were replaced by native Hungarian words, for example). New loanwords from the languages of those nations that were considered oppressors were banished—for instance, German words in Czech—while loanwords from nations that were considered kinsmen received a positive reception—for example, words from other Slavonic languages in Slovak. Purism was frequent. It was at its weakest in Polish (where it was noticeable only in technical and medical vocabulary) and strongest in Czech and Hungarian. Puristic doctrines can be viewed as a reflection of the complexes and reactions against cultural or political domination (see Thomas 1991: 45, 135–9). National considerations may find their expressions not only in language itself but also in linguistics as a science. Historical linguistics is a field where different national stances are expressed. Linguists from two different nations in dispute about a particular territory may try to claim that their nation was first or strongest there—for example, Poles and Germans in Pomerania, Hungarians and Romanians in Transylvania. There are cases when language historians try to prove the kinship of a language with one or more other languages, since this brings prestige—for example, in the Ural-Altaic hypothesis in Hungary. Or they may try to demonstrate the difference of a nation from a group with which it is otherwise usually associated—for example, Czambel's theories of the affiliation of the Slovak language with the South Slavonic group and not the West Slavonic, where Czech belongs. Another common example of nationalistically tinted linguistic discussions are the deliberations about the status of a variety as a dialect or a distinctive language; an example of this is the Kashubian issue.

In the model of national identity presented in the introduction, language was one of its many components. In the concrete realizations of this model in eastern central Europe, language appears as an extremely important element. In eastern central Europe at the beginning of the twenty-first century language and national identity most often (but not always) coincide, largely because of the artificial homogenization of the area since 1918, seen in the genocide of Jews and Roma, in warfare, and in population exchanges. Nevertheless, despite this artificial situation, language played a decisive role in the development of nationalisms in this area. Language was an important operating factor in the awakening of nationalism and in the processes of nation-building in this part of Europe, but never on its own, only in combination with several other factors, which could fortify or considerably weaken its significance. Its role was to a great extent the result of the three functions of language: a medium of communication, a common marker of ethnic identity, and an integrating symbol for group unity and distinctiveness.

10.

'A people exists and that people has its language'*: Language and Nationalism in the Balkans

CATHIE CARMICHAEL

10.1. State Formation in the Balkans

For the purposes of this chapter the term 'the Balkans'[1] is used to denote Bulgaria, Romania, Albania, Macedonia, Kosovo, the Federal Republic of Yugoslavia (Serbia-Montenegro), Bosnia-Hercegovina, Croatia, and Slovenia. It is unlikely that the inhabitants of the latter two would define themselves as 'Balkan'; indeed the call to be part of 'Europe' formed an important part of the process of rejection of Yugoslavia (and in particular of Slobodan Milošević's vision for a future Yugoslavia) in the two northern republics in the countdown to the break-up of 1991. Despite different traditions and orientations, all of these states are products of relatively recent political changes (the most important of which occurred during the nineteenth and twentieth centuries), but all also enjoy rich cultural and linguistic histories that are infinitely more complicated than the individual backgrounds to state formation would suggest.

Contemporary Balkan geopolitics grew from the circumstances surrounding the formation and subsequent decline of multinational empires. Albania, Romania, Serbia, and Bulgaria sprang from the collapsing Ottoman Empire, in which religion and loyalty to the state rather than language were the defining bases for active inclusion in the state. The first Yugoslavia grew from the remnants of the Ottoman Empire but also from the Habsburg Monarchy, which valued religion and loyalty to the Emperor (*Kaisertreue*) more highly than language and

---

* '. . . postoji narod i taj narod ima jezik', (Katičić 1987: 33). I am indebted to Igor Biljan, Nebojša Čagorović, Rajko Muršič, Mark Thompson and Peter Vodopivec for their comments on this chapter.

[1]   It is not the purpose of this chapter to deconstruct the term 'Balkans', although I acknowledge that this is a problematic term. I do not intend to impute any value to it, either negative or positive. The subject of the use of the word 'Balkan' and 'balkanize' has been covered in some depth by John Allcock (1991). For the purposes of this chapter the term will not cover Greece and Turkey, which are considered in Chapter 11. The port of Trieste in Italy, which in many ways resembles the Balkans in its culture, is not included here for historical and political reasons.

ethnicity, at least before the latter half of the nineteenth century. The Habsburg and Ottoman states were, according to Ernest Gellner (1991: 127), 'largely indifferent to the national principle ... faith and dynasty were held to be natural, adequate and appropriate foundations of political order'.

The states created on their ruins were beset by national problems from the start and characterized by political instability after 1918. The Versailles settlement, influenced as it was by what Eric Hobsbawm (1990) has called the Wilsonian–Leninist 'principle of nationality', meant that other more autonomist and potentially democratic currents in political life (such as the formation of peasant parties across the region) were eventually submerged, and all the states of the Balkans succumbed to dictatorships in the inter-war period. Ahmet Bey Zogu proclaimed himself King Zog of Albania in 1928, but the first independent Albania was swallowed up by fascist Italy in 1941. The Serbian-dominated Yugoslavian regime, which had been established as the Kingdom of Serbs, Croats, and Slovenes in 1918, was plagued by national problems. In 1934 King Aleksandar was assassinated in Marseilles by Macedonian terrorists, who had been financed by the Croatian fascist *Ustaša*. Both groups opposed the hegemony of Belgrade in the affairs of the state. This ethnically unstable state collapsed in 1941 and was carved up between Mussolini's Italy, the Third Reich, a rump Serbia, and the fascist puppet state of Croatia under the selfstyled *Poglavnik* (*Il Duce*) Ante Pavelić. Romania succumbed to the native fascism of the Iron Guard during the inter-war period, and Bulgaria allied itself with the Axis powers during the war.

The war itself was a terrifying episode of what has since become known as ethnic cleansing, when sadistic crimes were perpetrated by one ethnic group against another. Of the million or more Yugoslavs killed during the war, probably only one-tenth met their deaths at the hands of occupying forces. The cruelty of the Croatian *Ustaša* against Jews, Muslims, and Serbs was considered to be excessive even in Berlin, and, as a German minister Siegfried Kasche remarked, the *Ustaša* was 'filled with a blind destructive will against real or imagined enemies of the state, above all Serbs' (Trifković 1993: 539). It was at this time that many of the Balkan Jewish and Romani communities were completely destroyed. Symbolic cruelty, which surfaced again in Croatia, Kosovo, and Bosnia during the Yugoslavian Wars of Dissolution (1991–9),[2] occurred at this time as Serbian nationalist *Četnici* tortured Muslims by impaling them on stakes, in a deliberate imitation of the supposed judicial practices of the Ottoman Empire.[3]

[2] In Bratunac in 1992, 'the local Muslim cleric was reportedly tortured in front of the townsfolk, who had been rounded up in the soccer stadium, was ordered to make the sign of the cross, had beer forced down his throat, and then was executed' (Cigar 1995: 59). Similar occurrences were recorded throughout the recent war in Bosnia.

[3] This 'memory' of Ottoman cruelty was in part kept alive by the work of the Nobel prize winning Bosnian novelist Ivo Andrić, who describes the practice in some detail in his *Na Drini Ćuprija*, (Andrić 1947). The Bosnian Muslims have faced 'ethnic cleansing' from Serbian and Croatian extremists more recently, which has involved the obliteration of their cultural inheritance. The ancient Ottoman bridge at Mostar was deliberately destroyed as part of a continuing Croatian attempt to 'cleanse' Hercegovina of traces of its Islamic past (see Jezernik 1995a: 470–84).

All the states under consideration were reconstructed by Communists after the end of the Second World War. Bulgaria and Romania were largely dependent on the fraternal aid of the Red Army in the restoration of order, and Albania and Yugoslavia were liberated by pro-Soviet partisans. In the immediate aftermath of the war the future geopolitical shape of the Balkans was undetermined. In 1947, when the Yugoslavian leader Tito met his Bulgarian counterpart Dimitrov at Lake Bled in Slovenia, they discussed the possibility of forming a Balkan federation. The two men communicated amicably in Russian and thought in terms of a Soviet-style federation. All attempts to unite the region into a superstate were quashed in 1948 when Yugoslavia was expelled from Cominform. Albania, which had been promised Albanian-speaking Kosovo by the Yugoslavians in 1944–5, retains its postwar boundaries at the time of writing, as do Romania and Bulgaria. Yugoslavia disintegrated in 1991, when Tito's vision of a multiethnic state united by common struggle against external enemies, a monolithic political party, and an artificial Communist-inspired *bratstvo i jedinstvo* (brotherhood and unity) collapsed in the face of competition by élites in Zagreb, Belgrade, and Ljubljana, who adopted an ardent kind of parochialism wearing the oversized clothes of early medieval rulers. Serbian nationalist rhetoric revolves around the 'martyr-dom' of the Serbs at Kosovo polje in 1389, whereas Croatian nationalists claim to be re-establishing the '1,000 year state' (*tisućljetna država*) of Croatia. In Slovenia in the late 1980s there were even those who fantasized about a *Nova Karantanija* (that is, the re-creation of an early medieval state, in which the Slovenes were predominant), although on the whole Slovenian nationalists did at least use the vocabulary of democratization, while at the same time stressing their distinctive-ness (Carmichael 1995). The growth of nationalism amongst these ethnic groups was in part the result of the nationality policies of the post-1945 regimes. In Yugoslavia all nations were not equal. As Milovan Djilas once suggested, if the Communists had really had the will to break down the old nationalisms, they would have moved the capital from Belgrade to Sarajevo.

10.2. The Languages of the Balkans

In linguistic terms, the Balkans initially appears to be very fragmented—a meet-ing ground between language families. The Slavonic languages of Bulgarian, Macedonian, Serbian, Montenegrin, Croatian, Bosnian, and Slovene are similar and might have been unified into a single language, like the disparate dialects that were forged into modern German or English, had not separate state formations prevented this. Indeed, four of the languages were codified as 'Serbo-Croat', but the concept of this single language did not survive the demise of the second Yugoslavia after 1991. Romanian, Vlach, and Ladino (Judaeo-Spanish) are related to other Romance languages. Albanian is said to be the surviving descendant of the ancient Illyrian language, although its lexicon is largely derived from languages belonging to other groups.

In the Balkans it is important to make the distinction between languages that are the official languages of states, and those that are not. German was once spoken across the region as a lingua franca, especially in towns but also in some village settlements.[4] In addition, dialects of Ruthenian (which can be regarded as varieties of Ukrainian) and Slovak are also found in some villages in Vojvodina. Romani[5] is still spoken, particularly in the south of the region. The Ladino of the Sephardic Jews, which is a close relative of Spanish, was once more widespread in the Balkans, but its use has almost died out since 1945 (see Elazar *et al.* 1984). According to the writer Aleksandar Tišma from Vojvodina: 'Novi Sad had had 3,500 Jews and they *all* went to camps. Today there are a hundred or so. The Jewish Street, as it was called, simply does not exist any more. A whole community had its spiritual and physical life here; its customs, its physiognomy were brushed away like so many crumbs of bread' (Thompson 1992: 239). Vlach, a relative of Romanian, was found across the Balkans, although its use had largely dwindled by the 1980s to an estimated 50,000 speakers, who are to be found in Macedonia, Greece, and (nominally) in Croatian Istria (Winnifrith 1987: 7, see also Chapter 11, this volume).

Although we can refer here to discrete languages from different language groups, the popular idioms of the Balkans have experienced a great deal of admixture during historic times. Scholars have frequently defined the Balkans in terms of one or more *Sprachbünde*.[6] This has been defined by Ronelle Alexander (1983: 13) as 'cohesive convergence areas whose shared features embrace morphology, syntax and phraseology, as well as certain phonological and lexical features'. The characteristic use of the infinitive verb is often given as an example of a *Sprachbund* phenomenon in this region, as it has similar forms in Slavonic and non-Slavonic languages. In his memoirs Elias Canetti, who came from a Ladino- and German-speaking family in Rustschuk, recounts how as a child he had been horrified by fairy tales told to him by Bulgarian-speaking servants. As an adult he retained no practical knowledge of Bulgarian, but could still remember the content of the stories vividly (Canetti 1979: 15). This autobiographical fragment may indicate how *Sprachbünde* work at a mundane level, where people come to understand the languages and dialects of the people who live around them because of close contact, and because they understand their daily experiences and emotions. It is clear, not just from studies of linguistic structures but also from analysis of vocabularies, that Balkan peoples greatly influenced each other's languages. Slavonic dialects spoken around the Macedonian shore of Lake Ohrid have been influenced by Macedonian, Albanian, Turkish and Arumanian (Vlach)

---

[4] For studies of German-speaking villages in the Balkans and the overall decline of the language, see Teutsch (1924), Castellan (1971), Gaffney (1979), Šmitek and Krnel-Umek, (1987).

[5] One of the largest Romani communities in the Balkans is in Macedonia. For a guide to the language, see Saip and Kepeski (1980).

[6] The concept of a *Sprachbund* was first introduced in Trubetzkoy (1939), although the earlier scholarship of Kristian Sandfeld (1930) pointed to comparisons between the Balkan languages.

(P. Hendriks 1976). Albanian, which putatively stems from the Illyrian branch of Indo-European languages, has a large number of words from Serbian, Italian, Greek, and Turkish (Krajni 1966; Pellegrini 1992: 101–51). It is particularly noteworthy that the language has few native words for maritime activities: *peshk* (fish) and *natoj* (swim) are of Romance origin, *lopate* (oar) is of Slavonic origin, and *gjemi* (ship) is of Turkish origin (Cabej 1982: 166 ff.; Weigand 1927: 233).

10.3. Linguistic Profiles of the contemporary Balkan States

10.3.1. *Bulgaria*

According to the census carried out in Bulgaria in 1992,[7] of a total population of 8.5 million, about 85 per cent were ethnically Bulgarian. Nine per cent declared themselves to be Turkish, 300,000 declared themselves to be Romani, and 14,000 declared themselves to be Armenian (see Wyn Jones 1997: 238). Until the 1980s, Bulgaria was probably the most stable country in the Balkans, having avoided the excesses of Ceauşescu's Romania and the ever-volatile ethnic situation in Yugoslavia, as well as the extremism that characterized Communist Albania. In 1984 the Bulgarian leader Todor Zhivkov decided to launch a policy of 'Bulgarizing' Turks, primarily by making them adopt Slavonic surnames. This policy backfired when the regime received widespread international criticism and some 300,000 Turks fled the country in the summer of 1989. Many Turks subsequently returned, and in 1993 five police officers were charged with violating the rights of ethnic Turks during the mid-1980s during the forcible assimilation phase. This was the first trial of its kind, but indicates that, since the fall of Zhivkov in 1989 and the end of the Communist monopoly of political power, the Bulgarians are anxious to maintain a good international record on human rights.

10.3.2. *Bosnia-Hercegovina*

The former Yugoslavian Republic of Bosnia-Hercegovina is divided between the Croatian–Muslim federation, which administers the south-west of the region, and the Serbian Republic (*Republika Srpska*). The political settlement, which has effectively divided the old Bosnia along national/ethnic lines, was reached at the end of 1995, after war had broken out in the spring of 1992, although the settlement does not recognize the former ethnic composition of the region in which communities of Muslims, Orthodox, and Catholic Christians lived together, often intermarrying. The war completely destroyed the delicate ethnic fabric of old Bosnia. Areas in the east of the republic, which had been Islamic for several centuries, were cleansed of Muslims by the Bosnian Serb army and Serb paramilitaries, whereas the monuments of the ancient Islamic cities and towns were destroyed by Croat or Serb paramilitaries. The language of *Republika Srpska* is now defined as

---

[7] All the census data in this chapter are derived from Wyn Jones (1997).

'Serbian', whereas 'Croatian' and 'Bosnian' are spoken in the Federation territory. Until the late 1980s it was rare to perceive linguistic differences between the ethnic and religious groups in Bosnia, although Robert D. Greenberg (1996) has indicated that there was an increase in ethnocentric dialect studies after the 1960s, which, he felt, undermined the Novi Sad Agreement of 1954 in which a unified Serbo-Croatian language was promoted by the Yugoslav state, albeit with 'Western' and 'Eastern' variants. Indeed, the text of the agreement stated 'narodni jezik Srba, Hrvata i Crnogoraca jedan je jezik' (the national language of the Serbs, Croats, and Montenegrins is a single language) (Nikčević 1993*b*: 81), thus omitting the Muslims altogether, who were considered to have primarily a religious ethnicity.[8] During the 1991 census, most of the inhabitants of the republic volunteered 'Bosnian' (*bosanski*) as their language,[9] rather than Serbo-Croat, on the advice of the primarily Muslim Party of Democratic Action, which led the move for independence the following year (see Sučić 1996: 13). At this time 43.8 per cent declared their ethnicity as 'Muslim', 31.5 per cent as 'Serb', 17.3 per cent as 'Croat', and 7 per cent as 'Yugoslav' (Ramet 1996: 187). However, since the disintegration of Yugoslavia, ethnically specific features in language have been sought by the representative intellectuals of each group, such as the re-emphasis of a fricative *h* in *bosanski*, so that coffee becomes *kahva*, instead of *kava* or *kafa* (Isaković, 1993: 6).

10.3.3. *Albania*

Contemporary Albania is over 98 per cent Albanian-speaking. Historically Albanians have leaned more towards French and Italian cultural centres than Central or Eastern Europe—hence *Bulevardi Zhan D'Ark* (Boulevard Jeanne d'Arc) in Tirana. Modern unified literary Albanian was created in 1972 during Enver Hoxha's leadership as a 'literary *koine*', although the language was first codified in the sixteenth century (Kostellari 1973: 58), uniting elements of the two main dialect groups of Albanian: Gheg and Tosk. Of the estimated 3.4 million Albanians, approximately 1.7 million speak Gheg (although their numbers are swelled by the estimated 3.3 million Albanians in Kosovo and elsewhere in the successor states of the former Yugoslavia). Tosk is spoken in the south of the country by about 1.7 million people. The two dialect groups are usually described as very similar, although they might have been even closer before the nineteenth century (Prifti 1990: 12–18). Some scholars have argued that the modern literary language owes more to Tosk than to Gheg (see Pipa 1989), although the latter is usually viewed as dominant.

---

[8] The term *Muslimani po etničkom smislu* (Muslim in the ethnic sense) was used in the census data.

[9] Friedrich Krauss, who was responsible for much of the early collating of folk materials in the South Slavonic areas, noted in 1886 that Bosnians referred to 'their' language or 'Bosnian', suggesting that this declaration in 1991 was not a radical departure from previous practice. On Krauss, see Isaković (1993: 18).

10.3.4. *Slovenia*

The Republic of Slovenia is ethnically and politically the most stable state under consideration here, having fought a brief war in the summer of 1991 to leave the Yugoslavian Federation. Although classed as a South Slavonic language, along with the other Slavonic languages of the former Yugoslavia, Slovene is also close to the West Slavonic languages (Czech, Polish, Slovak, and others), and hence shows similarities both to Czech and to the Kajkavian dialects of Croat. In the nineteenth century, some Slovene writers such as Stanko Vraz favoured linguistic assimilation with Serbo-Croat, whereas others, particularly the poet France Prešeren, wanted to retain the distinctiveness of Slovene. Inclusion in Yugoslavia between 1945 and 1991 meant, given the federal structure of this state, that the Slovene language remained autonomous. Although the popular language may have moved closer to Serbo-Croat, the official literary language retained highly distinctive characteristics, thanks largely to the work of state-sponsored academicians, such as the use of the archaic dual number (*dvojina*) in addition to singular and plural, which is not found in all Slovene dialects. In Slovenia itself the language is flourishing amongst a population that owns more books *per capita* than any other nation in Europe. By contrast, the use of Slovene in the Italian province of Friuli Venezia-Giulia and the Austrian province of Kärnten (Carinthia), both of which territories have had Slovene-speaking populations since the sixth century, waned drastically during the twentieth century. The Slovene Constitution of 1991 allows the two 'autonomous national groups' (Hungarians in Prekmurje and Italians in Istria) rights to cultural expression, links with the 'mother nation', but no right to self-determination. In the 1991 census, 87.8 per cent of the population of 1.7 million declared themselves to be Slovene. In addition there were 2.4 per cent who declared themselves as Serb, 2.8 per cent Croat, 1.4 per cent Muslim, 0.6 per cent 'Yugoslav', and 0.4 per cent Hungarian. Macedonians, Montenegrins, Albanians, and Italians together constituted a further 0.2 per cent of the total.

10.3.5. *Romania*

In the 1992 census in Romania, of a population of almost 23 million, almost 90 per cent described themselves as ethnically Romanian. Just over 7 per cent were ethnically Hungarian, with other groups listed as Romani, German, and Ukrainian. The regions of Wallachia and Moldavia formed the basis of the late-nineteenth-century state, which had been part of the Ottoman Empire. This was a multi-ethnic area, in which ethnic Romanians were largely peasants. After the dismemberment of Hungary by the Treaty of Trianon in 1919, Transylvania with its large Hungarian population was added, although the population defined themselves as Szeklers and had a distinctive border mentality (not unlike the Krajina Serbs, who were also separated from their ethnic brethren), and were isolated from the mainstream of Hungarian culture. German-speakers had also lived in Transylvania for centuries, which gave the region a more central European character than the earlier kingdom of Romania. In the twentieth century Romanian nationalism dominated the political character of this country and, under the Communists Dej and Ceauşescu, ethnic Romanians were favoured above other groups. Ceauşescu even wanted to alter the ethnic and linguistic character of Transylvania by destroying old villages and herding the population into 'agro-industrial complexes'. The Romanian revolution of 1989 ended the long night of Ceauşescu's nationalism, and overtly bad treatment of Romania's ethnic and linguistic minorities was curtailed under Iliescu, although Transylvania remains a potentially volatile region.

10.3.6. *Croatia*

In 1991 the Republic of Croatia had a population of almost 5 million, but the influx of the 'Croatian diaspora' from Serbia and Bosnia and the flight of an estimated 450,000 Serbs have made these figures unreliable. In 1991, 78.8 per cent of the population described themselves as Croats, 6.3 per cent as 'Yugoslav', and 12.2 per cent as Serbs, with the rest being made up of peoples from almost all areas of the former Yugoslavia. After the election victory of the leader of the nationalist *Hrvatska Demokratska Zajednica* (Croatian Democratic Union), Dr Franjo Tudjman, in 1990, Croatia left the Yugoslavian Federation. There followed five years of bitter warfare, during which the ancient city of Vukovar was destroyed and the historic port of Dubrovnik shelled. In the summer of 1995, almost the entire Serb population of Krajina, which had been held by rebels since 1990, fled in the wake of the victorious Croatian army. In effect, war in Croatia meant a series of localized struggles to decide the ethnic character of each region. Those areas where the fighting was heaviest were areas populated by *prećani* (the name given to Serbs/Orthodox Christians outside Serbia proper) who did not want to be part of an independent Croatian state, which they associated with fascism and/or Catholicism. The fears of the Serbs, often directly manipulated by extremists in Belgrade, were not allayed by the activities of the *Hrvatska Demokratska Zajednica*. Tudjman himself was the author of a 'post-modern' history, *Bespuća povijesne zbiljnosti* (*Wastelands of Historical Reality*), published by the Matica Hrvatska in 1989, which sought to minimize the crimes of the *Ustaša* Croatian fascist movement during the Second World War. His policy towards ethnic Serbs was undoubtedly clumsy and, given the strength of Serb nationalism at that time, circumstances combined to precipitate armed struggle, which revolved around 'ethnic cleansing'. Croatia is, since 1995, more ethnically homogeneous than it ever was in the historic past, although Italian is still spoken on parts of the Dalmatian coast. In the later nineteenth century, Hungarian was the official executive language, which aroused the passions of Croat autonomists and stimulated scholarship in their own language. A glimmer of Croatia's multicultural past survives within the Istrian Democratic Alliance, which was the only political party to oppose the ethnic reclamation of Serb-held Krajina in 1995. At the time of writing there is room for hope that a more open Croatia may arise, following the defeat of Dr Tudjman's party in elections in January 2000, after its leader's death the previous month.

10.3.7. *Macedonia (FYROM)*

The Republic of Macedonia, which seceded from the Yugoslavian Federation in 1992, has a population that numbers about 2 million. In the 1991 census 1.3 million described themselves as Macedonian, 0.44 million as Albanian, with the rest calling themselves Turkish, Romani, Serb, or Muslim. Macedonian national identity is one of the most complex in the Balkans. As a language, Macedonian is very similar to Bulgarian, but historically, since Serbia has been a stronger and more aggressive state than Bulgaria, Macedonia, and consequently its language, developed separately from Bulgaria, particularly since Macedonia's annexation by Serbia in 1912. The Communists eschewed the policy of King Aleksandar's regime to integrate the southern ethnic groups within the monarchy and created a separate Macedonian republic in 1946, which has helped to maintain the status of a separate Macedonian language (see Hill 1992).

10.3.8. *Federal Republic of Yugoslavia (Serbia-Montenegro)*

The Federal Republic of Yugoslavia (Serbia-Montenegro) is currently made up of the former Yugoslavian Republics of Montenegro and Serbia, the latter containing the two formerly autonomous regions of Vojvodina and Kosovo. Kosovo came under UN protection in the latter half of 1999. Although part of Serbia, Kosovo had a 90 per cent ethnic Albanian population, and in 1999 most of the remaining Serbs left. In the 1991 census in Yugoslavia (Serbia and Montenegro), 62.5 per cent of a total population of 10.4 million described themselves as Serb. Albanians made up 16.5 per cent of the population, with 5 per cent describing themselves as Montenegrin, 3.4 per cent as 'Yugoslav', 3.3 per cent as Hungarian and 3.2 per cent as Muslim. During the Communist period, Serb nationalism was suppressed, because Tito in particular feared the impact of its unrestrained growth. After 1987, Slobodan Milošević was able to defeat the 'bureaucratic old guard' in Montenegro, Serbia, Kosovo, and Vojvodina on a ticket of representing the Serbs of Kosovo, who were, according to his rhetoric, facing 'genocide' at the hands of the ethnic Albanians. Milošević managed to tap into an enormous upsurge of popular nationalism. For instance, at the rallies he held in the late 1980s, his supporters would chant 'Kill [Azem] Vllasi!' (the Kosovar leader) and other ethnic provocations. Serbia's intellectuals had already anticipated a change in their national fortunes and the infamous *Memorandum of the Serbian Academy* in 1986 described the suffering of the Serbs within Yugoslavia. The signatories were amongst the best-known Serbian intellectuals, including the 'Praxis' philosopher Zagorka Golubović. The novelist Dobrica Ćosić, whose own fictional work dealt with themes of fighting and honour, was another moving spirit behind the Memorandum and Vuk Drašković developed the thesis of Serbian martyrdom, comparing his people's sufferings to those of the Jews. If Milošević represented the mainstream, then the years of fighting that accompanied the end of Yugoslavia also saw the emergence of Serb paramilitary groups led by extremists such as Vojislav Šešelj (a presidential candidate in the 1997 elections, who was appointed as Deputy Prime Minister), who flaunted their sadistic feats of ethnic cleansing in Croatia and Bosnia quite openly. Since 1995, the Federal Republic has been beset by internal problems, with a strong autonomist movement emerging in Montenegro, which has sought to re-establish a separate identity and language.[10] The question of Kosovo was unresolved at the end of the twentieth century, with ethnic cleansing of the Albanian population intensifying after March 1998, and developing into full-scale war against the Kosovars in the spring of 1999.

10.4. *Ideologies of Nationalism in the Balkans*

From examining the languages of the Balkans as well as considering the histories of the individual states, it is evident that there is very little about the development of nationalism and thus nations themselves that is organic, or in turn related closely to actual linguistic or ethnic circumstances. For example, however historic the links are between the Serbs and Kosovo (Albanian Kosovë), epitomized in the 'memory' of the Battle of Kosovo polje in 1389, Kosovo was one of the most ethnically homogeneous regions in the entire Balkans, being over 90 per cent Albanian. It was difficult to justify the continued involvement of Belgrade in its affairs on any grounds, not least those of democratic representation, in particular as the population had been terrorized by the Serb-dominated police since at least 1981 (and probably even before), and the war of 1999 demonstrated the bloody intentions of the Milošević government.

The relationship between language and nationalism is part of an ideological complex. The Balkans are a region of Europe where the consequences of the clash between ideologies imported from outside and more or less autonomous currents in thinking and behaviour (tribalism, animistic religions, udalism, notions of honour and shame) have been immense and profound. These traditional mentalities, in particular udalism, or the belief by the peasantry that they 'own' the land because they farm it and their ancestors have farmed it and are buried there, account for the importance of territorial claims in Balkan nationalism, and go some way to explaining why ethnic cleansing took place in Croatia, Bosnia, and Kosovo. Serbs in Krajina were hostile to independent Croatia because they could not accept the authority of an alien government over their territory in a region where ancestor worship is particularly important and knowledge about family histories is strongly preserved in memory. At the beginning of the twentieth century the peasantry or at least rural dwellers such as pastoralists accounted for

---

[10] Nikčević (1993a). Čagorović (1996) discusses further the view implicit in this movement that, if a group considers itself to be a separate nation, it must have a distinct language with an appropriate name reflecting the name of the group.

the vast majority of the population in the Balkans.[11] During the early stages of industrialization or modernization, when peasants moved into the towns or to the factories, they often associated with people from their region or ethnic group by choice. Nationalism was, in these circumstances, often the result of a rapid transition. Instead of increasing ethnic homogenization (as happened, for example, in nineteenth-century England) or furthering the development of pan-Slavonic koines (as happened in Minnesota[12]), peasant ethnicities, which were often very ancient, became as it were 'fixed' because of the chronological overlap between modernization and ethnic consciousness. In some respects, therefore, Balkan nationalism has its roots in the peasantries, whose identities were subsequently reified by the intelligentsias of the regions. Imported ideologies (religion, cultural nationalism, historical materialism, and fascism) more or less fused with more autonomous currents to produce what will be described here as post-Communist nationalism, which can be seen as the propeller behind the creation of increasingly homogeneous states, which have come into existence during a period of renewed ethnic intolerance.

Although the dichotomy between native and non-native ideologies is rather crude, I will argue that is necessary to unravel the skeins before the elements of post-Communist nationalism can be properly analysed. This approach might also avoid lapsing into notions of a peculiarly Balkan ferocity and cruelty, a traditional Western European cliché that, according to Hermann Wendel (1925: 342), 'is as stupid as it is dangerous'. For reasons that are largely historical and due to the proximity between the Balkans and Western Europe and the geopolitical struggles that have taken place in the region since the early nineteenth century and even before, the role of 'alien' ideologies has been peculiarly virulent. Gale Stokes has talked about the 'unfortunate transformation of the superstructure before the base' in the Balkans, suggesting that ideas have generally travelled rather faster than material growth (Stokes 1984: p. iv).[13] The Balkans houses a vital interface between language and nationalism: the copious energy that Balkan élites have lavished upon themselves, the languages of their regions or villages, their people's music, upon their microcosms, could have gone instead into the pursuit of material wealth. Even the Communists, who believed in the possibility of material progress within the space of a few generations, were ultimately defeated by the national question in the Balkans and indeed were responsible for some of the worst violations of human rights.

---

[11] In the inter-war Balkans, 'peasants formed 80 per cent of the population in Bulgaria, 78 per cent of the population in Romania and 75 per cent of the population in Yugoslavia' (Swain and Swain 1993: 1). The figures for the Albanian peasantry were even higher.

[12] Slovak, Slovene, and Serb interacted to form a new koine amongst iron-workers. See Paternost (1976).

[13] The American satirist P. J. O'Rourke (1994: 256) rather accurately observed that 'Yugoslavia's ethnic wounds are . . . infected with idealism. There's a surplus of intellectuals in the region. Yugoslavia, like the rest of Eastern Europe, has more artists, writers, and teachers than it has art, literature, or schools. In the resultant mental unemployment, idealism flourishes.'

The Balkans cover the fault lines between three major religions, Catholicism, Islam, and Orthodoxy. However, so many of the factors that led to the creation of strong and dissenting (and eventually nationally cohesive) civil societies in the Protestant countries of Europe are almost entirely missing in this region. Alexander Solzhenitsyn's view that Russian history would have been 'incomparably more humane' had the Orthodox Church been less supine is probably also a valid sentiment when applied to the south-east of Europe (Alexander Solzhenitsyn, *New York Times*, 23 Mar. 1972: 6, cited in Pipes 1974: 245). Certainly the Serbian Orthodox Church has been slow to condemn the nationalist outrages of its brethren and in some cases has even condoned Serb ethnic violence as a lesser evil than Croat actions. The links between Croatian nationalism and the Catholic Church, particularly the Franciscan order, were criticized by the victorious Communists after 1945. However, since 1991 leading former 'comrades' in Zagreb are frequently to be seen at televised masses in the city's cathedral.

Nevertheless, religion was a vital part of the shaping of early linguistic consciousness in the Balkans, as it created distinct communities and was part of the dynamic behind the early codification of languages. The Ottomans established the millet system 'whereby the Orthodox Christians, and eventually the Jews as well, maintained their religious organizations and were permitted to adjudicate civil differences among their own believers. The Greek, Bulgarian, Serbian and Romanian Orthodox churches survived the Ottoman period and remain today living parts of the national sensibilities in each of those countries' (Stokes 1997: 11). The Counter-Reformation provided the impulse that first recorded the Albanian language, which was largely based on the Gheg dialect of Shkodër, in the mid-sixteenth century (Cabej 1968). At the beginning of the twentieth century, as a 'curious Ottoman anomaly', the Bible was one of the few books that was freely distributed in the Albanian language.[14] The first books to be printed in the Slovene language were catechisms and translations of the New Testament, and the moving spirits behind the codification were Lutherans based in Urach in Germany. It would therefore not be wholly exaggerated to state that the evolution of Slovene was not dissimilar to that of German and Czech where the early reformers, such as Martin Luther and Jan Hus, held the idea that an individual 'belonged' to a linguistic community (Dimnik 1984). The Slovene Protestant Primož Trubar refused to remove the Germanisms from his theological work in the sixteenth century on account of the fact that he was not writing for 'Croats, Bezjaks, Bohemians or Poles' (Stankiewicz 1980: 89).

Religion helped to create proto-nations, but without ever becoming the equivalent of the Church in Poland, which is so important in the preservation of popular national consciousness. The education and literacy of Bosnian Muslims

---

[14] The Sultan had granted an exception to the ban on Albanian language books to the Bible Society of London, in the mistaken belief that they would not bother to produce an Albanian version. However, 'Albanians, Christians and Moslems alike, crowded to buy the books, avid for any scrap of print in their own language' (Hodgson 1991: 16).

through Islam largely impeded the later development of Bosnian regionalism (*bošnajstvo*) (Friedman 1996: 64). However, the straw that finally broke the back of Ceauşescu's regime was the activities, including vigils in the church at Timişoara, of the Hungarian Protestant pastor László Tökés, and the existence of separate nationalities with different religions impeded the Romanian Conducator's 'Greater Carpathian' project. And again, since 1989, ethnic tension in Transylvania has led to sporadic outbursts of violence and the growth of Romanian nationalism in the form of the right-wing Romanian 'hearth' movement *Vatra Romaneasca*. Religion radicalized multi-ethnic regions such as Transylvania and Bosnia and prevented the formation of non-ethnic nations along Swiss lines.

Yet, despite the religious fault lines running through the Balkans, generations of folklorists, linguists, and ethnographers revealed traditions of shared meanings, of animism, and of mentalities revealed through language (Kitromilides 1996: 163–91). Folklorists have assumed that popular cultures have different kinds of 'borders', which do not correspond to the national or linguistic divides. The ethnologist Mary Edith Durham, who was christened the 'Queen of the Mountains' (*Kraljica e Maltsorëvet*) by her Albanian hosts, was a sensitive recorder of the close links between the cultures of the Slavonic Montenegrins and the Albanians, indicating that the area around Lake Skadar was what we might call now a 'soft border' (Durham 1909). Indeed, Noel Malcolm (1998: 10) has referred to a situation of 'ethnic osmosis' between Montenegrins and Albanians. Croatian scholar Maja Bošković-Stulli (1959–60: 293) has referred to a 'geographical complex' in popular beliefs that stretches from Friuli to the Gulf of Quarnero in Dalmatia (an area in which Romance and Slavonic dialects overlap and where the use of Vlach was once widespread). Traditionally, there are strong links between Slavonic and Greek Macedonians in terms of ideas and cultural practices (Abbott 1906).

Researchers into peasant community and native cultures were themselves infused with ideologies, particularly cultural nationalism, associated primarily with the work of Johann Gottfried Herder. Some also adopted local particularism, others supported commitments to larger units, such as Yugoslavism or Illyrianism. A sense of linguistic alienation and a desire for liberation was a common feature of these early nationalists. In the poem 'Istranom', written in 1869 by the young Istrian politician Matko Laginja, the hermit of Učke laments that in the Croat lands 'for the foreign lord all is done in a foreign language', and 'when the nation does not have its own language then the nation does not have qualities' (Žanić 1995: 115). In part, the illiteracy of the population of Habsburg Croatia allowed Hungarian, Italian, or German linguistic hegemony. In the hinterland of Split in 1880, 95 per cent of the population was estimated to be illiterate, and revivalist nationalists placed emphasis on organizing primary schools (Gross 1993: 270–92). Elsewhere in the Balkans, the schools and universities were important arenas for the activities of nationalists. Irena Livezeanu has argued that the growth of Romanian patriotism in the late nineteenth and early twentieth centuries led to an emphasis on the superiority of their 'Latin' heritage. This included the use of the term 'foreigner' to denote autochthonous minorities who had been living in an area for many centuries (Livezeanu 1995: 11). Onisifor Ghibu commented on the collection of Romanian folk songs *Arion*: 'A large part of the songs had a revolutionary character, which awakened and kept alive in children a spiritual state of permanent national pride and revolt, embroidered on the consciousness of our Latinity, of the necessity of unification of all Romanians and the great historical destiny of our people' (Livezeanu 1995: 144).

Fascist ideologies, which emerged in the Balkans after the First World War, also introduced notions of cultural value related to language, but were unconcerned about the possibility of future harmony between ethnic groups. Gabriele D'Annunzio, whose supporters occupied Rijeka/Fiume in 1919, described the struggle of the Italian people of the Adriatic against a 'barbarian usurper'—namely, the South Slavs—and the need to protect 'the furthest point of Latin culture' (D'Annunzio 1990: 264, 248). In majority South Slav areas occupied by Mussolini, intellectuals were transported to other regions and required to speak Italian. There was also discrimination against South Slavs in the economy and many Italianized their surnames in an attempt to compromise with the regime, although during the 1960s and 1970s names were changed back again. Balkan nationalisms have continued with the belief that one group rather than another has the ultimate right to live in an area and to destroy or drive out another group. Both Serbs and Croats believed that the Krajina was theirs and the issue of the ownership of the area was ultimately decided by force, with the result that hundreds of thousands of people were killed or displaced. Playing the numbers game in multi-ethnic regions such as Krajina, Vojvodina, Kosovo, or even Ulster, cannot be anything other than a recipe for conflict. Whether or not one group has a 'better' historical or even cultural claim to a territory is potentially menacing, unless it is accompanied by stringent protection for minorities.

The influence of historical materialism in the Balkans has also been profound, but it is possible to delimit two main stages in the influence of this philosophy. In the nineteenth century, the founding fathers of scientific socialism (particularly Marx and Engels) were largely scathing of cultures and communities outside Western Europe, regarding progress and homogenization as desirable. Unlike the fascists, they did not advocate the use of force to eliminate undesirable elements from Europe, but rather believed that the smaller Slavonic languages would disappear with the progress of languages of civilization. However, in the hands of the Russian Social Democratic and Labour Party, particularly with the publication of Joseph Stalin's *Marxism and the National Question* in 1913, historical materialism took an interesting diversion. Through the ideological stranglehold of the Comintern (1919–43), the notion that positive differences between nations should be legally recognized within devolved governmental structures crucially affected the Balkans. The Yugoslavian Constitution of 1946 gave the country a federal structure. Differences were encouraged by setting up academies in each of the regional capitals (except in Montenegro, whose academy was not founded until the 1970s) in which intellectuals thought about the meaning and consequences of their own national questions. This republican structure indicated that Tito was insufficiently Hegelian to impose a single culture, to 'make Yugoslavians', and that Stalinism actually impeded the creation of single national cultures using one language like those of Britain and France (which resulted in the weakening of ancient languages and cultures).

If 'Balkan nationalism' was a synthesis of ideas about national and ethnic identity that emerged in Europe after the middle of the eighteenth century, it also developed in part as a reaction against being defined as 'worthless' or 'savage' by outsiders, particularly descriptive writers (see e.g. Harry de Windt's *Through Savage Europe* of 1907). As Josiah Gilbert and Joseph Churchill (1864: 292) remarked in the early 1860s of Grintovec in the Slovenian Eastern Alps: 'It was a great disappointment to find the inn affording scarcely possible quarters for a lengthened stay, should we ever return to it. And besides, no one spoke anything but dreadful Sclavonic—all k's and z's. Our drivers themselves scarcely knew a word of German, and it was with difficulty we got anything to eat, the people being all, as it seemed to us, excessively stupid.'

Dismissive representations of south-eastern Europe are not just a historical curiosity. Belgium's former Foreign Minister Willy Claes discussed the 'latent Byzantine mentality of the peoples of Bulgaria, Serbia, and Romania, which makes them more naturally inclined towards despotism and abuse of legal powers' (Peter Beaumont, 'Tyrants Suit Slavs Says NATO Favourite', *Observer*, 25 Sept. 1994, 18). Native nationalisms, pan-Slavism, or even Yugoslavism were essentially reactions against a relationship of inequality between Western Europe and the Balkans, and arose from the desire of the region's intelligentsias to imitate the values of the academies of Western Europe as well as other features seen as 'European' such as types of town planning and architecture (Jezernik 1995*b*: 2–13). These movements were specific to the period after 1780, although some projections of larger national consciousness existed before that time in writers such as the seventeenth-century priest Juraj Križanić, an early if eccentric Panslavist, who publicized his views in Russia.

It is unlikely that relative values were given to particular languages at this time. Certainly foreigners travelling in the Balkans before the mid-eighteenth century do not appear to mock the primitivism of either the languages or the people, as they certainly do a century later. As one English gentleman remarked in 1737:

The language of the Croatians is the Sclavonick somewhat corrupted, but there is very little difference between them. The great extent of this language is something surprising. For it is talked not only here but likewise in Bosnia, Servia, Albania, Dalmatia, Moldavia, Wallachia, Bulgaria, in great parts of Hungary, Bohemia, Poland, Russia and (if one may believe travellers) in Tartary, and almost as far as China: and all these different countries have only so many different idioms of the original language.[15]

---

[15] Letter of 31 May 1737, Jeremiah Milles's Letters to the Bishop of Waterford, British Library Add. MS 15,774.

10.5. Ideologies and Language: 'Serbo-Croat'

To examine the interface between national ideologies and language, it is instructive at this point to examine a case study of the language that was habitually referred to in the former Yugoslavia (and elsewhere) as Serbo-Croat (i.e. *hrvatskosrpski* or *srpskohrvatski*). This language forms the basis for the newly established languages of *bosanski* (Bosnian), *crnogorski* (Montenegrin), *srpski* (Serbian), and *hrvatski* (Croatian), although several decades of a genuinely Yugoslavian culture helped to eliminate many regional disparities and ironically spoken 'Serbo-Croat' was more uniform by 1991 than in 1918 or 1945. The lexical variation between these languages is between 3 per cent and 7 per cent (Sito Sučić 1996: 13), all are mutually comprehensible, and dialect boundaries cut across state boundaries, so what is in a name?

Slavonic-speaking peoples arrived in the Balkans in the sixth century. Because of different settlement patterns, different religious and political traditions, and the consequent diversification of the spoken language, different languages and dialects emerged. In the case of Serbo-Croat, three main dialect groupings were distinguished in the nineteenth century: *štokavski*, *čakavski*, and *kajkavski*. These dialect groupings took their names from the various words for 'what'—that is, *ča*, *što*, and *kaj*. In addition, the *štokavski* has eastern and western variants, between which vowels differ markedly. Thus, for example, in the *ekavski* variant the word for milk is *mleko*, in the *jekavski* it is *mlijeko*, and in the *ikavski* (spoken in Dalmatia) it is *mliko* (Hawkesworth 1986: p. xviii).

Before the early modern period linguistic boundaries were less fixed and questions of codification were based upon the hope that communities of believers would understand the word of God. Early scholars working on a Croatian Bible project under the auspices of Primož Trubar in Germany felt that it was the Bosnian dialect *ikavska štokavština* that would make the most suitable unified variety for the *glagoljaši*—that is, those South Slavs who used the Glagolitic as opposed to the Latin or Cyrillic alphabets (Dimnik 1988: 380–99). In the nineteenth century, owing largely to the work of cultural nationalists, in particular Vuk Karadžić, a Serb scholar from western Hercegovina who urged his compatriots to 'write as you speak', the *štokavski* variant came into literary favour, with two main subvariants, the *jekavski* and the *ekavski*. This situation was not wholly without problems. As Ivo Banac (1994: 81) has remarked:

> the unique Croat dialectical situation, that is the use of three distinct dialects . . . could not be reconciled with the romantic belief that language was the most profound expression of the national spirit. Obviously one nation could not have three spirits, nor could one dialect be shared by two nationalities. It followed, therefore, that regardless of what their actual national consciousness might be, all stokavian speaking peoples were Serbs.

Despite the voluntary and cultural nature of early Yugoslavism or Illyrianism, the inherent danger of Serb domination dogged the unification of South

Slavonic dialects and goes some way to explain the subsequent fracture of Serbo-Croat.

The first Yugoslavia was the political result of several decades in the evolution of Illyrian or Yugoslav ideals, although in practice this state was highly centralized and Serb-dominated. Ideological commitment to Yugoslavia greatly affected academic discourse, with many authors claiming a common cause for all the South Slavs and representing Yugoslavia and the literary existence of Serbo-Croat as the culmination of natural impulses. As a government-sponsored grammar proclaimed in 1926, 'in spite of many statements to the contrary, Serbian and Croatian are one and the same language' (Prince 1929: p. ix). Those who disagreed with this found their work shunned. Josip Vidmar had his *Kulturni problem slovenstva* (*The Cultural Problem of Being Slovene*) banned after it was initially published in Ljubljana in 1932, because he disagreed with the 'three tribes' idea popularized by the Serb geographer Jovan Cvijić and adopted by the regime. At the beginning of the twentieth century a Serb linguist Aleksandar Belić defined the dialects of Macedonian as 'south Serb' (Belić 1905). By the 1930s, when Belić was President of the Serbian Academy, this view was universally adopted by the state and Macedonians were officially required to use Serbian in their daily life.

Tito's regime was to adopt the mid-nineteenth century Illyrian view that Serbian and Croatian were basically the same language, which led to a systemization of the languages after the Novi Sad Agreement in 1954, although as Marxist-Leninists they were prepared to add the element of 'agency' to the mystical brew of Yugoslavism, 'national unity', and royalism that King Aleksandar's regime had prepared.[16] In the 1960s there was a rise in Croatian linguistic consciousness, led by the *Matica Hrvatska* (Croatian Society) and the weekly newspaper *Hrvatski tjednik*. In 1971 the Matica even suggested that, if the language of command in the army was to be 'Serbian', then sailors ought to obey commands in 'Croatian' on the grounds that 80 per cent of the Yugoslavian navy operated in Croatian waters (Ramet 1992: 126). During Tito's lifetime nationalism was controlled by purging party ranks and sacking key journalists; nevertheless the language issue was to emerge again after the death of Tito with alarming frequency. In 1988 the Slovenian capital saw its largest ever post-war street demonstration in protest at the trial of journalists from the official 'youth' magazine *Mladina* (including the future Defence Minister Janez Janša) for leaking military documents to the public. Perhaps the greatest bone of contention, as far as the citizens of Ljubljana were concerned, was the use of Serbo-Croat at the trial rather than Slovene, which offended the real sense of national exclusiveness that had developed in the republic in the previous decade.

---

[16] Edvard Kardelj's pre-war view was that local cultures would eventually be superseded by larger states, and modern cultures reflect his own separation of 'state' and 'culture' (Kardelj 1939). In practice he and his fellow Communists preserved the political existence of the smaller nations, reflecting either a pragmatism born of their experiences during the war or a desire to add checks and balances at the level of the individual republics within the Yugoslavian Confederation.

Since the dissolution of the second Yugoslavia in 1991 the fortunes of 'Serbo-Croat' have waned. The government of Franjo Tudjman in Croatia sought to purge their language of alien words, especially those that might be considered to be shared with Serbian, echoing the practices of the Pavelić regime (Samardžija 1993). Citizens of Croatia, mostly Serbs, with 'un-Croat'-sounding names such as Jovanka and Jovan have changed them to Ivanka and Ivan (Ramet 1996: 210). Bosnian Serbs have attempted to purge their language of words originally derived from Turkish, but to do so they would have to do without many common things such as sugar (*šećer*), cotton (*pamuk*), or socks (*čarapa*) (Čengić 1994: i. 14). This later move is ironic, given that Vuk Karadžić had specifically not wanted to exclude Turkish loanwords when he codified the Hercegovinian *štokavski* (Peco 1987). As a kind of codification and a recognition that war and state formation have brought change, the text of the Dayton Peace Accords, signed at the end of 1995 by representatives of the central republics of the former Yugoslavia, was written in the languages of English and 'Serbo-Croat (Bosnian, Croatian and Serbian variants)' (Wyn Jones 1997: 98).

10.6. Post-Communist Nationalism

Post-Communist nationalism has constitutive elements from all the ideologies of nationalism as well as local features. The Iliescu regime in Romania was a version of the centralized state under a single party, without the cult of the personality that emerged under Ceauşescu. Bosnia's Muslims attempted to revive the first-among-equals status that they had previously enjoyed under the Ottoman millet system, and this was forcibly opposed by Serb and Croat extremists. Slobodan Milošević's regime in Serbia relies on corrupt political practices established during the Communist period, while he himself rose to power using the techniques associated with fascist regimes (use of *squadristi* at mass rallies, emotive rhetoric directed against other Yugoslavian ethnic groups, and so on). His regime relies on the tacit support of the Church, with his claim to be safeguarding monasteries and graves in Kosovo, and the active support of cultural nationalists in the Serbian Academy. Franjo Tudjman's government in Croatia was also characterized by ethnic intolerance, flaunting of democratic processes in local elections, nepotism, and the 'moral' use of force—for example, when evicting Serbs from flats formerly owned by the Yugoslavian People's Army. The provocative use of fascist symbolism, the re-emergence of kitsch folk art in Zagreb, with traditional costumes being donned at weddings and other festivals, as well as the rewriting of dictionaries and the reinstatement of the holy memory of Archbishop Stepinac (an *Ustaša* collaborator, but now considered by the Vatican to be worthy of beatification), are all elements of nationalism with historical roots.

It is possible, of course, to attempt to deconstruct the elements that have gone into modern Balkan nationalism and its relationship with language. Slovene national culture has elements of 'invented tradition', including the ritual climbing of Mount Triglav to announce 'Zdaj sem pravi Slovenec' (now I am a true Slovene), a practice wholly unknown before the nineteenth century. What is more difficult for the writer to convey is the passion with which people feel alienated from groups of 'others' whom they have lived beside for centuries and how less exclusive ideologies can be cynically manipulated and then discarded. It is simply insufficient to dismiss such passions as 'the narcissism of minor differences' (Judt 1994: 44). Nor is it sufficient to argue that historical 'memory' has been manipulated in a 'post-emotional' sense (Meštrović 1996), and that events from the past, particularly the Second World War, were used to stoke up ethnic rivalries. To argue that the Bosnian Serb General Ratko Mladić, whose father was killed by the *Ustaša*, is replicating the horrors of the Second World War, rather than avenging wrongs committed against his people or nation, surely misses the point about ethnic violence. Mladić may himself believe that he was fighting for a 'higher cause', and his troops may have had no compunction about slaughtering those they refer to as *Turci* (Turks—in this case Bosnian Muslims [17]) or *Ustaša*, but in the end they believed that the people they were slaughtering were less than human and therefore had lesser human rights.[18] Their sadism was cynically used by the governments in Belgrade and Zagreb to carve up new states from the former Yugoslavia with the gain of as much territory as possible. Such sadistic people probably exist in all societies at all times, but in times of political chaos their violence is directed at those whom they come to regard as 'other', whether that be Albanian (on the grounds of language or culture), or Bosnians and Croats (on the grounds of religion, history, and so). In effect, any real differences between people in these sort of circumstances are arbitrary.

As Slavoj Žižek (1990) has stated, ethnic nationalism reduces a 'multitude of dreams' to essential factors that are more or less unchangeable. In the Balkans as elsewhere in Europe it is possible to see the profoundly anti-democratic consequences of the politics of narrow constructions of identity, which privileges the single common denominator of etatist 'ethnicity' over region, religion, human rights, shared histories, and even shared languages.

[17] A separate word *Turjaši* for Anatolian Turks also exists.

[18] A naturalized Bosnian Serb, living in London, explained the attitude of his compatriots in a personal communication thus: 'They do not hate the Muslims. If you are walking along the street and accidentally step on and kill an insect, does that mean that you hate it?'

11.

Greece and European Turkey: From Religious to Linguistic Identity

PETER TRUDGILL

11.1. The Area

Many areas of Europe have seen a transition from ethnic identities based on traditional cultural practices and religion (with language playing some part), to
national identities with a strong territorial dimension, often with language as a
highly important marker of identity. A transition of this kind is particularly clear
in the area covered by the Greek and Turkish states, which are hence treated
together here. Their combined treatment is also merited by the long inclusion of
Greece within the Turkish-ruled Ottoman Empire.

11.2. Greece

11.2.1. *The Greek Nation: History and Self-Definition*

The issue of language and nationalism in Greece is quite naturally intimately
linked to the history of the modern Greek nation. The nation-state of Greece has
been in existence only since the 1830s, but its development as a nation has not
been a peaceful one. Indeed, 'few countries in Europe have had such a harrowing
and strife-torn recent history' (Clogg 1979: p. vii), and an examination of this
history suggests that it is not at all surprising that issues connected with nationalism, including those relating to language, can still arouse passionate argument and
debate in certain sections of Greek society today (see Woodhouse 1984).

Greece was part of the Turkish Ottoman Empire for approximately 400 years,
from the fifteenth century onwards. Towards the end of the eighteenth century,
however, events began to take place that were eventually to lead to Greek independence. The gradual breakdown of central control in the Empire led to a state
of anarchy in many places, which in turn led to the growth in power of the small
Constantinople (Turkish Istanbul) Greek élite known as the Phanariots, after the
Phanar area of the city. Because of its diminishing power, the empire was forced
to negotiate with the countries of the Christian West more than before and came

to rely increasingly on Greek interpreters for this purpose, who thus gained considerable control over Turkish foreign policy and eventually over the bureaucracy as a whole. Phanariot Greeks came to rule the Ottoman principalities of Moldavia and Wallachia with semi-regal pomp and status, and their courts in Iasi and Bucharest became important centres of Greek learning and culture, which were open to a certain amount of influence from the West. The Greek language became the commercial lingua franca of the Ottoman Balkans generally, and Greek culture was very influential, being looked up to by all in the Balkans who were Christian—that is, the majority. Indeed, at this time there were many Balkan Orthodox Christians who were 'Greek' by culture: their native language may have been Slavonic or Romanian, but they regarded themselves as Greek, because for them religion and culture were a more important determining factor than language (see Roudometof 1998).

Also of considerable importance during the same period was the gradual development of a class of mercantile Greeks who were active as traders both within and beyond the Empire, forming large colonies in places such as Livorno, Marseilles, Naples, Trieste, and Venice. There were also thousands of Greek traders and their families in Germany, in the Austrian Empire, and in Russia, especially around the Black Sea. These overseas Greek communities (although some of them consisted partly of Vlachs rather than exclusively of ethnic Greeks—see below) tended to be well provided with Greek schools, funded by wealthy merchants who were interested in the promotion of Greek language and culture as well as in the development of a commercial class of well-educated, literate Greeks.

Outside the Ottoman Empire, books had been published in Greek, particularly in Venice, since the sixteenth century—Venice controlled many Greek areas, including Crete, for some hundreds of years. But the eighteenth century saw an enormous increase in the number of books produced, as well as a change from religious to secular content, including translations of many of the most important philosophical works of the West European Enlightenment. Another important aspect of this secularization was the proud rediscovery by the small but growing Greek intelligentsia of their classical past, and an emphasis on classical texts and the study of Ancient Greek. Within Greece itself, however, this remained a minority, intellectual concern of little interest to the peasant majority, and it was also the target of hostility from the Orthodox Church, which regarded both the Enlightenment and an interest in pagan Ancient Greece as promoting dangerously secular atheistic and seditious tendencies.

The start of the nineteenth century also saw the beginnings of organized movements for Greek independence, influenced by the ideas of the Enlightenment and the French Revolution. The 'independence' under British control of the Ionian islands, including Corfu (Greek Kerkira), which came under British protection as a result of their capture from the French in 1815, was also influential, in that it showed that Greeks could manage their own affairs. These liberation movements were not universally popular with all Greeks. The Phanariots, for example, had little or nothing to gain by change; and many in the Orthodox Church went so far as to suggest that the Ottoman Empire had been created by the will of God. Nevertheless, unrest of various sorts increased, until a major series of uprisings began in earnest in 1821 in the Peloponnese.

After eleven years of difficult military struggle and the diplomatic and naval intervention of Britain, France, and Russia, independence was achieved for Greece in 1832 as a monarchy under a king of Bavarian origin. A feature of the struggle was the involvement of numerous individual philhellene volunteers who travelled from western Europe to Greece to fight against the Turks. Many of these were inspired to fight for Greek freedom by their classical education in Ancient Greek language, literature, and history, and not a few were disillusioned to find themselves fighting alongside illiterate modern Greek peasants and brigands.

Much of the history of Greece since 1832 has to do with the fact that the borders of the newly liberated Greece (see Map 3) contained none of the major Ottoman Greek centres of culture and commerce such as Alexandria, Istanbul, Thessaloniki, and Izmir (Smyrna), and that a majority of ethnic Greeks still remained unliberated in areas under Ottoman (or, in the case of the Ionian islands, British) rule. After the departure of its Turkish inhabitants—in what was to be but the first of a number of waves of ethnic cleansing in Greece—and an influx of Greeks from Constantinople and elsewhere wanting to enjoy freedom under the Greek flag, the population of the new state was about 750,000. Some 1,250,000 ethnic Greeks, however, still remained outside the country. One of the major themes of modern Greek history has been the *Megali Idea* or 'Great Idea': that the borders of Greece should be expanded so that it might include all ethnic Greeks.

It is probable that many Greeks outside Greece were initially not at all interested in this 'idea'. Many of the Asia Minor Greeks had become Greek only in name—they might have been Christians, but they had become Turkish-speaking. Strenuous efforts were made to rehellenize these Anatolian Christian Greeks through education, but the usage of *Katharevousa* Greek (see below) certainly did not help, and many 'Greek' communities in Asia Minor went through a process of language shift from Greek to Turkish as recently as the nineteenth century. Elsewhere, in Macedonia and Crete especially, there were Greek-speakers who, as a result of conversion on the part of their ancestors, were Muslims. Many Christian Greeks, too, continued to play an active role in the Ottoman Empire—the first Turkish ambassador to the new Greek kingdom was a Greek—and many Ottoman Greeks believed that irredentism on the part of the new country could be damaging to Ottoman Greeks and the interests of Greeks in general.

In 1864 the further territorial expansion of independent Greece began with the ceding of the Ionian islands to Greece by Britain. This increased the population of Greece to about 1,100,000. Greek attention then turned to the possibility of expansion into Thessaly, Epirus, Macedonia, and Crete, and in 1881, as a result of vari-

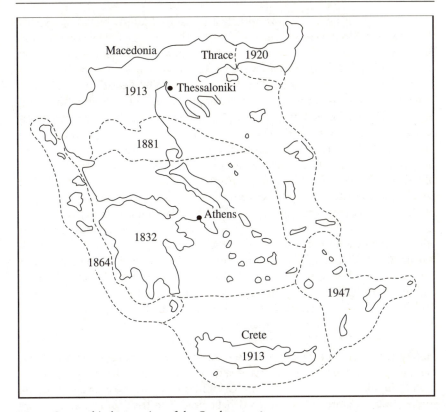

Map 3. Geographical expansion of the Greek state, 1832–1947

ous diplomatic and military events, Thessaly in the north and southern Epirus in the west, areas that were inhabited predominantly by ethnic Greeks, became incorporated into Greece (see Map 3). There were, however, particular worries in Greece amongst supporters of the 'Great Idea' about further northern expansion, because of the achievement of independence by Serbia and Bulgaria by 1878. This seemed to presage a three-way struggle between Serbia, Bulgaria, and Greece for Macedonia and the northern part of Epirus, which remained for the time being under Turkish control. Attempts were made by the competing nations to attract the loyalty of the populations of these areas, and Greeks made determined efforts to instil Hellenic consciousness into the Christian populations. In 1900 there were about 1,000 Greek schools in Macedonia with about 75,000 pupils, while schools run by the Bulgarian Church, newly independent of Constantinople Greek control, had about 40,000 pupils. There were also large numbers of Serbian schools, and even the Romanian government opened schools in areas inhabited by Vlachs (see below).

After years of sporadic guerrilla warfare between Greeks and Slavs, full-scale war broke out in 1912. This was initially a war waged jointly by Greece, Serbia, Bulgaria, and Montenegro against Turkey, but it was later followed by fighting between Bulgaria, on the one hand, and Romania, Greece, and Serbia, on the other. This led to a further expansion of Greece in 1913. Greece obtained Crete and most of the other predominantly Greek islands of the Aegean that had so far remained outside its control; most, but not all, of the rest of Epirus (the newly formed state of Albania was given the far north of this area); and a large area of Macedonia, which was now divided between Albania, Serbia, Bulgaria, and Greece (see Map 3). The land area of Greece was thus increased by about 70 per cent, and the population rose to about 4,800,000. For the first time, however, large numbers of people who were not ethnic Greeks were included within its frontiers. In 1912 Greeks had constituted only 43 per cent of the population of the now Greek part of Macedonia (Clogg 1979: 121). The newly Greek Macedonia had very large populations of Slavs and Turks in particular, as well as Greek-speaking Muslims whose ethnic loyalties were not at all clear. At the same time, many ethnic Greeks still remained outside Greece, notably in northern Epirus (Albania), especially in Agii Saranda (Sarandë), Argirokastro (Gjirokastër), and Koritsa (Korçë); in Thrace and Constantinople (European Turkey); and especially in Anatolia (Asian Turkey), where there were between 1 and 1.5 million, although, as we have seen, some of them were more Greek than others.

A majority of Asia Minor Greeks were to be found in the region of Smyrna. However, as a result of the disastrous war against the Turks of 1919–22, which was designed to incorporate the Smyrna area into Greece—as well, perhaps, as to win back Istanbul, the ultimate goal of the 'Great Idea'—this area was, in an enormous human tragedy, more or less entirely dehellenized. The Treaty of Lausanne of 1923 allowed Greece to expand its frontiers into western Thrace (see Map 3), which was at this time only about 17 per cent Greek, but it also provided for a compulsory exchange of populations. People of Greek Orthodox religion living in Turkey had to leave for Greece, and Muslims living in Greece had to leave for Turkey. The fact that religion was used as the criterion meant that many monolingual Turkish-speakers arrived in Greece, and many Greek-speaking Muslims left Greece for Turkey, Lebanon, and Syria. To this day, moreover, there are a number of Muslim Greek-speaking communities in northern Turkey. The only exceptions to these exchanges were the Turks of western Thrace, and the Greeks of Constantinople, who were allowed to remain where they were as protected minorities. It is thought that about 380,000 Muslims left Greece at this time, and there were also many Slavs who left Greek Macedonia and Thrace. About 1,100,000 Greeks arrived in Greece from Turkey, and Greek refugees also arrived from Bulgaria and Russia. This caused enormous problems, but many of the newcomers were settled in areas vacated by Turks and Slavs. This influx had the effect of raising the Greek population of Greek Macedonia to about 89 per cent of the total, and the Greek population of western Thrace to about 62 per cent. The total population of Greece in 1928 was 6,200,000.

11.2.2. *The Greek Language*

Greek is the only surviving member of the Hellenic branch of the Indo-European language family; indeed, it is not known if there ever were any other members. Scholars, for example, have variously speculated that the original language of the ancient Macedonians, before they became assimilated into mainstream Ancient Greek culture, was (*a*) a dialect of Ancient Greek, (*b*) a Hellenic language related to but distinct from Ancient Greek, or (*c*) not Hellenic at all but some other language altogether, such as Illyrian (which in turn may or may not have been the ancestor of modern Albanian). As is well known, the Ancient Greek dialects were in historical times for the most part subject to levelling, leading to the formation of the interdialectal koine, and modern Greek varieties are almost all descended from this koine (Browning 1969). Unlike Latin, however, Ancient Greek did not give rise to a number of different daughter languages. The only descendant of Ancient Greek is Modern Greek. This has had the consequence that the Greek language today is one of only a relatively small number of European languages that have the sociolinguistic status of Abstand languages, in the sense of Kloss (1967) and Trudgill (1992*a*). This means that Greek can be considered an independent and separate language for purely linguistic reasons without having to resort also to cultural, political, and historical factors, as has to be done with Ausbau languages (Trudgill 1992*c*). Greek has no close linguistic relatives, and it is not part of a dialect continuum that includes other languages in the manner of, say, Dutch and German (see Chapter 7).

The status of Modern Greek as an *Abstand* language is not without its significance for Greek nationalism and Greek identity. For most native speakers of Greek today, ethnicity is an unproblematic concept. Greeks are those whose mother tongue is Greek, whether they are citizens of Greece or are part of overseas communities, such as the long-established communities in Cyprus, Italy, the Balkans, Syria, Egypt, Turkey, Ukraine, and Georgia, or the more recently established communities in areas such as Australasia and North America. It is difficult for many Greeks to conceive of situations where language and ethnicity might be problematical or indeterminate. The unique Greek alphabet is also a factor in strengthening Greeks' perception of themselves and their language as being clearly and unambiguously distinct from all other peoples and languages.

This unambiguous identification of ethnicity is not necessarily shared by linguistic minorities in Greece (see below). It is also of relatively recent origin. When Crete, certain other islands, and parts of Macedonia were incorporated into Greece in 1913, many native Greek-speakers voluntarily left the country for Turkey, together with Turkish speakers and others, because they were Muslims (about 475,000 Muslims left altogether); religion was a more important factor for them in their subjective perception of their ethnic identity than their mother tongue.

As far as the language itself is concerned, there are two varieties of Greek that are sufficiently different from all others—that have a sufficient degree of

Abstand—that linguists might want to suggest that they are actually different languages. The first is Tsakonian (see B. Newton 1972), a Hellenic variety spoken in the eastern Peloponnese that is descended from Ancient Greek but not by way of the koine. Although Tsakonian is reported to be dying out, some schools in the area have acknowledged the degree of difference between it and other forms of Greek by providing pupils with teaching materials written in this variety. The second is Pontic. Although the term 'Pontic' originally applied only to the Black Sea varieties of Greek spoken in Georgia and northern Turkey, it is now also sometimes used to refer to varieties of Greek originating in central areas of Turkey such as Cappadocia (see Dawkins 1916; Sikkenga 1992). These varieties are very different from other dialects of Greek because of this long separation and because of considerable influence from other languages, notably Turkish. Some varieties, for example, demonstrate vowel harmony, a well-known feature of Turkish (Mirambel 1965). Both Tsakonian speakers and Pontics, however, regard themselves and are regarded as Greeks; and, although Pontics who have recently arrived in Greece do complain of discrimination, this ethnic identification appears to be uncontroversial.

11.2.3. *Language and Nationalism: The Competing Symbols of* Katharevousa *and* Dhimotiki

When Greece eventually achieved independence, a number of competing solutions were advanced to solve the problem of what form the standard written language of the nation should take. Language conflict of a kind had already been a feature in the Greek-speaking world for many centuries. In the progression from classical Ancient Greek to the Hellenistic Attic koine through New Testament Greek and on to Byzantine Greek, an ever-increasing gap had opened up between spoken and written forms of Greek. The written language, which to varying extents harked back to Classical Greek, lagged further and further behind the spoken language, which quite naturally underwent many internal changes and also borrowed extensively from Italian and Turkish.

With the first stirrings of Greek independence movements in the late eighteenth century, and with the beginning of publication of educational and non-religious texts in Greek under the influence of the Western European Enlightenment, the fact that contemporary vernacular Greek had hitherto been relegated to the status of a spoken language only (with the exception of some popular verse) came to be perceived as a problem. With the benefit of hindsight, it is possible to discern four different solutions that were advocated to this problem. First, there was the response of the conservatives who had been members of the Phanariot Greek élite in Istanbul and who advocated the continuing use of the archaic, Byzantine Greek that had been in written use at the Sultan's court whenever Greek rather than Turkish was employed. Secondly, inspired by the renewal of awareness of links with ancient Greece, there were a small number of intellectuals who advocated a complete return to Ancient Greek. They believed that it would be possible to persuade the population of Greece not only to write but also to speak the Classical language. Naturally, they had no success.

The third approach was that of the compromisers or purizers. Led by the Paris-based Adamantios Korais (1743–1833), who despised the Byzantine Orthodox tradition and who was greatly influenced by the French intelligentsia, they recommended that a modern Greek national language should be formed gradually by taking the current spoken vernacular and 'purifying' it of Turkish loans and regional dialect features at all linguistic levels. The result of this approach was a form of Greek known as the 'purifying' or *Katharevousa* language. This form of Greek was not then and never has been codified, but there were already many people who were employing a somewhat haphazard mixture of Ancient, New Testament, Byzantine, and modern vernacular Greek in their writings while trying to avoid the use of loanwords, particularly borrowings from Turkish.

The fourth approach represented a populist or vulgarist tendency that advocated the use of the ordinary everyday vernacular as the national language, as was perceived to be the case in west European countries. Poets in the Ionian islands of western Greece, which had remained for the most part outside the Ottoman Empire, were already writing in the vernacular. And in 1814 Yannis Vilaras, a scholar based in Epirus, published a 'Romaic Grammar' (for the term 'Romaic', see below) in which he laid down norms for a standardized Greek based on spoken dialects. Vilaras's grammar made little impact. Especially important for the populist approach, however, was the work of Yannis Psicharis (1854–1929), whose intention was to make a codified version of vernacular spoken, demotic Greek the only national language of Greece; this came to be known as *Dhimotiki*. He himself carried out no codification, but his famous novel *To Taxidhi Mou* (*My Journey*) (1888) was the first literary prose work to be published in *Dhimotiki* and was extremely influential. The language he used was a vernacular form that had developed as a result of dialect-mixing in the Peloponnese, the first area of Greece to be liberated, and especially in Nafplion, the first Greek capital, as people from all over the Greek-speaking world flocked to this area to fight the Turks and enjoy independence (see Jahr and Trudgill 1993). This koine also became the dominant form of Greek in Athens as it expanded from a small town to the national capital, replacing the original local dialect.

Although much of the fighting in the War of Independence took place in the Peloponnese and a majority of the fighters were from there, élite conservative Phanariot Greeks from Istanbul soon took control of the new government. This group was disconcerted by, as they saw it, the dangerous notion of using the language of the people as a national language, and Korais's purizing movement was therefore favoured by the government, although in fact in a more extreme form than he had ever intended. Thus, during the course of the nineteenth century, *Katharevousa* became institutionalized as the language of education, government, and the press. Linguistically it underwent considerable focusing and stabilization, but it remained an artificial form of language, full of hypercorrections and false archaisms.

In the meantime, Psicharis's approach received considerable support, particularly from the 1880s onwards, from intellectuals who were becoming very disenchanted with the artificial and difficult *Katharevousa*, especially in view of the educational problems it caused and the lack of success of any literature written in this variety. Following the publication of Psicharis's novel, there was therefore a very rapid move to the use of *Dhimotiki* in the writing of nearly all novels, poems, and plays.

Most of the language struggle in the twentieth century was, then, about the replacement of *Katharevousa* by *Dhimotiki* in the other, non-literary spheres. The struggle between the two forms of the Greek language has often been a bitter one, with governments intervening to impose one or the other in schools depending on their political complexion. The official language of schools during the century was as follows:

- pre–1909:   Ancient Greek only
- 1909–17:   *Katharevousa* only
- 1917–21:   *Dhimotiki* in primary schools
- 1921–23:   *Katharevousa* only
- 1923–35:   *Dhimotiki* in primary schools
- 1935–36:   *Katharevousa* only
- 1936–64:   *Dhimotiki* in primary schools
- 1964–67:   *Dhimotiki* only
- 1967–76:   *Katharevousa* only
- 1976–:   *Dhimotiki* only

Because of its close association with the deeply unpopular and enormously discredited military junta that was overthrown in 1974, *Katharevousa* has now more or less completely disappeared from the Greek scene—not, however, without having exerted a considerable amount of linguistic influence on the actual linguistic form of *Dhimotiki* as it is spoken and written today. It is now most usual to refer to this latter variety as Standard Modern Greek.

Of considerable interest to us is the fact that this struggle has often been conducted on the basis of issues intimately connected with nationalism (see Tsiouris 1989). *Katharevousa*, which harked back to the great days of the classical Greek past and which had attempted to remove all lexical signs of the humiliating period of Turkish colonial rule, was associated symbolically in the minds of many Greeks with Hellenism, the monarchy, Orthodox Christianity, and right-wing politics. *Dhimotiki*, on the other hand, was associated with republicanism, democracy, and left-wing politics.

The conflict in modern Greece between two competing perceptions of Greek identity and nationality *Ellinismos* and *Romiosini* (a reference to the fact that the Byzantine Empire was the successor to the empire of Rome) is especially interesting (see the discussion in Leigh-Fermor 1966), and has a definite though complex link to the language question. Without going into too much detail, we can say that a focus on Hellenic identity (*Ellinismos*) is one that stresses the classical Greek past and the Ancient Greek contribution to modern Western civilization, order, and logic. A remarkable manifestation of *Ellinismos* was the decision taken after Greek independence in 1833 to move the capital from Nafplion to Athens, at the time an unimportant and rather scruffy small town. A focus on Romaic identity, on the other hand, is one that stresses the Byzantine heritage and the heroism of the struggles against the Turks; it has a greater association with Greek peasant culture as well as with Orthodox mysticism. In modern times, this conflict was already visible in the war of independence against the Turks, during which there were also frequent outbreaks of fighting amongst the Greeks themselves. Particularly notable was the conflict between a 'military' camp (Clogg 1979: 59)—who wore traditional Greek dress, thought of themselves as waging a religious war against the Turks, and planned an oligarchic military state with considerable Church involvement for the new nation—and the civilian camp—who wore Western clothes, saw the war in nationalist rather than religious terms, and wanted a liberal constitution free from religious domination for post-war Greece. We can also say that the European philhellenes who were so influential in fighting for Greek independence from Turkey both politically and militarily were primarily motivated by Hellenism and their admiration for Ancient Greece and certainly not by *Romiosini*. Though the relationship is a complex one, links can be traced between support for *Katharevousa* and favourable attitudes towards *Ellinismos*. Similarly there are links between support for *Dhimotiki* and *Romiosini*-type sentiments.

More straightforward political issues connected with nationalism were also of considerable importance. The problem of wresting Macedonia from the Turks, and of whether control of this area would ultimately pass to Serbia, Bulgaria, or Greece, had a clear linguistic component. Most of the population of this area was mixed, as we have seen, with Greeks predominating only in the coastal areas. In laying claim to this area, the Serbs and Bulgarians could not, of course, base any claims on ancestry or direct descent from the Ancient Greeks. They could quite legitimately, however, lay claim to the inheritance of Byzantium, of which they had been a part. Anything that stressed the descent of the modern Greeks from pre-Byzantine Ancient Greece, such as *Katharevousa*, was therefore favoured by all Greeks who espoused the 'Great Idea'. Particular controversy was also aroused in Greece by the well-publicized claim of the Austrian politician and historian Jakob Fallmayer, who had a nationalist and racist agenda of his own—that modern Greeks 'did not have a drop of genuine and pure Greek blood' in their veins and that they were instead descended from Slavs, Albanians, Turks, Romanians, and others. Genetically, of course, this is obviously not without some truth, but its effect on Greek public opinion was enormous, not least because it seemed to directly contradict all the positive sentiments associated with Hellenism. Support for *Dhimotiki* was thus often seen, particularly by those on the political right, as representing support for the Slavs and constituting anti-national subversion.

The Greek Orthodox Church also had an important part to play. During the centuries of Muslim Turkish occupation, the Church had played a leading role as the only organized body that could act as a symbol of Greek identity and resistance, and as a guardian of Greek culture and nationality. *Katharevousa* was much more similar to the language of the scriptures and church services than was *Dhimotiki*, and any attack on *Katharevousa* could be construed as an attack on the Church. Thus, support for *Dhimotiki* could be perceived as hostility to Christianity, treachery to the nation, and support for pan-Slavism. When a demotic translation of the gospels was published in 1901, there were riots in the streets of Athens in which eight people were killed. And in 1903 there were further riots leading to one death following a performance of Aeschylus' *Orestia* in a demotic translation. Mobs marched through the streets of Athens shouting, amongst other things, 'death to the Slavs!'

11.2.4. Language and Nationalism: The Perceived Threat of the Minority Languages

Modern Greece has always been a multilingual country. Unfortunately, accurate information on how multilingual it has been and continues to be is very difficult to obtain. This is partly the result of the fact that no Greek census since 1951 has included a question about language. It is also a result of the distortion of some of the academic research on this topic by anti-minority Greek nationalism. In the context of modern Greek history—the ethnic cleansing of Greece, Bulgaria, and Turkey in the 1920s, the fixing of the present borders only since 1947 (see Map 3), the conflict over Cyprus, and the unrest in former Yugoslavia—many Greek writers, whether they claim the status of scholars or not, sadly fail quite miserably to achieve objectivity on the subject of linguistic and ethnic minorities.

This is undoubtedly matched by a similar lack of objectivity on the part of writers in neighbouring countries. But even on the part of academic linguists and sociologists, there is a surprising amount of paranoia in Greek writings on the subject, by European standards. As Exarchos (1992) quite rightly says in connection with the lack of linguistic support given to the Vlach minority (see below) in Greece, 'here in Greece, if you speak about something like [the conservation of the minority language Romansh in Switzerland], people will accuse you of stirring up trouble and will want to know which hostile power you are acting as a secret agent for' (author's translation). As Karakasidou (1993: 17) also points out, with reference to the work of contemporary Greek academics on the subject of the slavophone minority: 'The extremist and militant tone of most articles is alarming. It is striking that much of the rhetoric coming out of Greece . . . has progressed markedly little beyond the simplistic and reductionist notions that inflamed the Balkan Crisis at the turn of the century.'

We also find obfuscation that is totally contrary to the spirit of academic enquiry. Andriotis (1966), for example, would have us believe that Greek Macedonia was never, ever penetrated by Slavs. The Greek Foreign Minister, too, at an official press conference in 1998, denied the existence of a Macedonian minority in Greece (see Friedman 1999: 22). Others, slightly more cunning in their approach to the Slavonic minority, resort to a commonly used phrase in Greece, saying that 'people in border areas are often bilingual'. There is also a strong tendency to a bias so obvious that it is hard to credit. For instance, Angelopoulos (1979), writing in an academic journal, tells us without any trace of irony that, while members of the Slavonic-speaking minority in northern Greece left for Bulgaria in the period 1913–18 'to escape punishment for atrocities perpetrated', members of the Greek-speaking minorities further north 'were driven into Greece from Bulgaria and Yugoslavia by the occupying armies'. And there is also a regrettable and illiberal lack of acceptance of the concept of the multi-ethnic state. For example, Angelopoulos (1979) writes, again with no hint of irony, in a scholarly journal intended for an international readership that 'Greece represents, in Europe, a country with practically ideal ethnic, linguistic and religious homogeneity and unity'. There is also a failure on the part of some Greek academics to recognize the true nature of ethnicity and nationality. As Karakasidou (1993: 17) quite accurately points out: 'most Greek scholars do not regard ethnicity (or even nationality, for that matter) as a historical construct, and many fail to recognize the fundamental truth that reality—just like our cultural representations of "self" and "other"—is constructed.'

In 1994 the International Helsinki Federation for Human Rights issued a report extremely critical of the Greek state's treatment of minorities (see *Guardian*, 12 May 1994). It cites harassment of Slavs in the north-west of the country; the refusal of Greek authorities to cooperate with European and other international bodies concerned with minority rights; and the prosecution six times in the space of four years of a Greek Slav for claiming that Greece has a Slavonic minority. It also mentions multiple prosecutions of a former Turkish Greek MP from western Thrace. Within Greek society at large there is a commonly encountered failure to distinguish between citizenship and ethnicity, and recent prosecutions seem to indicate that members of the Turkish-speaking minority are permitted to identify themselves as 'Muslims' but not as 'Turks'.

Some of the linguistic minorities in Greece are only marginally involved in issues to do with language and nationalism. Romani, the Indo-Iranian language of the Roma, is spoken by many of the Roma in Greece. Indeed, many of them do not speak Greek (see Tressou-Milona 1992); praiseworthy small-scale projects are under way in some areas of Greece to bring literacy in both Greek and Romani to the children of some Roma groups. Other Roma are native speakers of Bulgarian (see below). The number of Roma in Greece is difficult to determine, for the reasons given above. The Commission of the EC reports a figure of 20,000 in Greek Thrace alone. How many of them actually speak Romani, however, is simply not known (Lunden (1993) guesses 10,000). In the absence of any Roma state or nationalist movement, the Romani language plays no role in Romani nationalism, nor in Greek counter-nationalism.

The same can be said for those few remaining speakers of Ladino (Judaeo-Spanish). In 1912 Ladino speakers were the largest single linguistic group in Thessaloniki, outnumbering both Greeks and Slavs. And in 1928 Ladino was the third largest minority language in Greece after Turkish and Slavonic—the official census suggests about 65,000 speakers—and there were thriving communities of speakers, not only in Thessaloniki, but also in other urban areas (see Kerem 1996). Most of its speakers were, however, exterminated by the Nazis during the Second World War. The 1951 census showed about 1,300 speakers of 'Spanish' in Greece, while Lunden (1993) suggests, perhaps optimistically, a current figure of about 5,000.

The same is also true of Armenian. Official Greek census figures suggest that there were 30,000 speakers in Greece in 1928 and about 9,000 in 1951—many Armenian speakers had by then emigrated to Armenia. The current situation is, of course, unknown, but a community of Armenian speakers survives in Thessaloniki and does produce a small number of publications in that language (Mackridge 1985)—the only non-Greek-speaking language community in Greece to do so apart from the Turkish-speakers.

There are, however, four other minority language communities that are intimately connected with issues to do with language and nationalism in Greece. Of these, two groups—the Vlachs and the Albanians—have been regarded as relatively unthreatening by Greek nationalists during the twentieth century, for reasons that will be explained below. The two other groups—the Slavs and the Turks—have been more heavily involved in issues of language and nationalism.

11.2.5. *Minority Languages: Balkan Romance*

Varieties of Balkan Romance spoken in the southern Balkans are generally referred to by linguists (see Mallinson 1988) as (*a*) Arumanian for those varieties found in the Pindus mountains of Greece and in Thessaly, and (*b*) Megleno-Romanian for those varieties spoken in Macedonia. Speakers of these varieties are known as Vlachs and are to be found in Albania, former Yugoslavia, and Bulgaria as well as Greece (Nandris 1987; Scarlatiou 1992). There are also small communities in Romania and Turkey, as well as emigrant communities in North America and Australia. The origins of the Vlachs remain mysterious (see Winnifrith 1987), particularly since it is known that, under the Roman Empire, the boundary between the Greek-speaking areas and Latin-speaking areas lay to the north of modern Greece. Obviously, then, they must be either direct descendants of Roman garrisons stationed in the mountainous areas of central Greece or, as seems more likely, descendants of some original Balkan population group who were romanized, and who migrated south during the intervening period.

In historical times, they have traditionally been transhumant shepherds, with the largest concentration in Greece lying in the Pindus mountains, focusing on Metsovo, today the only major town that is Vlach speaking. The number of speakers of *Vlachika*, as it is called in Greek, is difficult to determine, for the reasons outlined above and because of their migratory lifestyle. Census returns and other sources suggest a population in Greece today of at least 50,000. There is also a population in northern Greece of transhumant Greek-speaking shepherds known as Sarakatsans, who are also of mysterious origins, but whose culture suggests that they may in origin be hellenized Vlachs.

Most Vlachs, whether in Greece or outside, have a relatively weakly developed—or perhaps deeply concealed—notion of their own ethnic identity, tending to assume, at least for public consumption, the ethnicity of those around them. Winnifrith (1993) describes them as a 'minority which never achieved ethnic identity', although he also suggests that it may have been mainly wealthy Vlachs who identified with Greece, and on whom Greece relied for support—for example, in Macedonia in the nineteenth century—while poorer Vlachs were more inclined to be 'pro-Vlach'. Certainly, many Vlachs were very active on the Greek side in the wars of independence from Turkey, and some are regarded as national heroes by Greeks today who do not necessarily know that they were Vlachs. Rigas Velestinlis, also known as Pheraios, who was executed by the Turks for his role in promoting the struggle for Greek independence in the late eighteenth century, was a Vlach. The wealthy Vlach Georgios Averoff donated large sums of money for the purchase of a Greek battleship in the 1890s. Yannis Kolettis, the first Prime Minister of Greece, who played a very important part in the struggle against the Turks and in the revolutionary governments of the 1820s as well as in post-independence governments, and who was a passionate advocate of the Greater Greece 'Great Idea', was a Vlach. And Andreas Tzimas, one of the leaders of the left-wing anti-German guerrilla army during the Second World War, was also a Vlach. Many of the Greek merchants in eighteenth-century Europe were also actually Vlachs.

The submerged nature of Vlach ethnicity has also led to a number of misunderstandings. It is often reported in Greece, for example, that the town of Bitola (Greek Monastiri) in the Republic of Macedonia (formerly in Yugoslavia) has or had a sizeable Greek population. The vast majority of them, however, turn out to have been Vlachs (Winnifrith 1993). This submerged ethnicity has also led to increasing language shift in modern times, and many younger Vlachs now have only passive competence in the traditional language. The Vlach Head Teacher of the High School in Metsovo reports (personal communication) that no attempt is being made there to save the language and that he has no interest in doing so. The extent of this language shift should not be exaggerated, though. A majority of the inhabitants of Metsovo still speak *Vlachika*, and in nearby Anelio the children are mostly fluent native speakers (Winnifrith 1993). Interestingly, some Vlach villages in the Meglen region on the Greek side of the border with the Republic of Macedonia have become linguistically Slavicized rather than Hellenized (Winnifrith 1993).

From a sociolinguistic point of view, there is the interesting Ausbau linguistic problem of whether Arumanian and Megleno-Romanian are dialects of Romanian or not (see Lazarou 1986; Trudgill 1992*a*, *b*). The Greek practice of referring to the language as *Vlachika* has the effect of implying that they are not Romanian, which is of course something that certain Greek nationalists would want to stress. This linguistic problem naturally has parallels with the ethnic question of whether Vlachs are 'really' Romanians or not. Certainly, earlier in this century, the Romanian government, who of course had some interest in claiming that the Vlachs had a Romanian identity, established Romanian-medium schools in some areas of what is now Greece, as noted above, and argued, with some linguistic justification, that the dialects spoken by the Vlachs are indeed dialects of Romanian, although mutual intelligibility is by no means always easy. Since the 1920s, however, there have been no such schools, except for one that survived more or less by accident in Ano Grammatiko (Greek Macedonia) until 1945 (Winnifrith 1993), and most of the Pindus Vlachs, at least, would not today support the idea that they are ethnically Romanian. This was not always so, however, particularly in the Meglen. In the period of population movements after the First World War, a large number of Meglen Vlachs emigrated to Romania, less or more willingly, and the Greek government was particularly keen to remove from Greece those Vlachs who did identify with Romania, and to replace them with Pontic Greek refugees. Some Meglen Vlach villages were forcibly evacuated during the Second World War, which also resulted in considerable population movement. In addition, some Meglen Vlachs were Muslims and left for Turkey in 1924.

11.2.6 *Minority Languages: Albanian*

The position of the Albanian-speaking minority in Greece is in some ways very similar to that of the Vlachs, in that their sense of separate identity is weak and their feelings of connection with Albania for the most part are non-existent. They are all Christians—at least 20,000 Muslim Albanians, mostly from northern Greece, have left the country since the 1920s—and this aids their sense of identification with Greek culture and society, given that a majority in the state of Albania traditionally identified themselves as Muslims. Indeed, many Albanian-Greeks have played a prominent role in modern Greek life. George Koundouriotis, for example, was an Albanian-Greek from the island of Hydra who was president of one of the revolutionary governments established in the 1820s during the war of liberation from the Turks. Admiral Koundouriotis, from the same family, was president of Greece in the 1920s.

Linguistically, there is no doubt that their language is a variety of Albanian; the degree of linguistic *Abstand* between it and the dialects of southern Albania is so relatively small that mutual intelligibility is usually possible—problems are caused mainly by the usage of Greek loanwords—and the identification is much less controversial than that of *Vlachika*. Nevertheless, all Greeks have adopted the interesting practice of referring to the language of this minority not as *Alvanika* (Albanian) but as *Arvanitika*, and the people themselves not as Albanians but as *Arvanites* (singular *Arvanitis*). (Writers in English sometimes use the term

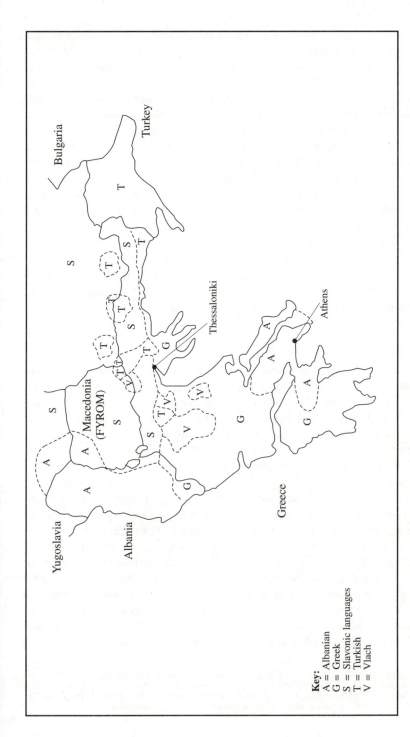

Map 4. Dominant languages in rural areas of mainland Greece, 1820
Source: Hasluck and Morant (1929).

Key:
A = Albanian
G = Greek
S = Slavonic languages
T = Turkish
V = Vlach

'Arberol'.) This, as in the case of *Vlachika*, has the effect of implying that *Arvanitika* is an autonomous language—a language that, though not Greek, is a 'language of Greece'—rather than a dialect of Albanian, the national language of a neighbouring country (see Trudgill 1992*b*).

The *Arvanites* have been in what is now Greece since medieval times (see Trudgill and Tzavaras 1977), and the biggest concentration of *Arvanites* today is in the areas where they were formerly the dominant element in the population—in Attica, Biotia, and much of the Peloponnese (see C. Williams 1992)—and indeed many of the suburbs of Athens are, or were until recently, *Arvanitika* speaking (see Map 4). Until the 1880s at least, electioneering politicians in this region would address public meetings in *Arvanitika*.The number of Athenians with at least some *Arvanitis* ancestry is very large indeed. The number of speakers is, once again, difficult to determine. The 1951 census gives a figure of 23,000, but this is certainly too small. There are, of course, complications, due to the fact that nearly all *Arvanites* are now bilingual and that many younger members of the community no longer speak the traditional language (Tsitsipis 1983). But my own research in the 1970s in the villages of Attica and Biotia alone indicated a figure of at least 30,000 speakers (see Trudgill and Tzavaras 1975, 1977). Lunden (1993) suggests 50,000 for Greece as a whole.

11.2.7. *Minority Languages: South Slavonic Languages*

Of all the linguistic minorities in Greece, it is the speakers of Slavonic languages who have been regarded with the greatest suspicion by centralizing and hellenizing Greek governments.[1] They occupy an area that was incorporated into Greece only as recently as 1912, and, in spite of the fact that under the Ottoman Empire many of them thought of themselves as 'Greeks', at a time when that term could be taken to mean simply 'Orthodox Christians', their occupation of areas bordering on other countries has been perceived as providing a threat to the territorial integrity of Greece.

During the course of the sixth and seventh centuries, peoples speaking southern Slavonic languages penetrated and overran large areas of what is now modern Greece as part of a general southward movement that saw them enter also into parts of Asia Minor. Some Slavs reached as far as Crete, but the areas that saw heaviest in-migration were Macedonia, Thrace, and the Peloponnese. In most parts of Greece, these Slavonic-speaking peoples were gradually assimilated into the original populations. Large areas of northern Greece, however, remained predominantly Slavonic speaking for 1,200 years or so, until the present century. For example, the first Slavonic literary language, Old Church Slavonic—the language into which the Apostles Cyril and Methodius translated the Scriptures

---

[1] I will provisionally refer to the language or languages concerned as 'Slavonic', and to the people who speak them as 'Slavs'. This will, however, require revision, since these labels also refer to a number of other languages and their speakers, but it reflects the undifferentiated label *Slavika* in Greek. I return below to the question of a more satisfactory labelling of the languages and people.

from Greek—was based on the Slavonic dialects spoken in the region of Thessaloniki. Under the Ottoman Empire, Slavonic speech continued to predominate in northern Greece. For instance, as recently as 1892, schools in Kastoria (Macedonian Kostur) prepared teaching materials in the local Slavonic dialect for use with pupils; the local Greek bishop, however, did not approve of this, nor of church services in Slavonic, and had the school closed down. The areas of rural Greece which remained predominantly Slavonic speaking in the early years of this century can be seen from Map 4.

After the Balkan Wars, which succeeded in liberating those areas of the Balkans that had remained under Turkish control and subsequently in dividing up the liberated areas between Albania, Serbia, Greece, and Bulgaria, it is estimated that in 1913, on the Greek side of the border, there were somewhere between 300,000 and 500,000 Slavonic speakers (see Breatnach 1991), including a sizeable Slavonic-speaking minority in Thessaloniki. According to the Treaty of Neuilly, Greece undertook to defend the rights of the national minorities within its borders and, in the 1920 Treaty of Sèvres (which was never ratified), promised to open schools for minority-language pupils. In 1925 the government of Greece submitted copies of a school primer, which was written in a Slavonic variety[2] for use with Slavonic-speaking minority pupils and published by the Greek Ministry of Education, to the League of Nations as evidence that they were carrying out these obligations. Unfortunately, this tolerant attitude towards the Slavonic-speaking minority in Greece did not last long. During the 1930s, under the totalitarian dictatorship of Metaxas, education in Slavonic languages was made illegal, as indeed was the use of a Slavonic language for any purpose whatsoever, including in the home. Speakers of Slavonic languages are reported to have been fined and imprisoned simply for speaking their own language. In at least one village in the area of Florina, where the vast majority of locals spoke Macedonian, 'all villagers were forced to attend night school to study Greek . . . Anyone "caught" speaking Slavo-Macedonian was forced to drink castor-oil and some were even tortured. Youths who used Slavo-Macedonian at school were thrashed. In the evenings, an individual was assigned to make rounds of the village to listen for people speaking Slavo-Macedonian at home' (Karakasidou 1992: 2). Slavonic family names were also compulsorily changed to Greek ones (Hill 1992). In addition, between 1924 and 1935, the Communist Party of Greece had a policy of advocating autonomy or independence from Greece for Macedonia, which aroused considerable opposition and suspicion from the political right and hostility towards Slavs.

In 1913 a proportion of the Slavonic-speaking population of northern Greece were Muslims. During the resettlements that took place between 1913 and 1922, most of these left for Turkey (see above), religion being, as for Greek-speaking Muslims, a more important feature in their subjective ethnicity than language. By 1926, about 50,000 Christian Slavonic speakers had also left for Bulgaria and

---

[2] See below for further information on the language of this primer.

Yugoslavia, although a majority of the Christian Slavonic-speaking population remained in Greece. Not surprisingly, though, the repression under Metaxas led to further emigration to Yugoslavia. It also led to considerable resentment, much of which found expression during the Second World War and the subsequent Greek Civil War. In Slavonic-speaking areas of Greece liberated by partisans from the Germans, at least one newspaper was published in the local Slavonic dialect, and Slavonic-language schools were set up in Slavonic-speaking areas. In 1944 a number of schools in the Kastoria and Florina (Macedonian Lerin) districts were using a Slavonic-language primer. On the other hand, the fact that the Bulgarian forces who occupied Greek Macedonia in support of the Germans during the war imported numbers of Bulgarian settlers into northern Greece did the Slavs' cause no good at all.

During the Greek Civil War, there was, not surprisingly, considerable support for the anti-government forces in the Slavonic-speaking areas, and Slavonic speakers were well represented in the Leftist army, constituting about 40 per cent of the force. The defeat of the Left, however, was a disaster for the Slavonic-speaking Greeks, and very large numbers of them fled to Yugoslavia or overseas. There are today, for example, sizeable Slavonic-speaking communities of Greek origin in Australia and Canada. At a conservative estimate, at least a quarter of a million Slavonic speakers have left Greece during the course of this century. The current situation of Slavonic speakers in Greece is difficult to determine. The official Greek census figures show a Slavonic-speaking population of about 100,000 in 1928 and 1940, and about 60,000 in 1951. Estimates for the current Slavonic-speaking minority in Greece range from 60,000 to 90,000; the figure of 210,000 given in Bright (1992), is certainly too high.

In Greek Macedonia today, Slavonic speakers are almost all bilingual in Greek and a Slavonic language, and many of them probably regard themselves as ethnically and/or culturally Greek: many of those for whom a Slavonic identity was particularly important have tended to leave Greece during the past eighty years. Repression continues, however. Many Slavonic-speaking political refugees who fled to Yugoslavia in the civil-war years have not been allowed to return to Greece and rejoin their families (Karakasidou 1993). Slavonic-speakers, moreover, are often even today not permitted to dance their folk dances or sing their folk songs in public. And approaches by Slavonic-speakers to the EU have been met by personal reprisals on the part of the Greek civil service (Karakasidou 1993: 13). It is not impossible that in time this repression will become counterproductive. Most Slavonic-speaking activists have wanted only recognition of their ethnic identity, and linguistic minority rights, but it is not entirely impossible that the politicization of culture by Greek authorities—for example, the Florina-based cultural association Shelter of Macedonian Heritage has been declared illegal by the Greek Supreme Court—might lead to stronger demands (Karakasidou 1993).

One problem in researching this minority is the strong tendency on the part of Greek authorities to deny the existence of Slavonic-speaking minorities in Greece at all. This tendency, sadly, is not confined to politicians, as we saw above. My own research and enquiries on this topic show—as do those of Karakasidou (1993)—that Slavonic-speaking villages are, nevertheless, still to be found in many areas of Greek Macedonia, and towns such as Florina, Kastoria, Edessa (Macedonian Voden), and even Verria certainly contain sizeable numbers of Slavonic speakers, although they tend to conceal their ability to speak a Slavonic language in public situations. Current estimates (see Lunden 1993) suggest a Slavonic-speaking population in Greek Macedonia of about 50,000. Karakasidou estimates that 80 per cent of the population of the Florina area of north-western Greece are either Slavonic-speaking or descended from Slavonic-speaking families.

There is also a community of Slavonic speakers in Greek Thrace. This is a Muslim community known as the Pomaks, 20,000 strong in 1951, perhaps 10,000 today (some estimates suggest as many as 40,000), who live in the area around Xanthi; there are also Pomaks in Bulgaria. As Muslims, they receive their education in Turkish and tend to send their children to Turkey for their higher education (Lunden 1993). There are also Roma who are native Slavonic-speakers, as indicated above.

So far, I have used the imprecise term 'Slavonic' to refer to the language or languages spoken by these minorities in northern Greece. However, there is, of course, the very interesting Ausbau sociolinguistic question as to whether the language they speak is Macedonian or Bulgarian, given that both these languages have developed out of the South Slavonic dialect continuum that embraces also Serbian, Croatian, and Slovene. In former Yugoslav Macedonia and Bulgaria there is no problem, of course. Bulgarians are considered to speak Bulgarian and Macedonians Macedonian. The Slavonic dialects of Greece, however, are 'roofless' dialects whose speakers have no access to education in the standard languages. Greek non-linguists, when they acknowledge the existence of these dialects at all, frequently refer to them by the label *Slavika*, which has the implication of denying that they have any connection with the languages of the neighbouring countries. It seems most sensible, in fact, to refer to the language of the Pomaks as Bulgarian and to that of the Christian Slavonic-speakers in Greek Macedonia as Macedonian.

Of course, in Greece itself, particularly in the 1990s after the achievement of independence by the former Yugoslav republic of Macedonia, the name 'Macedonian' for the Slavonic language, as well as 'Macedonia' for the former Yugoslav republic, gave rise to a certain amount of nationalist controversy. Greek linguists have sensibly for the most part adopted the disambiguating practice when writing in Greek of referring to the language as *Slavomakedhonika*, since the most obvious meaning of the Greek word *Makedhonika* would be 'the dialect of Greek spoken in Greek Macedonia'. Certain non-linguists, on the other hand, including politicians, have recently taken to arguing that, given the recent Ausbau development of Macedonian, there 'is no such language' and that Slavonic-speakers in 'Skopja', as they refer to the former Yugoslav republic of Macedonia, are really speakers of Bulgarian (or Serbian). It is, therefore, interesting to note that, at earlier periods, different Greek governments have been at pains to distinguish between Macedonian and Bulgarian. The 1928 census gave figures for speakers of Bulgarian and Macedonian-Slav separately. And the 1925 Slavonic primer referred to above was written in a variety of South Slavonic quite distinct from Bulgarian—that is, it more closely resembled the modern standard Macedonian language—and was, interestingly, written in the Latin alphabet, both steps obviously taken in an attempt to stress the lack of connection between Bulgaria or Serbia and the Slavonic population of Greece. Ironically, during the course of the nineteenth century, printers and publishers in Thessaloniki played a very important role in developments that were eventually to lead to the standardization of Macedonian in the 1940s.

11.2.8. *Minority Languages: Turkish in Greece*

Hundreds of thousands of Turkish-speakers left Greece at various times during the period 1821–1923, by no means all of them simply part of an urban-based occupying power. Map 4 shows that, even in the early years of the twentieth century, large areas of rural Greek Macedonia were predominantly Turkish speaking. In the Peloponnese, too, they constituted about 10 per cent of the population in 1820—there were 40,000 or so Turkish inhabitants to about 360,000 Greeks (Clogg 1979: 35). Today, however, the only Turkish speakers in Greece are in western (Greek) Thrace (Sella-Mazi 1992). Here, alone of all Greek minorities, they have protected status, with rights to practise their own religion and to use their own language, including in the education system, as a result of the Treaty of Lausanne. They also elect members to the national Parliament in Athens. It is sometimes difficult to distinguish between Turks and the Slavonic-speaking Pomaks (see above), who tend to be able to speak Turkish also (for a similar problem in Bulgaria, see Konstantinov *et al.* 1991). Census returns give figures for native Turkish speakers of 190,000 in 1928, 230,000 in 1940, and 180,000 in 1951. These Turkish-speakers look to Istanbul rather than Athens for many purposes, and typically young people go there to study rather than to universities in Greece. There are also well-known but not officially recognized communities of Muslim Turkish-speakers on Kos and Rhodes.

11.3. European Turkey

Most of Turkey is, of course, in Asia, but the fact that a proportion of the country is located in Europe (eastern Thrace, including much of Turkey's largest city Istanbul), and the existence of a Turkish diaspora of several millions in Germany and elsewhere, justifies its inclusion in this volume. As a nation-state, Turkey is an even more recent creation than Greece, dating only from 1923. Prior to that, what is now modern Turkey had simply been part of the multi-ethnic Ottoman Empire, in which, although it was controlled by Turks, ideas of Turkish nationalism and ethnicity traditionally played a very small role. The area of modern Turkey, moreover, was by no means necessarily the most important part of the Empire. The hub of the Empire was undoubtedly Istanbul, but at many periods in history, and for many purposes, the European parts of the Empire were politically, culturally and economically the more important, and cities such as Thessaloniki (Turkish Salonika) were highly influential.

For centuries, just as Christianity was the most important identifying characteristic within the Empire for the people we today call Greeks, Bulgarians, and Serbs, so the ancestors of the modern Turks thought of themselves as Muslims first, Ottoman citizens second, and Turks hardly at all. Any sentiments of Turkish ethnicity that may have been present amongst the original Turkic populations that migrated from Central Asia into Anatolia were submerged after their conversion to the Muslim faith under a pan-Islamic identity. To this was added, at a later date, sentiments of loyalty to the Ottoman Empire and the Sultan (see Lewis 1968).

Within the Ottoman Empire, citizens' native languages were of little importance as compared to their religious affiliation, and ethnicity relatively meaningless. Muslims were the privileged caste, while Christians and Jews, although generally treated with considerable tolerance, were second-class citizens. Turkish nationalism as such dates only from the nineteenth and twentieth centuries, and awareness of ethnic as opposed to religious identity developed only during the same period. Indeed, even in the early years of the modern Republic, speakers of Slavonic or Albanian or Arabic who were Muslims were accepted as Turks, while Christians and Jews, even if they were Turkish-speaking, could be considered as Turkish citizens, but never as Turks (Lewis 1968: 357).

11.3.1. *The Turkish Language*

Turkish is a member of the Turkic branch of the Altaic language family: Turkic languages are mainly spoken in Central Asia; examples are Kazakh, Kirghiz, Tatar, Uzbek, and Yakut (Deny 1955). The closest linguistic relatives of Turkish are Azeri, Gagauz (spoken in Moldova), and Turkmenian (Kornfilt 1987). Turkish has close to 50 million native speakers, most of them in Turkey, but there are sizeable indigenous communities also in Cyprus, Greece (see above), Bulgaria, and the Republic of Macedonia.

Like modern Greek, the modern Turkish language has been the object of attempts at lexical and other forms of 'purification' (C. Gallagher 1975). Unlike in the case of Greek, however, these attempts have been relatively successful. This is certainly because the motivation in the two cases was rather different. With Greek *Katharevousa,* as we have seen, the impulse was largely derived from a nationalistic harking back to the golden age of classical Greece and the sloughing-off of linguistic reminders of Ottoman rule, in spite of the fact that Turkish and Italian loanwords had become an integral part of the Greek vernacular. The abortive attempts at the removal of these loans from modern Greek had the effect, as mentioned above, of rendering *Katharevousa* almost impossible for native speakers to learn without years of formal education. The motives for the 'purification' of Turkish, on the other hand, were functional as well as nationalistic. It involved the removal from the literary language and formal spoken styles of learned Persian and Arabic vocabulary that had, in most cases, never become part of the spoken vernacular language, thus making standard Turkish easier for the majority of the population to acquire (for parallels with Norwegian, see Jahr and Trudgill 1993). Nevertheless, in cases where Persian and Arabic loans were part of everyday Turkish, attempts to create new forms, often by compounding indigenous lexical items, were often unsuccessful. The changes, however, were so extensive that the written Turkish of fifty years ago may be relatively incomprehensible to younger Turkish-speakers today.

There was also, however, a nationalistic motivation behind these lexical changes. Indeed, they were an important part of the modernizing and secularizing moves made by the Turkish leader Kemal Atatürk that followed from the creation of the Turkish state in the 1920s and that were designed to remodel Turkey along the lines of a western European nation and to instil national consciousness into the population. As part of the same movement, by government decree the Turkish language was written in the Latin alphabet from 1929 onwards rather than in the Arabic alphabet, as had previously been the case. The deliberate fostering of sentiments of Turkish nationality and ethnicity often came into conflict with older, more conservative ideas of a wider Islamic identity, and the abolition of the Arabic script and the removal of Arabic vocabulary items were highly symbolic in this respect.

11.3.2. *Minority Languages in European Turkey*

Non-Turkish language communities were thriving and numerous under the highly polyglot Ottoman Empire. The minority language communities in European Turkey today, however, are few and are almost exclusively concentrated in Istanbul. There is, for example, a sizeable community of Jewish Ladino speakers in the city. Happily, unlike similar communities in Yugoslavia, Romania, and Greece (see above), this community was not exposed to the horrors of the Nazi extermination campaign, although it has been somewhat reduced in size as a result of emigration to Israel. These Ladino speakers are the descendants of Jews who were expelled from Spain and Portugal *en masse* from 1492 onwards and who found a welcome in the much more tolerant Ottoman Empire. Their language, also known as Judaeo-Spanish, bears the same kind of relationship to Spanish as Yiddish does to German. The Istanbul community continues to enjoy a cultural and literary life focused on the Ladino language, and they are not involved in any issues to do with language and nationalism in the modern Turkish state.

Armenian, an Indo-European language that, like Greek, has no close relatives, was formerly spoken by a very large minority community indeed in Ottoman Anatolia, but Armenian speakers are now relatively few in number in modern Turkey as a result of a number of massacres of Armenians by Turks, notably the appalling massacre of 1915 when a million and a half Armenians were killed. It is not, of course, a coincidence that these massacres of what had initially been conceived of as a loyal, albeit Christian, Ottoman population occurred at a time when notions of language and ethnicity were becoming more and more powerful in determining the attitudes of the Turkish-speaking population to their nation-state. Another significant factor in the reduction of the community, as in Greece, has been the emigration of Armenian speakers to the former Soviet Armenian Republic. As far as European Turkey is concerned, however, we must note that a community of Armenian-speakers does still survive in Istanbul.

Survivors from the Greek-speaking minority that was allowed to remain in Turkey after the 1923 population exchanges (see above) are still found today in Istanbul as well as in Imroz (Greek Imbros) and Bozcaada (Greek Tenedos), two islands at the entrance to the Dardanelles. This Greek minority has shrunk considerably over the years. In spite of their protected status, they have been placed under various types of nationalistic pressure, both official and unofficial. The infamous capital levy of 1942, for example, was an emergency tax that required non-Muslims to pay up to ten times as much as Muslims; defaulters were severely punished, whether they were able to pay or not (Lewis 1968: 297–301). Most defaulters, quite naturally, were Greek, Jewish, and Armenian merchants who were simply unable to pay. There were also anti-Greek riots in Istanbul in 1955, and many Greeks left for Greece as a result of tensions between Greece and Turkey arising from the Cyprus crisis, especially in 1963 and 1974. The Greek-speaking population of Istanbul declined from over 100,000 in 1923 to 70,000 in 1960, to no more than 10,000 now.

11.4. Conclusions

Greece and Turkey represent an area in which ethnic identities have long played a major role in politics and society. Until modern times the most salient element of such identities was traditional religious affiliation, with language differences play-ing a much smaller role. Over the last two centuries, however, ethnic groups, delimited to a great extent by religion, within a single political unit, the Ottoman Empire, have given way to different nations, still distinguished by religion, but to a diminishing degree, and with language becoming ever more salient as a marker of national identity. As an illustration of the changes, today one state, Greece, has a troubled relationship with Orthodox Christian speakers of Macedonian, who in the nineteenth century could even have carried the label 'Greek', which could be applied to all Orthodox Christians. Greece and Turkey demonstrate how language and national identity are becoming ever more closely related in much of Europe.

12.

Coming to Terms with the Past: Language and Nationalism in Russia and its Neighbours[*]

CATHIE CARMICHAEL

12.1. Introduction

A comprehensive account of the role of language in national identity in the former Soviet Union would require another book of comparable dimensions to this one. The territory is vast, and is home to a large number of ethnic groups, many distinguished from others at least in part by the use of distinct languages. It might be argued that, apart from the majority populations of the former Union republics, not many of these groups can be described as nations, at least in the sense which that term may have further to the west; the group may be very small, there may be little aspiration to autonomy or independence, the extent of a putative national territory might be highly debatable. An adequate treatment would nevertheless have to outline the characteristics of each group, and the circumstances of each group, which vary greatly, would have to be discussed.

In view of the impossibility of including an adequate treatment here, it has been decided to restrict discussion to those parts of the former Soviet Union that have close links with the rest of Europe: Ukraine, Belarus, Moldova, the Russian Federation, and the Baltic states of Estonia, Lithuania, and Latvia. Lithuania, Ukraine, Belarus, and Moldova actually border on other European states; Estonia has close linguistic and cultural ties to Finland, as does Moldova to Romania. Lithuania and parts of modern Ukraine were in the past united politically with Poland (see Section 9.3). As the major Orthodox Christian power from the end of the fifteenth century onwards, Russia exercised a great influence on the other Orthodox peoples of Europe, such as the Greeks, Bulgarians, Serbs, and Romanians. Russian, or Soviet, thinking in many spheres, including on questions of nationality and language, was influential throughout the Communist states of Cold War Europe, from Bulgaria to the German Democratic Republic, from Poland to the former Yugoslavia (see Gustavsson 1990).

* I am grateful to Stephen Barbour for comments on earlier drafts of this paper, and to Dunstan Brown for much invaluable information on linguistic matters. All the census data in this chapter comes from Wyn Jones (1997).

We have excluded from discussion those republics of the former Soviet Union that are conventionally held to lie entirely in Asia: Kazakhstan, Kirghizia, Uzbekistan, Turkmenistan, and Tadzhikistan. Although the boundary between Europe and Asia is, to a great extent, conventional and arbitrary, and while the republics in question experienced great influence from Russia in the Soviet period and earlier, including extensive in-migration of Russians and others, such as ethnic Germans,[1] they remain nevertheless rather different in most respects from Europe, and, as states with majority Muslim populations, have perhaps more in common with states to the south, such as Iran, than they have with Europe.[2]

A further area excluded is the Caucasus, some of which at least is often considered to be part of Europe. I exclude not only the former Union republics of Azerbaijan, Armenia, and Georgia, but also the Caucasus region of the Russian Federation, approximately the autonomous republics of Dagestan, Chechnya, North Ossetia, Kabardino-Balkaria, and Karachai-Cherkessia. The major reason for excluding the Caucasus is its extreme linguistic diversity, a diversity arguably quite different in kind from any found elsewhere in Europe: members of two of the world's major language families, Altaic and Indo-European, are found in this region, the former represented by Azeri, which closely resembles Turkish, the latter by Russian and Armenian, an Indo-European language without any close relations. However, apart from these, there are three entire language families, each with several members, found only in the Caucasus: North-East Caucasian, North-West Caucasian, and Kartvelian. Of the languages in these three families, only Georgian, a Kartvelian language, has a number of speakers reaching several millions. Over all there are at least forty distinct languages in the Caucasus, Dagestan being particularly linguistically diverse (Comrie 1981: 196–7).

The Russian Federation, though it represents only part of the former Soviet Union, is still, in terms of land area, the largest sovereign state on earth, showing great linguistic and ethnic diversity. As there is not scope here for full discussion of that diversity, I focus chiefly on only one language of the Federation, Russian, whose speakers are arguably the only group in the Federation that constitutes a nation comparable to other European nations. In particular, languages and ethnic groups found only in the Asiatic part of Russia, Siberia, such as the so-called Paleo-Siberian languages and their speakers, are not discussed here, although I would reiterate that the conventional boundary between Europe and Asia, generally following the Ural Mountains, has little real political or cultural significance.

---

[1] At the end of the Soviet period the Kazakh ethnic group formed less than 50% of the population of Kazakhstan. This was the only union republic in which the nominal majority 'nationality' was no longer a numerical majority, but in some other republics, both in Europe and Asia, the population belonging to minority nationalities was close to 50%

[2] The term 'Europe' is used in a loose sense here and is fixed by discursive definition rather than geography or politics.

12.1.1. *The Legacy of the Past*

All the states discussed here share a common recent history: as provinces of the Romanov Empire until 1917, as republics of the Soviet Union, and as new states founded on the ashes of the Soviet Union. With the exception of the Baltic states (Estonia, Latvia, and Lithuania), they have since continued to cooperate as members of the Commonwealth of Independent States.

All the non-Russian ethnic and linguistic groups now share a complex relationship with the formerly dominant language of the region, Russian, and the post-communist period is characterized by a process of coming to terms with centuries of Russian hegemony and the ubiquitous presence of Russian-speakers. Russian has not always dominated in this region. As Harold Haarman (1992: 12) reminds us, 'the cultural trends among non-Russian peoples in the European part of the (former) Soviet Union have not always been characterized by dependence on or interference from Russian . . . the early progress of regional cultures did not coincide with the development of Russian literacy'. However, the Russian presence is hard to ignore, even if Soviet military hegemony has gone. The ethnic Russian diaspora in the 'near abroad' is estimated to be about 25 million and a further 10 million use Russian as their first language (Tolz 1998: 267, 280). Russian movement into other areas was particularly marked after the Second World War. It is estimated that in 1939, what is now Estonia had a population that was 88.2 per cent Estonian-speaking, whereas now that figure is less than 65 per cent (Park 1994: 71–2). In the 1970s the Soviet authorities also followed a policy of Russification in the non-Russian-speaking parts of the Soviet Union, and it is possible to see that the independence moves of 1991 were a backlash against late Stalinization (Misiunias and Taagepera 1993: 213). However, it would be unfair to see these Russians in the 'near abroad' merely as a kind of ethnic fifth column, as 'Russians have made serious efforts to join their non-Russian neighbours in the creation and strengthening of new states' (Bremmer 1994: 262).

All of the European states of the CIS, and the Baltic states, also have a small minority of Yiddish-speaking Jews (usually less than 1 per cent of the population). Before 1941, the vast majority of the Soviet Union's Jews were Ashkenazim, speaking Yiddish, which is closely related to German, but which also has Slavonic and Hebrew elements and is written in Hebrew characters. By the turn of the seventeenth century, the centre of European Jewry had become the Polish Crown lands, and it was in the area that is now Ukraine that probably 100,000 Jews were massacred between 1648 and 1654 under the directions of Bohdan Hmelnitskii. This was to begin an intermittent tradition of physical persecution, which was to last until the Second World War. When these areas were incorporated into the Russian Empire in the eighteenth century, restrictions on the Jewish community led to the development of sectarian Hasidism and later in the nineteenth century to Zionism. In the nineteenth and early twentieth centuries, the Jews of the Russian Empire were subject to periodic outbursts of instigated ethnic fury, known as pogroms, which radicalized them as a community. Millions of the Jews who once lived in this area (and gave it many of its cultural and social characteristics) were wiped out during the Second World War or emigrated outside Europe. To give a brief example of just how drastically the population altered in the twentieth century, it would be well to remember that in 1926 Jews constituted 40.2 per cent of the population of the Soviet Republic of Belorussia and outnumbered the Belorussians in the capital Minsk, where they represented 43.6 per cent as opposed to 40 per cent of Belorussians in the urban population (Carrere d'Encausse 1992: 198–9).

Another significant diaspora was German-speakers, encouraged to settle to introduce new technologies at various times—for example, during the reign of Catherine the Great (1762–96). Although they were always rather dispersed, there was nevertheless a concentration on the lower Volga, where there was an Autonomous Volga German Republic between the two world wars. Since many German-speakers joined the advancing German armies during the Second World War, they understandably suffered reprisals after the war, many being resettled in the Russian Arctic, in Siberia, and in Central Asia. A high proportion left for Germany after the relaxing of travel restrictions in the late 1980s.

12.1.2. *The Origins of Russian Hegemony*

The first state to organize the Eastern Slavs was Kievan Rus, with Kiev, now in Ukraine, as its capital. Russians, Ukrainians, and Belorussians trace their origins back to this state and in the tenth century the Kievan King Volodymyr converted to Orthodox Christianity. Although this state collapsed in 1240 in the face of Tatar forces, most of the earliest Eastern Slavonic literature dates from the Kievan period. This includes the Chronicles of Nestor (1113) and the law code *Russkaya Pravda* from the eleventh and twelfth centuries (Haarman 1992: 20). The centre of Eastern Slavonic literacy then moved to the Hanseatic town of Novgorod. The reigns of Ivan III and Ivan the Terrible consolidated the Muscovite state in the fifteenth and sixteenth centuries respectively at the expense of Novgorod, and this state, with its capital in Moscow, then began a prolonged period of expansion into neighbouring territory. Its rulers also took upon themselves the mantle of protectors of Orthodox Christianity after the fall of Constantinople in 1453, which legitimized their expansionist pretensions.

Orthodox Christianity has had important linguistic consequences for Russia. For Orthodox Christians who speak Slavonic languages, the language of the Bible and the liturgy is Church Slavonic, which also fulfilled this function for Orthodox speakers of Romanian. Church Slavonic derives ultimately from the written language codified by the missionaries Cyrïl (or Constantine) and Methodius in the ninth century, which is known as Old Church Slavonic, but it has developed significantly different variants in the different areas in which it is used, so that we can speak of Russian Church Slavonic, Serbian Church Slavonic, and so on (see Vlasto 1983: 1–10). Old Church Slavonic can be regarded as a South Slavonic language, sharing an origin with Bulgarian, Macedonian and the other Slavonic languages of former Yugoslavia. It hence cannot be seen as an early form of Russian, but nevertheless, perhaps partly since the Slavonic languages of the ninth century had not yet diverged greatly, it does not seem alien to speakers of modern Russian, and can seem like an archaic form of their own language. Indeed Russian Church Slavonic served as a written language of Russia until the eighteenth century (see below). In 1717, during a visit to France, Peter the Great was presented with a missal, originally brought from Kiev, which lay in the Cathedral at Rheims, and which was written in tenth-century Old Church Slavonic. He read out fluently from it to the astonishment of the assembled clergy (Massie 1980: 654). The use of Church Slavonic entailed the adoption of the Cyrillic alphabet, which Russian shares with Belorussian, Serbian, Macedonian and Bulgarian (and which was used for Romanian until the nineteenth century), and which serves to mark a cultural divide even today between these Eastern European Slavonic languages and their close linguistic relatives, such as Polish, Czech, Slovak, Croatian, and Slovene, to the west. The alphabetic divide continued under Communism, with non-Slavonic languages of the USSR—Kazakh, for example—being transcribed in the Cyrillic alphabet. Church Slavonic remains a source of neologisms in Russian and other Slavonic languages, in much the same way that Latin and Ancient Greek provide neologisms in the languages of western Europe (Latin and Greek fulfil this role in eastern Europe too) (Vlasto 1983: 251–99).

Between the seventeenth and the nineteenth centuries, the Romanov monarchy, which had come to power in 1613, expanded its territory to the east, incorporating huge tracts of Siberia, which was chiefly populated by peoples speaking Uralic and Altaic languages. By 1900 Russian hegemony of the region had been capped by the completion of a Trans-Siberian railway. In the eighteenth century the Russian monarchy also moved southwards, achieving a presence in the Black Sea region with the foundation of the port of Odessa in the 1790s. The Russian state also found its 'window on the West' with the building of St Petersburg, a city that Karl Marx was later to refer to as the Russian Empire's 'eccentric centre' (Engman 1993: 75). St Petersburg was founded in 1703 by the modernizing Tsar Peter the Great, in an area that had previously been subjugated by Teutonic Knights in the early Middle Ages. Russian conquest of the Baltic region was confirmed by the Treaty of Nystad in 1721. The Baltic areas had a German-speaking nobility, while the Estonian, Lithuanian, and Latvian peasantry remained tied to elements of the old feudal system even after the Emancipation of the Serfs in 1861. St Petersburg subsequently became the most multinational of the cities of the Empire, as opposed to Moscow, which largely retained its Russian linguistic and cultural character (Engman 1993: 78–9).

With the partitions of the Kingdom of Poland between 1762 and 1795, the Romanov dynasty acquired much of what is now Ukraine, Belarus, and eastern parts of Poland (Poland was to become independent again after the First World War). Previously these lands had been united in an enlarged Polish kingdom. In the early nineteenth century, the Romanovs obtained Bessarabia between the Prut and Dniestr rivers from the Ottomans, although the Romanov attempt to take Western Moldova was thwarted by defeat in the Crimean War. In these different ethnic territories, the Romanovs pursued various levels of official Russification, a policy first envisaged by Catherine the Great in the 1760s, enforcing primary education in Russian after the Polish uprising of 1863 in Polish-speaking and Ukrainian-speaking areas.

The Baltic Provinces were never subjected to the same measure of official Russification, where the feudal privileges of the German-speaking landlords were more or less respected by the state until the introduction of Russian state institutions in 1889, which ironically promoted the interests of peasants who spoke the vernaculars rather than Russian. Industrialization and a spread of literacy in the latter half of the nineteenth century brought with them the Russian language to previously non-Russian-speaking parts of the Empire with the proletariat who arrived to work in the newly established factories. Yiddish-speaking Jews often adopted the Russian language as a lingua franca. The spread of Russian coincided with the growth of cultural nationalism among all the subject peoples, which was very often directed into revolutionary politics with organizations such as the Jewish socialist Bund and the Armenian socialist Dashnaksium, which were organized separately from the Russian Marxists. The 1905 revolution, which almost brought the collapse of the Romanov dynasty, was strong in all the regions of the Empire, although anti-Tsarist rather than specifically nationalist in its tone.

12.1.3. *The Soviet Period*

The Russian Revolution was famously the revolution in which the workers' councils or Soviets of 'Red Petrograd' brought the monarchy to an end and then proceeded to remove a Provisional Government committed to war on the Eastern Front, electing Lev Trotskii to lead the Soviet in September 1917. The subsequent seizure of power by the Bolsheviks led by Vladimir I. Lenin under the slogan of 'all power to the Soviets' was followed by a revolutionary wave across the country. In July 1917 the Soviet movement spread to Belorussia, where workers organized themselves in a Rada (council), which was subsequently dissolved when the Bolsheviks retook the republic in November of that year. A nationalist or autonomous movement resurfaced when the Belorussian lands were ceded to the Germans under the terms of the Treaty of Brest–Litovsk, but re-Sovietized in January 1919 (although parts of Belorussian ethnic territory were ceded to the newly independent Poland). The Second World War and the subsequent exodus of Poles to Poland, the near destruction of the Jewish community, and an influx of ethnic Russians altered the ethnic balance of the Belorussian Republic. In 1917 the Moldovans had looked towards Romania rather than Communist Russia for future protection and the status of their people, although their pro-Romanian ambitions were quashed by the Nazi–Soviet Pact of 1939, which united the existing Moldovan Soviet Republic with parts of Bessarabia and Bukovina.

Under the influence of Austro-Marxist theory and their own brand of anti-Tsarism, (Lenin had declared the Romanov monarchy a 'prison of peoples' on the eve of the First World War), the Bolsheviks had committed themselves to a nominal self-determination of the different nationalities living in the Empire. Despite their hostility towards Tsarism, their own nationalities policy did not live up to the early 'organicism' set out in Stalin's 'On the National Question' in 1913, and the Stalin era (1924–53) was a period of far greater Russification than the pre-Revolutionary period. The federal mechanisms of the Soviet Union, but also the dominance of the Communist Party apparatus, guaranteed the predominance of Russian in political life (just as in federal Yugoslavia all Communist politicians habitually used Serbo-Croat in federal political life). Erik van Ree has argued that Stalin's early work 'shows interesting similarities' to that of Nikolai Danielevskii, whose book *Rossiia i Evropa*, published in 1871, elevated the idea of a particular national 'soul' (van Ree 1994: 228–9). This, in effect, meant that Stalin reintroduced the idea that language was one of the 'constitutive elements of nationhood'. In 1929 he predicted the 'flourishing of nations for the socialist era, which would only be fused together with the world-wide victory of socialism' (van Ree 1994: 230). However, in practice, the citizens of the Soviet Union would have to wait for the world and accept Russian. In official Soviet jargon, Russian became known as *jazyk meznacionalnogo obsčenija* (language of international communication) or even more pompously *istočnik razvitija i obgasčenija jazykov narodov SSSR* (a source for the development and enrichment of the languages of the peoples of the USSR). For Lenin 'Latinization' of the alphabet was 'the revolution in the East' (Haarman 1992: 33–4), but Stalin's Russian chauvinism meant that projects such as the adoption of a Latin alphabet for minority languages waned, especially after 1934 when the Soviet regime abandoned most of its vestiges of pluralism (Imart 1966). It was the great irony of the Bolshevik Revolution of 1917 that it actually speeded up the integration of the Russian state, spreading the Russian language and the Cyrillic alphabet far more effectively than the Russification policies of the Romanovs. But its republican structure also had within it the seeds of its own destruction and the potential for the creation of republican élites who were antithetical to the centralized state.

The Soviet Union operated several contradictory policies. For example, there was a theoretical right of the Union republics to secede, and a theoretical equality between Russian and the national languages of the Union republics, but there was simultaneously strong and increasing central control that in practice intensified the domination of Russian. Languages other than these national languages were in theory protected, but in practice most suffered serious decline as Russian flourished. A further contradiction lay in the simultaneous promotion of a discourse of brotherhood and internationalism coupled with a rigorous classification of all Soviet citizens as members of particular nationalities, independently of their place of residence. A result of these contradictory policies can be seen in the reports of ethnic Germans leaving the Soviet Union for Germany in the 1980s and 1990s; they were officially registered as Germans in the Soviet Union and claimed to suffer discrimination on the basis of nationality, yet a high proportion of them were actually monoglot Russian-speakers.

In the process of de-Stalinization and the restructuring of the 1980s under the leadership of Mikhail Gorbachev, republic élites emerged as stronger than ever before (Kappeler 1994: 323–7) Opposition to the Communists emerged in the form of 'Popular Fronts' in the Baltic states in the late 1980s, and a Soviet military crackdown on the television station in Vilnius, which resulted in civilian deaths, radicalized the populations of neighbouring Latvia and Estonia. Mikhail Gorbachev maintained a strong anti-nationalist line, but his attempt to steer a middle course between reform and conservatism left him vulnerable, and he eventually oversaw the disintegration of the Soviet Union on 24 December 1991, just months after an aborted coup against him in August 1991 in reaction to his proposals for a looser Union of Sovereign States to replace the Soviet Union. The Baltic states had already left the federation by this time, having been admitted to the United Nations in September 1991. In Ukraine the reform-minded Party chairman Leonid Kravchuk used the failed August coup to call for a referendum on Ukrainian independence on 1 December 1991. Ninety-two per cent of the republic's population voted for independence, and even in Donets'k and Crimea (Krim) (with their large number of Russian speakers) there was a clear majority in favour (Magocsi 1996: 674). Belarus retained its close emotional ties with the Soviet Union after 1991 and its President Aliaksandr Lukashenka signed a bilateral treaty in May 1995 with Russia, creating a 'Minsk–Moscow' axis.

In view of the contradictory ethnic policies of the Soviet Union, it is surprising that the break-up of the Union has not seen more violence and repression. Romanov and Soviet policies bequeathed to all of the successor states a strongly ethnic and linguistic view of national identity, but in practice identities may be highly complex, given that a sense of ethnic belonging may not be matched by a command of a distinct language. The majority populations of the former Union republics have now achieved an independence that may satisfy nationalist aspirations, but at the cost of discrimination against minorities, including Russians in other republics. Groups that are in a weaker position—for example, minorities within Russia—represent a serious potential for discord; they may be too small or weak to achieve independence, and may feel frustration at being left with permanent minority status.

I now present sketches of the language–nationalism relationship in the various European republics, with a more detailed exemplary discussion of Ukraine, which illustrates well the complexities this relationship may entail.

12.2. The Post-Soviet states and their Languages

12.2.1. *Belarus, Ukraine, and Russia*

Of the languages spoken in this region, Belorussian, Ukrainian, and Russian belong to the Eastern Slavonic group of languages and share many similarities. All share the Cyrillic alphabet and show strong influence from Church Slavonic (see above). One view commonly held by Russian linguists in particular is that a proto-Russian existed from the eighth or ninth century onwards that had experienced regional fragmentation by the thirteenth century. Subsequent political division of these lands, particularly between Muscovy and the lands of the Polish Crown, broke up this linguistic unity still further, and Ukrainian and Belorussian were separately codified in the nineteenth century (Wexler 1992: 45). Modern Russian as a literary language can be dated from linguistic reforms of Mikhail Lomonosov, who published his grammar in 1755 (see Greenfeld 1992: 244), and the poetry of Pushkin in the early nineteenth century, although the political domination of Muscovy and the 'Muscovite koine' from the late fifteenth century onwards ensured its early unification as a spoken language (see Timberlake 1993: 827). Similarly the poetry of the Belorussians Yanka Kupala (1882–1942) and Yakub Kolas (1882-1956) and the Ukrainian Taras Shevchenko (1814–61) gave their respective languages a firm basis for codified deviation from Russian, and 'Alphabetical orthographical and grammatical norms' for modern Belorussian were established in the journal *Naša Niva* in 1906–14 (Mayo 1993: 888).

Before Lomonosov's reforms, much writing by Russian-speakers is in Russian Church Slavonic (see above), but some texts can be viewed as Russian, others as representing intermediate varieties; given that Russian and Church Slavonic are quite close linguistically anyway, the unambiguous assignment of a text to one or other language is not always possible. The language of a text depends on the period of writing and the nature and purpose of the text. In earlier centuries Russian and the Russian variety of Church Slavonic were not so clearly distinct, but by the eighteenth century Church Slavonic doubtless seemed remote from everyday language, and the adoption at this time of a written standard language that was much more clearly Russian in character, albeit with many elements of Church Slavonic origin, is an important step in the establishment of language as a marker of national identity (see Vlasto 1983: 365–93).

Russian takes more of its neologisms from Church Slavonic than do Belorussian and Ukrainian, which, in their turn, show more of German and Polish influence. Ukrainian shows both common Slavonic features and those not found in other languages such as the suffix *-enko,* commonly found in surnames. Russian, Belorussian, and Ukrainian all derive from a Common Slavonic that was probably spoken in the sixth or seventh century (Wexler 1992: 45). It is clear that all the languages have coexisted for most of their histories, and might have been codified into a single tongue in different historical circumstances. There is regional variation within Ukrainian and Belorussian. Ukrainian spoken in L'viv absorbed Polish and Habsburg influences. Some dialects of modern Belorussian can have so much in common with dialects of neighbouring languages that they could have been classified as variants of those languages given the appropriate political circumstances; the Poleshchuk dialect, for example, could have been classified as Ukrainian.

Ideologies of a common Slavonic identity have arisen at various times. Alexander Solzhenitsyn advocated the retraction towards a Slavonic nucleus for the state in his book *Kak nam obustroit' Rossiiu?* (*How Can We Reconstruct Russia?*) (Tolz 1998: 275). Even now the leader of the extreme nationalist *Derzhava* movement Alexander Rutskoi expresses hope for the *svobodnoe triedinstvo* (three-in-one free will and unity) of the Russians, Belorussians and Ukrainians (Tolz 1998: 278). Conversely, Belorussian and Ukrainian nationalists have dismissed such reciprocal ideologies as a disguise for overarching Russian domination.

The Russian Federation is a patchwork of different ethnic and linguistic groups. It has eighty-nine major administrative divisions, twenty-one autonomous republics, six provinces (*krai*), fifty regions (*oblast*), the two federal cities of Moscow and St Petersburg, and ten autonomous districts (*okrug*); the autonomous republics have little real political autonomy, but are intended to allow a degree of self-rule for distinct ethnic groups. Minority languages include those from the Uralic language family. Of these Karelian, Finnish, Veps, Mordvin, Mari, Udmurt, and Komi belong to the so-called Finnic group of languages, and Khanty and Mansi are Ugric languages. Speakers of these languages have generally been Orthodox Christians in recent centuries. In the Arctic region Nenets and Selkup as well as a few related dialects form part of the Samoyedic language group within the Uralic family. In both western and eastern parts of the Russian Federation, Altaic languages are also spoken, the most significant being Tatar; this family includes the Turkic group, to which Azeri, Kazakh, Kirghiz, Turkmen, and Uzbek belong, as well as Tatar. Of the population of the Russian Federation 17.4 per cent are estimated to be non-Russians (Tolz 1998: 279), although the use of Russian as a lingua franca is almost universal.

According to the Soviet census of 1989, Ukraine had a population of which 72.7 per cent spoke Ukrainian as their first language, while a further 22.1 per cent spoke Russian as a mother tongue. There were also significant minorities who spoke Yiddish and Belorussian. The ethnic situation in Ukraine is extremely complex for many reasons, which are discussed further below. As Andrew Wilson (1997: 21) has argued Ukraine is 'a society that is both bi-ethnic and bilingual, but which on the other hand is not strictly bipolar because the ethnic and linguistic divides between the Ukrainian and Russian spheres do not coincide'. In the case of Ukraine, language is only one of the elements that have become the markers of a separate national culture, and is not necessarily the most important.

In the 1989 census, Belarus had a population of which 77.9 per cent spoke Belorussian as their first language. A further 13.2 per cent of the local population spoke Russian as their first language, with additional Ukrainian- and Polish-speaking minorities. In practice, however, these figures might be misleading. Belarus experienced greater Russification than perhaps any other former republic of the Soviet Union. In the 1980s its *Nomenklatura* were unreceptive towards *glasnost* and behaved as if Belarus was simply *Zapadnaya Rossiya* (Western Russia). When surveyed in 1992 60 per cent of the citizens of Belarus preferred to use

Russian in daily life and 75 per cent favoured bilingualism in state institutions (Burant 1995: 1133).

12.2.2. *Estonia, Latvia, and Lithuania*

Latvian and Lithuanian belong to the Baltic group of Indo-European languages. Estonian belongs to the Finnic group of the Uralic Languages. There are several distinctive dialects of Estonian: Tallinn and Tartu, spoken in the towns of those names, and coastal Estonian, which is close to Finnish. Setu is spoken near the Russian border and Setu-speakers tend to be Orthodox in religion, whereas other Estonians adopted Lutheranism in the sixteenth century. Lithuanian can be divided into four major dialects; the language of the Aukstaiciai became the basis for modern literary Lithuanian in the sixteenth century, with a Roman Catholic catechism being produced in 1547. Other dialects have been heavily influenced by Polish in historic times. Latvian is closely related to Lithuanian (the Latvian dialect of Latgalian is comprehensible to Lithuanians), although the largely Protestant culture of Latvia, contrasting with Lithuanian Catholicism, ensured their separate development. Latvian has more neologisms from Slavonic languages than does Lithuanian.

In 1994, Estonia had a population of which only an estimated 63.9 per cent spoke Estonian as their first language. Almost 30 per cent of the population had Russian as their first language and there were also a number of Ukrainians, Finns, and Belorussians. Of these Russian-speakers, many are not ethnic Russians *per se* but people from throughout the former Soviet Union using Russian as their first language. Estonia's relatively peaceful transition to post-Communism has been put down to 'a tradition of pragmatic . . . individualism . . . which is suspicious of grand visions' and a 'deeply embedded belief—shared both by Estonians and non-Estonians—that Estonia would achieve relative economic prosperity much more quickly without Russia' (Park 1994: 70). According to the section of the Citizenship Laws passed in 1993 pertaining to language, in order to obtain Estonian citizenship 'an applicant's spoken Estonian must be clear enough to understand but he or she may take time to find a suitable word, repeat and reword a phrase and make mistakes in grammar and syntax'. Despite this, according to a survey undertaken the previous year, only 9.2 per cent of Russians in Estonia knew Estonian fluently and 33 per cent had almost no knowledge (Park 1994: 73–4). Resentment against the Russophone population occasionally spilled over during the Communist period, especially as some Estonians thought that other Soviet peoples had migrated to the region in search of a 'long rouble' or quick buck. On New Year's Eve a ditty would be shouted on the streets that translated as 'Out, get out of this republic's reach all eaters of Estonia's bread who do not use its speech' (Misiunias and Taagepera 1993: 215). While some Estonian nationalists refer to the Russophone population as *Gastarbeiter*, Estonian governments have approached the language questions pragmatically (for instance, by abandoning plans to deliver all teaching in secondary schools in Estonian in 1995), particularly given the importance of predominantly Russian-speaking Talinn in the economy (D. Smith 1998: 7–14).

According to 1994 estimates, 54.2 per cent of the population of Latvia spoke Latvian as their first language, while a further 33.1 per cent were first-language Russian-speakers. There were also significant numbers of other nationalities from the former Soviet Union, including Lithuanians. Rules about achieving Latvian citizenship were quite strict and the number of Russians who can apply for naturalization is numerically limited every year. In the mid-1990s there were an estimated 150,000 people who were denied official residency status, perhaps in the hope that they would drift towards the Russian Federation (Barrington 1995: 738–9).

In 1995 Lithuania contained an estimated 81.3 per cent of the population who spoke Lithuanian as their first language, with additional minorities who spoke primarily Russian or Polish as their first languages. Although language requirements were not particularly stringent when related to citizenship, it was impossible for Russians who applied to become Lithuanian citizens also to hold a passport of the Russian Federation and in addition they had to sign a loyalty statement, stating a respect for Lithuania's language, culture, customs, and traditions (Barrington 1995: 733).

12.2.3. *Moldova*

Moldovan is a Romance language, which can be regarded simply as a variety of Romanian, although the language has had rather different recent histories in the two states. Moldova also had small minorities who were defined as Gagauz- or Turkish-speaking Christians and speakers of Yiddish. In 1859 in Romania, the Cyrillic script was jettisoned in favour of the Latin, although in Moldova it continued to be used (van Meurs 1998: 40). A Soviet Moldovan identity was promoted from the 1920s, which emphasized the historic experiences of the Moldovan people, promoted the idea of a Moldovan language, and opposed the 'bourgeois' language of the neighbouring Romanian state (King 1995). According to the 1989 Soviet census, 64.5 per cent of the population of Moldova spoke Moldovan as first language, while approximately a further 13 per cent spoke Russian and 14 per cent spoke Ukrainian; 3.5 per cent of the population spoke Gagauz and 2 per cent Bulgarian.

In the post-war period Moldova, with its capital Chişinau (Kishinev), became something of a cultural backwater, not known for its national or irredentist tendencies. After the Russification of the Stalin years and the promotion of historical interpretations that emphasized the Slavonic element in Moldovan ethnogenesis, during the *perestroika* movement in Soviet Moldova, 'in 1988–9, the political leadership in Chisinau reluctantly recognised the Moldovan language as the state language of the republic and allowed the use of Latin script. These concessions *de facto* boiled down to a recognition that the Moldavian and Romanian languages were in fact identical' (van Meurs 1998: 52).

12.3. National Ideologies: A Case Study of Ukraine

In order to demonstrate the complex interaction of language and nationalism typical of the former Soviet Union, I now focus briefly on one area of particular complexity, Ukraine.

The term 'Ukraine', originally meaning frontier or border lands, was first used in the twelfth century to denote borders between the Slavonic principalities and the Tatars. Modern Ukraine emerged as an independent state from the ashes of the Soviet Union in 1991. Southern and Eastern Ukraine (for example, Crimea and Donets'k) have a largely Russian ethnic character. Crimea was given to Ukraine by Khrushchev in 1954 to commemorate the 300th anniversary of the Treaty of Pereiaslav, which united the two peoples, and Donets'k experienced a wave of Russian immigration in the latter half of the nineteenth century in the wake of industrialization. Western Ukraine, which was part of Habsburg Galicia is more ethnically Ukrainian in character. However, as Andrew Wilson reminds us, it is unproductive to talk about ethnicity in Ukraine in bipolar Russian–Ukrainian terms. The Russian and Ukrainian languages are closely related, millions of Ukrainians are effectively bilingual, and millions speak varieties that cannot unambiguously be assigned to either Russian or Ukrainian, known as *surzhyk* (Wilson 1997: 22). Nevertheless, as George Shevelov (1993: 991) reminds us, 'modern Ukrainian is still closer in its word stock to Polish than any other Slavonic language'.

The histories of Ukraine and Russia have been interwoven for many centuries, and, in nationalist terms, these Slavonic peoples could be said to share the same ethnogenesis in Kievan Rus' and a shared Orthodox Christian identity. After the modernization of the Russian economy in the late nineteenth century, Ukraine became the breadbasket of the Romanov domains, and Lenin often chose to compare the relationship between the two regions as being similar to that between Britain and Ireland. Even in the late Soviet period, Ukraine supplied some 25 per cent of Soviet grain (as well as 20 per cent of industrial production) (Bremmer 1994: 262). One tendency amongst Ukrainians has been to define themselves as 'Little Russians' (from the geographical term *Malorus'*) and famous Ukrainians such as the nineteenth-century prose-writer Nikolai Gogol chose to write in Russian, rather than Ukrainian, with its image as a language of the peasantry. It has been argued, however, that there is a linguistic 'dualism' in his work and unconscious Ukrainianisms (Hrishko 1973). In contrast, Shevchenko, who was born a serf, struggled with Russian prose before finding his *métier* in the spoken Ukrainian of the peasants. His popular, original, and inspirational poetry gave him something of the status of a Burns, Mickiewicz, or Prešeren in terms of the place he made for himself in the Ukrainian national revival and the elevation of a romantic *Volksgeist*. The exploration of a Herderian link between the peasant and the nation continued in the work of Olekssander Potebnja, who published his *Mysl i jazyk* (*Philosophy and Language*) in 1862, the year of Shevchenko's death. In the early nineteenth century it was commonplace to define Ukrainian as *juznorusskii jazyk* (South Russian), although the Russian Academy debated the differences between the two languages as early as 1805.

Decrees after the Polish uprising of 1863 restricted the use of Ukrainian. Before this date the *Hromada* (Society) had secretly produced the *Kievskii Telegraf*, which was inspired by the *émigré* writer Alexander Herzen. Professor Mykhailo Drahomanov envisaged continuing ties between the nations of the Russian Empire within a sort of socialist federative structure. In the Tsarist period the Ukraine was an ethnically mixed land. According to the census of 1897, less than 23 per cent of Kiev's population was ethnically Ukrainian; by 1959 this had risen to 60 per cent and to 72 per cent by 1989 (Wilson 1997: 20). In the eighteenth century laws relating to Jewish settlement in the Romanov Empire had largely restricted Jews to this area. Although by law the Jews could not take part in certain professions, the nineteenth century saw a rapid rise in Russian-language literacy among Jews and more social movement. The late nineteenth and early twentieth centuries also saw outbreaks of horrific acts of social violence against Jews, vividly recalled in the painting of Marc Chagall. Nikita Khrushchev recalled a pogrom in his native village of Yuzovka in the Ukraine in 1905, which, he claimed, was instigated by the proto-fascist Black Hundreds and involved the (largely) Russian-speaking proletariat (Khrushchev 1971: 234–5).

In 1905 after the Revolution, the ban on publications in Ukrainian was lifted and *Nova Hromadska* was published in Kiev. After the fall of the Romanov dynasty, the Ukrainians organized themselves in a *Rada* (soviet), which broke ranks with the Bolsheviks over the peace negotiations with Germany in January 1918. A temporary government under the 'Hetman' Pavlo Skoropadskii was set up, but collapsed with the defeat of Germany at the end of 1918, and Ukraine was reabsorbed by the Soviets in 1919–20 after a bitter civil war involving Polish, Ukrainian, and Allied forces. A separate Ukrainian republic was then set up as part of the Soviet Federal structure. 'Paradoxically, therefore, the Ukrainians achieved a kind of ersatz statehood through external agency, without having progressed significantly beyond the level of national consolidation that had proved insufficient to win independence in 1917–20' (Wilson 1997: 17). Ukraine flourished during the 1920s under the New Economic Policy and its language also enjoyed a golden age (by 1932, 89 per cent of all its children were studying at Ukrainian language schools (Wilson 1997: 16). Ukraine then suffered immensely during the collectivization period and the Second World War, although it regained western territory after the war.

The events of Ukrainian history are perhaps not sufficient to have created a separate Ukrainian nation and we must also look to other tendencies to define the Ukrainians as a national group. Biological conceptions of ethnicity have historically been quite strong among Ukrainians. The *Prosvita* leader Pavlo Morchan stated, 'a person who speaks a foreign language is incomplete, that is to say that a Ukrainian who speaks perfect Russian can (still) never be a genuine Russian' (Pirie 1996: 1081).

Although there have been centuries of cohabitation between Russians, Ukrainians, and (historically) Jews, there have been differences in collective mentalities that have been noted by many writers. As Sir Laurens van der Post (1984: 214) noted perspicaciously in his travels in the Soviet Union in the early 1960s,

Finns, Ukrainians, the Greater Russians all have similar environments, yet they all three differ because they bring with them from the past different conceptions of the value and meaning of life. The difference between the Russians and Ukrainians is summed up by something that Tikhomirov wrote in 1888. The Greater Russian, he said, cannot imagine life outside his society, to betray his village or commune is for him the unpardonable sin, to go against it is all wrong. The Ukrainian on the other hand says 'What belongs to all belongs to the devil'. The greater Russian takes his idea of his rights from the idea of public welfare whereas the Ukrainian takes as his starting point the exigencies of his individual rights. No wonder Stalin's attempt to impose collective farming was so desperately resisted in the Ukraine . . .

Symbols of Ukrainian statehood (such as the blue and yellow flag) vary from region to region and are historically contested (Krawchenko 1990; Serhiichuk 1992). Again, here mentalities already existing within the peasant population may be more important than symbolic parameters, which have a more nominal function.

By the late 1990s, Ukraine had a strong Russian element that coexisted in various respects with its Ukrainian identity, which was also perhaps integral to the Ukrainian national character. In Kiev in 1992, 49 per cent of the inhabitants claimed that they primarily used Russian, and 40 per cent Ukrainian, leaving 10 per cent of people who used both languages equally (Bremmer 1994: 268). In 1994 only 27 per cent of newspapers in circulation were in Ukrainian (Wilson 1997: 156) and people still chose to tune into Russian-language television. According to a sociological survey conducted between 1993 and 1994, 57 per cent of the adult population of Ukraine considered themselves to exclusively Ukrainian by ethnicity, 11 per cent exclusively Russian, 25–26 per cent of respondents considered themselves to be both Russian and Ukrainian simultaneously, whereas 6 per cent (like Jean-Jacques Rousseau!) saw themselves as citizens of the world (Pirie 1996: 1087–90). Ukrainian nationalists continue to emphasize the importance of *ukrainstvo* (Ukrainian identity) over multiple loyalties. As one member of the L'viv branch of the Organization of Ukrainian Nationalists put it, 'It is impossible to serve simultaneously both God and Mammon' (Vasyl' Volodymyrovich Ventsel', interviewed in Shulman 1998: 619). In other words, a 'good' Ukrainian should make a historical choice to become a Ukrainian rather than a national hybrid. Despite these sort of sentiments, Ukrainian nationalism remains a 'minority faith' (Wilson 1997).

12.4. Conclusion: Language and Nationalism in the CIS and Baltic States

The break-up of the Soviet Union in 1991, like the collapse of the European empires in 1918, was a time of enormous opportunity for positive change. But, like the post-Versailles landscape in 1918, there was also the potential for 'Sudeten'-type problems across the territory, with potential Russian discontent being exploited by unscrupulous nationalists from Moscow such as the leader of the inappropriately named Liberal Democrats Vladimir Zhirinovskii, whose extreme nationalism has fascistic overtones. This scenario may even yet be precipitated by gloomy and distorted Western prognoses of the situation in the CIS (D. Smith 1998: 14–15). In addition, the near universal condemnation of the Soviet period could have left those people living outside their 'homelands' as a result of Communist-inspired migration looking like unwelcome aliens, the residue of past experiments that failed (Park 1994: 70). As the economies of the region have spiralled downwards, the potential for nationalists to exploit discontent is evident.

However, at the beginning of the twenty-first century, it appears that this region has largely avoided violence and the need for widespread recrimination, with certain spectacular exceptions, including Chechnya. If the peoples of the CIS can hold out long enough, they may live to see the collapse of single and narrow identities that were first forged in the industrial age and construct complex and regional identities more characteristic of a post-modern age dominated by the free flow of uncensored (but often qualitatively very poor) information. As one ethnic Russian in the Ukraine put it, 'We are talking here about how a person defines himself. And here, it seems many people say to themselves "I make a double choice. I consider equally native Ukrainian and Russian language, Ukrainian and Russian culture" ' (M. I. Beletskii, quoted in Shulman 1998: 621).

13.

Conclusions: Language and National Identity in Europe

CATHIE CARMICHAEL

> My Czechness is a given. If I had lived during the national revival of the nine-teenth century, my Czechness might still have been a matter of personal choice, and I might have tormented myself with the question of whether it was 'worth the effort'. The problem of whether we should develop the nation or simply give up on it is not something that I have to solve. These matters have already been decided by others.
>
> (Havel 1990: 178–9)

All of the chapters in this book have considered ways in which certain languages have become dominant as national languages. In addition, the relationship between language, ethnicity, and state formation over several centuries of European history has been examined. Contained within these narratives are the stories of the waning of some peripheral languages, the codification of standard languages, and the increasing use of English as a lingua franca across Europe. In other words, the overall emphasis is on change in language use rather than stasis.

Sometimes changes in language use have happened more or less through evolutionary processes. Kashubian, Sorbian, or Rhaeto-Romance began to wane to a large extent because of economic modernization, rather than deliberate and concerted attempts to wipe them out. It is also fair to remind ourselves that we cannot also refer to a language (such as 'English') as anything other than a float-ing signifier: we may talk about the prose of Geoffrey Chaucer as 'English' and the poetry of Robert Burns as 'Lallans', but both are distant from modern English although also somehow still related to it. The labels we give to either of these liter-ary landmarks are subjective from a contemporary perspective and depend largely upon what we want to convey. When writing about such a pertinent and sensitive subject as nationalism we should also be acutely aware of the fact that there have been historical circumstances in which languages were almost extinguished through force or acts of social violence (Yiddish or Irish) and this should be considered as a crucial, if deplorable part of the process of state formation. As we know from the above chapters, violence was an integral part of the history of the creation of Spain (the expulsion of Muslims), the creation of Germany (the Franco-Prussian War), and the creation of Croatia (the expulsion of Serbs). The narratives have therefore traced the triumph of some languages, the establishment of nation-states, and the erection of crude and simplistic political boundaries.

But our story does not end with state formation. Ethnicity and language did not cease to be important in Spain in 1492 or in Germany in 1871 or even in Croatia in 1995. A far more complex scenario is evident. Existing states have experienced (and will continue to face) challenges on different levels. The EU and the development of numerous Euro-regions have led to the emergence of new ties and identities. Simple state categories ('German', 'French', 'Spanish'), describing not only people's citizenship but also by inference their cultural practices, were never wholly adequate, but regionalism and a re-emergence of formerly waning languages have made the complexity of identities even more evident.

One of the characteristics of late modernity has proved to be the creation of complex subcultures. Since the late 1960s, European intellectuals (with a great deal of help from post-colonial theorists) have been deeply immersed in the politics of redefining identity and of constructing metanarratives of emancipation. The shame of not conforming ethnically—and here one remembers that John Millington Synge had to listen through the floorboards to hear his Irish compatriots speak freely—has been partially lifted just as the range of other available identities is much greater. It is no coincidence that in an era when people can openly define themselves as homosexual or non-Christian, options that were scarcely available to their grandparents, ethnic identity has been reconstructed in a more complex manner.

In the past thirty years a vast academic discourse about nationalism and all attendant phenomena has been created, written by specialists in all the social sciences (sociology, history, anthropology, linguistics, and so on). This discourse has been enormously fruitful in terms of encouraging both microstudies and synthetic and comparative works. Implicit in much of the early work on nationalism was the idea that somehow those who took part in this discourse had evolved so far as to have rejected nationalist feeling. In other words, there was a general sense in which it was believed that a writer could tackle a subject like national identity in an objective and unbiased (i.e. non-national) fashion.

Eric Hobsbawm in his *Nations and Nationalism since 1780* took a rather scathing view of the emotions that have stirred in the breasts of so many Europeans since that date, but in so doing adopted a tone reminiscent of Karl Marx and Friedrich Engels in 1848–9 in their well-known series of articles in the *Neue Rheinische Zeitung*[1] with all its concomitant sense that nationalism was a bourgeois sentiment that had not somehow contaminated the historical materialist. Typical

[1] In an article, 'Democratic Pan-Slavism' in the *Neue Rheinische Zeitung* on 16 Feb. 1849, Friedrich Engels wrote, 'the Austrian Slavs have never had a history of their own . . . they are entirely dependent on the Germans and Magyars for their history, literature, politics, commerce and industry' (see Fernbach, 1973: 236–7).

of Hobsbawm's overarching self-confidence was his contemptuous description of the new nations of Eastern Europe—those that, as Mark Thompson put it, 'have dared to individuate themselves in our sight' (Carmichael 1993: 72)—as 'welcome to philatelists' (Hobsbawm 1990: 32).

A generally distant attitude towards nationalism was also found in Benedict Anderson's (1991) thesis of 'imagined communities', and the idea of 'the invention of tradition' explored by Hobsbawm himself and some distinguished colleagues (Hobsbawm and Ranger 1992). Both of these studies emphasized the constructed nature of national cultures, their role in modern bourgeois societies, and the ways in which patriotism was manipulated for imperial territorial purposes. Although these ideas were enormously creative and led to what Roy Porter has described as a 'mini-tradition' of finding invented ceremonies wherever the researcher cared to look (Porter 1992), in the end they failed to take nationalism seriously enough as a phenomenon. As Hugh Trevor-Roper (1992: 24) remarked in his essay 'The Highland Tradition of Scotland':

[In 1745], the British government decided . . . to destroy finally the independent Highland way of life. By various acts of Parliament . . . not only were the Highlanders disarmed and their chiefs deprived of their hereditary jurisdictions, but the wearing of highland costume—'plaid, philibeg, trews, shoulder-belts . . . tartans or partly-coloured plaid or stuff' was forbidden throughout Scotland under pain of imprisonment without bail for six months and, for a second offence, transportation for seven years . . . By 1780 the Highland dress seemed extinct and no rational man would have speculated on its revival.

As Trevor-Roper continued, 'history is not rational: or at least it is rational only in parts', and by doing so conferred on himself as the historian the right to judge the past by his own standards of rationality rather than looking at the real emotional need that the 'invention' of a separate, albeit quasi-historical Scottish identity fulfilled and the acts of social violence that preceded this movement. In this scenario the Scots (some of them Lowlanders, including Sir Walter Scott) were individuating themselves by adopting tartan in the early nineteenth century, but are condemned by posterity for not being more rational, but this notion of rationality is a purely ideological fantasy. And those who indulge in such fantasies will only be disappointed by the past, the present and the future.

Since these seminal works appeared, there are signs that writers about nationalism are adopting a more historically lenient viewpoint. This trend began perhaps with the work of the late Ernest Gellner, who saw nationalism as part of the modernization process and interpreted the growth of national standard languages as part of the need for modern states to have functionally literate citizens. Although he shared a great deal in common with Hobsbawm in terms of the emphasis on modernization, he adopted more textual distance than the latter. An anthropological approach has informed the work of Geoffrey Hosking and George Schöpflin, who have looked at the role of national myths in Europe. As the latter has stated, there are elements of rationality within nationalist discourse:

there has to be some factor, some event, some incident in the collective identity to which (national) myth makes an appeal; it is only at that point that the reinterpretation can vary very radically from a closer historical assessment. It is hard to see how the Czechs and Slovaks, say, could define their mythopoeias by inventing a strong seafaring tradition. (Schöpflin 1997: 26)

As a reply to Trevor-Roper here one could add that the Highland dress would not have been banned after Culloden if it had not been seen as a political threat and that the supposedly 'invented tradition' of wearing tartan kilts that flourished in the nineteenth century *bore some resemblance* to the dress of the past and certainly represented something distinctive and a symbolic resistance against homogenization.

Some writers have even predicted the end of national feeling or perhaps even its effusion into something a bit more tolerable, but at the same time displaying more empathy towards the phenomenon. As Gale Stokes (1997: 184–5) has stated:

. . . in a little more than thirty years this new (European) community has become not just a strong economic unit, but also a vertical structure for containing the passions that burst the traditional European system of empires apart earlier in the century. Today, if you live in Florence, for example, you can be a booster of your neighbourhood or city, a Tuscan patriot, a citizen of Italy and an advocate for Europe, all at the same time, or singly on the appropriate occasions. One may fear that the increasingly inward-looking preoccupations of the European Community will eventually turn Europeans into multinational nationalists, but the absurdity today of Germans shooting Frenchmen or Italians bombing Spaniards, both commonplaces of our fathers' time, is obvious.

In this analysis, nationality becomes simply a question of identity, choice, and introspection. Nationalism also becomes something that people had faith in, but only in the past (and in a past that should not be judged too sternly by the present). Gale Stokes also concedes that one may even become what he describes as a 'multinational nationalist' without apparent contradiction. As Edward Said noted ironically, questions of identity became so 'de-centred' among American college students that one '[could] become a Marxist, a feminist, an Afrocentrist, or a deconstructionist with about the same effort and commitment required in choosing items from a menu' (Said 1993: 389).

However, at a time when scholars are looking at homogenization, globalization, the dominance of the Internet, the so-called decentring of centres, viewing nationalist discourse in a historically lenient manner and most crucially placing nationalism within the politics of identity, there has been a parallel recrudescence of extreme violent nationalism, ethnic cleansing, and other political phenomena that have caused so much destruction in some regions of Europe, but also discomfort to Western academics and diplomats. It is indeed discomforting that the Kosovo Liberation Army, or the Basque ETA movement, or, until recently, the various paramilitary groups in Northern Ireland, should behave so badly and spoil things for those nations ready to live in the postmodern condition and ready, to paraphrase Václav Havel, to accept the bacteriological role of love, peace and forgiveness. It is certainly strange that while a 'multinational nationalist' might exist in Florence or elsewhere in the EU, on the other side of the Adriatic the climate in Croatia is so rarefied and intolerant that in 1997 a beauty contest winner was barred from international competition by the Croatian authorities on the grounds of her Muslim heritage. It seems that, although we may be close to moving into a new historical epoch—defined by the French philosopher Jean-François Lyotard (1984) as postmodernity—there is still a great deal of unfinished business to take place before a nationalism can be entirely consigned to the dustbin of history.

As Bill Schwarz (1992: p. viii) has reminded us, 'Modernity is still organized by differing histories and uneven development. We need more than ever to think historically and at the same time globally.' As was noted earlier, Václav Havel has written that he felt that the struggle for Czech national emancipation was something that was handed to him by history and not something he had a choice about. Milan Kundera spoke similarly about the need for national emancipation that was far more pressing for him than for an individual who lived in an older or more well-established state:

The Czech national anthem begins with a simple question: where is my homeland? The homeland is understood as a question. As an eternal uncertainty. Think of the British national anthem 'victorious, happy and glorious . . . You see if you are English you never question the immortality of your nation because you are English. You may question England's politics but not its existence'. (McEwan 1983 : 26)

Despite the dominance of English in information technology and as a kind of international lingua franca in some parts of Europe, the struggle for national emancipation is still not completed. Although we live in a time of globalization, we are experiencing that phenomenon in Europe of state formation and reformation (and the possible disintegration of the third Federal Republic of Yugoslavia, the United Kingdom, and Spain). More importantly, questions of national identity still dominate the daily lives of some Europeans, whereas others have consigned the question to the back of their minds. Changes to existing states have come about in part because of an incredible tenacity of certain cultures and a simple refusal to homogenize. In these circumstances the issue of language is often crucial. As Jeremy MacClancy (1993: 106–7) has noted: 'there is no creation more strictly and permanently national, present and lived, popular and collective, than the national language. Since the time of Machiavelli it is an extremely well-known political counsel, and one which works infallibly, that to kill a nation there is nothing more deadly than to kill its national language.'

Of course this is precisely what General Franco tried to do in Catalonia—to 'kill a nation' by curbing the public use of the Catalan language—but apparently with little historical success. Even in cultures where the language all but died out (such as Ireland), a spirit of difference lived on with a wholesale adaptation of

Gaelic idioms to English, so ably represented in the plays of Synge. Language is the main vehicle for a national culture—the wisdom of centuries preserved—so much so that when it dies what replaces it is not a new linguistic culture, but something intermediate—perhaps resembling the old culture more than the new apparently hegemonistic one, and making a new language.

Without doubt, there is a strong emotional interface between language and identity. With good reason Roger Chickering gave his book on the *Alldeutscher Verband* the subtitle 'we men who feel most German'. The instinctive universalism of both Max Weber and Karl Marx was befuddled by German patriotism. The great masters of a 'national' prose have an enormous pull for speakers of that language. Most adult English-speakers will consciously and subconsciously refer to Shakespearian passages in everyday conversations. Phrases from Wordsworth, learnt at school, have often come back to me with an almost biblical resonance. And any individual who has travelled beyond their linguistic capabilities will understand Heinrich Heine's 'In der Fremde' ('In a Foreign Land'):

> Ich hatte einst ein schönes Vaterland,
> Der Eichenbaum
> Wuchs dort so hoch, die Veilchen nickten sanft,
> Es war ein Traum.

> Das küßte mich auf deutsch und sprach auf deutsch,
> (Man glaubt es kaum,
> Wie gut es klang) das Wort: 'Ich liebe dich!'
> Es war ein Traum.[2]

But if language inhabits the realm of emotions, it is also involved in state formation and in functioning as a citizen in a modern unified (i.e. linguistically unified) state. Arguably, one could not function as a citizen of the United Kingdom without English, but nor could one define oneself as British without knowledge of this language. It is, in effect, the *conditio sine qua non* of inclusion and self-belief, but also of daily existence. In the mid-twentieth century it was not uncommon to encounter a monolingual Welsh-speaker. In practice Welsh speakers at the beginning of the twenty-first century would have to enter the emotionally dubious area of bilingualism to function as citizens of the UK, but it is unlikely now that they would abandon the Welsh language altogether, as many of their forebears did.[3] Indeed, even beyond the UK, individuals who do not learn English nowadays (just like the illiterate individual in societies undergoing industrialization in Europe

---

[2] Heinrich Heine, 'In der Fremde', in Forster (1961) 330: 'Once upon a time I had a fine country where I was at home. The oaks grew tall there, the violets beckoned gently. It was a dream. It kissed me in German and said in German—It's hard to believe how good it sounded—the words "I love you". It was only a dream.'

[3] Recent requirements for public employees in some Welsh counties to be proficient in the Welsh language have doubtless contributed to a new lease of life for the language, but prevent the further integration of the United Kingdom, and, as it were, halt the 'march of progress'.

before 1914) may never be able to cultivate much more than regional identities and may be economically and professionally tied to their region. There is a crucial difference, however, in that there is no political movement demanding the exclusive use of English in all circumstances, parallel to earlier nationalist campaigns for the exclusive use within states of the national language.

Most writers would probably concur that ideologies of nationalism inhabit a space between the gaining and maintenance of power and modes of political expression. And yet, almost as a philosophical point of departure, these ideologies have usually based themselves on notions of 'essence'. The 'essence' of language and its relationship both to citizenship and ideologies of nationalism is historically grounded. Medieval kings ruled territories by the grace of God, not through ethnic kinship, although the royal territory and the territory of a supposed kinship group often overlapped to a considerable extent. As Leon Poliakov (1974) argued, pre-modern cultures were acutely aware of ethnic borders, hence the German words *Welsche* and its cognates for foreigners to the west and *Wenden* or similar words for those to the east.

Although consciousness about ethnicity manifested through language is as old as the Tower of Babel, which has given weight to recent theories about 'primordial ethnicity' (van den Berghe 1969; Grosby 1991), cultural nationalists in the latter half of the eighteenth century made the study of ethnicity into a branch of scientific knowledge. The most famous amongst them, Johann Gottfried von Herder (1744–1803), indeed stated that one's true homeland is one's language, but in so doing implied that one could only ever have one *Volksgeist*, fixed in the mists of the Pripet marshes or the Black Forest.

There was also a decisive link between Herderian cultural forms of national ascription and later Hegelian political forms of nationalism, although Isaiah Berlin made a celebrated distinction between the two (Gardels 1991: 19–23). But as John Edwards (1995: 131) has rather coyly observed of Herder, 'that the high priest of cultural and linguistic nationalism was himself prone to, shall we say, lapses of taste, is indicative of the dark side of that phenomenon. That while logic does not require that fellow-feeling be accompanied by disdain for out-groups, a sense of groupness has usually had such an accompaniment.'

Like the search for the holy grail, the search for a pure identity (or essence/*Geist*) will ultimately be in vain and will be a waste of intellectual energy. It would involve a process of continual readjustment to cope with awkward historical facts such as the Polish ethnic identity of Joseph Conrad, who is considered to be one of the finest writers of English prose, or the fact that the leader of the Easter Uprising in Dublin in 1916, James Connolly, was born in Scotland. After two centuries of ethnic essentialization—Heinrich von Treitschke's remark that the English confused soap with civilization being a typical example of this (Blackbourn and Eley 1984: 3)— national and cultural boundaries are being broken down. In their everyday lives Europeans often have more than one linguistic identity. Many pass between dialect and standard language with no problem, but, perhaps more significantly, many use different languages at work or at study, like medieval monks inscribing Latin or nineteenth-century diplomats negotiating in French. The Centre for the Study of Nationalism, founded by Ernest Gellner at the Central European University in Prague, used English almost exclusively. Any business in Europe that uses computers or the Internet will communicate in English. The EU, despite the official status of other languages and the hordes of translators in Brussels and Luxembourg, is increasingly an English-speaking club. Arguably, it was the so-called American circle in Bosnian politics (that is, politicians such as Ejup Ganić and Haris Siljadžić who had studied in North America) whose skilful propaganda in the USA during the war turned the tide against the Bosnian Serbs.

Potentially, Europeans have a greater range of identities on which to draw than ever. If people in southern Germany use English throughout their professional career and communicate in Alemannic dialect at home, in what sense do they remain German? Of course, they master *Hochdeutsch* at school, vote for their Chancellor, and listen to the national news, but in many important ways they function at a regional and international level before a national one. Across the continent, subcultures have sprung up that defy simplistic characterization. Beside Baker Street Underground Station in London is the intriguingly named 'Treffpunkt Froso', which claims to be a German-Greek restaurant. There are millions of Anatolians in Western Europe who have not only introduced new words into the national languages but have retained many of their old cultural patterns. Parts of France have the culture and languages of the Maghreb imported wholesale, and contemporary youth cultures in Britain use words of Afro-Caribbean origin that are not yet codified but are universally understood.

Political destabilization has not occurred because of the number of people who have moved to Europe in the wake of decolonization. Inter-ethnic tensions such as the Brixton Riots or the anti-Turkish aggression of the far right in Germany are numerically insignificant in Europe compared with the USA. As Stephen Barbour has argued (Chapter 1 this volume), ethnic consciousness among immigrants from beyond Europe is not considered here under the heading of 'nationalism', because these groups do not usually aspire to form states or even to use their languages in place of the nationally established language. In Europe, the impulse for new state formation (or at the very least the destabilization of existing states) has chiefly come from what we might cautiously refer to as autochthonous ethnic groups, such as the Basques in Spain and the Albanians in the Federal Republic of Yugoslavia. It has come from the nations that have existed without states for hundreds of years. Although new cultures and languages are becoming established, particularly in the urban areas of Western Europe, autochthonous cultures are simply not on the wane any more either. During the 1990s fifteen new states were created in Europe alone,[4] and

---

[4] The Czech Republic, Slovakia, Slovenia, Croatia, Bosnia-Hercegovina (incorporating Republika Srpska and the Muslim-Croat Federation), the Former Yugoslav Republic of Macedonia, the Federal

there are numerous borders and boundaries that were being contested at the end of the twentieth century.[5]

We are witnessing two parallel and apparently contradictory phenomena: the abandonment of nationalism and the re-emergence of nationalism. But, as Kundera (McEwan 1983) reminds us, individuals can only doubt the form of their state once they are sure that state really exists and, more pragmatically, can offer them the benefits of citizenship. Florentines can allow themselves to become Tuscan patriots because they can be fairly confident that neither Tuscany, nor Italy, nor even the EU will cease to exist in the next decade. A citizen of the Republic of Croatia faces quite a different level of existential doubt and may have even experienced dislocation or ethnic cleansing.

We can see very clearly from the chapters in this volume that the formation of national identity is a historical process and there can be no date in history by which no good new nations are made. In any case, despite the ahistorical nature of much nationalist propaganda, most of the new nations are only new in a political sense, rather than a cultural one. In the nineteenth century, to paraphrase d'Azeglio, Italians were 'made', but not from nothing. Similarly in the twentieth century Slovaks were 'made', but again not from nothing.

All nations are formed by cultural processes—language and ethnicity will never be an essence—and one day we might even have new types of polity based on other elements of identity. But the denial of national self-determination is an act of denial that defines the actions of others as deviant, abnormal or irrational. Democratic progress for Europe demands a recognition of the rights of smaller cultures and non-national languages before antagonistic situations develop into war and it is then left to the international community to patch up problems. It is no coincidence that the international community began to examine the position of Kosovo's Albanians only after March 1998, when the Kosovo Liberation Army (KLA) began a military campaign against the Serb-dominated regime in the Federal Republic of Yugoslavia. When the KLA abandoned the policy of dialogue (which had been pursued by Ibrahim Rugova), the rest of the world examined the plight of the Kosovars, which had largely been ignored since the imposition of military law in 1981. The issue was foolishly omitted from the Dayton Peace Accords in 1995, which settled the war in Bosnia. In other words, the right to self-determination for the Kosovars was not recognized as a right until they tried to seize it for themselves. The war over Kosovo in 1999 resulted from a failure to recognize a violation of basic human and democratic rights, until it was too late to solve the problem in any other way apart from military confrontation.

Republic of Yugoslavia (Serbia-Montenegro), the Federal Republic of Germany (incorporating the GDR), Moldova, the Ukraine, Belarus, the Russian Federation, Estonia, Lithuania, and Latvia.

[5]   There are contested boundaries across Europe, but particularly in Catalonia, the Basque Country, Gibraltar, Corsica, Ulster, Wales, Scotland, Montenegro, Kosovo, Cyprus, Istria, Alto-Adige, which may emerge as even more pressing political problems in the next few years.

The postmodern vision of truly decentred centres and the supremacy of information technology implies the use of different languages for different activities in different circumstances: perhaps a regional language at home, the official language of the state or English at work, English on the Internet. For this to work in practice it will be necessary to end the attrition of the languages of smaller groups. Nationalism shaped modern Europe, but nationalism is still at work in the creation of the new postmodern order.

References

Abbott, G. F. (1906), *Macedonian Folklore* (Cambridge: Cambridge University Press).

Abrams, D., and Hogg, M. A. (1988), 'Language Attitudes, Frames of References and Social Identity: A Scottish Dimension', in W. B. Gudykunst (ed.), *Language and Ethnic Identity* (Clevedon: Multilingual Matters), 45–57.

Alexander, R. (1983), 'On the Definition of Sprachbund Boundaries: The Place of Balkan Slavic', in N. Reiter (ed.), *Ziele und Wege der Balkanlinguistik* (Berlin: Osteuropa-Institut an der Freien Universität Berlin), 13: 10–27.

Alladina, S., and Edwards, V. (1991), *Multilingualism in the British Isles* (2 vols.; London: Longman).

Allcock, J. B. (1991), 'Constructing "the Balkans" ', in J. B. Allcock and A. Young (eds.), *Black Lambs and Grey Falcons: Women Travellers in the Balkans* (Bradford: Bradford University Press), 170–91.

Allum, P. (1973), *Italy, Society without Government?* (London: Weidenfeld and Nicholson).

Ameri, S. M. (1991), *Die deutschnationale Sprachbewegung im Wilhelminischen Reich* (Berne: Lang).

Ammon, U. (1995), *Die deutsche Sprache in Deutschland, Österreich und der Schweiz* (Berlin: de Gruyter).

Anderson, B. (1991), *Imagined Communities* (London: Verso).

Andrić, I. (1947), *Na Drini Ćuprija* (Višegrad: Višegradska Hronika).

Andriotis, N. (1966), *The Federative Republic of Skopje and its Language* (Athens).

Angelopoulos, A. (1979), 'Population Distribution of Greece Today According to Language, National Consciousness and Religion', *Balkan Studies*, 20: 123–32.

Ari P. Kristinsson (1992), 'Islandsk sprogrøgt over for en ny verden', in E. Bojsen *et al.* (eds.), *Språk i Norden* (Oslo: Cappelen), 18–28.

Auty, R. (1980), 'Czech', in A. Schenker and E. Stankiewicz (eds.), *The Slavonic Literary Languages* (New Haven: Yale Concilium on International and Area Studies), 163–82.

Baldur Jónsson (1988), 'Isländsk språkvård', in E. Bojsen *et al.* (eds.), *Språk i Norden 1988* (Oslo: Cappelen), 5–16.

Balibar, R. (1996), *Histoire de la littérature française* (Paris: Presses Universitaires de France).

Ball, M. J. (1993), *The Celtic Languages* (London: Routledge).

Banac, I. (1994), *The National Question in Yugoslavia: Origins, History, Politics* (Ithaca, NY: Cornell University Press).

Barany, G. (1990), 'The Age of Royal Absolutism', in P. F. Sugar (ed.), *A History of Hungary* (Bloomington, Ind.: Indiana University Press), 174–208.

Barbour, S. (1991), 'Language and Nationalism in the German-Speaking Countries', in P. Meara and A. Ryan (eds.), *Language and Nation* (British Studies in Applied Linguistics, 6; London: British Association for Applied Linguistics, CILT), 39–48.

—— (1992), 'The Rôle of Language in European Nationalisms: A Comparative Study with Particular Reference to the German-Speaking Area', in R. Lippi-Green (ed.), *Recent*

Developments in Germanic Linguistics (Current Issues in Linguistic Theory, 93) (Amsterdam: Benajmins), 1–9.

—— (1993), ' "Uns knüpft der Sprache heilig Band": Reflections on the Rôle of Language in German Nationalism, Past and Present', in J. L. Flood, P. Salmon, O. Sayce, and C. Wells (eds.), *'Das unsichtbare Band der Sprache': Studies in German Language & Linguistic History in Memory of Leslie Seiffert* (Stuttgart: Heinz), 313–32.

—— (1996), 'Language and National Identity in Europe: Theoretical and Practical Problems', in C. Hoffmann (ed.), *Language, Culture and Communication in Contemporary Europe* (Clevedon: Multilingual Matters), 28–46.

—— and Stevenson, P. (1990), *Variation in German* (Cambridge: Cambridge University Press).

—— —— (1998), *Variation im Deutschen* (Berlin: de Gruyter).

Barrington, L. (1995), 'The Domestic and International Consequences of Citizenship in the Soviet Successor States', *Europe-Asia Studies*, 47: 731–63.

Bartol-Jarosińska, D. (1991), 'Język jako wyznacznik przynależności narodowej w świadomosci Polaków', unpublished paper presented to the conference of the Polish Linguistic Society, Warsaw, 15–16 Apr.

Baudouin de Courtenay, J. (1983; orig.1904), 'Kurzes Resumé der kaschubischen Frage', in *Dzieła Wybrane* (Warsaw: PWN), v. 187–222.

Bauer, D. (1993), *Das sprachliche Ost-West-Problem* (Berne: Lang).

Bauer, O. (1924), *Die Nationalitätenfrage und die Sozialdemokratie* (Vienna: Europaverlag).

Belić, A. (1905), *Dijalekti istočne i južne Srbije* (Belgrade: Srpska kraljevska akademija).

Benkö, L., and Imre S. (1972), *The Hungarian Language* (The Hague: Mouton).

Berghe, P. van den (1969), *The Ethnic Phenomenon* (New York: Elsevier).

Bergman, G. (1968), *Kortfattad svensk språkhistoria* (Stockholm: Prisma).

Berruto, G. (1974), *La Sociolinguistica* (Bologna: Zanichelli).

Billigmeier, R. H. (1979), *A Crisis in Swiss Pluralism* (The Hague: Mouton).

Bister-Broosen, H. (1993), 'Aspekte von Dialektverlust und Dialektresistenz: Erosion des niederländischen Sprachguts im Dialekt von Krefeld', in R. Dirven, M. Pütz, and S. Jäger (eds.), *Mit fremden Augen* (Frankfurt: Lang), 319–30.

Blackbourn, D., and Eley, G. (1984), *The Peculiarities of German History: Bourgeois Society and Politics in Nineteenth-Century Germany* (Oxford: Oxford University Press).

Blanchet, P. (1998), 'Evaluer la vitalité des variétés régionales du domaine d'oïl', in J.-M. Eloy (ed.), *Évaluer la vitalité, Variétés d'oil et autres langues. Actes du Colloque international, 29–30 nov.1996* (Amiens: Université de Picardie-Jules Verne, Centre d'Études Picardes), 23–43.

Bliss, A. (1984), 'English in the South of Ireland', in P. Trudgill (ed.), *Language in the British Isles* (Cambridge: Cambridge University Press), 135–51.

Bojsen, E., *et al.* (eds.), *Språk i Norden 1992* (Oslo: Cappelen).

Bošković-Stulli, M. (1959–60), 'Kresnik-Krsnik, ein Wesen aus der kroatischen und slovenischen Volksüberlieferung', *Fabula*, 3: 275–98.

Breatnach, D. (1991) (ed.), *Contact Bulletin*, 8 (Dublin: European Bureau for Lesser Used Languages).

Bremmer, I. (1994), 'The Politics of Ethnicity: Russians in the New Ukraine', *Europe-Asia Studies*, 46: 261–84.

Bright, W. (1992) (ed.), *International Encyclopaedia of Linguistics* (Oxford: Oxford University Press).

Browning, R. (1969), *Mediaeval and Modern Greek* (London: Hutchinson).

Brozović, D. (1965), 'O karakteru kašupske književnosti', *Studia z filologii polskiej i slowian-skiej*, 5: 245–54.

Bugge, P. (1994), 'Czech Nation-Building, National Self-Perception and Politics 1780–1914', doctoral dissertation (Aarhus: Aarhus Universitet, Det humanistisk Fakultet).

Burant, S. R. (1995), 'Foreign Policy and National Identity: A Comparison of Ukraine and Belarus', *Europe-Asia Studies*, 47: 1125–44.

Burke, P. (1987), 'The Uses of Literacy in Early Modern Italy', in P. Burke and R. Porter, *The Social History of Language* (Cambridge: Cambridge University Press), 21–42.

Çabej, E. (1968) (ed.), *Meshavi i Gyon Buzukut* (2 vols.; Tirana: State University Publishers).

—— (1982), *Studime Etimologjike në Fushe të Shqipes* (Tirana: Akademia Shqipërisë).

Caesar (1996), *Seven Commentaries on the Gallic War*, trans. C. Hammond (Oxford: Oxford University Press).

Čagorović, N. (1996), 'Crna Gora pred izazovom ljudskih prava', in M. Špadijer (ed.), *Crna Gora pred izazovima Budućnosti* (Cetinje: Matica Crnogorska), 96–102.

Calvet, L. J. (1974), *Linguistique et colonialisme: petit traité de glottophagie* (Paris: Payot).

Camerlynck, L. (1993), 'Französich-Flandern oder Flandern in Frankreich', in R. Dirven, M. Pütz, and S. Jäger (eds.), *Mit fremden Augen* (Frankfurt: Lang), 287–318.

Canetti, E. (1979), *Die gerettete Zunge: Geschichte einer Jugend* (Frankfurt am Main: Fischer).

Caritat, M. J. A., Marquis de Condorcet (1994; 1st pub. 1791), *Cinq mémoires sur l'instruction publique*, ed. C. Coutel and G. F. Kintzler (Paris: Flammarion).

Carmichael, C. (1993), 'An Interview with Mark Thompson', *South Slav Journal*, 14: 71–6.

—— (1995), 'Some Thoughts on the Creation of a Slovenian National Culture', *Glasnik slovenskega etnološkega društva*, 35: 7–14.

Carrere d'Encausse, H. (1992), *The Great Challenge: Nationalities and the Bolshevik State 1917–1930* (New York: Holmes and Meier).

Castellan, G. (1971), 'The Germans of Rumania', *Journal of Contemporary History*, 6: 52–75.

Čengić, H. (1994), 'Bosanski, a ne materinji jezik', *Večernje Novine*, 1: 14.

Certeau, M. de, Julia, D., and Revel, J. (1975) (eds.), *Une politique de la langue: La Révolution française et les patois* (Paris: Gallimard).

Chase, B. (1996), 'Walter Scott: A New Historical Paradigm', in B. Schwarz (ed.), *The Expansion of England* (London: Routledge), 92–129.

Chickering, R. (1984), *We Men who Feel Most German: A Cultural Study of the Pan-German League 1886–1914* (Boston, Mass.: Allen & Unwin).

Chlebowczyk, J. (1980), *On Small and Young Nations in Europe* (Wroclaw: Ossolineum).

Cigar, N. (1995), *Genocide in Bosnia: The Policy of 'Ethnic Cleansing'* (College Station, Tex: Texas A&M University Press).

CIS (1994): Centro de Investigaciones Sociológicas, *Conocimiento y uso de las lenguas en España* (Madrid: CIS).

Clark, M. (1984), *Modern Italy 1871–1982* (London: Longman).

Clausén, U. (1978), *Nyord i färöiskan: Ett bidrag till belysning av språksituationen på Färöarna.* (Stockholm: Almqvist & Wiksell International).

Clogg, R. (1979), *A Short History of Modern Greece* (Cambridge: Cambridge University Press).

Clyne, M. (1995), *The German Language in a Changing Europe* (Cambridge: Cambridge University Press).

Colley, L. (1992), *Britons* (New Haven: Yale University Press).

Comrie, B. (1981), *The Languages of the Soviet Union* (Cambridge: Cambridge University Press).

Condorcet, Marquis de: *see* Caritat.

Contact Bulletin (1997), *Contact Bulletin of The European Bureau for Lesser Used Languages* (Dublin: European Bureau for Lesser Used Languages), 14: 2.

—— (1998), *Contact Bulletin of The European Bureau for Lesser Used Languages* (Dublin: European Bureau for Lesser Used Languages), 15: 1.

Conversi, D. (1990), 'Language or Race? The Choice of Core Values in the Development of Catalan and Basque Nationalisms', *Ethnic and Racial Studies*, 13/1: 52–70.

—— (1993), 'The Influence of Culture on Political Choices: Language Maintenance and its Implications for Basque and Catalan Nationalist Movements', *History of European Ideas*, 16: 189–200.

Coulmas, F. (1991), *A Language Policy for the European Community: Prospects and Quandaries* (Berlin: Mouton de Gruyter).

Crick, B. (1997), 'The English and the Others', *The Times Higher Education Supplement*, 2 May, 1997: 15.

Crowley, T. (1996), *Language in History* (London: Routledge).

Crystal, D. (1987), *The Cambridge Encyclopedia of Language* (Cambridge: Cambridge University Press).

Dann, O. (1992), *Nation und Nationalismus in Deutschland* (Munich: Beck).

D'Annunzio, G. (1990), 'La Constitution de Fiume', in A. Londres, *D'Annunzio, Conquérant de Fiume* (Paris: Julliard).

Dardano, M. (1991), *Manualetto di linguistica italiana* (Bologna: Zanichelli).

Davies, N. (1981), *God's Playground: A History of Poland* (2 vols.; Oxford: Clarendon Press).

Dawkins, R. (1916), *Modern Greek in Asia Minor* (Cambridge: Cambridge University Press).

De Mauro, T. (1963), *Storia linguistica dell'Italia unita* (Bari: Laterza).

—— (1992), *L'Italia delle Italie* (Rome: Editor Riuniti).

Deny, T. (1955), *Principes de grammaire turque* (Paris: Adrien-Maisonneuve).

Deprez, K. (1993), 'Standardsprache in Flandern', in R. Dirven, M. Pütz, and S. Jäger (eds.), *Mit fremden Augen* (Frankfurt: Lang), 227–42.

Deutsch, K. W. (1966), *Nationalism and Social Communication* (Cambridge, Mass.: MIT Press).

Diamanti, I., and Segatti, P. (1994), 'Orgogliosi di essere italiani', in *A che serve L'Italia— Perché siamo una nazione* (Special Issue of *Limes—Rivista italiana di geopolitica*) (Rome: Editrice Periodici Culturali), 15–36.

Diez, M., Morales, F. and Sabin, A. (1977), *Las lenguas de España* (Madrid: Ministerio de Educación).

Dimnik, M. (1984), 'Gutenberg, Humanism, the Reformation and the Emergence of the Slovene Literary Language, 1550–1584', *Canadian Slavonic Papers*, 26: 141–59.

—— (1988), 'Primož Trubar and the Mission to the South Slavs', *Slavonic and East European Review*, 66: 380–99.

Djupedal, R. (1964), 'Litt om framvoksteren av det færøyske skriftmålet', in A. Hellevik and E. Lundeby (eds.), *Skriftspråk i utvikling. Tiårsskrift for Norsk språknemnd* (Oslo: Cappelen), 144–86.

Donaldson, B. (1983), *Dutch: A Linguistic History of Holland and Belgium* (Leiden: Nijhoff).

Duneton, C. (1982), *Parler croquant* (Evreux: Stock & Plus).

Durand, J. (1996), 'Linguistic Purification, the French Nation-State and the Linguist', in C.

Hoffman (ed.), *Language, Culture and Communication in Contemporary Europe* (Clevedon: Multilingual Matters), 75–92.

Durham, E. M. (1909), *High Albania* (London: Edward Arnold).

Ďurovič, L. (1980), 'Slovak', in A. Schenker and E. Stankiewicz (eds.), *The Slavonic Literary Languages* (New Haven: Yale Concilium on International and Area Studies), 211–28.

—— (1986), Reformationen: Frihetskamp och överhet'. *Folkets Historia, Skriftserie*, 1: 9–19.

—— (1992), 'Rosa and Doležal', in A. W. Mackie, T. K. McAuley, C. Simmons (eds.), *For Henry Kucera: Studies in Slavonic Philology and Computational Linguistics* (Ann Arbor: Michigan Slavonic Publications), 179–90.

—— (1993), 'Začiatky spisovnej slovenčiny v XVII. a XVIII storoči', *Slovenské pohl'ady*, 109: 88–101.

EBLUL (1993): European Bureau for Lesser Used Languages, *Mini-Guide to the Lesser Used Languages of the EC* (Dublin: European Bureau for Lesser Used Languages).

Edelman, M. (1977), *Political Language: Words that Succeed and Politics that Fail* (New York: Academic Press).

Edwards, J. (1985), *Language, Society and Identity* (Oxford: Blackwell).

—— (1995), *Multilingualism* (Harmondsworth: Penguin).

Eiríkur Rögnvaldsson (1988), 'Islandsk sprogpolitik', in E. Bojsen *et al.* (eds.), *Språk i Norden 1988* (Oslo: Cappelen), 56–63.

Elazar, J. D. *et al.* (1984), *The Balkan Jewish Communities: Yugoslavia, Bulgaria, Greece and Turkey* (Lanham, Md.: London University Press of America).

Elias, H. J. (1970), *Geschiedenis van de Vlaamse gedachte* (Antwerp: De Nederlandsche Boekhandel).

Eloy, J.-M. (1998) (ed.), *Evaluer la vitalité, Variétés d'oïl et autres langues: Actes du Colloque international, 29–30 nov.1996* (Amiens: Université de Picardie-Jules Verne, Centre d'Etudes Picardes).

Engels, F. (1973; orig. 1849), 'Democratic Pan-Slavism', in D. Fernbach (ed.), *The Revolutions of 1848* (Harmondsworth: Penguin), 236–7.

Engman, M. (1993), ' "An Imperial Amsterdam"? The St Petersburg Age in Northern Europe', in T. Barker and A. Sutcliffe (eds.), *Megalopolis: The Giant City in History* (London: Macmillan), 73–85.

Enloe, C. H. (1980), 'Religion and Ethnicity', in P. F. Sugar (ed.), *Ethnic Diversity and Conflict in Eastern Europe* (Oxford: Clio Press), 347–71.

Eriksen, T. H. (1993), *Ethnicity and Nationalism: Anthropological Perspectives* (London: Pluto Press).

European Commission (1996), *Euromosaic Report* (Luxembourg: Office for Official Publications of the European Communities).

Exarchos, G. (1992), 'Afti ine i Vlachi: 5', *Eleftherotypia*, 29 Aug.

Fairclough, N. O. (1989), *Language and Power* (London: Longman).

Favereau, F. (1994), 'Langue bretonne, nation française, république jacobine et perspective européenne'. *Revue internationale d'éducation* (Sèvres: Centre International d'Études Pédagogiques), 3: 75–84.

—— (1996), *Langues et parlers de l'ouest* (Rennes: Presses Universitaires de Rennes).

Feitsma, A., Jappe Alberts, W., and Sjölin, B. (1987), *Die Friesen und ihre Sprache* (Nachbarn, 32; Bonn: Royal Netherlands Embassy).

Fernbach, D. (1973) (ed.), *The Revolutions of 1848* (Harmondsworth: Penguin).

Ferrer, F. (1985), *La persecució política de la llengua catalana* (Barcelona: Ediciones 62).

Fishman, J. A. (1980), 'Social Theory and Ethnography', in P. F. Sugar (ed.), *Ethnic Diversity and Conflict in Eastern Europe* (Oxford: Clio Press), 347–71

—— (1989), 'Language and Nationalism: Two Integrative Essays', in J. A. Fishman, *Language and Ethnicity in Minority Sociolinguistic Perspective* (Clevedon: Multilingual Matters), 97–175, 269–367.

Foret, M. (1991), 'Mährens uppvaknande', *Röster från Tjeckoslovakien*, 25: 47–8. Also published in *Lidové noviny*, 12 Apr. 1991.

Forster, L. (1961) (ed.), *The Penguin Book of German Verse* (Harmondsworth: Penguin).

Friedman, F. (1996), *The Bosnian Muslims: The Denial of a Nation* (Boulder, Colo.: Westview Press).

Friedman, V. (1999), *Linguistic Emblems and Emblematic Languages: On Language and Flag in the Balkans* (Columbus, Oh.: Ohio University Slavic Department).

Gaffney, C. (1979), 'Kisker: The Economic Success of a Peasant Village in Yugoslavia', *Ethnology*, 18: 135–51.

Gallagher, C. (1975), 'Language Reform and Social Modernisation in Turkey', in J. Rubin and B. Jernudd (eds.), *Can Language be Planned?* (Honolulu: Hawaii University Press), 111–300.

Gallagher, T. (1983), *Portugal: A Twentieth Century Interpretation* (Manchester: Manchester University Press).

Gardels, N. (1991), 'Two Concepts of Nationalism: An Interview with Isaiah Berlin', *New York Review of Books*, 21 Nov. 1991: 19–23.

Gellner, E. (1983), *Nations and Nationalism* (Oxford: Blackwell).

—— (1991), 'Nationalism and Politics in Eastern Europe', *New Left Review* (Sept.–Oct.), 127.

Gerner, K. (1987), 'Nationalities and Minorities in the Soviet Union and Eastern Europe', *Nordic Journal of Soviet and East European Studies*, 4: 5–30.

Geyl, P. (1964), *History of the Low Countries* (London: Macmillan).

Gilbert, J., and Churchill, J. (1864), *The Dolomite Mountains: Excursions through Tyrol, Carinthia, Carniola and Friuli in 1861, 1862 and 1863* (London: Longman, Roberts & Green).

Gilroy, P. (1987), *There Ain't no Black in the Union Jack* (London: Hutchinson).

Goossens, J. (1976), 'Was ist Deutsch—und wie verhält es sich zum Niederländischen?', in J. Göschel and W. Veith (eds.), *Zur Theorie des Dialekts (Zeitschrift für Dialektologie und Linguistik*, 16) (Wiesbaden: Steiner), 256–82.

—— (1977a), *Deutsche Dialektologie* (Berlin: De Gruyter).

—— (1977b), *Inleiding tot de Nederlandse Dialectologie* (Groningen: Wolters-Noordhoff).

Gorter, D., Jelsma, G. H., van der Plank P. H., and de Vos, K. (1988), *Language in Friesland* (Leeuwaarden: Fryske Akademy).

Greenberg, R. D. (1996), 'The Politics of Dialects among Serbs, Croats and Muslims in the former Yugoslavia', *East European Politics and Societies*, 10: 393–415.

Greenfeld, L. (1992), 'The Scythian Rome: Russia', in L. Greenfeld, *Nationalism: Five Roads to Modernity* (Cambridge, Mass.: Harvard University Press), 189–274.

Grillo, R. (1989), *Dominant Languages* (Cambridge: Cambridge University Press).

Grosby, S. (1991), 'Religion and Nationality in Antiquity', *European Journal of Sociology*, 32: 229–65.

Gross, M. (1993), 'The Union of Dalmatia with Northern Croatia: A Crucial Question of the Croatian National Integration in the Nineteenth Century', in M. Teich and R. Porter (eds.), *The National Question in Europe in Historic Context* (Cambridge: Cambridge University Press), 270–92.

Gustavsson, S. (1990), 'Socialism and Nationalism: Trends and Tendencies in the Language, Nationality and Minority Policy of the Socialist Countries in Post-War Europe', *Sociolinguistica*, 4: 50–83.

Guthier, S. L. (1979), 'The Popular Basis of Ukrainian Nationalism in 1917', *Slavic Review*, 38: 30–47.

Gwiazda, A. (1994), 'Poland's Policy towards its National Minorities', *Nationalities Papers*, 22: 435–44.

Haarman, H. (1992), 'Historical Trends of Cultural Evolution among the Non-Russian Languages in the European Part of the Former Soviet Union', *Sociolinguistica*, 6: 11–41.

Hætta, O. M. (1993), *Samene: Historie, kultur, samfunn* (Oslo: Grøndahl Dreyer).

Haiman, J. (1988), 'Rhaeto-Romance', in M. Harris and N. Vincent (eds.), *The Romance Languages* (London: Routledge), 351–90.

Hall, S. T., Hobson, D. & Willis, P. (1980) (eds.), *Culture, Media, Language* (London: Hutchinson).

Hammel, E., and Gardy, P. (1994), *L'Occitan en Languedoc Roussillon* (Perpignan: Editorial Trabucaire).

Hardie, K. (1996), 'Lowland Scots: Issues in Nationalism and Identity', in C. Hoffmann (ed.), *Language, Culture & Communication in Contemporary Europe* (Clevedon: Multilingual Matters), 61–74.

Haritschelhar, J. (1994), 'La Construction de l'Europe et la politique linguistique de la France le cas Basque', *Revue internationale d'éducation* (Sèvres: Centre International d'Études Pédagogiques), 3: 85–92.

Harris, J. (1984), 'English in the North of Ireland', in P. Trudgill (ed.), *Language in the British Isles* (Cambridge: Cambridge University Press), 115–34.

Hasluck, M., and Morant, G. (1929), 'Measurements of Macedonian Men', *Biometrika*, 21: 322–6.

Haugen, E. (1966), *Language Problems and Language Planning: The Case of Modern Norwegian* (Cambridge, Mass.: Harvard University Press).

—— (1972), *The Ecology of Language: Essays*, ed. by Anwar S Dil (Stanford, Calif.: Stanford University Press).

—— (1976a), 'Dialect, Language, Nation', in J. B. Pride and J. Holmes (eds.), *Sociolinguistics* (Harmondsworth: Penguin), 97–111.

—— (1976b), *The Scandinavian Languages: An Introduction to their History* (London: Faber & Faber).

Haumann, H. (1991), *Geschichte der Ostjuden* (Munich: dtv).

Havel, V. (1990), *Disturbing the Peace: A Conversation with Karel Hvizdala* (New York: Knopf).

Hawkesworth, C. (1986), *Colloquial Serbo-Croat* (London: Routledge).

Heida, M. (1976), 'De ondergang van het Nederlands in het Nederrijngebied', *Ons erfdeel*, 19: 539–48.

Hempton, D. (1996), *Religion and Political Culture in Britain and Ireland* (Cambridge: Cambridge University Press).

Hendriks, J. B. (1997), Immigration and Linguistic Change: A Sociohistorical/Linguistic Study of the Effect of German and Southern Dutch Immigration on the Development of the Northern Dutch Vernacular in sixteenth and seventeenth century Holland' doctoral dissertation (Madison: University of Wisconsin).

Hendriks, P. (1976), *The Radožda Verćani Dialect of Macedonian: Structure, Texts, Lexicon* (Lisse: Peter de Ridder).

Hermans, K. (1993), 'Holländer und Flamen: Die gescheiterte Wiedervereinigung', in R. Dirven, M. Pütz, and S. Jäger (eds.), *Mit fremden Augen* (Frankfurt: Lang), 207–26.

Hermans, T. (1992) (ed.), *The Flemish Movement: A Documentary History 1780–1990* (London: Athlone).

Herr, R. (1992) (ed.), *The New Portugal: Democracy in Europe* (Berkeley: IIS).

—— and Polt, J. (1989) (eds.), *Iberian Identity* (Berkeley: IIS).

Hill, P. (1992), 'Language Standardization in the South Slavonic area', *Sociolinguistica*, 6: 108–50.

Himka, J.-P. (1982), 'Young Radicals and Independent Statehood: The Idea of a Ukrainian Nation State', *Slavic Review*, 41: 219–35.

Hobsbawm, E. (1990), *Nations and Nationalism since 1780* (Cambridge: Cambridge University Press).

—— & Ranger, T. (1992) (eds.), *The Invention of Tradition* (Cambridge: Cambridge University Press).

Hodgson, J. (1991), 'Edith Durham, Traveller and Publicist', in J. B. Allcock and A. Young (eds.), *Black Lambs and Grey Falcons: Women Travellers in the Balkans* (Bradford: Bradford University Press), 8–28.

Hoffmann, C. (1991), 'Language and Identity: The Case of the German *Aussiedler*', in P. Meara and A. Ryan (eds.), *Language and Nation* (British Studies in Applied Linguistics, 6; London: British Association for Applied Linguistics, CILT), 49–60.

Horak, S. M. (1985), *Eastern European National Minorities 1919/1980: A Handbook* (Littleton, Colo.: Libraries Unlimited).

Horst, J. M. van der, and Marschall, F. J. (1989), *Korte geschiedenis van de Nederlandse taal* (Amsterdam: Nijgh and Van Ditmar).

Hrishko, W. (1973), 'Gogol's Ukrainian Russian Bilingualism and the Dualism of Gogolian Style', doctoral dissertation (Washington: Washington University).

Hroch, M. (1985), *Social Preconditions of National Revival in Europe* (Cambridge: Cambridge University Press).

Hunt, L. (1984), *Politics, Culture, and Class in the French Revolution* (Berkeley and Los Angeles: University of California Press).

Imart, G. (1966), 'Le Mouvement de "latinisation" en U.R.S.S.', *Cahiers du monde russe et sovietique*, 6: 223–39.

Innes, A. (1995), 'An Alternative Perspective on the Break-up of Czechoslovakia', *The ASEN Bulletin*, 8: 19–23.

Isaković, A. (1993), *Rječnik karakteristične Leksike u Bosanskome Jeziku* (Sarajevo: Svjetlost).

Isotta, P. (1994), 'Una lingua straniera? L'Italiano', *Il corriere della sera*, 7 Sept., 1.

Israel, J. (1995), *The Dutch Republic: Its Rise to Greatness and Fall 1477–1806* (Oxford: Clarendon Press).

Jacobsen, H. G. (1973), *Sprogrøgt i Danmark i 1930rne og 1940rne* (Copenhagen: Gyldendalske Boghandel).

Jahr, E. H. (1989), *Utsyn over norsk språkhistorie etter 1814* (Oslo: Novus forlag).

—— and Trudgill, P. (1993), 'Parallels and Differences in the Linguistic Development of Modern Greece and Modern Norway', in E. H. Jahr. (ed.), *Language Conflict and Language Planning* (Berlin: Mouton de Gruyter) 83–98.

Jakobson, R. (1968), 'The Beginning of National Self-Determination in Europe', in J. A. Fishman, (ed.), *Readings in the Sociology of Language* (The Hague: Mouton), 585–97.

Jernsletten, N. (1993), 'Sámi Language Communities and the Conflict between Sámi and Norwegian', in E. H. Jahr (ed.), *Language Conflict and Language Planning* (Trends in Linguistics, Studies and Monographs, 72; Berlin: Mouton De Gruyter), 115–32.

Jezernik, B. (1995*a*), 'Qudret Kemeri: A Bridge between Barbarity and Civilization', *Slavonic and East European Review*, 73: 470–84.

—— (1995*b*), ' "Evropeizacija" Balkanskih mest kot vzrok za njihovo "Balkanizacijo" ', *Glasnik slovenskega etnološkega društva*, 35: 2–13.

Johansson, R. (1993*a*), 'Nationer och nationalism: Teoretiska och empiriska aspekter', in S. Tägil (ed.), *Den problematiska etniciteten* (Lund: Lund University Press), 15–61.

—— (1993*b*), 'Nationalitetsproblemets rötter', in K. G. Karlsson (ed.), *Det förvandlade Europa* (Moheda: Fontes), 19–32.

Johnston, O. W. (1990), *Der deutsche Nationalmythos* (Stuttgart: Metzler).

Johnstone, R. (1994), *The Impact of Current Developments to Support the Gaelic Language* (London: CILT).

Jón H. Jónsson (1988), 'Tendenser og tradisjoner i islandsk orddannelse', in E. Bojsen *et al.* (eds.), *Språk i Norden* 1988 (Oslo: Cappelen), 21–33.

Jónsson: *see* Baldur Jónsson *and* Jón H. Jónsson.

Judge, A. (1993), 'French: A Planned Language?' in C. Sanders (ed.), *French Today: Language in its Social Context* (Cambridge: Cambridge University Press), 7–26.

—— (1994), 'La Planification linguistique française: Traditions et impact de la communauté européenne', *Revue internationale d'éducation* (Sèvres: Centre International d'Études Pédagogiques), 3: 33–46.

—— (1996*a*), 'The Institutional Framework of *la Francophonie*', in L. Ibnelfassi and N. Hitchcott (eds.), *African Francophone Writing* (Oxford: Berg).

—— (1996*b*), 'La Francophonie: Mythes, masques et réalités', in B. Jones, A. Miguet, and P. Corcoran (eds.), *Francophonie: Mythes, masques et réalités* (Paris: Publisud), 19–43.

—— and Judge, S. (1998), 'The Impact of European Linguistic Policies on French', in D. Marley, M. A. Hintze and G. Parker (eds.), *Linguistic Identities and Policies in France and in the French Speaking World* (London: Association for French Language Studies, CILT), 291–317.

Judt, T. (1994), 'The New Old Nationalisms', *New York Review of Books*, 26 May, 44.

Kann, R. (1950), *The Multinational Empire* (2 vols.; New York: Columbia University Press).

Kappeler, A. (1994), *La Russie: Empire multiethnique* (Paris: Institut d'Études Slaves).

Karakasidou, A. (1993), 'Politicizing Culture: Negating Ethnic Identity in Greek Macedonia', *Journal of Modern Greek Studies*, 11: 1–28.

Kardelj, E. (1939), *Razvoj slovenskega narodnega vprašanja* (Ljubljana: Naša založba).

Karker, A. (1993), *Dansk i tusind år* (Copenhagen: C. A. Reitzels forlag).

—— Lindgren, A.-R., and Løland, S. (1997) (eds.), *Nordens språk* (Oslo: Novus forlag).

Kassabov, I. (1987), 'On the Problem of Defining the Core of the Vocabulary of the Bulgarian Language', *Balkansko ezikoznanie*, 30: 51–5.

Katičić, R. (1987), 'O hrvatskom književnom jeziku', *Jezik*, 35/2: 33.

Kerem, Y. (1996), 'The Greek–Jewish Theatre in Judeo-Spanish, ca. 1880–1940', *Journal of Modern Greek Studies*, 14: 31–46.

Kersten, K. (1992), *Zydzi, Polacy, Komunizm* (Warsaw: Niezalezna Oficyna Wydawnicza).

Kertzer, D. (1988), *Ritual, Politics and Power* (New Haven: Yale University Press).

Keskitalo, A.-I. (1981), 'The Status of the Sámi Language', in E. Haugen, J. D. McClure and D. Thomson (eds.), *Minority Languages Today* (Edinburgh: Edinburgh University Press), 152–62.

Khrushchev, N. S. (1971), *Khrushchev Remembers*, ed. and trans. Strobe Talbott, with an introduction by Edward Crankshaw (London: André Deutsch).

Killilea, M. (1994), *Killilea Report*, Doc. A 3 0042/94 PR 963/fin, 9 Feb. 1994 (Luxembourg: Office for Official Publications of the European Communities).

King, C. (1995), 'The Politics of Language in Moldova, 1924–1994', doctoral dissertation. (Oxford: University of Oxford).

Kirkness, A. (1984), 'Aliens, Denizens, Hybrids and Natives: Foreign Influence on the Etymological Structure of German Vocabulary', in C. V. J. Russ (ed.), *Foreign Influences on German* (Dundee: Lochee), 1–26.

—— (1993), 'The Native and the Foreign: German Vocabulary in the European Melting Pot', in J. L. Flood, P. Salmon, O. Sayce, and C. Wells (eds.), *'Das unsichtbare Band der Sprache': Studies in German Language and Linguistic History in Memory of Leslie Seiffert* (Stuttgart: Heinz), 411–30.

Kitromilides, P. M. (1996), ' "Balkan Mentality": History, Legend, Imagination', *Nations and Nationalism*, 2: 163–91.

Klinge, M. (1985), 'Finska språket i Finland under 1800-talet', in Nordisk språksekretariat, *De nordiske skriftspråkenes utvikling på 1800-tallet 2. Behovet for og bruken av skrift i 1800-tallets forvaltning, næringsliv og privatkommunikasjon* (Oslo: Nordisk språksekretariat), 7–24.

Kloeke, G. G. (1927), *De Hollandsche expansie in de 16e eeuw en 17e eeuw en haar weerspiegeling in de hedendaagsche nederlandsche dialecten* (The Hague: Nijhoff).

Kloss, H. (1967), 'Abstand Languages and Ausbau Languages', *Anthropological Linguistics*, 9/7: 29–41.

—— (1969), 'Völker, Sprachen, Mundarten', *Europa Ethnica*, 26: 146–55.

—— (1978), *Die Entwicklung neuer germanischer Kultursprachen seit 1800* (Düsseldorf: Schwann).

Konstantinov, Y., Alhaug, G., and Igla, B. (1991), 'Names of the Bulgarian Pomaks', *Nordlyd*, 17: 8–117.

Kornfilt, J. (1987), 'Turkish and the Turkic languages', in B. Comrie (ed.), *The World's Major Languages* (London: Croom Helm), 619–44.

Kossman, E. H. (1978), *The Low Countries 1780–1940* (Oxford: Clarendon Press).

Kostellari, A. (1973), 'La Langue littéraire albanaise contemporaine et les problèmes fondamentaux de son orthographie', *Studia Albanica*, 10: 33–89.

Krajni, A. (1966), 'Bref aperçu des emprunts turcs à l'albanais', *Studia Albanica*, 3: 85–96.

Krawchenko, B. (1990), 'National Memory in the Ukraine: The Role of the Blue and Yellow Flag', *Journal of Ukrainian Studies*, 11: 1–21.

Krejci, J. (1990), *Czechoslovakia at the Crossroads of European History* (London: I. B. Tauris).

Kremer, L. (1983), *Das Niederländische als Kultursprache deutscher Gebiete* (Nachbarn, 27; Bonn: Presse- und Kulturabteilung der königlichen Niederländischen Botschaft).

Kren, J. (1990), *Konfliktní spolecenství* (Toronto: Sixty-Eight Publishers Corporation).

Kristinsson: *see* Ari P. Kristinsson.

Kuhn, H. (1982), 'Die Tchsechoslowakei zwischen Unitarismus and Föderalismus', in G.

Brunner and B. Meissner (eds.), *Nationalitätenprobleme in der Sowjetunion and Osteuropa* (Cologne: Markus), 99–118.

Lazarou, A. (1986), *L'aroumain et ses rapports avec le grec* (Thessaloniki: Institute for Balkan Studies).

Leff Skalnik, C. (1997), *The Czech and Slovak Republic: Nation versus State* (Boulder, Colo.: Westview Press).

Lehr-Splawiński, T., Piwarski, K., and Wojciechowski, Z. (1947), *Polska-Czechy: Dziesięć wieków sąsiedztwa* (Katowice, Wroclaw: Wyd. Instytutu Śląskiego).

Leigh-Fermor, P. (1966), *Roumeli: Travels in Northern Greece* (London: Murray).

Lékó, I. (1992), 'Mellan likgiltighet och hat', *Röster från Tjeckoslovakien*, 30–1: 84–6. Also published in *Lidové noviny* 23 June 1992.

Lemaire, J., *et al.* (1991), *Eauze, Terre d'histoire* (Nogaro: Conseil Général du Gers).

Lepschy, L., and Lepschy, G. (1977), *The Italian Language Today* (London: Routledge).

Levi, C. (1982), *Christ Stopped at Eboli* (London: Penguin).

Lewis, B. (1968), *The Emergence of Modern Turkey* (2nd edn., Oxford: Oxford University Press).

Lindgren, A.-R. (1990), 'What can we Do when a Language is Dying?', in E. H. Jahr and O. Lorentz (eds.), *Tromsø Linguistics in the Eighties* (Oslo: Novus forlag), 259–70.

Linz, J. (1973), 'Early State-Building and Late Peripheral Nationalism against the State: The Case of Spain', in N. Eisentadt and S. Rokkan (eds.), *Building States and Nations* (Beverley Hills, Calif: Sage), ii. 32–116.

Livezeanu, I. (1995), *Cultural Politics in Greater Romania* (Ithaca, NY: Cornell University Press).

Lockwood, W. B. (1976), *An Informal History of the German Language* (London: André Deutsch).

Lodge, A. (1993), *French, from Dialect to Standard* (London: Routledge).

Lunden, T. (1993), *Språkens landskap i Europa* (Lund: Studentlitteratur).

Lyotard, J.-F. (1984), *The Postmodern Condition* (Manchester: Manchester University Press).

MacClancy, J. (1993), 'Biological Basques, Sociologically Speaking', in M. Chapman (ed.), *Social and Biological Aspects of Ethnicity* (Oxford: Oxford University Press), 92–129.

McCagg, W. O., Jr. (1989), *A History of Habsburg Jews, 1670–1918* (Bloomington: Indiana University Press).

McEwan, I. (1983), 'An Interview with Milan Kundera', *Granta*, 11: 20–37.

Macháček, J. (1993a), 'Vad menar de mähriska partierna?', *Tjeckiska och slovakiska röster*, 33: 33–4. Also published in *Lidové noviny*, 11 Feb. 1993.

—— (1993b), 'Partiernas åsikter om Mährens och Schlesiens delning går isär', *Tjeckiska och slovakiska röster*, 33: 35–6. Also published in *Lidové noviny,* 15 Mar. 1993.

Mackridge, P. (1985), *The Modern Greek Language* (Oxford: Oxford University Press).

Magocsi, P. R. (1978), *The Shaping of National Identity: Subcarpathian Rus, 1848–1948* (Cambridge, Mass.: Harvard University Press).

—— (1996), *A History of Ukraine* (Toronto: Toronto University Press).

Maiden, M. (1995), *A Linguistic History of Italian* (London: Longman).

Majewicz, A. E. (1996), 'Kashubian Choices, Kashubian Prospects: A Minority Language Situation in Northern Poland', *International Journal of the Sociology of Language*, 120: 39–53.

Malcolm, N. (1998), *Kosovo: A Short History* (London: Macmillan).

Mallinson, G. (1988), 'Romanian', in M. Harris and N. Vincent. (eds.), *The Romance Languages* (London: Routledge), 391–419.

Marley, D. (1995), *Parler Catalan à Perpignan* (Paris: L'Harmattan).

Mar-Molinero, C. (1994), 'Linguistic Nationalism and Minority Language Groups in the "New" Europe', *Journal of Multilingual and Multicultural Development*, 15: 319–29.

—— (1995), 'Catalan Education Policies: Are Castilian-Speakers Persecuted?', *Journal of the Association of Contemporary Iberian Studies*, 8: 49–56.

—— and Smith, A. (1996) (eds.), *Nationalism and the Nation in the Iberian Peninsula* (Oxford: Berg).

—— and Stevenson, P. (1991), 'Language, Geography, and Politics: The "Territorial Imperative" Debate in the European Context', *Language Problems and Language Planning*: 162–77.

Marti, R. (1993), 'Slowakisch und Tschechisch vs. Tschechoslowakisch, Serbokroatisch vs. Kroatisch und Serbisch', in *Slavische Studien zum XI. internationalen Slavistenkongress in Preßburg/Bratislava* (Cologne: Böhlau Verlag), 289–316.

Massie, R. K. (1980), *Peter the Great* (London: Sphere Books).

Mayo, P. (1993), 'Belorussian', in B. Comrie and G. G. Corbett (eds.), *The Slavonic Languages* (London: Routledge), 887–946.

Mečnyk, S. M. (1994), *Radechiščyna u borot'bi za samostijinu ukrains'ku deržavu* (L'viv: Universum).

Melucci, A. I. (1985), 'The Symbolic Challenge of Contemporary Movements', *Social Research*, 52: 789–816.

—— (1988), 'Getting Involved: Identity and Mobilization in Social Movements', in *From Structure to Action: Comparing Social Movement Research Across Cultures 1. International Social Movement Research*, 329–48.

Meštrović, S. G. (1996) (ed.), *Genocide after Emotion: The Post-emotional Balkan War* (London: Routledge).

Meurs, W. van (1998), 'Carving a Moldavian Identity out of History', *Nationalities Papers*, 26: 39–56.

Mirambel, A. (1965), 'Remarques sur les systèmes vocaliques des dialectes néo-grecs d'Asie Mineure'. *Bulletin de la société linguistique de Paris*, 51: 18–45.

Misiunas, R. and Taagepera, R. (1993), *The Baltic States: Years of Dependence 1940–1990* (London: Christopher Hurst).

Mitchinson, R. (1982), *A History of Scotland* (London: Routledge).

Moser, M. (1995), 'Anmerkungen zur "Prosta mova" ', in *Slavia*, 1–2: 117–23.

Nandris, J. (1987), 'The Aromani: Approaches to the Evidence', in R. Ruhr (ed.), *Die Aromunen: Sprache, Geschichte, Geographie* (Hamburg: Buske).

Nelde, P. H. (1996), 'Language Conflict' in F. Coulmas (ed.), *The Handbook of Sociolinguistics* (Oxford: Blackwell), 285–300.

Newton, B. (1972), *The Generative Interpretation of Dialect* (Cambridge: Cambridge University Press).

Newton, G. (1987), 'The German Language in Luxembourg', in C. V. J. Russ and C. Volkmar (eds.), *Sprache und Gesellschaft in deutschsprachigen Ländern* (York: Goethe-Institut), 153–79.

—— (1990), 'Central Franconian', in C. V. J. Russ (ed.), *The Dialects of Modern German* (London: Routledge), 136–209.

Nic Craith, M. (1995), 'The Symbolism of Language in Northern Ireland', in U. Kockel (ed.), *Landscape, Heritage and Identity: Case Studies in Irish Ethnography* (Liverpool: Liverpool University Press), 11–46.

Niederhauser, E. (1982), *The Rise of Nationality in Eastern Europe* (Budapest: Corvina Kiadó).

Nikčević, V. (1993*a*), *Crnogorski jezik* (Cetinje: Matica Crnogorska).

—— (1993*b*), 'Zaključci Novosadskog Dogovora iz 1954. godine', in V. Nikčević, *Piši kao što zboriš: glavna pravila crnogorskoga standardnoga jezika* (Podgorica: Crnogorsko Društvo Nezavisnih Književnika), 81.

Oftedal, M. (1981), 'Is Nynorsk a Minority Language?', in E. Haugen, J. D. McClure and D. Thomson (eds.), *Minority Languages Today* (Edinburgh: Edinburgh University Press), 120–9.

Ó Laoire, M. (1995), 'An Historical Perspective of the Revival of Irish outside the Gaeltacht, 1880–1930, with Reference to the Revitalization of Hebrew', *Current Issues in Language and Society*, 2: 223–35.

Ó Riagáin, D. (1999), 'Highly Successful Language Conference in Belfast', *Contact Bulletin, The European Bureau for Lesser Used Languages*, 15/3: 3–4.

O'Rourke, P. J. (1994), 'Multiculturalism', in P. J. O'Rourke, *All the Trouble in the World* (London: Picador).

Panzer, B. (1992), 'Zur Geschichte der russischen Standardsprache. Identität, Kontinuität, Entwicklung', *Sociolinguistica*, 6: 1–10.

Park, A. (1994), 'Ethnicity and Independence: The Case of Estonia in Comparative Perspective', *Europe-Asia Studies*, 46: 69–87.

Paternost, J. (1976), 'Slovenian Language on Minnesota's Iron Range: Some Linguistic Aspects of Language Maintenance and Language Shift', *General Linguistics*, 16: 96–150.

Pearson, R. (1983), *National Minorities in Eastern Europe* (London: Macmillan).

Peco, A. (1987), *Turcizmi u Vukovim Rječnicima* (Belgrade: Vuk Karadžić).

Pelinka, A. (1990), *Zur österreichischen Identität* (Vienna: Ueberreuter).

Pellegrini, G. B. (1992), 'Sull'elemento latino dell' Albanese', in G. B. Pellegrini, *Richerche linguistiche balcanicodanubiane* (Rome: La Fenice), 101–51.

Penny, R. (1991), *A History of the Spanish Language* (Cambridge: Cambridge University Press).

Péter, K. (1990), 'The Later Ottoman Period and Royal Hungary', in P. F. Sugar (ed.), *A History of Hungary* (Bloomington: Indiana University Press); 100–200.

Petit Larousse (1972), *Petit Larousse en couleurs* (Paris: Librairie Larousse).

Picard, L. (1963), *Evolutie van de Vlaamse beweging van 1795 tot 1950* (Antwerp: Standaard).

Pileri, S., Schmidtke, O., and Ruzza, C. (1994), 'From System Opposition to a State Party: The Leagues and the Crisis of Italian Politics', *Telos* (Spring) 86–100.

Pipa, A. (1989), *The Politics of Language in Socialist Albania* (New York: Columbia University Press).

Pipes, R. (1974), *Russia under the Old Regime* (Harmondsworth: Penguin).

Pirie, P. S. (1996), 'National Identity and Politics in Southern and Eastern Ukraine', *Europe-Asia Studies*, 48: 1079–1104.

Poliakov, L. (1974), *The Aryan Myth* (New York: Basic Books).

Popowska-Taborska, H. (1980), *Kaszubszczyzna* (Warsaw: PWN).

Porter, R. (1992) (ed.), *Myths of the English* (Cambridge: Polity).

Post, L. van der (1984), *Journey into Russia* (Harmondsworth: Penguin).

Poulsen, J. H. W. (1981), 'The Faroese Language Situation', in E. Haugen, J. D. McClure, and D. Thomson (eds.), *Minority Languages Today* (Edinburgh: Edinburgh University Press), 144–51.

Prat de la Riba, E. (1986; orig. pub. 1906; Castilian translation 1917), *La nacionalitat catalana* (Barcelona: Aymá SA).

Price, G. (1984), *The Languages of Britain* (London: Arnold).

Prifti, P. R. (1990), 'A Commentary on Prof. Pipa's Critique of Unified Literary Albanian', *South Slav Journal*, 13: 12–18.

Prince, J. D. (1929), *Praktična gramatika srpskohrvatskogo jezika* (Belgrade: Državna Štamparija).

Pynsent, R. B. (1994), *Questions of Identity: Czech and Slovak Ideas of Nationality and Personality* (London: Macmillan).

Ramet, S. P. (1992), *Nationalism and Federalism in Yugoslavia* (Bloomington: Indiana University Press).

—— (1996), *Balkan Babel: The Disintegration of Yugoslavia from the Death of Tito to Ethnic War* (Boulder, Colo.: Westview Press).

Ranelagh, J. O'B. (1994), *A Short History of Ireland* (Cambridge: Cambridge University Press).

Ree, E. van (1994), 'Stalin and the National Question', *Revolutionary Russia*, 7: 214–38.

Reuter, M. (1981), 'The Status of Swedish in Finland in Theory and Practice', in E. Haugen, J. D. McClure, and D. Thomson (eds.), *Minority Languages Today* (Edinburgh: Edinburgh University Press), 130–7.

—— (1992), 'Swedish as a Pluricentric Language', in M. Clyne (ed.), *Pluricentric Languages: Differing Norms in Different Nations* (Berlin: Mouton De Gruyter), 101–16.

Rickard, P. (1974), *A History of the French Language* (London: Hutchinson University Library).

Rögnvaldsson: *see* Eiríkur Rögnvaldsson.

Romano, S. (1994), 'Perché gli Italiani si disprezzano', in *A che serve l'Italia—Perché siamo una nazione* (Special Issue of *Limes—Rivista Italiana di Geopolitica*) (Rome: Editrice Periodici Culturali), 159–63.

Rossillon, P. (1995), *Atlas de la langue française* (Paris: Bordas).

Roudometof, V. (1998), 'From Rum Millet to Greek Nation: Enlightenment, Secularization, and National Identity in Ottoman Balkan Society, 1453–1821', *Journal of Modern Greek Studies*, 16: 11–48.

Rouquette, Y. (n.d.), *Histoire des pays de langue occitane* (Saint-Amand: Photos-Jeunesse Documents).

Russ, C. V. J. (1987), 'Language and Society in German Switzerland: Multilingualism, Diglossia and Variation', in C. V. J. Russ and C. Volkmar (eds.), *Sprache und Gesellschaft in deutschsprachigen Ländern* (York: Goethe-Institut), 94–121.

—— (ed.) (1989), *The Dialects of Modern German* (London: Routledge).

Russell, P. (1995), *An Introduction to the Celtic Languages* (London: Longman).

Ruys, M. (1994), 'Belgian Federalization', in F. Deleu (ed.), *The Low Countries* (Rekkem: Stichting Ons Erfdeel), 118–23.

Ruzza, C. (1996), 'Collective Identity Formation and Community Integration in the *Lega Lombarda*', in G. M. Breakwell and E. Lyons (eds.), *Changing European Identities: Social Psychological Analyses of Social Change* (International Series in Social Psychology; Oxford: Butterworth Heinemann), 195–207.

—— and Schmidtke, O. (1993), 'Roots of Success of the *Lega Lombarda*: Mobilization Dynamics and the Media', *West European Politics*, 16: 1–23.

—— —— (1996), 'The Northern League: Changing Friends and Foes and its Political

Opportunity Structure', in M. Fulbrook and D. Cesarani (eds.), *Citizenship, Nationality and Migration* (London: Routledge), 179–208.

Said, E. (1993), *Culture and Imperialism* (London: Chatto & Windus).

Saip, J., and Kepeski, K. (1980), *Romani gramatika—Romska gramatika* (Skopje: Nasa knjiga).

Salvador, G. (1987), *Lengua española y lenguas de España* (Barcelona: Ariel).

Samardžija, M. (1993), *Jezični purizam u NDH* (Zagreb: Hrvatska sveučilisna naklada).

Sandfeld, K. (1930), 'Concordances entre différentes langues balkaniques en dehors du lexique', in K. Sandfeld, *Linguistique Balkanique: Problèmes et résultats* (Paris: Eduard Champion), 100–62.

Sandøy, H. (1977), 'Island: Historia ligg gjømt i språket', in L. S. Vikør (ed.), *Språkpolitikk på fem kontinent* (Oslo: Det Norske Samlaget), 75–98.

—— (1992), 'Faroese—a Minority Language or a National Language? The Socio-Political Problem of Becoming and Being a Fully-Fledged Small National Language', in G. Blom *et al.* (eds.), *Minority Languages—The Scandinavian Experience* (Oslo: Nordic Language Secretariat), 57–74.

Scarlatiou, E. (1992), 'Les Parlers des minorités roumanophones du nord de la Grèce et leurs rapports avec le grec', *Plurilinguismes*, 4: 192–202.

Schenker, A., and Stankiewicz, E. (1980) (eds.), *The Slavonic Literary Languages* (New Haven: Yale Concilium on International and Area Studies).

Schieder, T. (1992), *Nationalismus und Nationalstaat* (Göttingen: Vandenhoeck & Ruprecht).

Schmidtke, O. (1996), *Politics of Identity: Ethnicity, Territories and the Political Opportunity Structure in Modern Italian Society* (Pforzheim: Pro Universitate Verlag).

Schöpflin G. (1997), 'The Functions of Myth and a Taxonomy of Myths', in G. Hosking and G. Schöpflin (eds.), *Myth and Nationhood* (London: Christopher Hurst), 19–35.

Schwarz, B. (1992), 'Latin America: Exiled from Historical Time', *History Workshop Journal*, 34: pp. iii–viii.

—— (ed.) (1996), *The Expansion of England* (London: Routledge).

Sella-Mazi, E. (1992), 'La Minorité turcophone musulmane du nord-est de la Grèce et les dernières évolutions politiques dans les Balkans', *Plurilinguismes*, 4: 203–31.

Serhiichuk, V. (1992), *Natsional'na symvolika Ukraïny* (Kiev: Veselka).

Shevelov, G. Y. (1993), 'Ukrainian', in B. Comrie and G. G. Corbett (eds.), *The Slavonic Languages* (London: Routledge), 947–98.

Shuken, C. (1984), 'Highland and Island English', in P. Trudgill (ed.), *Language in the British Isles* (Cambridge: Cambridge University Press), 152–66.

Shulman, S. (1998), 'Competing versus Complementary Identities: Ukrainian–Russian Relations and the Loyalties of Russians in Ukraine', *Nationalities Papers*, 26: 615–32.

Siguán M. (1993; orig. pub. 1992), *Multilingual Spain* (Amsterdam: Swets & Zeitlinger).

Sikkenga, E. (1992), 'Structural Influence of Turkish on Asia Minor Greek', paper presented at NWAVE 21 Conference, University of Michigan, Ann Arbor.

Simonsen, D. F. (1996), *Nordens språk i EUs Europa. Språkplanlegging og språkpolitikk mot år 2000* (Nordisk språksekretariats rapporter 22; Oslo: Nordisk språksekretariat).

Sito Sučić, D. (1996), 'The Fragmentation of Serbo-Croatian into Three New Languages', *Transition*, 29 Nov., 10–16.

Šmitek, Z., and Krnel-Umek, D. (1987), *Kruh in Politika: Pozglavja iz Etnologije Vitanja* (Ljubljana: Partizanska knjiga).

Smith, A. D. (1983), *Theories of Nationalism* (New York: Holmes & Meyer).
—— (1986), *The Ethnic Origins of Nations* (Oxford: Basil Blackwell).
—— (1991), *National Identity* (Harmondsworth: Penguin).
—— (1995), *Nations and Nationalism in a Global Era* (Cambridge: Polity).
—— (1998), 'Russia, Estonia and the Search for a Stable Ethno-Politics', *Journal of Baltic Studies*, 26: 3–18.
Smith, G. (1994) (ed.), *The Baltic States: The National Self-Determination of Estonia, Latvia and Lithuania* (London: Macmillan).
Smith, R. A. (1997), 'Indigenous and Diaspora Élites and the Return of Carpatho-Ruthenian Nationalism, 1989–1992', *Harvard Ukrainian Studies*, 21: 141–55.
Sol'chanyk, R. (1985), 'Language Politics in the Ukraine', in I. T. Kreidler (ed.), *Sociolinguistic Perspectives on Soviet National Languages* (Berlin: Mouton de Gruyter), 57–105.
Sonntag, S. K. (1991), *Competition and Compromise amongst Elites in Belgian Language Politics* (Bonn: Dümmler).
Stankiewicz, E. (1980), 'Slovenian', in A. M. Schenker and E. Stankiewicz (eds.), *The Slavic Literary Languages: Formation and Development* (New Haven: Yale Concilium on International and Area Studies), 89.
Stokes, G. (1984), *Nationalism in the Balkans: An Annotated Bibliography* (New York: Garland).
—— (1997), *Three Eras of Political Change in Eastern Europe* (Oxford: Oxford University Press).
Stone, G. (1972), *The Smallest Slavonic Nation: The Sorbs of Lusatia* (London: Athlone).
Sugar, P. F. (1980) (ed.), *Ethnic Diversity and Conflict in Eastern Europe* (Oxford: Clio Press).
Swain G., and Swain, N. (1993), *Eastern Europe since 1945* (London: Macmillan).
Szporluk, R. (1992), 'The National Question', in T. J. Coulton and R. Levgold (eds.), *After the Soviet Union: From Empire to Nations* (New York: W.W. Norton), 84–112.
Szücs, J. (1981), *Nation und Geschichte* (Budapest: Corvina Kiadó).
Tandefelt, M. (1992), 'The Finland-Swedes—the Most Privileged Minority in Europe?', in G. Blom *et al.* (eds.), *Minority Languages—The Scandinavian Experience* (Oslo: Nordic Language Secretariat), 21–42.
Tarajło-Lipowska, Z. (1994), 'Dyglosja czeska na tle problemów narodowych', *Slavonica Wratislaviensis*, 87: 87–95.
Tarrow, S. I. (1989), *Democracy and Disorder: Protest and Politics in Italy 1965–1975* (Oxford: Clarendon Press).
Teutsch, F. (1924), *Die Siebenbürger Sachsen in Vergangenheit und Gegenwart* (Hermannstadt: W. Krafft).
Thomas, G. (1991), *Linguistic Purism* (London: Longman).
Thompson, M. (1992), *A Paper House: The Ending of Yugoslavia* (London: Hutchinson Radius).
Thomson, D. S. (1994), 'Attitudes to Linguistic Change in Gaelic Scotland', in M. M. Parry, W. V. Davies and R. A. M. Temple (eds.), *The Changing Voices of Europe* (Cardiff: University of Wales Press), 227–35.
Timberlake, A. (1993), 'Russian', in B. Comrie and G. G. Corbett (eds.), *The Slavonic Languages* (London: Routledge), 827–86.
Tolz, V. (1998), 'Conflicting "Homeland Myths" and Nation-State Building in Postcommunist Russia', *Slavic Review*, 57: 267–94.
Topolińska, Z. (1980), 'Kashubian', in A. Schenker and E. Stankiewicz (eds.), *The Slavic Literary Languages* (New Haven: Yale Concilium on International and Area Studies), 181–94.

Törnquist-Plewa, B. (1992), *The Wheel of Polish Fortune: Myths in Polish Collective Consciousness during the First Years of Solidarity* (Slavonic Monographs, 2; Lund: Lund University Slavonic Department).

Torp, A. and Vikør, L. S. (1994), *Hovuddrag i norsk språkhistorie* (Oslo: Ad Notam Gyldendal).

Townsend, L. (1990), *A Description of Spoken Prague Czech* (New York: Columbus).

Trefulka, J. (1991), 'Ett nytt försök med Mähren', *Röster från Tjeckoslovakien*, 25: 30–2. Also published in *Lidové noviny*, 27 Feb. 1991.

Tressou-Milona, E. (1992), 'I didaskalía tis ellinikís glóssas se pedhiá Rom', in M. Makri-Tsilipakou (ed.), *Proceedings of the Sixth International Symposium on the Description and/or Comparison of English and Greek* (Thessaloniki: Aristotle University), 181–212.

Trevor-Roper, H. (1992), 'The Invention of Tradition: The Highland Tradition of Scotland', in E. Hobsbawm and T. Ranger (eds.), *The Invention of Tradition* (Cambridge: Cambridge University Press), 15–41.

Trifković, S. (1993), 'Rivalry between Germany and Italy in Croatia', *Historical Journal*, 36: 537–59.

Trubetzkoy, N. S. (1939), 'Gedanken über das Indogemanenproblem', *Acta Linguistica*, 1: 81–2.

Trudgill, P. (1977), 'Creolization in Reverse: Reduction and Simplification in the Albanian Dialects of Greece', *Transactions of the Philological Society* (1976–7), 32–50. Reprinted as 'Language Contact in Greece' in P. Trudgill, *On Dialect: Social and Geographical Perspectives* (Oxford: Blackwell, 1983), 108–26.

—— (1992a), 'Ausbau Sociolinguistics and the Perception of Language Status in Contemporary Europe', *International Journal of Applied Linguistics*, 2: 167–78.

—— (1992b), 'The Ausbau Sociolinguistics of Minority Languages in Greece', *Plurilinguismes*, 4: 167–91.

—— (1992c), 'The Ausbau Sociolinguistics of Greek as a Minority and Majority Language', in M. Makri-Tsilipakou (ed.), *Proceedings of the Sixth International Symposium on the Description and/or Comparison of English and Greek* (Thessaloniki: Aristotle University), 213–35.

—— (1994) (ed.), *Language in the British Isles* (Cambridge: Cambridge University Press).

—— and Tzavaras, G. (1975), *A Sociolinguistic Study of Albanian Dialects Spoken in the Attica and Boitia Areas of Greece* (London: Social Science Research Council).

—— —— (1977), 'Why Albanian-Greeks are not Albanians', in H. Giles (ed.), *Language, Ethnicity and Intergroup Relations* (London: Academic Press). Reprinted as 'Language Contact, Language Shift and Identity: Why Arvanites are not Albanians', in P. Trudgill *On Dialect: Social and Geographical Perspectives* (Oxford: Blackwell, 1983), 127–40.

Tsiouris, E. (1989), Modern Greek: A Study of Diglossia', doctoral dissertation (Exeter: University of Exeter).

Tsitsipis, L. (1983), 'Language Shift among the Albanian Speakers of Greece', *Anthropological Linguistics*, 25: 288–308.

Tyson Roberts, G. (1996), ' "Under the Hatches": English Parliamentary Commissioners' Views of the People and Language of Mid-Nineteenth-Century Wales', in B. Schwarz (ed.), *The Expansion of England* (London: Routledge), 171–97.

Udvari, J. (1993), 'Rusyns in Hungary and the Hungarian Kingdom', in B. R. Magocsi (ed.), *The Persistence of Regional Cultures: Rusyns and Ukrainians in their Carpathian Homeland and Abroad* (New York: Columbia University Press), 105–38.

Valverdú, F. (1984), 'A Sociolinguistic History of Catalan', *International Journal of the Sociology of Language*, 47: 13–29.

Vekeman, H. and Ecke, A. (1993), *Geschichte der niederländischen Sprache* (Bern: Lang).

Venås, K. (1993), 'On the Choice between Two Written Standards in Norway', in E. H. Jahr (ed.), *Language Conflict and Language Planning* (Trends in Linguistics. Studies and Monographs, 72; Berlin: Mouton De Gruyter), 263–78.

Verbeke, L. (1970), *Vlaanderen in Frankrijk* (Antwerp: Standaard).

Verwey, G. (1983), *Geschiedenis van Nederland* (Amsterdam/Brussels: Elsevier).

Vikør, L. S. (1993), *The Nordic Languages: Their Status and Interrelations (Nordisk språk-sekretariats skrifter 14) (Oslo: Novus forlag)*. (Third edition 2001.)

Vlasto, A. P. (1983), *A Linguistic History of Russia to the End of the Eighteenth Century*, (Oxford: Clarendon).

Vooys, C. G. N. de (1952), *Geschiedenis van de Nederlandse taal* (Groningen: Wolters).

Vries, J de (1984), *European Urbanization 1500–1800* (Cambridge, Mass.: Harvard University Press).

—— Willemyns, R. and Burger, P. (1994), *Het verhaal van een taal* (Amsterdam: Prometheus).

Wal, M. van der and Bree, C. van (1992), *Geschiedenis van het Nederlands* (Utrecht: Aula).

Waldenberg, M. (1992), *Kwestie narodowe w Europie środkowo-wschodniej* (Warsaw: PWN).

Walicki, A. (1982), *Philosophy and Romantic Nationalism: The Case of Poland* (Oxford: Clarendon Press).

—— (1990), 'The Three Traditions in Polish Patriotism', in S. Gomulka and A. Polonsky (eds.), *Polish Paradoxes* (London: Routledge), 21–39.

Walter, H. (1988), *Le Français dans tous les sens* (Paris: Robert Laffont).

—— (1994), *L'Aventure des langues en Occident* (Paris: Robert Laffont).

Wande, E. (1992), 'Ecological and linguistic aspects of Tornedal Finnish in Sweden', in G. Blom *et al.* (eds.), *Minority Languages—the Scandinavian Experience* (Oslo: Nordic Language Secretariat), 43–56.

Wardhaugh, R. (1987), *Languages in Competition* (Oxford: Blackwell).

Weber, E. (1977), *Peasants into Frenchmen* (London: Chatto & Windus).

Weidenfeld, W. (1983) (ed.), *Die Identität der Deutschen.* Bonn: Bundeszentrale für politische Bildung; Munich: Hanser).

Weigand, G. (1927), 'Sind die Albaner das Nachkommen der Illyrer oder der Thraker?', *Balkan-Archiv*, 2: 66–116.

Weijnen, A. A. (1966), *Nedelandse dialectkunde* (Assen: van Gorcum).

Wells, J. C. (1982), *Accents of English* (Cambridge: Cambridge University Press).

Wendel, H. (1925), *Der Kampf der Südslawen um Freiheit und Einheit* (Frankfurt am Main: Frankfurter Societäts-Drückerei).

Wessén, E. (1965), *De nordiska språken* (Stockholm: Ahlqvist & Wiksell).

Wexler, P. (1992), ' "Diglossia et schizoglossia perpetua"—the Fate of the Belorussian Language', *Sociolinguistica*, 6: 42–51.

Widding-Jacobson, A. (1983) (ed.), *Identity: Personal and Socio-Cultural* (Stockholm: Almqvist & Wiksell).

Williams, C. (1992), 'On the Recognition of Minorities in Contemporary Greece', *Planet*, 94: 82–90.

Williams, C H. (1990), 'The Anglicisation of Wales', in N. Coupland (ed.), *English in Wales* (Clevedon: Multilingual Matters), 19–47.

Williams, G. A. (1985), *When was Wales?* (Harmondsworth: Penguin).

Williams, R. (1961), *The Long Revolution* (Harmondsworth: Penguin).

Wilson, A. (1997), *Ukrainian Nationalism in the 1990s: A Minority Faith* (Cambridge: Cambridge University Press).

Windt, H. de (1907), *Through Savage Europe* (London: T. Fisher Unwin).

Winkel, J. te (1901), *Inleiding tot de geschiedenis van de Nederlandsche taal* (Culemborg: Blom & Olivierse).

Winnifrith, T. (1987), *The Vlachs: The History of a Balkan People* (London: Duckworth).

——— (1993), 'The Vlachs of the Balkans: A Rural Minority which never Achieved Ethnic Identity', in D. Howell (ed.), *Roots of Rural Ethnic Mobilisation* (Dartmouth: New York University Press), 58–73.

Woodhouse, C. (1984), *The Story of Modern Greece* (3rd edn., London: Faber).

Wyn Jones, G. (1997) (ed.), *Eastern Europe and the Commonwealth of Independent States* (London: Europa).

Yevtukh, V. (1993) (ed.), *Etnopolitychna sytuatsiia v Ukraini* (Kiev: Int).

Žanić, I. (1995), 'The Curse of King Zvonimir and Political Discourse in Embattled Croatia', *East European Politics and Societies*, 9: 90–122.

Žižek, S. (1990), 'Eastern Europe's Republics of Gilead', *New Left Review*, 183: 50–62.

Index

Where alternative place names are in use either in English, in relevant historical literature, or in border regions then more than one version has been supplied (e.g. Rijeka/Fiume).